SOURCES IN BRITISH POLITICAL HISTORY 1900–1951

Volume 6
First Consolidated Supplement

Compiled for the British Library of Political and Economic Science by

CHRIS COOK

MACMILLAN

First published 1985

Published by
THE MACMILLAN PRESS LTD
Houndmills, Basingstoke, Hampshire RG21 2XS
and London
Companies and representatives
throughout the world

Typeset by
Styleset Limited
Warminster, Wiltshire
Printed in Great Britain
at the University Press, Oxford

British Library Cataloguing in Publication Data
Cook, Chris
    Sources in British political history 1900–1951.
    Vol. 6
    1. Archives—Great Britain   2. Great Britain
    —-History—20th century—Sources
    3. Great Britain—Politics and government—
    20th century—Sources

    I. Title
    941.082   DA566.7

Volume 6: ISBN 0-333-26568-8
6-volume set: ISBN 0-333-38789-9

CONTENTS

FOREWORD

This book is the first supplement to the earlier series of five volumes which reported the results of a major survey of twentieth-century British political archives. This was undertaken from 1970 to 1977 by the British Library of Political and Economic Science with the generous support of the Social Science Research Council. This supplement was gradually compiled between 1977 and 1984, again with financial help for part of this period from the Social Science Research Council, to bring the volumes up to date to 1 July 1984.

The original project stemmed from a meeting of archivists, historians and librarians held in October 1967 on the initiative of Nuffield College, Oxford. As a result of this meeting a Political Archives Investigation Committee was established to explore the possibility of making a major effort to locate and list modern British political manuscripts and encourage their preservation.

With the assistance of a grant from the Social Science Research Council a two-year pilot project, directed by Dr. Cameron Hazlehurst, was begun at Nuffield College in 1968, with the object of locating the papers of cabinet ministers who held office between 1900 and 1951. The Political Archives Investigation Committee acted as an advisory body to the project. The survey of cabinet ministers' papers was an undoubted success and a guide to the papers was published in 1974.[1]

In view of the favourable outcome of the pilot project, the Committee had no hesitation in recommending that a more comprehensive survey should be undertaken; and particularly bearing in mind the bibliographical facilities and geographical convenience of London, as well as the number of scholars active in relevant fields, working in the London School of Economics, it was proposed that this phase of the investigation should be carried out under the auspices of the British Library of Political and Economic Science.

A generous grant was accordingly made to the BLPES by the Social Science Research Council and on 1 October 1970 a research team directed by Dr. Chris Cook began work on a six-year project intended to locate the papers of all persons and organisations influential in British politics between 1900 and 1951, encourage their preservation, and publish guides.

The records of political parties, societies, institutions and pressure groups were described in the first volume in this series. The second volume was concerned with the private papers of senior public servants, colonial administrators, diplomats and senior officers of the armed forces. The third and fourth volumes were devoted to reporting the findings of a comprehensive search that was made for the papers of all members of the House of Commons between the general elections of 1900 and

---

[1] Cameron Hazlehurst and Christine Woodland, *A Guide to the Papers of British Cabinet Ministers, 1900–1951* (London: Royal Historical Society, 1974).

1951. The fifth volume dealt with the papers of selected writers, intellectuals and publicists, religious leaders, leading trade unionists, businessmen and others.[2]

Inevitably, within a few years, some of the information contained in these volumes had become outdated, through the changes of address of owners, through deposits, or through the reorganisation of library or record services. The need for a supplement volume became very readily apparent and, with the aid of a further grant from the Social Science Research Council, Dr. Chris Cook was appointed research officer for a six-month period, beginning 1 January 1980. The results of that research are contained in this volume.

Doubtless, as the years go by, yet further papers will become available and will themselves form the basis of subsequent supplement volumes. I would hope, therefore, that those who have so generously provided information over the years will continue to do so in the coming years by writing to the Librarian, British Library of Political and Economic Science, 10 Portugal Street, London WC2A 2HD. The resulting file of up-to-date information will be made available to enquirers.

It remains for me, on behalf of the British Library of Political and Economic Science, to thank Dr. Cook for his part in ensuring the successful outcome of this supplementary research.

D. A. Clarke
Librarian
British Library of Political and Economic Science

July 1984

---

[2] Chris Cook with Philip Jones, Josephine Sinclair and Jeffrey Weeks, *Sources in British Political History, 1900–1951*
Vol. 1: A Guide to the Archives of Selected Organisations and Societies (London: Macmillan, 1975).
Vol. 2: A Guide to the Private Papers of Selected Public Servants (London: Macmillan, 1975).
Vols. 3 and 4: A Guide to the Private Papers of Members of Parliament (London: Macmillan, 1977: A–K and L–Z).
Vol. 5: A Guide to the Private Papers of Selected Writers, Intellectuals and Publicists (London: Macmillan, 1978).

ACKNOWLEDGEMENTS

This book is the sixth in the series, and like its predecessor volumes could not have been compiled without a grant from the Social Science Research Council, and the help and guidance of Derek Clarke, Librarian of the British Library of Political and Economic Science. The facilities of that Library have been essential to the success of this project, and I owe its staff a major debt. I must also thank the members of the Political Archives Investigation Committee for their advice and guidance in connection with this first supplement volume.

This volume has been completed only with the unstinting help of many individuals, and it would be impossible to thank them all by name. I am, however, especially indebted to the following: H. Cobb at the House of Lords Record Office; D. S. Porter of the Bodleian Library, Oxford; A. E. B. Owen of Cambridge University Library; Daniel Waley, Keeper of Manuscripts at the British Library; J. K. Bates, Secretary of the National Register of Archives (Scotland); J. S. Ritchie at the National Library of Scotland; D. O'Luanaigh at the National Library of Ireland and G. M. Griffiths at the National Library of Wales; the Keeper and the staffs at the Public Record Office and the India Office Library, London and their colleagues at the Public Record Office of Northern Ireland. I also enjoyed considerable help from some staff at the Historical Manuscripts Commission and I must record my deep debt to them.

The project has enjoyed the closest possible cooperation with the Modern Records Centre at the University of Warwick. I am personally indebted to the Centre's archivist, Richard Storey, for his willing advice and help. The excellent guide to the Centre's holdings should be used to supplement the brief entries given in this volume.

It goes without saying that I owe a major debt to the archivists and staff of various county record offices and specialist libraries. Particular thanks are due to Patricia Methven of the Liddell Hart Centre for Military Archives, King's College, London; Rod Suddaby, Department of Documents, Imperial War Museum; Dr. R. A. Morriss at the National Maritime Museum; R. F. Barker and A. E. Cormack at the Royal Air Force Museum, Hendon; Julia Sheppard and Richard Palmer at the Wellcome Institute; Miss T. M. Thatcher at the Centre for South Asian Studies, Cambridge; Gillian Grant at the Middle East Centre, St. Antony's College, Oxford; N. Higson at the Brynmor Jones Library, University of Hull; Jean Ayton at Manchester Public Library; Glenise Matheson at the John Rylands University Library, Manchester; Miss J. Coburn at the Greater London Record Office; Dr. Felix Hull at Kent County Record Office and Ailsa Holland at University College, Dublin.

Amongst individuals who have given of their time and specialist knowledge I must thank Stephen Brooks, Richard Clayton, Philip Jones, Peter Morgan, Jeffrey Weeks and Judith Woods. The whole of the secretarial work for the book was done by Jean Ali with her usual efficiency and good humour.

Additionally, I must thank my colleagues Angela Raspin and Linda Bell at BLPES not only for answering my many questions but also for tolerating with such good nature my temporary intrusion into the Manuscript Reading Room.

CHRIS COOK
July 1984

PART I

A Guide to the Papers of Organisations, Societies and Pressure Groups

ABORTION LAW REFORM ASSOCIATION

Since the entry in *Sources* Vol 1, p 1, the papers covering the period 1935 to 1978 have been placed in the Contemporary Medical Archives Centre at the Wellcome Institute.

ADAM SMITH CLUB

Minute books, covering the period 1891 to 1939, and other papers are in Glasgow University Library. The collection also includes three notebooks of James Bonar, the political economist. For Bonar's other papers, *see Sources* Vol 5, p 20.

AFRICA BUREAU

On the closure of the Bureau on 31 December 1978, the surviving records were deposited in Rhodes House Library, Oxford (ref MSS Afr s 1681). A list is available (NRA 24727). The deposit contains the associated records of the Africa Educational Trust, the Africa Protectorates Trust and the Africa Publications Trust as well as seven boxes of records of the African Development Trust, created by the Bureau in 1952. N.B. *see also* entry Scottish Council for African Questions.

AGRICULTURAL ORGANISATION SOCIETY

Since the entry in *Sources* Vol 1, p 166, some records have been located at the Institute of Agricultural History, University of Reading. They were deposited by the National Farmers' Union between 1974 and 1976 (*see* NRA 20988) and form part of its own deposit. The collection consists of minute books of the Society, Executive Committee minutes, Finance and General Purposes Committee minutes and the Joint Committee with the Farmers' Central Trading Board.

ALLIED CIRCLE

The records were deposited in Westminster City Library in 1981 (ref Acc. 1196). A list is available (NRA 26033). The group dated from 1941, when informal meetings took place of exiled members of foreign governments and armed forces to discuss wartime problems and post-war reconstruction. The Circle was formally constituted in 1942. The papers include bye-laws, membership records, notes concerning the organisation's foundation, minutes (mainly post-war), material relating to finance and some private correspondence, mainly relating to Mrs McNeil Robertson (at whose home the Circle held its meetings). The Circle was dissolved in 1963.

AMALGAMATED SOCIETY OF BRUSH MAKERS

Since the entry in *Sources* Vol. 1, p 187, the Society has amalgamated with the Furniture, Timber and Allied Trades Union. The records are now with this Union at its London district office, 14 Jockeys Fields, London WC1R 4BP.

AMALGAMATED SOCIETY OF MILL SAWYERS, WOOD-CUTTING MACHINISTS AND WOOD-TURNERS

A collection of records, 1899-1963, is deposited in Lancashire Record Office.

AMALGAMATED SOCIETY OF WIREDRAWERS AND KINDRED WORKERS

The surviving records of the society (the oldest trade union operating in the wire industry) have been placed in South Yorkshire Record Office. A list is available (NRA 26196). The organisation was originally founded in 1840 as a friendly society. Its headquarters were always at Sheffield. The records, covering the period 1906 to 1955 include Executive Council minutes (6 vols, 1918–1953), registers of members, statements of accounts etc.

AMALGAMATED UNION OF ENGINEERING WORKERS

Although the main archive of the AUEW Engineering Section is still retained at the union's Peckham headquarters, the Modern Records Centre, University of Warwick, has acquired the archives of the AUEW (Foundry Section) (ref MSS 41). The collection includes various series of minutes of the Amalgamated Union of Foundry Workers, (later AUEW, Foundry) 1860–1972, London United Brass & General Metal Founders, 1850–1940, with annual and monthly reports. There are also Amalgamated Society of Moulders and Foundry Workers reports, together with rule books, files and correspondence of these and associated organisations.

The Modern Records Centre also has some records of the AUEW (Technical, Administrative and Supervisory Section) (ref MSS 101). The collection comprises 77 archive boxes of local and central conference proceedings, mainly post-war, and an incomplete run of the journal.

AMNESTY INTERNATIONAL

Enquiries concerning certain recent records should be made to the Modern Records Centre, University of Warwick, which has some material (ref MSS 34).

ANGLICAN AND EASTERN CHURCHES ASSOCIATION

The society was founded in 1864 as the Eastern Churches Association. The records, unlisted and unsorted, are with the present Secretary, the Reverend A. T. J. Salter, 137 Liverpool Road, London N1. The records would appear to include minutes, selected correspondence, some letters of H. J. Fynes-Clinton and copies of various journals, including *The Christian East, Christian News From Israel* and *Eastern Church Newsletter*. There are also some early photographs of pre-revolutionary Russia. *See* C. Kitchin, *The Central Records of the Church of England*.

ANGLICAN EVANGELICAL GROUP MOVEMENT

The records of this Anglican pressure group have been acquired by the Brynmor Jones Library, Hull University. The collection, which covers the period 1926–70, includes minutes, 1927–67; minutes of the Group Movement, 1907–11, and of the Group Brotherhood, 1920–26; committee files, 1927–51; finance, 1927–72; study outlines, 1948–66; correspondence, 1937–62; publications, *c.* 1927–62 (including *The Liberal Evangelical*, 1933–62); and files, 1927–70. A list is available (NRA 23221).

ANGLICAN PACIFIST FELLOWSHIP

Some records of the Fellowship, which was founded in 1937, survive in the possession of the General Secretary at the Fellowship's offices, 29 Great James Street, London WC1N 3ES. Minutes date from formation, but only the earliest are made available for inspection. Other material includes news-sheets, annual reports, some filed material and photographs. There is no list.

ANGLO-CONTINENTAL SOCIETY

The surviving records, covering the period 1844–1932, have been placed in Lambeth Palace Library.

ANGLO-EGYPTIAN ASSOCIATION

No archive has been located, but a memorandum by Herbert Addison, entitled *The Anglo-Egyptian Association and its kindred associations: a historical note* is in the Middle East Centre, St Antony's College, Oxford.

ANGLO-HELLENIC LEAGUE

Certain papers relating to Greece covering the period 1915–1944, are in the archives of King's College, London.

ANGLO-ISRAEL ASSOCIATION

According to Philip Jones, *Britain and Palestine* (OUP, 1979) there is almost no material in the Association's records prior to 1950. However, there is relevant material in the papers of the Association's founder, Sir Wyndham Deedes (see *Sources* Vol. 2, p. 64), in the Parkes papers (*Sources* Vol. 5, p. 152) and in the Webster papers (*Sources*, Vol. 5, pp. 202–203). The Association was founded by Wyndham Deedes in 1949 to promote goodwill towards Israel and to educate the British people about Israel.

ANGLO-SOVIET PUBLIC RELATIONS ASSOCIATION

Some relevant material is to be found amongst the Gollancz papers at the Modern Records Centre (ref MSS 157/3/ASP/1. The papers include the minutes of general meetings, with some attendance lists, and the executive committee minutes; papers relating to the aim and constitution of the Association; a file on the Treasurer's work containing finance sub-committee minutes (December 1941); abstracts of the sub-committee's reports; a list of cheques received and donors and some correspondence. The 'Association notices' file includes a list of members and circulars regarding the establishment of local groups and the 'Executive notices' file contains both policy documents and routine circulars. There is some correspondence between the Association and the Soviet ambassador, Maisky, regarding the latter's attendance at Association functions plus an exchange of messages of support.

ANIMAL DEFENCE VIVISECTION SOCIETY

The Wellcome Institute has a minute book of the executive council, 1911–16.

ANTI-BOUNTY ASSOCIATION

See *West India Committee*

ANTI-OPIUM SOCIETY

The minutes of the Society for the Suppression of the Opium Trade, 1891–97 are in Friends House Library, (Temp MSS 33/2).

ANTI-PARTITION LEAGUE

Some material concerning this Irish Republican organisation can be found in the Mulvey papers in the Northern Ireland Public Record Office. The same Record Office also has the minutes and correspondence, 1945–55, of the County Armagh branch of the Anti-Partition League.

ASSISTANT MASTERS ASSOCIATION (Incorporated Association of Assistant Masters in Secondary Schools)

Since the entry in *Sources* Vol 1, pp 124–125 a collection of records has been deposited in the library of the University of London Institute of Education, 11–13 Ridgmount Street, London WC1E 7AM. The papers date from 1899 to the 1960s. Access to some of the papers is restricted.

ASSOCIATED BLACKSMITHS, FORGE AND SMITHY WORKERS SOCIETY

Since the entry in *Sources* Vol 1, p. 5, Miss Angela Tuckett has deposited the records in the Modern Records Centre, University of Warwick. The collection includes financial reports, 1857–1909, 1960–1, quarterly reports, 1873–80, 1927–60, monthly and annual reports, 1910–24, rule books, 1857–1968, and registration books, 1857–1919. There are also files on piecework earnings, the union's centenary, and papers of rules revision committees, 1924, 1926, 1929, 1955. The collection also includes minutes of the Temporary Executive Council and of the General Council of the Amalgamated Union of Shipbuilding, Engineering and Constructional Workers, 1921.

ASSOCIATED SHIPWRIGHTS' SOCIETY

After the entry in *Sources* Vol. 1, p 4, the records were placed in Strathclyde Regional Archives in November 1975. They had originally been deposited with Northumberland Record Office by the Secretary of the Boilermakers and Ship-wrights Union. The deposit comprises records of the Glasgow Shipwrights Society (founded 1853), the Associated Shipwrights of Scotland (amalgamated 1876) and the Associated Shipwrights (instituted 1882). For the Glasgow Shipwrights' Society the records include minutes and accounts, 1853–83; branch business, general and financial, 1875–83; external business 1877; strike material 1874–78; Partick branch records, 1871–83; Govan branch records, 1872–76.

For the Associated Shipwrights of Scotland there are only general minutes and accounts, 1876–82. For the Associated Shipwrights there are reports, 1882–85; branch business records, general and financial, 1882–90; and external business, 1880–90.

ASSOCIATION FOR THE EDUCATION OF WOMEN IN OXFORD

The records of this women's pressure group, covering the period 1878–1920, have

6

been placed in the Bodleian Library, Oxford (ref Dep b 213 c 483–497 d 378–386 e 176–95 f 31). The Bodleian Library also has the minute books of the Oxford University Delegacy for Women Students, 1910–16 (ref Dep d 387–388).

ASSOCIATION OF ASSISTANT MISTRESSES
In addition to the records cited in *Sources* Vol 1, p 123, the Association has deposited on indefinite loan in the Modern Records Centre, University of Warwick (ref MSS 59) selected records of the Anna Westmacott Trust, a charity established by the will of Mrs. Westmacott (proved 1897) for the benefit of 'female teachers in High Schools or other schools for the higher education of girls', to provide allowances or temporary pensions at the discretion of the trustees of the Teachers' Guild.

ASSOCIATION OF BRITISH MALAYA
See British Association of Malaysia and Singapore

ASSOCIATION OF COUNTY MEDICAL OFFICERS OF HEALTH FOR ENGLAND AND WALES
For the papers in the Wellcome Institute, *see* Society of Medical Officers of Health. The Wellcome Institute also has certain papers of the successor body, the Association of Area Medical Officers of Health. *See* NRA 25579.

ASSOCIATION OF HEAD MISTRESSES
At the time of writing, the Association was proposing to merge with the Headmasters' Association as the Secondary Heads Association and the papers were to be deposited in the North London Collegiate School. Since the entry in *Sources* Vol 1, p 124, some regional records have been deposited in the Modern Records Centre, University of Warwick (ref MSS 188). These records comprise Midland Branch minutes, 1914–77, including committee minutes, 1933–71, and employment committee minutes, 1929–35. A list is available (NRA 24513).

ASSOCIATION OF JEWISH EX-SERVICEMEN AND WOMEN
Certain papers are believed to be held by the Secretary. Enquiries should be addressed to the AJEX secretary, Beaumont Hall, Beaumont Grove, London E1. In addition, AJEX minutes, memoranda and correspondence (1934–56) are included in the Board of Deputies' archives (ref E1/11–12). The Association was founded in 1929 to foster good fellowship between all ex-servicemen and women, to unite Jewish veterans for communal activities, to assist them in settlement on land in Palestine and to fight anti-semitism.

ASSOCIATION OF METROPOLITAN AUTHORITIES
See Association of Municipal Corporations

ASSOCIATION OF MUNICIPAL CORPORATIONS
The surviving records were placed in the Public Record Office (ref PRO 30/72) in

1975 by the successor organisation, the Association of Metropolitan Authorities. The Association was formed on 27 February 1873 when a meeting took place attended by 102 representatives from 48 cities and boroughs, at which a decision was taken to form an Association of Municipal Corporations 'in order, by complete organisation' more effectually to watch over and protect the interests, rights and privileges of municipal corporations as they may be affected by public Bill legislation, and in other respects to take action in relation to any other subjects in which municipal corporations may be generally interested'. Its function was to administer the central affairs of local government on behalf of urban local authorities. In its earlier years the Association, through MPs, was able to secure the promotion of Bills, a number of which passed into law, among them the Private Street Works Act 1892 and the Public Health Act 1925. The most important theme, however, has been boundaries and areas of local government reorganisation generally.

On 1 April 1974 the Association of Municipal Corporations became the Association of Metropolitan Authorities to come in line with current local government reorganisation.

The deposit includes an almost complete set of minutes and reports of annual meetings (1877–1972). These volumes contain minutes and reports by the representatives of municipal corporations on the various committees: Education, Children, Fire Service, General Purposes, Health, Housing, Law, Police, Rating, Welfare and Town Planning.

The question and answer books contain questions from local authorities and replies by the Secretary. There is also material on the Conference on Slum Areas (1929) and the Conference of Chairmen of Police Authorities (1931–34). There are no restrictions on access. A list is available (NRA 23367).

ASSOCIATION OF POST OFFICE WOMEN CLERKS

Some records covering the period 1901–1932 are with the Fawcett Library collection now deposited in the City of London Polytechnic.

ASSOCIATION OF PRINCIPALS OF TECHNICAL INSTITUTIONS

The records of the Association 1921–1965 have been deposited in the Greater London Record Office. These include minutes of General Meetings, Executive (later Council) meetings, membership records and annual reports. There are also minutes of the Midland and South/South-Eastern branches. No documents less than twenty-five years old can be produced to non-members of the Association without the written permission of the Honorary Secretary. The Association was founded in 1920 to confer on all matters relating to the work conducted in Technical Institutions and take such action as seemed desirable. It was later renamed the Association of Principals of Colleges.

ASSOCIATION OF SCIENTIFIC, TECHNICAL AND MANAGERIAL STAFFS

Since the entry in *Sources* Vol 1, pp 16–17, the principal surviving archives have been deposited in the Modern Records Centre, University of Warwick (ref MSS 79), in a number of instalments. Deposited records include minutes of the National Foremen's Association, 1918–42; ASSET General Purpose, Finance, Industrial Relations and other committee minutes, c 1945–60; post-war agreement files and subject and company files, mainly 1960s; minutes of various ASTMS district councils, 1960–66, 1969–72; head office circulars, 1968–77; reports to the NEC, files re other unions and organisations, including material on the Foremen's and Staff Mutual Benefit Society, 1944–69; case files involving individuals and files re applications to the National Industrial Relations Court. The surviving records of the Association of Scientific Workers have been transferred to the Modern Records Centre from the History and Social Studies of Science Division, University of Sussex. The deposited material at the Modern Records Centre also includes varied series of minutes of the Guild of Insurance Officials from foundation in 1919, correspondence files (mainly post-war) and the union journal; some material from the ASTMS Pearl Section, including the *Pearl Agents Gazette*, 1926–1950s; minutes (and the Journal) of the Medical Practitioners' Union; extensive minutes and the journal of the United Commercial Travellers' Association; some material relating to the ICI Staff Association and the Union of Speech Therapists. Courtaulds Group I Staff Association minutes are held as a separate accession (ref MSS 201).

Note   In addition to the above records in the Modern Records Centre, some corresponding records for Ireland have been deposited in University College, Dublin (ref TU 6). The deposit (4 boxes, 1939–77) incorporates records of the Prudential Agency Staff Protective Association and the Industrial and Life executive council and administrative council agendas and minutes (1939–74); analyses of income and expenditure (1947–77); statements of account on various funds including the emergency and benefit fund, strike fund, legal defence fund, loan fund, licence deposit fund and contingency fund (1942–74); copies of the union *Bulletin* (1947–73).

ASSOCIATION OF TEACHERS OF DOMESTIC SCIENCE

The records have been deposited in the Modern Records Centre, University of Warwick. The Association originated in 1896 as a technical sub-committee of the National Union of Women Workers and adopted its present title in 1897. The deposit includes Executive Committee minutes, 1896–1949, Council minutes, 1911–38, audited accounts, 1929–71, and various account books, 1935–62. There is a large collection of correspondence, 1936–74. Because of the bombing of the Association's office in 1940, very little correspondence survives for the earlier period. Among the subjects covered are relations with other teachers' unions, such as the National Union of Teachers, international congresses, travelling scholarships and various aspects of domestic science teaching. The collection is completed by runs of the Association's publications, the *Year Book*, 1907–43, and the magazine from 1925. A list is available (NRA 23183).

ASSOCIATION OF UNIVERSITY TEACHERS

In addition to the information given in *Sources* Vol 1, p 17, further material has now been deposited in the Modern Records Centre, University of Warwick (ref. MSS 27). Besides the 36 transfer cases of inter-war correspondence files, the AUT has deposited a complete run of Council minutes from 1919–75. A set of Executive Committee minutes for this period has been retained at head office.

ASSOCIATION OF UNIVERSITY TEACHERS (SCOTLAND)

The records were deposited in Glasgow University Library in 1974. The collection, covering the period 1922–72, includes minute books, papers, correspondence etc.

BANKING, INSURANCE AND FINANCE UNION

Since the entry in *Sources* Vol 1, p 191, the records have been deposited in the Modern Records Centre, University of Warwick (ref MSS 56). The collection includes NEC minutes, 1919—50s, General Purposes Committee minutes, 1936—74, minutes of committees dealing with individual banks, Finance Committee minutes, records of expenditure, and the Union's journal, the *Bank Officer*, 1919—69. There is also considerable correspondence, mainly originating with the Union's Research Department. In April 1976, when the Union moved its headquarters, a second deposit of material was made in the Modern Records Centre. This later deposit included subject files on various banks, and on geographic areas of the union's organisation, as well as material on incomes policy, national negotiating machinery, equal pay, pensions and safety at work, mainly covering the later 1960s—early 1970s.

BRITAIN IN EUROPE

Some 350 box files of the papers of this all party pro-Europe co-ordinating group were deposited in the House of Lords Record Office in 1975 (ref Hist. Coll. 255). The 'Britain in Europe' movement was established in January 1975 to organise a strong and positive vote in the Common Market Referendum. The Director of the movement was Sir Con O'Neill and its Secretary Mr. Cecil Dawson. The movement was disbanded on 13 June 1975 and a board of trustees was established to administer its remaining funds and records. The main classes of records are: minutes of campaign meetings, records of the budget and executive committees, a large collection of press-cuttings, correspondence about the campaign, transcripts and tapes of broadcasts, advertising vouchers, posters and propaganda leaflets and records of the activities of local *Britain in Europe* committees. There are some pre-1975 papers of the member organisations.

BRITISH AND COLONIAL ANTI-BOUNTY ASSOCIATION

See **West India Committee.**

BRITISH ASSOCIATION COMMITTEE ON WOMEN'S EMPLOYMENT

Some records of the committee are in the library of Nuffield College, Oxford, to whom any enquries should be addressed.

BRITISH ASSOCIATION FOR EARLY CHILDHOOD EDUCATION

Enquiries should be addressed to BLPES, who acquired some surviving records in 1980 (ref M1466). The records, covering the period 1923—67, include the archives of the Nursery Schools Association of Great Britain and Ireland. The Public Record Office of Northern Ireland has *c* 500 documents of correspondence and reports of the Northern Ireland Committee of the Nursery Schools Association, *c* 1939—70.

BRITISH ASSOCIATION FOR THE ADVANCEMENT OF SCIENCE

Since the entry in *Sources* Vol 1, pp 22—23, the papers, covering the period 1831—1970, have been placed in the Bodleian Library. The collection consists of 3 vols of Council meeting minutes (1841—1924), 2 vols of minutes of the committee of recommendations (1835, 1903—22), minutes of the Toronto Committee of Council 1923—4, plus 16 minute books of the different sections of the Association (various periods 1864–1970) eg sections on Mathematics, Chemistry, Geology, Zoology. There are 4 notebooks regarding arrangements for annual meetings (1832–35) and lists of members (1831–45). Financial papers include a volume of membership subscriptions (1839–1957) an investment ledger (1924–37) and 10 vols labelled 'ledger' (1831–1948). 18 boxes of correspondence (1831 and various periods 1905–68) exist on a variety of topics including annual meetings, post-war education, miscellaneous correspondence (1912–62) and correspondence with local secretaries. Printed material includes volumes of press cuttings c 1905–72.

BRITISH ASSOCIATION OF MALAYSIA AND SINGAPORE

Further details are now available of the surviving records of the Association, deposited in the India Office Library (ref MSS Eur F 168), to whom they were presented by the Association's Secretary, W. C. S. Corry. Originally formed as the Association of British Malaya, 1920, the Association came to an end in 1973. The collection, covering the period 1920–74, consists of a complete set of minute books and c 90 correspondence files, 1941–74. The subjects dealt with include the relief fund established by the Association to aid victims of the Japanese invasion, war damage claims, educational and cultural links with Malaysia and Singapore, correspondence with the Colonial Office, etc.

BRITISH COUNCIL

The records of the Council for the period 1934–49 have been deposited in the Public Record Office (ref BW 1–66). A list has been prepared (NRA 20892). The British Council was established in 1932 and incorporated by Royal Charter in 1940. Its function is to promote a wider knowledge of the United Kingdom and the English language overseas and to develop cultural relations with other countries. It also administers educational programmes etc. on behalf of the Ministry of Overseas Development, the UN etc.

The collection is very extensive. Amongst much other material, there is a General Series (BWI) of 29 files, covering a wide variety of topics, but including auditors' reports, estimates, the allocation of funds and the Colonial Office vote for 1946–47. BWI/36 and 37 also deal with payments by government departments and the allocation of funds, 1946–47.

There are 49 files on Council committees and sub-committees (BW2/5–54) and the minutes of many of the committees. Also in BW2 are 9 files dealing with Council Members, particularly Lord Lloyd, and General Meetings of the Council 1936–1946. Files on Lord Lloyd's visits to the Middle East 1942–43, and Luxembourg 1937–39 are closed for 50 years.

Thirteen files on education cover relations with various universities, while 17 files deal with British and foreign propaganda, much of it in war time. Six financial files for the years 1934–47 relate to subjects such as the Foreign Office grant, donations and appeals for funds from industry, 10 files appertain to the Colonial Office, Foreign Office and Treasury 1935–1945.

A host of subject headings describe the series of files with such varying titles as 'Gramophone Records', 'Visitors', 'Drama', 'Bursaries'. Six reports exist on Lord Lloyd's Italian and Near Eastern tours (1937–39) and Sir Malcolm Robertson in the Middle East and Turkey (1943). There are files on the Home Division of the Council and 9 files relating to the Empire generally, including three (BW2/313–315) on colonial policy (1940–46), dominions policy (1941–46) and empire policy (1941–45). In a series of files on Council Committees BW2/323–332, the agenda and minutes of the Finance Committee (1943–48) and composition of the Executive Committee (1946–1948) may be found.

Sixty-six files (BW4) cover the production and distribution of films by the Council and its relations with various government departments (1940–1946) regarding this activity.

There is a series of files on the various activities of the Council in each of nearly 60 countries.

The minutes exist for a number of the Council Committees. These include minutes of meetings of the Governing Board (later the Executive Committee) 1934–1935 (ref BW68/1–4); Executive Finance and Agenda Committee 1934–1947 (BW69/1–12); the Books and Periodicals Committee 1936–1946 (ref BW70/1–2); the Conference of Allied Ministers of Education 1942–45 (BW74/1–2); and the Joint Standing Committee of the Colonial Office and British Council 1942–1945 (BW77/1).

BRITISH COUNCIL FOR PEACE IN VIETNAM
See **Campaign for Nuclear Disarmament**

BRITISH DENTAL ASSOCIATION
Certain papers have been deposited in the Wellcome Institute. These include minutes and papers of the Representative Board, 1944–51, and minutes of the Joint Advisory Dental Council 1946–47 and the Incorporated Dental Society 1942–47.

BRITISH ECOLOGICAL SOCIETY
See **Environment and Planning**

BRITISH EMPIRE PRODUCERS' ASSOCIATION
See **Commonwealth Producers' Association**

BRITISH FIELD SPORTS SOCIETY
See **Environment and Planning**

BRITISH GAS STAFF ASSOCIATION
Further records of the Association have now been acquired by the Modern Records Centre, University of Warwick (see *Sources*, Vol 1, pp 166–167). The deposit at Warwick (ref MSS 109) was extended when Mr. H. J. Arnold, first general secretary of the Association, donated minutes of the Gas Staff Association, 1943–46, and minutes of the Co-ordinating Committee of Gas Light and Coke Co. Staff, 1944–47. This deposit also included the text of H. J. Arnold's unpublished autobiography.

BRITISH IRON AND STEEL FEDERATION
The records now form part of the archive of the British Steel Corporation.

BRITISH LEAGUE FOR A FREE PALESTINE

Yale University Library holds papers of the Palestine Statehood Committee in-cluding the American League for a Free Palestine. The collection in 14 boxes includes a little material on the activities of the British League for a Free Palestine. Formed in World War II, the League was sponsored by a group of Palestinian Jews led by Peter H. Bergson (Hillel Kook) and allied to similar organisations in the United States and France. These bodies and others campaigned for a Jewish army not under British command to fight against the Axis powers together with the rescue and re-patriation in Palestine of European Jews and the re-establishment of the Hebrew nation in an independent Palestine.

BRITISH LEAGUE FOR THE SUPPORT OF ULSTER AND THE UNION

Although no central archive has been located, reference should be made to the papers of the moving spirit of the League, the 19th Lord Willoughby de Broke. These papers were deposited in the House of Lords Record Office by his son, the present Lord Willoughby de Broke, in June 1973. A handlist has been published in the form of House of Lords Record Office Memorandum No. 58 *The Political Papers of the 19th Lord Willoughby de Broke* (HLRO 1977) a copy of which is filed at the NRA (21684). Although there is little directly bearing on the organisa-tion and administration of the League, there is a great deal of correspondence between de Broke and Unionists, both Irish and English, of every station, on the Irish question. These appear in his general correspondence for 1912 and 1913 (WB/5 and 6) of which there are 19 letters, plus WB/7 and 8, letters referring to Ireland January and February 1914 (26 letters) and WB/10, 16 letters 'concerning Irish Home Rule', 6 March 1914 to 27 July 1914.

BRITISH LEYLAND TRADE UNION COMMITTEE

Certain records of this committee have been placed in the Modern Records Centre, University of Warwick (ref MSS 228). The deposit comprises 26 files of minutes, correspondence and reports, 1949—78, including records of such earlier organisa-tions as the Nuffield Combine Shop Stewards Committee and the MBC Joint Shop Stewards Committee. The deposit complements the Etheridge collection (*q.v.*).

BRITISH MARITIME LAW ASSOCIATION

Records for the period 1947—71 are in University College Library, London.

BRITISH SAFETY FIRST ASSOCIATION
See **Royal Society for the Prevention of Accidents**

BRITISH UNIVERSITIES INDUSTRIAL RELATIONS ASSOCIATION

Certain records have been deposited by the Association in the Modern Records Centre, University of Warwick (ref MSS 52). The collection covers selected records, either originals or copies, from its beginnings in 1950, including minutes of annual meetings and several subject files. Access is only possible with the permission of the Secretary of the Association.

CAMBRIDGE REFUGEE COMMITTEE

The minutes of the Committee, covering the period 1938–53, have been placed in Cambridge University Library. Enquiries concerning access should be directed to the Librarian.

CAMPAIGN FOR NUCLEAR DISARMAMENT

In addition to the material in the BLPES, cited in *Sources* Vol 1, pp 32–33, the main archive of records is now housed in the Modern Records Centre, University of Warwick (ref MSS 181). The material includes Executive Committee Minutes 1958–74; National Council Minutes 1961–75; Income and Expenditure Accounts 1958–68; Annual Conference papers 1968; Publications *Sanity* (1961–8, 1975–8), *Bulletin* (1958–60), *Monthly Notes* (1963–5, 1967), *The Month* (1963–6), *Briefing* (1967–71), various other journals and pamphlets and 2 files of CND ephemera. Also in the collection are a cash book (1965–7), letters of support and lists of supporters (1968) of the British Council for Peace in Vietnam/National Vietnam Campaign Committee.

CAMPAIGN FOR THE ADVANCEMENT OF STATE EDUCATION (CASE)

The records of this group, whose national existence dates from January 1962, have been deposited in the Modern Records Centre, University of Warwick. The records comprise correspondence, papers, material re relations with other national bodies and minutes, *c* 1963–73. The organisation was originally known as the Confederation for the Advancement of State Education.

CENTRAL ASSOCIATION OF MASTER BUILDERS OF LONDON

See **National Federation of Building Trades Employers**

CENTRAL BRITISH FUND FOR GERMAN JEWRY

See **Central British Fund for Jewish Relief**

CENTRAL BRITISH FUND FOR JEWISH RELIEF

Relevant material can be found in the archives of the Board of Deputies of British Jews (see *Sources* Vol 1, pp 20–21). These records (1933–40) include correspondence with the Central British Fund concerning the European situation and refugees (ref E1/26–27). The Board's archives also contain minutes, notices, memoranda, financial statements, etc. (1940–41) of the 'Central Council for Refugees'. The organisation was founded in 1933 as the Central British Fund for German Jewry. The Fund worked until 1948 to rescue German and Austrian refugees.

CENTRAL BUREAU FOR THE SETTLEMENT OF GERMAN JEWS IN PALESTINE

The records of the Bureau, which was an agency of the Zionist Organisation in

London, are held by the Central Zionist Archives in Jerusalem (ref L13). They cover the period 1933–37.

CENTRAL DISCHARGED PRISONERS AID SOCIETY
See **National Association for the Care and Resettlement of Offenders**

CENTRAL LABOUR COLLEGE
In addition to the Central Labour College records, cited in *Sources* Vol 1, p 174, some records have been deposited by the National Union of Railwaymen in the Modern Records Centre, University of Warwick, (ref MSS 127/LC). A list is available (NRA 21635). The College was founded in 1909 by the A.S.R.S. and the South Wales Miners Federation. The records passed to the NUR when the College closed in 1929. The collection comprises 4 volumes of minutes, 1912–30; 22 volumes of financial records, 1919–30, including account books, records of income and expenditure, Secretary's cash book, wages book, buildings maintenance expenses, book allowances statements, and a file of cheque and cash receipts.

CHAMBERS OF COMMERCE AND TRADE
Further information is now available on the records of local chambers of commerce and trade. This includes:

Belfast Chamber of Commerce
Minute books, covering the period 1783–1937, are in the Northern Ireland Public Record Office.

Bradford Chamber of Commerce
Records, 1851–1970, are in Bradford Central Library.

British Latin American Chamber of Commerce
The records have been promised to the library of University College, London.

Bury St Edmunds Chamber of Commerce
Minute books, 1909–51, are in Suffolk Record Office, Bury St Edmunds branch.

Cheltenham Chamber of Commerce
Minute books, 1902–62, are in Gloucestershire Record Office (NRA 21968).

Derby Chamber of Commerce
The surviving records, 1867–1967, have been placed in Derby Public Library.

Dublin Chamber of Commerce
Minutes, annual reports, etc. 1820–1948, are in the Public Record Office of Ireland, Dublin.

Dundee and Tayside Chamber of Commerce
Minute books, cash books, registers, etc., 1819–1960 are in Dundee District Archives.

Glasgow Chamber of Commerce
The records are in the Mitchell Library, Glasgow. *See* NRA 24187.

Greenock Chamber of Commerce
Minute books, 1814–1971, and other records are in the Watt Library, Greenock (ref TD 508).

Kirklees and Wakefield Chamber of Commerce
Records in Kirklees Metropolitan Library, Huddersfield.

Leeds Chamber of Commerce
The records, cited in *Sources* Vol 1, p 13, have been deposited in the Brotherton Library, University of Leeds. There are early minute books and letter-books, 1785–1938 (34 items); an account book, 1857–68 (184 ff); minute books and letter-books, 1938–64 (11 vols); and MBs, 1942–62, 4 vols.

Leicester Chamber of Commerce
Cash books, 1848–50, 1860–1905, are in Leicestershire Record Office (ref DE 2334). A list is available (NRA 26163). The minute books (from 1854) of the Leicestershire Trade Protection Society are also believed to have survived (*see* NRA 1043).

Leyton Chamber of Commerce
Records, 1912–27, are in Waltham Forest Public Library.

Liverpool: American Chamber of Commerce
Established in 1801, the organisation was dissolved in 1908. Four minute books, the first with a list of rules and signatures of the original subscribers, 1801–1908, are in Liverpool Record Office (NRA 9702).

London Chamber of Commerce
The records cited in *Sources* Vol 1, p 13, have now been deposited in the Guildhall Library, London.

Louth Chamber of Trade
Minute books, accounts, etc. have been deposited in Lincolnshire Archives Office.

North Shields Chamber of Commerce
Minutes, 1939–59, are in North Shields County Archives.

Nottingham Chamber of Commerce
Miscellaneous papers, 1916–58, have been placed in Nottingham University Library.

Portsmouth Chamber of Commerce
Minute books, 1879–1950, are deposited in Portsmouth City Record Office.

St. Marylebone Chamber of Commerce
Minute books, 1931–1967, are in Westminster Public Library.

Sheffield Chamber of Trade
The records deposited in Sheffield City Library include minutes, 1864–1948, and correspondence. A list is available (NRA 22712).

Stepney Chamber of Commerce
Records, including records of the Union of Stepney Ratepayers, are in Tower Hamlets Local History Library. *See* NRA 26569.

Stockport Chamber of Trade
Formed as the Stockport Tradesmen's Association, 1897. The Chamber of Trade was formed in December 1919 and the Chamber of Commerce in March 1928. The records deposited in Stockport Public Library include minutes, 1898–1920, agenda and notes for minutes, 1910–20, Chamber of Trade minutes, 1919–48, 5 vols and Chamber of Commerce minutes after 1928.

Sunderland Chamber of Commerce
Minute books, correspondence, etc., 1879–1937, have been deposited in Tyne and Wear Record Office.

Tyne and Wear Chamber of Commerce
Minutes, 1819–1967, have been deposited in Tyne and Wear Record Office. *See* NRA 26360.

Warrington Chamber of Commerce
Minute books, 1876–1915, 5 vols, are in Warrington Public Library.

CHANNEL TUNNEL ASSOCIATION
The papers of this pressure group together with the papers of the Channel Tunnel Company were deposited in Churchill College, Cambridge in April 1980. A list is available (NRA 25829). The Company papers (sections 1–5) contain correspondence, press-cuttings, articles, statistics and plans mainly concerning the 1930 scheme (defeated in the House of Commons by only 7 votes). Most of the Company's early papers were destroyed in a fire at their London office in 1941. The records of the Association (section 6 of the deposit) include papers and publications since its formation in 1962.

CHILD EMIGRATION SOCIETY
The Society, which was renamed the Fairbridge Society Inc., in 1949, has placed its records with Liverpool University Archives. These include minutes (since 1925), individual case files, 1913 onwards, and printed annual reports.

CHINA ASSOCIATION
Since the entry in *Sources* Vol 1 p 36, the papers pertaining to the China Association have been deposited in the Library of the School of Oriental and African Studies. The papers include 13 vols of the Association's Annual Reports (1889–1962)

6 vols of its minutes (1889–1929) General and Executive Committee Minutes (1929–37, 1943–45), miscellaneous minutes and circulars (1945–52), general circulars (1907–27) and circulars to the Executive Committee (1943–45), Bulletins (1946–56) and General Committee Papers (1927–1945). There is a letter book (1893–1898). There are minutes, papers and correspondence (1946–53) of the British Community Interests Committee, relating mainly to Shanghai, and minutes, memos and correspondence (1960–69) of the Sino-British Trade Council. Amongst some other miscellaneous material are 2 volumes of press cuttings on the Far East (1939–1945).

CHINA INLAND MISSION

The few surviving records of the Mission are held by the Overseas Missionary Fellowship, Newington Green, London N16. The Mission, which was founded in 1865 by James Hudson Taylor (1832–1905), was forced to leave China in 1951. Its activities were subsequently extended to other countries in East Asia. Apart from the various publications of the Mission, very few original manuscript records survive. There are, however, various 'Missionaries Journals', copies of journals and letters written by James Hudson Taylor, 1850–74, (11 vols), biographical material concerning Taylor, material on the development of the Church in China etc.

CHRISTIAN SOCIAL UNION

In addition to the records in Pusey House described in *Sources* Vol 1, p 37, many records have been retained in the society's offices and library, St. Katharine Cree Church, Leadenhall Street, London EC3A 3DH. The records include minutes of the Navvy Mission from 1877, the main committee from 1897 and the finance committee from 1894. Records of the Christian Social Union include central executive minutes from 1895, council minutes from 1893, records of the Maurice Hostel from 1901 and records of the Westminster Group of the Christian Social Union 1911–17. Records of the Industrial Christian Fellowship include council, main committee and finance minutes from 1919. The society was originally formed as the Navvy Mission Society in 1877. It adopted the title Industrial Christian Fellowship in 1918. From 1919 it incorporated the Christian Social Union.

CHURCH COMMITTEE FOR DEFENCE AND INSTRUCTION
See Church Defence Institution

CHURCH DEFENCE INSTITUTION

There are records of the Institution held at Church House, Dean's Yard, Westminster, London SW1P 3NZ. The records include minutes of the Church Defence Institution, 1859–96 and annual reports, 1868–1921. In addition Church House holds the minutes of the Central Church Committee, 1894–96 and minutes of the Church Committee for Defence and Instruction, 1896–1923. There is also a complete run of the magazine *National Church*, 1872–1922. A list is available (NRA 24406).

CHURCH OF ENGLAND COUNCIL FOR FOREIGN RELATIONS

The records of the Council, which was founded in 1933 but since 1972 has been an independent secretariat of the Archbishop are held in the offices of the Archbishop of Canterbury's Counsellors on Foreign Relations, Palace Court, 222 Lambeth Road, London SE1 7LB. According to C. Kitchin, *The Central Records of the Church of England*, the records include files which contain much information on modern relations between the Church of England and other churches throughout the world. The records of the Nikaean Club and the Philip Usher Memorial Fund are also retained here. The material is not listed. Since many of the files are highly confidential, requests for access must be presented, though the Chaplain, to the Archbishop. As a general rule, no files less than 40 years old are available for consultation.

CHURCH OF ENGLAND PURITY SOCIETY

The records, since 1887, are held at Church House Record Centre, Dean's Yard, Westminster.

CHURCH OF ENGLAND TEMPERANCE SOCIETY

The records, 1907–67, have been placed in Lambeth Palace Library.

CHURCH OF SCOTLAND FOREIGN MISSIONS

An extensive collection of records has been deposited in the National Library of Scotland. A list has been prepared (NRA 10528). The papers are filed according to the denominations with which they originated.

(a) *Church of Scotland* – Letter books 1877 to 1895; 1895 to 1897; 1911 to 1929 with gaps; 6 volumes of the Convenor's letter books 1876–1907. Letter books relating to Africa 1888–1926; Darjeeling 1888–1926; Poona 1888–1904, Calcutta 1896–1925 and China 1896–1925.

The minutes survive for the Foreign Mission Committee – Sub Committee 1918–1922 and the Foreign Mission Committee Bombay Corresponding Board (with some Accounts) 1836–1858. The accounts of the Committee on the General Assembly: India Mission 1839–1848 survive, as does the Foreign Missions Ledger 1878–79 and the letter books of the Foreign Mission Treasurer 1895–1898 (2 vols).

There are letters received by the Foreign Mission Committee between 1918 and 1926 and the East India Mission letters (3 vols) 1829–1842.

(b) *United Presbyterian Church*
These consist of Foreign Mission Office foreign letter books 1851–1882 and 1882–1931 (with gaps); Foreign Mission Office general letter book 1882–1936 (with gaps) and Mission Board letter books for 1847–1851, 1858–1859, 1860–1865, 1867–1869, 1870–1879.

(c) *Free Church of Scotland*
Two letter books 1856–1920; 12 vols of letters 1869–1910, letter book of the Livingstonia Mission 1901–34, and the minute book of the Livingstonia Mission Sub-Committee 1877–90. There are 11 box files on the Livingstonia Mission which deal, amongst other things, with the Missions committees 1875–1900, accounts and a deputation to the government in 1887.

Fifteen box files exist on various locations and also on the Mission to Bombay

(1889–1900) and Poona (1880–1900). There is also a general box file for 1884–9. The records also contain 3 letters from David Livingstone 1861, 62, and 1872.

Women's Organisations – 6 volumes of letter books 1876–1899, with gaps, of the Ladies Society for Female Education in India and South Africa, and 3 volumes of letter books of that society's Glasgow Committee, for the years 1878–1895. Women's Foreign Mission Letter Book (2 vols) 1899–1901; (39 vols) 1901–1917; (13 vols) 1917–1927. Women's Foreign Missions General Book 1927–1930. Womens Foreign Missions Deputations (2 vols) 1921–1925 and 1929 to 1930. Womens Foreign Missions Accounts (2 vols) 1901–1911.

(d) *United Free Church of Scotland*
Box files on Foreign Missions Committees on Manchuria 1924–26; South Africa 1926; Rajputana 1926. German Mission 1924, General Letters 1924–1925. Home Organisation 1926, Salaries 1922–23, Candidates (2 vols) 1924–32, Lovedale (1900–1908).

There are 10 bundles of incoming letters from Britain and overseas.

Women's Organisations – Womens Missionary College Letter Book (2 vols), 1910–16; Household Accounts 1894–1908; Foreign Society Calabar 1919–1924; Foreign Mission Manchuria (1928–29) and Bengal (1925–9).

There is a miscellaneous collection of letter books, cash books etc. and a Report on the Establishment of the East African Scottish Mission 1891–92.

CHURCH REFORM LEAGUE

The surviving records are housed in Church House, Dean's Yard, Westminster. In 1929, the Church Reform League merged with the Incorporated Free and Open Church Association (IFOCA) to become the Church Self-Government League. The collection at Church House includes not only minutes of all these organisations but also some records of the League of Loyalty and Order, which itself later became the Westminster Group. The Church Reform League records include minutes, 1895–1929, an executive agenda and attendance book, 1901–09, records of the central representative council, 1899–1917, 1927–29, and accounts from 1897. There are minutes of the League of Loyalty and Order, 1927–28 and Westminster Group minutes, 1928–37; IFOCA minutes, 1917–29 and an agenda book, 1912-28. For the Church Self-Government League there are minutes, 1929–37, annual meetings, 1929–39 and finance committee minutes, 1929–34. A list is available (NRA 24408).

CHURCH SELF GOVERNMENT LEAGUE
See **Church Reform League**

CHURCH SOCIETY

The records of the Society have been retained in its offices, 7 Wine Office Court, Fleet Street, London EC4A 3DA. The Society was founded in 1950 by a merger of the Church Association (founded in 1865) and the National Church League (founded 1906). The National Church League was itself an amalgamation of the National Protestant Church Union (founded 1893) and the Church of England League (founded in 1904 and formerly the Ladies League, 1899). These in turn had as their predecessors the Protestant Association (1835) and the Protestant Education Institute (1870). The records retained at the offices of the Church Society consist mainly of relatively full sets of minutes, magazines etc., with apparently little original correspondence. A rough list of minutes, which are subject to a 40 year rule, is available. Details can be found in C. Kitchin, *The Central Records of the Church of England*. Among other organisations and conferences whose minutes are with the Church Society archive are the Cheltenham/Oxford Conference of Evangelical Churchmen (1916–   ) and the Federation of Diocesan Evangelical Unions (1945–   ).

CIVIL SERVICE UNION

Since the entry in *Sources* Vol 1, p 42, the union has deposited some records in the Modern Records Centre, University of Warwick (ref MSS 111). The first deposit comprised files on the contract cleaning issue *c* 1960–70.

COAL MERCHANTS' ASSOCIATION OF SCOTLAND

The records have survived in private hands. *See* NRA 23867.

COAL OWNERS' ASSOCIATIONS

See **Colliery Owners' Associations**

COBDEN CLUB

Since the entry in *Sources* Vol 1, pp 42–43, the papers have been deposited in West Sussex Record Office. The collection includes minutes of Committee and Annual Meetings, July 1866–August 1886 and January 1887–March 1896. There is also a Cobden Club dinner book, 1877–1880, the minutes of the Special Committee of the International Free Trade Congress, 1908, minutes of the Club's Annual Meetings, 1911–34, three Annual Reports (1936–38), various lists of subscribers to local Liberal Associations, a subscription book, 1921–50, an account book, 1913–19 and an account book of the South West Free Trade Union, 1936–39. There are also some records of the National Reform Union (*q.v.*).

COLLIERY OWNERS' ASSOCIATIONS

In addition to the various papers described in *Sources* Vol 1, p 44, the following additional records have been located:

Ayrshire Coal Owners' Association

Certain records are in Glasgow University Archives. These include financial records, 1946–55, and a 1946 list of members. A list is available (NRA 25551).

Durham Coal Owners' Association

An important collection of records is deposited in Durham Record Office (ref Acc. 1228 (D)). A list is available (NRA 25854). The deposit comprises 137 volumes of cash books, ledgers, minutes, records of area groups etc., the earliest dating back to February 1872.

Erewash Valley Colliery Owners' Association

The records have been acquired by Nottinghamshire Record Office.

Lanarkshire Coal Masters' Association

A collection of records is in Glasgow University Archives. The deposit includes 20 volumes of minutes (1886–1954) and annual reports, (1887–1953). A list is available (NRA 25550).

Midland Counties Colliery Owners' Association

The records have been acquired by Nottinghamshire Record Office, to whom enquiries should be addressed.

Northumberland and Durham Colliery Owners' Association

Records for the period 1857–91 have been placed in Northumberland Record Office.

South Yorkshire Colliery Owners' Association

In addition to the records cited in *Sources* Vol 1, pp 45–46, some three boxes of material on the Association can be found in the archives of Newton Chambers & Co. Ltd., in Sheffield Central Library (National Coal Board Deposit). A list is available (NRA 14792).

West Yorkshire Colliery Owners' Association

The records are in the Brotherton Library, University of Leeds. The collection includes the deed of association, lists of members, output statements, minutes and papers, 1889–1955.

COLONIAL CIVIL SERVANTS ASSOCIATION

The papers of the Association are in Rhodes House Library, Oxford (ref MSS Brit Emp S 100–121). The collection includes the constitution, minutes of conferences, circulars, bulletins and correspondence.

COMMITTEE FOR ARAB AFFAIRS

Although no surviving archive has been located for this pro-Arab pressure group, which was active in London in the 1940s, there is relevant material in the Spears papers in the Middle East Centre, St. Antony's College, Oxford. This includes minutes and agenda (1945–46), correspondence (mainly 1946) and membership records (1945–48).

COMMITTEE FOR THE HERBREW UNIVERSITY, LONDON

The records of the Committee, which was an agency of the Zionist Organisation in London and was founded in 1919, are held by the Central Zionist Archives, Jerusalem (ref L12). They cover the period 1919–34. Reference should also be made to the records of the Friends of the Hebrew University (*q.v.*).

COMMITTEE ON WOMAN POWER

Two volumes of minutes and papers of this all-party group of women MPs, covering the years 1940–45, were placed in BLPES in February 1978 by Graham Hoare Esq.

(ref Coll Misc 548). The Committee, which met at the House of Commons under the chairmanship of Irene Ward, was formed to investigate the problems and possibilities of women's war work.

COMMONS, OPEN SPACES AND FOOTPATHS PRESERVATION SOCIETY

An extensive collection of records of this pressure group has been deposited in the House of Lords Record Office, to whom enquiries should be addressed. *See also* NRA 24471 and **Environment and Planning.**

COMMONWEALTH AND CONTINENTAL CHURCH SOCIETY

The surviving records of the Society have been deposited in the Guildhall Library, London. The Society was founded in 1861 as the Colonial and Continental Church Society by the merger of two earlier bodies — the Colonial Church Society (formerly the Western Australia Missionary Society and later the Australian Church Missionary Society) and the Church of England Society for the Education of the Poor in New-foundland and the Colonies (formerly known as the Newfoundland School Society). Although some records were destroyed by bombing, the material in the Guildhall Library includes minutes, 1839–42, 1850–1933, various committee and sub-committee records, annual reports since 1905 (with gaps) and the magazine *Greater British Messenger*, 1902–60. There are also correspondence files by area, although these are almost all modern. The Chaplain's books (registers) are also mainly for the modern period.

COMMONWEALTH COUNTRIES LEAGUE

The surviving papers have been deposited in the Fawcett Library, City of London Polytechnic.

COMMONWEALTH INDUSTRIES ASSOCIATION

Since the entry in *Sources* Vol 1, p 47, the records have been deposited in the Modern Records Centre, University of Warwick. A list is available (NRA 24412).

COMMONWEALTH PRODUCERS' ASSOCIATION

Since the entry in *Sources* Vol 1, p 49, the records of this organisation (formerly the British Empire Producers' Association) have been deposited with the Royal Commonwealth Society. On the dissolution of the organisation in 1975, the records handed over included Council minutes, 1916–74; Executive Committee minutes, 1916–19, 1941–75; minutes of subsidiary bodies; the *Newsletter*, 1948–67; and a run of *Commonwealth Producer* (and earlier titles), 1916–75. A list is available (NRA 25316).

CONFEDERATION FOR THE ADVANCEMENT OF STATE EDUCATION

See **Campaign for the Advancement of State Education**

CONFEDERATION OF BRITISH INDUSTRIES

Since the entry in *Sources* Vol 1, p 50, a very important collection of records has been deposited in the Modern Records Centre, University of Warwick. The deposit includes the papers of the three constituents of the CBI : the Federation of British Industries; the British Employers Confederation; and the National Association of British Manufacturers. Cataloguing is not fully complete but it has been possible to identify the separate archives of the three predecessors and the distinct records series within them (such as the papers of Presidents, Directors General, departments, industrial advisers committees, publications etc. 1,500 archive boxes remained after weeding, but only a proportion has yet been catalogued in any detail. There are also extensive local and regional deposits.

CONFEDERATION OF EMPLOYEE ORGANISATIONS

Certain records have been acquired by the Modern Records Centre, University of Warwick (ref MSS 61). The Confederation was established in June 1973 to meet a demand from non-aligned unions, staff and professional associations for a voice with government. It was wound up in 1979, and the records subsequently deposited, but they were closed until January, 1985.

CONFEDERATION OF HEALTH SERVICE EMPLOYEES (COHSE)

Since the entry in *Sources* Vol. 1, p 50, an important deposit of material has been made to the Modern Records Centre, University of Warwick (ref MSS 229). It includes COHSE minutes to the 1960s and minutes of predecessor organisations. An outline history by M. Carpenter, *All for One*, was published in 1980. A list is available (NRA 24978).

CONFERENCE OF BRITISH MISSIONARY SOCIETIES

The archives of the organisation, described in *Sources* Vol 1, p 51, have been placed on loan in the Library of the School of Oriental and African Studies. The collection includes a section of Joint CBMS/International Missionary Council Africa and India Archives, 1910–45, the period of the work of J. H. Oldham and William Paton in Edinburgh House.

CONSERVATIVE PARTY

Since the entry in *Sources* Vol 1, p 53, the central records of the Party have been deposited in the Bodleian Library, Oxford. The collection is at present being catalogued and enquiries concerning access should be addressed to the Bodleian.

The following new information on constituency records is now available:

Accrington Conservative Association

The records (some dating from 1882) have been deposited in the John Rylands University of Manchester Library (NRA 25954).

Armagh Conservative Association

Minute books for the period 1906 to 1927 are in the Northern Ireland Public Record Office.

Banbury Conservative Association

Xeroxes of minute books, 1837–1932, are in Oxfordshire County Record Office.

Bedford Conservative Club

Minutes, articles of association, etc., 1894–1934, are in Bedfordshire County Record Office.

Bedfordshire Conservative Association

Minute books/accounts, 1933–69, are in Bedfordshire County Record Office.

Blackburn Conservative Association

Records, 1906–62, are in Lancashire Record Office.

Bradford Conservative Association

The records of the Association, 1870–1940, have been deposited in Bradford Archives Department.

Bristol Conservative Association

Minutes, 1920–53, have been placed in Bristol Record Office.

Buckingham Conservative Association

Registers and correspondence, 1837–74, are in Buckinghamshire Record Office.

Camborne Conservative Association

Records, 1919–34, are in Cornwall Record Office.

Carshalton Conservative Association

The records are now deposited in Surrey Record Office.

Caterham Conservative Association

A minute book, 1874–92, is in Surrey Record Office.

Chelmsford Conservative Association

Records, 1886–1977, are in Essex Record Office.

Cornwall South-East Conservative Association

Records, 1925–60, are in Cornwall Record Office.

Denbigh Conservative Association

Minute books, etc., 1923–69, are in the Clwyd Record Office at Ruthin.

Derby Conservative Association

Minute books, 1911–39, are now in Derbyshire County Record Office (*see* NRA 24133).

Derbyshire West Conservative Association

Minute books, 1907–73, accounts, 1912–73, papers on constituency organisation, etc., are deposited in Derbyshire County Record Office.

Down North Unionist Association
Minute books, 1929–73, are in the Public Record Office of Northern Ireland.

Dundee Moderate Group/Progressive Party
Minute books, 1948–70, are in Dundee District Archives.

Ealing South Conservative Association
Minute books, reports, etc., 1915–54, are in Greater London Record Office.

Essex North Conservative Association
The agent's records for 1865 are in Essex Record Office.

Fermanagh and Tyrone Unionist Association
Correspondence, etc., of R. A. Parke (1920–49), agent for the constituency are in the Northern Ireland Public Record Office.

Fylde Conservative Association
The papers of J. R. Almond, agent for the Association, and other papers, 1883–1972, are in Lancashire Record Office.

Glasgow Conservative Club
Records retained by the Club include 26 minute books of the Management Committee, 1880–1976, and a minute book of the Political Committee, 1895–1916.

Hatfield Conservative Association
The records, 1900–48, are held by Hertfordshire Record Office.

Lancashire North-East Conservative Registration Association
Records, 1876–86, are in Lancashire Record Office.

Leeds West Conservative Association
Minute books, 1927–48, are deposited in Leeds City Archives.

Leicester Constitutional Club
Accounts, minute books, correspondence, etc., 1886–1974, are in Leicestershire Record Office.

Long Eaton Conservative Club
Minute books/correspondence, 1887–91, are in Nottingham University Library.

Manchester Withington Conservative Club
Minutes, 1889–1918, are in Manchester Central Library.

Mid-Yorkshire Conservative Federation
Some records have been placed in the West Yorkshire Record Office.

Newbury Conservative Association
Records, 1934–75, are in Berkshire Record Office.

Newcastle-under-Lyme Conservative Club
Minute books, 1883–1950, have been placed in Staffordshire Record Office.

Newcastle West Conservative Association
Records, 1918–80, are in Tyne & Wear Record Office. *See* NRA 26629.

Northwich & District Conservative & Unionist Association
Records, 1905–65, are in Cheshire Record Office.

Pembrokeshire Conservative Association
Records, 1837–92, in the deposit of Higgon of Scolton are in Pembrokeshire Record Office.

Pontefract Conservative Club
Ten minute books, 1890–1958, are in West Yorkshire Record Office (NRA 20563).

Reigate Conservative Association
In addition to the earlier records, deposited in Surrey Record Office, more recent records deposited include AGM minutes, 1948–71, Executive Committee minutes 1964–71, etc.

St Marylebone Conservative Association
Records, 1929–81, are in Westminster Public Library.

Scottish Universities Conservative Association
Records, 1906–47, are in Glasgow University Library.

Sheffield Eccleshall Conservative Association
The records, 1885–1929, have now been placed in Sheffield University Library.

Sheffield Hallam Conservative Association
The records, 19th and 20th century, are in Sheffield Central Library.

Sheffield Park Conservative Association
Minutes, 1906–70, are in Sheffield City Library.

Stafford and Stone Conservative Association
Records, 1889–present, are in Staffordshire Record Office.

Stockport Conservative Club
Minutes, 1919–34, are in Stockport Central Library.

Todmorden Conservative Association
Records, 1875–83, are in Calderdale Public Library.

Truro Conservative and Unionist Association
Minutes and accounts, 1918–68, are in Cornwall Record Office.

Tyrone East Unionist Association
Accounts and pamphlets, 1904–21, are in the Northern Ireland Public Record Office.

Uxbridge Conservative Association
Contrary to the information in *Sources* Vol 1, p 70, the records remain with the Association.

Wanstead and Woodford Conservative Association
Records, 1924–82, are in Essex Record Office.

Warwick and Leamington Conservative Association
Records from 1885 have been placed in Warwickshire Record Office.

Woolwich West Conservative Association
Records, 1935–60, are in Greenwich Local History Library.

York Conservative Association
Minute books and other material, 1880–1945, are in York City Library.

COTTON EMPLOYERS' ASSOCIATIONS

Several Cotton Employers' Associations have deposited their records in the John Rylands University Library of Manchester. They include the following:

Ashton-under-Lyne Cotton Employers' Association
Two vols, general minutes, 1891–1908; nine vols, General Committee minutes, 1912–44; six vols, 'special' minute books, 1898–1943; and 'memoranda relating to holidays', 1929–54.

Glossop, Hyde and District Cotton Employers' Association
Minutes of meetings, 1898–1920, minutes of Committee Meetings, three vols, 1898–1921. In 1921 the Association amalgamated with the Ashton and District C E A

Manchester and District Cotton Employers' Association
Minutes, 1892–1949.

Stockport and District Cotton Employers' Association
Minutes, 1892–98, 1920–34, 1934–42, 1950–58; agenda books, 1924–45, 1945–53.

Wigan and District Cotton Employers' Association
Minutes, ten vols, 1907–35.

COTTON MANUFACTURERS' ASSOCIATIONS

An extensive collection of records of a variety of local organisations can be found in the archives of Blackburn Cotton Manufacturers' Association, deposited by the Secretary in Lancashire Record Office in 1977 (ref DDX 1115/1–2). A list is available (NRA 20851).

The collection includes 10 volumes of minutes, 1877–1966; Annual Reports, 1942–71; 17 letter books 1906–51; 4 rule books and 30 correspondence files on specific subjects. There are 2 ledgers for 1903–63, 4 cash books, 1904–55, and levy record 1899–1950. 13 volumes of minutes, 1927–35, of the Cotton Spinners and Manufacturers' Association (Manchester) joint meetings are held. The minutes (1896–1960) and correspondence (1912–20, 1958–60) of the Accrington and District Cotton Spinners and Manufacturers' Association, form part of the collection. There also exist a levy and subscription book (1912–60) and 30 statements of account (1920–49) of the Accrington Association. The minutes of the Clitheroe Cotton Employers' Association 1906–30, 1964, and of the Great Harwood Masters' Association, 1893–1914 are held. Also in the collection are the papers of Frank Longworth J.P., relating to his chairmanship of the Blackburn District Cotton Employers' Association 1941–46, and as a member of Manchester Chamber of Commerce and other regional bodies.

COUNCIL FOR THE AMELIORATION OF THE LEGAL POSITION OF THE JEWESS

Anglo-Jewish Archives at the Mocatta Library, University College, London, hold some records (ref AJ/13) including correspondence (1922–26) with organisations in Palestine, and press cuttings, general correspondence etc. (1923–46). The Council was founded in 1922 to campaign for practical help for Jewish women suffering from hardship and discrimination.

COUNCIL FOR THE PROTECTION OF RURAL ENGLAND

Since the entry in *Sources* Vol 1, pp 81–82 the council has deposited several hundred of its administration files, dating back to its formation in 1926 with the Institute of Agricultural History and Museum of English Rural Life, Reading University. A list is available (NRA 24450). *See also* **Environment and Planning**.

COUNCIL FOR THE RESCUE OF JEWS IN POLAND

The surviving records have been placed in the Central Zionist Archives in Jerusalem.

COUNCIL OF BRITISH SOCIETIES FOR RELIEF ABROAD

Certain records have been deposited in the Bodleian Library, Oxford, (ref BAG). The collection (19 boxes) include financial records, comprised of stores account book, subscription book, salaries books (1945–50) petty cash book (1946–50), general account books (1943–51), audited accounts and monthly bank statements (1949–51). There is a file index (1942–50) on 'Home-finance' including files of auditors reports, financial statements, Treasury grants, treasurer's file, and subsidies to Council and conference. There is a similar file index (1942–50) on 'Home Societies' including material on the British Red Cross, the Foreign Office, International Refugee Organisation and Catholic Committee for Relief Abroad. There are 3 files listed as 'Appeals-UNAC' and various administrative files eg. Transport, Office stationery. Files on 'Home-Grants' fill 3 boxes and relate to a large number of organisations including the Salvation Army, Y.W.C.A., British Red Cross and the Boy Scouts Association. The files (including agenda, minutes and notices) of various committees, and of the chairman, deputy chairman and treasurer are held, together with documents relating to the Relief Supplies Fund including receipt books, bank files and statements, account books and food schedules 1947/8. Files are also held on 'Home Societies' (1942–50); miscellaneous material on post war relief work; Germany 1949–50 (including minutes and agenda of various meetings, files on policy, 'displaced persons' 'locations', a diary and circulars); and 'general' files on various countries including Greece, Austria, Italy, Holland, Malaya and Palestine.

COUNCIL OF FOREIGN BONDHOLDERS

Since the entry in *Sources* Vol 1, p 84, the records have been deposited in the Guildhall Library, London.

COUNCIL OF MARRIED WOMEN

The records are with the Fawcett Society collection, now deposited in the City of London Polytechnic. A list is available (NRA 20625). The Council was founded in 1952 to support marriage as an institution, to promote equalisation of the sexes and to promote legislation for legal and economic justice for women. The collection includes minutes of the Executive Committee (1 vol. 1952–59); minutes of AGMs, 1952–64; Chairmen's reports, 1956–59. There are papers relating to the formation of the Council and its early years ; Bank statements, 1961–67, and the Annual Report and accounts for 1969. Correspondence includes files on specific topics 1957–61, mainly on the effects of various legislative acts on the position of women; and general correspondence, 1953–61. Various publications and printed matter are held, including a series of the *Monthly Bulletin* of the Council, 1952–59.

COUNCIL OF POST OFFICE UNIONS (COPOU)

A collection of records has been deposited at the Modern Records Centre, University of Warwick (ref MSS 89). The collection includes circulars and minutes of meetings (1922–68) of the Post Office Engineering Federation, subsequently the P.O. Engineering and Store Departmental Whitley Council; General Purposes Committee minutes (1932–1961) 'Whitley Bulletins', (1954–55, 1960–69), P.O. Departmental Whitley Council, Staff Side minutes (1920–69) with the secretary's reports for the 1950s and 1960s; the Executive Committee and Reorganisation Committee minutes of the Staff Side (1966–69); minutes of meetings of the Staff Side with the Official Side (1920–26, 1932–68) and the minutes of the following committees and sub-committees: Clerical sub-committee (1933–67); Postal (1967–69); Training and Education (1945–64) and Welfare (1947–69). A quantity of correspondence files exist on various topics including standard files for the 1930s, the Committee on the Women's Question, promotion procedure, productivity, staffing, regionalisation etc. The records include procedural agreements and substantive agreements prior to 1971. On the cessation of COPOU on 31 December 1981, recent administrative files and unsigned committee minutes, 1969–80, were added to the deposit.

COUNTRY LANDOWNERS' ASSOCIATION

Further details are now available of the papers, cited in *Sources* Vol. 1, p 85, at the Institute of Agricultural History, University of Reading. The collection, which is now listed (NRA 20987), is divided into four main parts: A (administrative), B (legal), C (social and personal), D (publications and publicity material). Among the more important records are minutes of the Council (1922–55), Executive Committee minutes (1908–58, 28 vols), minutes of the Land Committee, 1910; 26 box files relating to branch and regional offices, sub-committees etc., mainly 1950s–60s. There are files of the taxation sub-committee, 1949–59, reports of AGMs, 8 volumes of legal opinions on various matters, a typescript history of the Association, 1907–47 and a run of the *Journal*, 1923–50.

COUNTY COUNCILS ASSOCIATION

See **Environment and Planning**

DONOVAN COMMITTEE ON TRADE UNIONS AND EMPLOYERS' ASSOCIATIONS

The papers, 1965–68, are in the Library of Nuffield College, Oxford. They are not at present available for research.

DUBLIN UNIVERSITY DEFENCE COMMITTEE

The records of the Committee are in the Library of Trinity College Dublin. A list is available (NRA 21056). The Defence Committee was formed when a scheme of university reform, arising out of the Dublin University Commission of 1906 (the Fry Commission) and sponsored by James Bryce, the Chief Secretary for Ireland, was under consideration by the Liberal government in 1906. This was for the transformation of Trinity College, Dublin, into a federal university, to include a new college which would be regarded by the Roman Catholic church authorities as suitable for Roman Catholics. The honorary secretaries of the Defence Committee were Edward John Gwynn, fellow (later Provost) and Edward Parnall Culverwell, fellow and professor of education, and the honorary assistant secretary was Robert Malcolm Gwynn, fellow. The committee was active until late in 1908 when, having secured its object by the abandonment of the Bryce scheme, it dissolved itself.

The papers of the committee consist of 2 boxes of miscellaneous material (memoranda, circulars, pamphlets etc.) and a box of correspondence, (ref MS 2666), a memorandum book of one of the honorary secretaries, E. J. Gwynn (MS 2665), a register of letters received (MS 2664) and 6 volumes of lists of names and addresses (MSS 2658–63). No general minute book of the committee's meetings appears to have survived. Other relevant material is in the Herbert Greene papers (MS 2501), the A. F. Dixon papers (MS 3332) and the papers of Professor John Joly (MS 2304), all in the Library of Trinity College, Dublin.

DURHAM COUNTY COLLIER ENGINEMENS', BOILER MINDERS' AND FIREMENS' ASSOCIATION

See **National Union of Mineworkers**

EDUCATIONAL INSTITUTE OF SCOTLAND

An extensive archive has been retained by the Institute, the oldest teachers' organisation in the world. The Institute was founded in 1847 by Leonard Schmitz 'to promote sound learning in Scotland', but some of the records pre-date 1847. The collection includes annual reports (since 1847), membership lists from 1920, cash books and ledgers, records of committees, including the Parliamentary Committee from 1901, correspondence concerning relations with international bodies such as the World Federation of Education Associations and material concerning other organisations such as the Scottish School Books Association.

ELECTRICAL ELECTRONIC TELECOMMUNICATION AND PLUMBING UNION

Since the entry in *Sources* Vol 1, p 88, the first deposit of records of the Union has been made in the Modern Records Centre, University of Warwick. The initial deposit comprised records of the United Operative Plumbers' Association from the second half of the nineteenth and the first years of the twentieth century. Included are circulating executive and branch minute books or accounts and membership records from Birmingham, Blyth, Bolton, Brighton, Colwyn Bay, Doncaster, Edinburgh, Exeter, Grantham, Hull, Manchester, Newcastle, Preston, Sunderland, Torquay, North Wales and West Central. In addition files are held on a conference with employers, 1896, concerning the National Plumbers' Society, and the National Union of Operative Heating and Domestic Engineers and General Metal Workers, with minute books and other items from the East London Society of Operative Plumbers. Registration books and blank proposition books are held for the Scottish Plumbers.

ENGINEERING EMPLOYERS' FEDERATION

Since the entry in *Sources* Vol 1, p 90, the extensive surviving historical records (prior to 1950) have been placed in the Modern Records Centre, University of Warwick.

ENVIRONMENT AND PLANNING

With funds from the Social Science Research Council, a survey has been undertaken of the records of a wide variety of organisations and societies active in the area of environment, ecology and planning. The survey was carried out by Philippa Bassett on behalf of the Centre of Urban and Regional Studies, Birmingham University and the Institute of Agricultural History at Reading University. Lists of the surviving archives have been prepared for the following organisations: Council for the Protection of Rural England (NRA 24450); Scottish Rights of Ways Society (NRA 24451); Scottish Youth Hostels Association (NRA 24452); British Ecological Society (NRA 24453); British Field Sports Society (NRA 24454); Royal Town Planning Institute (NRA 24455); County Councils Association (NRA 24456); Cyclists Touring Club (NRA 24458); Fauna Preservation Society (NRA 24459); National Farmers Union of Scotland (NRA 24460); Men of the Trees (NRA 24461); Norfolk Naturalists Trust (NRA 24462); Countrywide Holidays Association (NRA 24463); Caravan Club Ltd (NRA 24464); Youth Hostels Association (NRA 24465); Council for National Parks (NRA 24466); Society for the Protection of Ancient Buildings (NRA 24467); Holiday Fellowship (NRA 24468); National Society for

Clean Air (NRA 24469); Friends of the Lake District (NRA 24470); Commons, Open Spaces and Footpaths Preservation Society (NRA 24471); Town and Country Planning Association (NRA 24472); Pedestrians Association (NRA 24474); Roads Beautifying Association (NRA 24475); Royal Society for the Protection of Birds (NRA 24476); and the Geographical Association (NRA 24477). Among other entries concerned with environment in this volume, *see* Society for Checking the Abuses of Public Advertising. In addition, a variety of records of local protest groups have also been deposited. Amongst these are the Stansted Airport Action Group (deposited in Essex University Library) and the Anti-Concorde Project (Modern Records Centre, University of Warwick, ref MSS 32). The 'Save the Broad St—Richmond Line Committee' is in the Greater London Record Office and the Blackheath Motorway Action Group in the Lewisham Archives and Local History Collection, while Essex Record Office has records of the Southend Railway Travellers Association (*see* NRA 25272).

EUROPEAN MOVEMENT
See **Britain in Europe**

EXIT
See **Voluntary Euthanasia Society**

FAIRBRIDGE SOCIETY INC.
See **Child Emigration Society**

FEDERAL UNION
The records were given to the University of Sussex Library through the agency of Dr R. Pryce in a series of deposits between 1966 and 1974. In 1984, however, these records may be transferred to the British Library of Political and Economic Science, to which enquiries should be directed. Federal Union was founded in 1938 to advance the cause of federal government among democratic states as a means of achieving international peace, economic security and civil rights. It devoted particularly strenuous efforts to the cause of European integration and Britain's entry into the European Economic Community. The records are essentially the complete archive of the Federal Union and its educational charity, the Federal Educational and Research Trust. To these have been added the personal papers of R. W. G. Mackay MP. The files of the archive have been arranged in groups under broad descriptive headings and have been numbered. A list is available (NRA 20019).

FEDERATION OF COMMONWEALTH CHAMBERS OF COMMERCE
The records, 1911—74, have been deposited in the Guildhall Library, London.

FEDERATION OF JEWISH RELIEF ORGANISATIONS
Although much correspondence etc., has been destroyed, the federation still holds a set of minutes from 1919 and also some books of press cuttings, at its offices,

139 Elgin Avenue, London W9 1JH. These records are to be placed in the Anglo-Jewish Archives. The Federation was founded in 1919 and embraces those organisations which give assistance to Jewish victims of war and persecution. For the records of such organisations, *see*, for example, the **Jewish Refugee Committee**, the **Central British Fund for Jewish Relief**, and the **Society for the Protection of Science and Learning** (*Sources*, Vol 1, p 243). For a detailed description of the many other organisations see P. Jones, *Britain and Palestine* pp 151–152.

FEDERATION OF SAILMAKERS OF GREAT BRITAIN AND IRELAND

Certain records of this small and now defunct trade union were acquired by the Modern Records Centre, University of Warwick, from a Yorkshire bookseller in 1975 (ref MSS 87). The Union was formed in 1889 and subsequently made its headquarters in Hull. It ceased functioning in 1926/27. The collection includes 4 minute books, 1889–99 (2 gaps in sequence), printed minutes of 9 Conferences, 1892–1918, some balance sheets, 1890–1923, some copies of monthly reports and wage rates, mainly 1916–18, and Federation rule books for Belfast, Hull and Liverpool. In addition, there are *c* 660 items of correspondence, 1892–1923. Topics covered include the local state of the trade, negotiations over pay and hours, Admiralty dockyard employment, the employment of women, the use of machines, war-time conditions and the problems of the Federation's future.

FEDERATION OF WOMEN CIVIL SERVANTS

The records, covering the period 1920–59, have been placed in the Fawcett Library Collection in the City of London Polytechnic.

FELLOWSHIP OF EVANGELICAL CHURCHMEN

The Fellowship has no permanent office and the few surviving records migrate with the Secretary. Virtually no records are known to survive, except minute-books for 1932–33 and from 1963 onwards. *See* C. Kitchin, *The Central Records of the Church of England.*

FELLOWSHIP OF ST. ALBAN AND ST. SERGIUS

An interesting collection of records has been retained by the Fellowship at St. Basil's House, 52 Ladbroke Grove, London W11 2PB. The collection includes minute books and accounts from its foundation, many files of correspondence, especially for the 1930s, records of the Russian Clergy and Church Aid Fund 1931–35 and some private papers of Nicholas Zernow. The Fellowship was founded in 1927 to promote understanding between the Churches of the West and the East.

FILE FORGERS UNION

A collection of records has been deposited at Sheffield Central Library, (ref MD 4020–4023). The collection consists of the minutes of general and quarterly and special meetings 1879–1915, minutes of committee meetings 1843–1918, a minute book 1889–99, the minutes of executive, general and other meetings 1890–1945, and the Carlton Main Colliery Company Shareholders' minute book.

There are wage lists for 1866 and 1873. MD 5846 is the Article of Agreement to found the File Forgers Branch Association, June 1831.

FLAX AND OTHER TEXTILE WORKERS' TRADE UNION

The surviving records, covering the period 1890–1953, are in the Public Record Office of Northern Ireland. The Union was known as the Flax Roughers' Trade Union from 1890–1906 and the Flax Roughers' and Yarn Spinners' Trade Union from 1906–24. The collection (12 vols. and *c* 300 documents) includes minute books, 1894–1953; cash books 1912–*c* 1952; correspondence, financial statements, annual returns, etc., *c* 1890–*c* 1940.

FREEDOM GROUP

Some papers of the organisation are reported to be in the International Institute of Social History, Amsterdam.

FREEDOM PRESS

The archives are reported to be being microfilmed by the Harvester Press Ltd.

FREELAND LEAGUE FOR JEWISH TERRITORIAL COLONISATION (BRITISH SECTION)

No central archive has been located, but Dr. H. Lowenthal, London N2, one-time Chairman of the organisation has unpublished memoirs of the Freeland Movement and is willing to be interviewed (*see* P. Jones *Britain and Palestine*.) Established in 1935, the League aimed to direct the migration of Jews from Eastern and Central Europe into one of the empty spaces of the world and to establish there a concentrated Jewish settlement on a large scale and a co-operative basis.

FRIENDS OF THE HEBREW UNIVERSITY OF JERUSALEM

The surviving records have been retained at the Friends' Office, 3 St. John's Wood Road, London NW8 8RB. The organisation was founded in 1926 'to further the development of the Hebrew University of Jerusalem, of the Haifa Technical Institute, and of the Daniel Sieff Research Institute of Rehoboth'. The surviving records comprise annual reports, committee minutes from 1925 and photographs etc. Case work records are closed. Enquiries should be addressed to the Administrative Secretary.

GEOGRAPHICAL ASSOCIATION

See **Environment and Planning.**

GERMAN EDUCATIONAL RECONSTRUCTION

The records of the Group, 47 packets, covering the period 1941–58, are in the Institute of Education Library, University of London. The records include correspondence, minutes, reports etc. of the joint group of German emigrants and British representatives for the reconstruction of the German educational system. The collection is almost entirely post-war. A detailed list is available (NRA 20822).

GLASGOW RATEPAYERS' AND CITIZEN'S UNION

Since the entry in *Sources* Vol. 1, p 103, a collection of papers has been deposited with Strathclyde Regional Archives (ref TD 488) per Messrs. Bird Son and Semple, Writers, Glasgow, in August 1977.

The papers of the Glasgow Ratepayers' Federation include a Director's minute book 1903–1922, 3 volumes of press cuttings, a cash book 1936–1966 and a box of typed and printed papers, accounts, deeds etc. The papers of the Citizen's Union include a minute book 1898–1903, an out-letter book 1899–1902 and a volume of printed pamphlets.

GLASGOW TYPOGRAPHICAL ASSOCIATION

The records have been deposited in Strathclyde University Library. A list is available (NRA 24814). The records include minute books, 1817–1946, contribution books, 1845–1881, Quarterly Reports since 1874, chapel records etc.

GUILLEBAUD COMMITTEE ON RAILWAY PAY

Papers relating to the Committee, 1958–59, are in the Library of Nuffield College, Oxford, to whom enquiries should be addressed.

HEADMASTERS' ASSOCIATION

Since the entry in *Sources* Vol 1, pp 104–105, certain records have been deposited on indefinite loan in the Modern Records Centre, University of Warwick (ref MSS 58). The deposit includes some post-war correspondence files and runs of various publications, including the *Bulletin* and the triannual *Review* as well as pamphlets on matters of professional interest. A list is available (NRA 24512). *See also* **Association of Head Mistresses.**

HOWARD LEAGUE FOR PENAL REFORM

Since the entry in *Sources* Vol 1, p 106, extensive additions have been made to the material deposited in the Modern Records Centre, University of Warwick (ref MSS 16). The additions include executive and other committee minutes 1927–55; 3 box files of correspondence and papers, one of which relates to the League of Nations in the 1930s; the minutes (1923–48) and related papers of the National Council for the Abolition of the Death Penalty; balance sheets 1925–35 and annual reports and the (war time) *Bulletin*, 1–28. Also included in papers relating to the Howard League are 9 notebooks of Secretaries (1895–1905) a survey of prison conditions (1943–4); 2 box files of returns; a file on mental health in prisons, 1948; and the 1911 and 1913 Annual Reports of the Penal Reform League.

IMPERIAL FEDERATION LEAGUE

In addition to the material described in *Sources* Vol. 1, p 108, records for the period 1884 to 1894 have been acquired by the British Library (Add MSS 62778-62783).

IMPERIAL MARITIME LEAGUE

Although no central archive has been located, reference should be made to the Horton-Smith collection of 28 volumes of pamphlets and press cuttings in the National Maritime Museum. Horton-Smith was Secretary of the Imperial Maritime League (see *Sources* Vol 5, p 103).

INDEPENDENT LABOUR PARTY

Since the entry in *Sources* Vol 1, pp 109–111, a collection of papers has been deposited with the BLPES (ref Coll Misc 464). It includes the minutes of the National Administrative Council, 1893–1950; Head Office reports, 1898–99; accounts, ballot papers regarding federation with the SDF, and summaries of branches and membership, 1918–21. Certain branch minutes are also held (see below for details), as well as minutes of the Metropolitan District Council, 1906–09. There are also a number of circulars, reports, minutes and correspondence on various topics from Head Office, 1904–22.

The following additional information is now available on branch records:

Birmingham ILP
Finance Committee minutes, 1912–15; branch reports for Kings Heath 1906–19 and Hay Mills, 1908–11, in Birmingham Public Library.

Bradford Manningham ILP
A minute book, 1899, is in Bradford Archives Department.

Bristol ILP
Minutes, 1906–18 (microfilm at BLPES).

Cambridge ILP
Minutes, 1906–12; balance sheets, 1911–12 in Cambridgeshire County Record Office.

Clifton and Swinton ILP
Minutes, including accounts, balance sheets etc., 18 May 1919–27 February 1921 are in the local public library.

Dowlais ILP
Minutes, 1901–03, are in the South Wales Miners Library, University College, Swansea.

East Anglia ILP
Minutes 1931–51, are in BLPES (Coll Misc 497).

Edinburgh Central ILP
Minutes, correspondence and other papers, 1911–34, are in the National Library of Scotland (Acc 5436, 5241).

Finsbury Central ILP
Minutes, 1899–1902, are in BLPES.

Gillingham (Kent) ILP
Minutes, 1920–31, are in BLPES.

Halifax ILP
Minutes, 1936–53, and accounts, 1895–1946, are in Calderdale Public Library. *See* NRA 25443.

Keighley ILP
Records, 1892–1950, have been placed in Bradford Central Library.

Neath ILP
Minutes, 1923–30, are in the South Wales Miners Library, University College, Swansea.

Preston ILP
Minutes, 1899, are in BLPES.

Stockport ILP
Surviving early records have been placed in Stockport Central Library. These include minutes and accounts, 1896–98 and 1916–1922.

Vale of Leven ILP
A minute book February 1904 – May 1906, is in the Mitchell Library, Glasgow.

Wrexham ILP
Minute books, 1912–21, are in Clywd Record Office.

Note The Harvester Press has embarked on a microfilming programme of those branch records which are part of the central ILP archive. Those available on microfiche include: Bilston, 1926–33, 1948–68; Birmingham, 1924–28, 1941–48; Ilford, 1919–28; London District, 1892–93; London Federation, 1894–98; Shettleston, 1905–16, 1935–51; Southall 1922–25 and West Bromwich 1925–35.

INDIA, PAKISTAN AND BURMA ASSOCIATION

Certain surviving records were placed on permanent loan in the India Office Library in 1972 by the Association (ref MSS Eur F 158). The collection is closed to access for 20 years. The papers, dated 1941–70, comprise 1050 files of administrative papers and subject files on trade and politics. The collection is not yet listed. Reference should also be made to the collection at the Modern Records Centre, University of Warwick (ref MSS 200/IPBA).

INDIAN TEA ASSOCIATION

An important collection of records, comprising 1,000 volumes and 600 files, has been deposited in the India Office Library (ref MSS Eur F 174). The collection comprises files, c 1900—74 on a wide variety of subjects including tea taxes, labour relations, wage boards and family planning, production figures, etc. There are annual reports etc., not only of the Association itself but of other organisations which shared its Secretariat — e.g. the Indian Tea Association (Calcutta), the Dooars Planters Association, the United Planters Association of Southern India and the British Tea Producers Association.

INDUSTRIAL CHRISTIAN FELLOWSHIP
See **Christian Social Union**

INDUSTRIAL LIFE OFFICES ASSOCIATION
The organisation was established as the Association of Industrial Assurance Companies and Collecting Friendly Societies in 1901. Its present title was adopted in 1950. It played a prominent part in the organisation of national health insurance in 1911 and in the campaign against nationalisation, 1949—50. Its records, including minutes of committees, 1901—58, and correspondence, 1901—49, are retained at the Association's offices, Aldermary House, London EC4N 1TP.

INLAND WATERWAYS ASSOCIATION
The organisation was founded in 1946 to campaign for the restoration, retention and development of inland waterways. Some records, together with some from the Inland Shipping Group, have been deposited in BLPES.

INSTITUTE OF ENGINEERS AND SHIPBUILDERS IN SCOTLAND
The records, including minute books, records of council etc. since 1857 have been deposited in Glasgow University Archives. A list is available (NRA 25306).

INSTITUTE OF PERSONNEL MANAGEMENT
An important collection of the surviving records of the Institute has been deposited in the Modern Records Centre, University of Warwick (ref MSS 97). The Institute originated in a conference held at York in 1913. However, the main series of minutes dates from 1917, following a conference held at Leeds in August of that year. In addition to central minutes, some branch records are held, including 2 volumes of minutes of the Liverpool Welfare Workers' Association, 1916—19, and a volume of minutes of the Scottish branch of the Welfare Workers' Institute, 1921—28. The Scottish Association of Welfare Workers (Women) and the Scottish Society of Welfare Supervisors are each represented by a volume of minutes (1917—21 and 1918—24 respectively) and the London Association of Welfare Workers by a minute book for 1917—19.

Many of the Institute's records were lost during the Second World War, hence there is very little pre-1945 correspondence. However, this is partly compensated in the miscellaneous papers of four individuals prominent in the work of the Institute in the inter-war period. In addition, the original collection has been supplemented by a deposit of records from its Birmingham branch. These include AGM minutes, 1951—54, 1958—69, and correspondence and papers, 1960's—70's.

INTERNATIONAL ARBITRATION LEAGUE

The papers are reported to be with the London-based 'Mondcivitan Republic'.

INTERNATIONAL BOOKBINDERS' UNION

An extensive collection of records, 1907–1953 is housed at the International Institute of Social History, Amsterdam. The material includes a complete set of Bulletins, rules, reports and minutes. A list is available for consultation. The Union was founded at Nürnberg in 1907. In 1949 it merged in the International Graphical Federation.

INTERNATIONAL CONFEDERATION OF FREE TRADE UNIONS

The archives for the period 1949–67 are in the International Institute of Social History, Amsterdam.

INTERNATIONAL FEDERATION OF INDUSTRIAL ORGANISATIONS AND GENERAL WORKERS UNIONS

The archives for the period 1923–64 are in the International Institute of Social History, Amsterdam.

INTERNATIONAL FEDERATION OF LEAGUE OF NATIONS SOCIETIES

The records of the Federation are with the surviving archive of the League of Nations, United Nations Library, Geneva. The Federation was founded in 1919, and its activities seem to have ceased in 1940. The secretariat was situated first in Bordeaux, then in Brussels, then in Brussels and Geneva, and finally in Geneva alone. The collection, in 44 boxes, covers the period 1921–40, but there are numerous and important gaps. Thus there are files on only seven of the at least 22 Assemblies held by the Federation, and parts of the general correspondence have been preserved only for some of the 1930s. Two of the boxes constitute in reality a separate archive group, the records of 'Föreningen Nordisk Folkhögskola i Genève' (the Association for the Scandinavian Adult Continuation School in Geneva), 1930–1932. The languages of those records are Danish, Norwegian and Swedish.

The archive also contains the records of the International Association of Journalists accredited to the League of Nations. The Association, founded in 1921, was still active in January 1940. Only journalists working for daily newspapers or agencies and broadcasters were admitted. The records, covering the period 1921–39, are housed in 12 boxes.

INTERNATIONAL FEDERATION OF LITHOGRAPHERS, PRINTERS AND SIMILAR TRADES

An extensive archive covering the period 1896–1949 is housed at the International Institute of Social History, Amsterdam. The material includes Executive Committee minutes, financial statements and reports, sets of Bulletins and papers re. Congresses. There are no papers relating to Harrap's period as Secretary, but a very near complete set of papers of J. Roelofs (General Secretary 1945–49) with much material on reconstruction after the war. A list is available for consultation. The Federation was founded in London in August 1896, with C. Harrap as first Secretary. The organisation moved to Berlin in 1907.

INTERNATIONAL FINANCIAL SOCIETY

The records have been deposited in the Brynmor Jones Library, Hull University. The Society, founded in 1863, had close links with the Imperial Ottoman Bank and the Credit Mobilier in Paris, and was active in channelling British investment funds into Middle Eastern enterprises. The records include minute books of Board Meetings, 11 May 1863 to 24 October 1912, (12 vols); minute books of Committee Meetings, 25 May 1863 to 15 May 1882, (4 vols); a draft minute book, 29 October 1863 to 16 January 1868, (1 vol.); account books: balance books, 3 September 1863 to 3 December 1878, (4 vols); capital journal, 1864 to 1886, (3 vols); cash books, 1867 to 1911, (11 vols); register of bills of exchange, 1865 to 1903 (1 vol.); register of bills payable, 1894 to 1908, (1 vol.).

INTERNATIONAL MARXIST GROUP

An extensive collection of papers has been acquired by the Modern Records Centre, University of Warwick. The main groups are as follows:

The International Marxist Group Deposit (ref MSS 128)

This collection comprises internal information bulletins, internal discussion bulletins and conference documents, 1973—75. There is also a run of Women's Liberation Newsletters. Unpublished documents may only be consulted with the written permission of the IMG. This deposit supplements the Whelan Collection (see below).

The Whelan Collection (ref MSS 95)

This collection which originated with the IMG Group, comprises complete records of IMG National Committee business, both minutes and related documents, 1970—73, internal discussion documents, 1967—73, IMG office archives, letters to members, notes to organisers etc. There are some regional archives, a complete file of international and internal documents of the Spartacus League (the IMG youth group). Certain restrictions on access exist.

The Tarbuck Collection (ref MSS 75)

This collection of Trotskyist records includes *c.* 150 internal documents of the Workers International League and the Revolutionary Communist Party, 1940—49, some Socialist Review Group (q.v.) material, and some WIL/RCP leaflets and press-cuttings, mainly concerning the 1944 apprentices strike. There are extensive runs of Trotskyist publications.

The Hyman Papers (ref MSS 84)

The deposit comprises duplicated Executive Committee minutes of the International Socialism group (known from January 1977 as the Socialist Workers' Party).

The Purdie Papers (ref MSS 149)

These papers contain correspondence, minutes and leaflets of the IMG concerning

Ireland, with other material on left-wing organisations (e.g. the Anti-Internment League, Vietnam Solidarity Campaign, Socialist Labour League etc).

INTERNATIONAL PEACE BUREAU

The archives of the International Peace Bureau (IPB) are with the League of Nations Archives, United Nations Library, Geneva. The IPB was founded in 1892 to serve as a permanent secretariat to the Universal Peace Congresses. Its headquarters were situated at first in Berne and in Geneva from 1924 onwards. Besides acting as liaison between various peace organisations, the Bureau assembled a valuable specialised library and published a considerable number of pamphlets, periodicals and books.

The International Union of Peace Societies, of which the IPB was the secretariat, was dissolved by decision of the (Swiss) Federal Tribunal on 18 June 1959. In 1961 the Swiss Government permanently deposited the library and the archives in Geneva.

The Archives of the Bureau, which cover the period 1889–1950 and amount to 41 linear metres, are open to research. They have not been listed and are only partially and provisionally classified. It is, however, possible to carry out certain research thanks to the box labels' and the correspondence diaries, which have been found for the periods 3 January 1913–21 August 1926; 1 January 1928–10 July 1933 and 22 July 1934–1 January 1942.

INTERNATIONAL RAILWAY CONGRESS ASSOCIATION

Some material concerning the Association can be found in the Public Record Office (ref RAIL 1023/24). The first congress of the Association was held at the instigation of the Belgian Government in 1884–85 and the Association was formally constituted in 1887. The record classes in the Public Record Office contain published proceedings and Bulletins of the Association.

INTERNATIONAL SHOE AND LEATHER WORKERS' FEDERATION

The archives are reported in the care of the Librarian of the Deutsche Gewerkschaftsbund, Düsseldorf.

INTERNATIONAL TRANSPORT WORKERS' FEDERATION (ITWF)

The records have been deposited in the Modern Records Centre, University of Warwick, by the Secretariat of the ITWF in London (ref MSS 159). The Federation was founded in 1896 as a federation of seafarers' and dockers' unions. It adopted its present title in 1898. Its headquarters were in England until 1904, then Germany and subsequently Amsterdam after 1919. Shortly before the Second World War its headquarters reverted to England.

The collection includes Executive and General Council minutes and correspondence files concerning national sections throughout the world, 1903–45. These include files concerning questions of international solidarity and the fight against Fascism. On Britain, the collection contains material on such specific topics as the transport workers' strike of 1911 and the 1926 General Strike. On the European labour movement, there is material on the Belgian seamen's dispute, the Russo-Polish war, the boycott of Hungary by transport workers in France, Germany and

Holland, the 1921 Norwegian seamen's strike, the 8-hour day campaign by French workers in 1922, the campaign in support of the Rand miners and the problems facing transport workers as a result of the Dawes and Young Plans. There is also material on refugees, the Second World War, the work of Hans Jahn, the organisation of German workers in the United Kingdom, post-war problems and the work of the ITWF Vigilance Committee.

To complete the collection, there are many ITWF publications, including *Fascism*, 1934–39, the ITWF *Bulletin*, 1923–33 and *Press Reports*, 1925–39. The Modern Records Centre has also acquired the papers of Paul Tofahrn, former Assistant General Secretary of the ITWF.

INTERNATIONAL UNION OF SOCIALIST YOUTH
The archives (1947–1958) of the International Press and Exchange Bureau of the Union have been placed in the International Institute of Social History, Amsterdam, through the good offices of Mr B. Bost.

INTERNATIONAL UNION OF STUDENTS
A collection of records 1946–1969, is housed in the International Institute of Social History at Amsterdam. The documents have been brought together mainly by the International Student Conference which deposited them in March 1969. The collection includes an important file from the NUS on the origins and early history of the International Union of Students.

INTERNATIONAL VOLUNTARY SERVICE
The records are reported to be with the organisation at its Leicester offices. The earliest records date from the 1930s. It is not known if access is granted.

INTERNATIONAL WOMAN SUFFRAGE ALLIANCE
Records of the organisation are reported to be with the successor organisation, the International Alliance of Women, 5th Floor, Parnell House, Wilton Road, London SW1.

IRISH BAKERS' UNIONS
The records of the following unions have been deposited with University College, Dublin:

Belfast Operative Bakers' Friendly and Allied Trades Society
These records (ref TU3) consist of minutes of committee and annual general meetings, 1912–20; and a financial ledger, 1912–18.

Cork Bakers' Benevolent Society
A ms. rule book c. 1860 (ref TU5).

Irish Bakers', Confectioners' and Allied Workers' Union (Dublin No. 1 Branch)

Includes membership rolls, 1806–1945; minutes and agendas, 1882–1939, of executive council, committee and general meetings; cash accounts, 1820–1946; contributions, 1856–1911; subscriptions and levies, 1912–45; benefit payments, 1880–1945; and payment to branches, 1890–1918; and the general secretaries' diaries, 1925–44 (ref TU2).

IBCAWU (Limerick Branch)

Includes minutes and attendance lists, 1844–1956, of executive council, committee and general meetings; and financial records, 1866–1960 (ref TU1).

Waterford Bakers' Union

Executive committee and general meeting minutes from 1861; financial records, 1826–1908; and rules and regulations from 1848.

IRISH BLEACHERS', DYERS' AND FINISHERS' ASSOCIATION

The records of the Association were acquired by the Public Record Office of Northern Ireland in 1974. The collection includes minute books, ledgers, cash books and correspondence for the period 1909–68.

IRISH LAND CLERKS ASSOCIATION

A minute book of the organisation, for the period 1891–1905, has been acquired by the National Library of Ireland.

IRISH LOCAL GOVERNMENT AND PUBLIC SERVICES UNION

The records have been acquired by the Public Record Office of Ireland, Dublin (ref. 1056). The collection, which includes minute books etc. covers the period 1901–70.

IRISH NATIONAL VOLUNTEERS

A minute book of executive committee meetings of the Belfast battalion, 1914–16, is in University College, Dublin (ref. P11/A).

IRISH PAINTERS AND INTERIOR DECORATORS UNION

The records have been acquired by the Public Record Office of Ireland, Dublin. The collection, which includes minutes, accounts and other papers, covers the period 1870–1950.

IRISH PLUMBING TRADE UNION

The records have been acquired by the Public Record Office, Dublin. The collection includes minutes, contribution books, correspondence, etc., covering the period 1931–72. In addition a minute book, 1890–1912, of the Belfast Master Plumbers Association is in the Public Record Office of Northern Ireland.

IRISH PROTESTANT NATIONAL TEACHERS UNION

A minute book for the period 1911–1926 has been placed in the Northern Ireland Public Record Office. The organisation was founded in 1901 to redress the grievances of Protestant teachers, of which, as the minute book reveals, the chief was the power of dismissal by the manager. Most of its membership was from Ulster. With the passing of the 1928 Northern Ireland Education Act, the managerial system began to disappear in Ulster and the organisation lost its main *raison d'être*.

IRISH SHOE AND LEATHER WORKERS' UNION

An extensive collection of records of the union(*c.* 15 boxes, 100 volumes) covering the period 1900 to 1977 has been deposited in University College, Dublin (ref. TU7). The collection, which incorporates some records of the National Union of Boot and Shoe Operatives (1900 onwards) relates to the organisation of workers in the footwear manufacturing industry in Ireland with specific reference to negotiations towards national agreements on wages and conditions (1936–68); executive council minutes and reports (1932–72), proceedings of delegate and national joint conferences (1934–72) and related correspondence files (1945–77); half-yearly statements of accounts (1948–75), branch accounts (1953–72), and records of appeal funds, special collections and benefit disbursements (1956–76).

IRISH TRANSPORT AND GENERAL WORKERS' UNION

Some records have been acquired by the National Library of Ireland, Dublin. The collection includes minute books, accounts etc., for the period 1913–38.

IRISH WOMEN WORKERS UNION

The records are in the Public Record Office of Ireland, Dublin. The collection includes minutes, reports, accounts, etc., covering the period 1913–60.

IRON AND STEEL TRADES CONFEDERATION

Since the entry in *Sources* Vol. 1, p 120, an extensive series of subject files (*c.*200 boxes) has been deposited in the Modern Records Centre, University of Warwick (ref. MSS 36). The collection includes material on wages and conditions by company/branch, relations with and information on other organisations, some documentation on overseas countries, material on such topics as overtime, hours of work, the tinplate trade pension scheme and the Cumberland blastfurnacemen. Other deposited files include correspondence with Sir Arthur Pugh in his retirement and material on the International Metalworkers' Federation.

JERUSALEM AND THE EAST MISSION

The Mission was founded in 1888 to support the work of the Anglican Church in Jerusalem. Some of its records are in the Middle East Centre, St. Antony's College,

Oxford, whilst other material is in Lambeth Palace Library. The material at the Middle East Centre, 1841–1974, includes papers on Palestine, Syria, Iraq, Jordan, Iran, Egypt and the Sudan, and Cyprus. Of particular significance is correspondence and memoranda on the political situation in Palestine, 1916–67. The papers at Lambeth Palace Library include the official correspondence and papers of Bishop John Wordsworth, Revd. William Sadler, 1889–1911, Bishop G. F. P. Blyth, 1881– 1915 and Bishop Samuel Gobat, 1844–78 (ref MSS 2327–41). There are also papers of the Association for the Furtherance of Christianity in Egypt (ref MSS 2539–40), the Baakleen Medical Mission to the Druses of the Lebanon, 1899–1916 (ref MSS 2608–10) and the Syria and Palestine Relief Fund, 1916–1918 (ref MSS 2611–13).

JEWISH COLONIAL TRUST

The archives of this important Zionist agency are in the Central Zionist Archives in Jerusalem (ref L50). Founded in 1902, the Jewish Colonial Trust (Jeudische Colonial Bank) was the financial instrument of the Zionist movement. It was later known as the Anglo-Palestine Bank and the Anglo-Israel Bank before becoming the Bank Leumi. The records in the Central Zionist Archives, covering the period 1899–1950, cover the Trust's activities in London.

JEWISH COLONISATION ASSOCIATION

Some records are available at the Association's offices, 46 Queen Anne's Gate, London SW1H 9AP. Founded in 1899 in Palestine, the association administered the Rothschild settlements and other Jewish communities until 1919. From 1920 to 1930, it concentrated its activities on encouraging and organising Jewish migration from Europe to South America and Canada. After 1929, it continued to work for the development of the Jewish home in Palestine.

The records held by the Association include files, correspondence and other reports concerning its various interests in Palestine (1914–48). The Annual Reports (and Board Briefings) are in good order, and provide a guide to material in the unsorted correspondence files. These are available to *bona fide* researchers.

The Central Zionist Archives hold other records of the Association, and the Anglo-Jewish Association's records (*q.v.*) include files covering relations with the Jewish Colonisation Association (1901, 1939–50).

JEWISH DEFENCE COMMITTEE

This Committee of the Jewish Board of Deputies was created in 1936, to take over the functions of the Press and Information Committee, and its object is the co-ordination of nearly all activities dealing with anti-semitism. The records form part of the Board of Deputies' archive, but no further details were available.

JEWISH PEACE SOCIETY

The Anglo-Jewish Archives at the Mocatta Library, University College, London, hold miscellaneous papers, mainly 1950s (ref AJ164). The Board of Deputies' archives contain earlier correspondence (1919–22 and 1928–30) of the Jewish Peace Society (ref E1/54 and 55). The Society was founded to unite Jews in Great

Britain and Ireland to work for the promotion of international peace and friendship between nations.

JEWISH REFUGEES COMMITTEE

Formed in 1933, the Committee which was also called the German Jewish Aid Committee, provided assistance to Jewish refugees from Germany and Austria, including welfare, training and settlement in Britain and overseas. Funds were raised by the Central British Fund for German Jewry. For surviving papers, reference should be made to the Central Zionist Archives, which has records of the Committee's relations with Zionism and Palestine, and also to Manchester Public Library, which has personal files and financial papers of the Guarantee Sub-Committee of the Jewish Refugees Committee, concerning its help to refugees from Nazi Germany *en route* to the United States, Palestine, etc. (1939—54). There are few papers at the Committee's new offices, Woburn House, Upper Woburn Place, London WC1.

JOINT AFRICA BOARD

Since the entry in *Sources* Vol. 1, p 123 the papers of the Joint Africa Board (formerly the Joint East and Central African Board), which was officially dissolved on 31 December 1973, have been deposited at the Royal Commonwealth Society. The archives are believed to consist of minutes, 1923—74, annual reports, 1924—64, and selected memoranda to government departments and the Chairman's Newsletter, 1953—74. *See also* **Africa Bureau.**

JUTE SPINNERS' AND MANUFACTURERS' ASSOCIATION

The records, 1918—77, are in Dundee University Library. This Library also has the surviving records of the Jute Importers' Association, 1892—1979.

LABOUR AND SOCIALIST INTERNATIONAL (THE SECOND INTERNATIONAL)

Material can be found in the International Institute of Social History, Amsterdam. The material includes files *re* Executive Meetings, 1921—23; files *re* meetings of the Bureau and Congresses etc.; files on the preparation of the International Socialist Congress at Hamburg; press cuttings; and some papers of Tom Shaw *re* the Labour Party, 1922—23 and a few private letters.

LABOUR PARTY

Since the entry in *Sources* Vol. 1, p 127, the headquarters of the Party have moved to 152 Walworth Road, London, S.E.17. The Party has retained its archive.

The following additional information on regional and constituency records is now available:

Aberdare Trades Council
Minute books, 1941—68, are in the Library of Swansea University.

Barrow & Dalton CLP

Minute books and other records, 1914—61, are in Cumbria Record Office, Barrow-in-Furness. The Trades Council records, 1924—73, are also deposited there.

Batley and Morley Labour Party

Minute books, 1918—29, 1941—49 have been deposited in Sheffield University Library (NRA 22343). There is also a minute book of Batley Labour Party and Trades Council, 1928—32.

Battersea Trades Council

The Annual Reports for 1896—1900, 1901—09, 1911 and 1916 are in Battersea Public Library. Annual Reports for 1898—9, 1903—4 are in BLPES. Recent minute books (1948-date) are retained by the Trades Council.

Beccles and District Trades and Labour Council

Minute books, 1918—73 and accounts 1918—74, are in Suffolk Record Office (Ipswich).

Beeston Trades and Labour Council

A minute book, 1900—1907, has been deposited in the Modern Records Centre, University of Warwick.

Bermondsey Labour Party

The surviving records *c* 1900—1975, are in Southwark Local Studies Library. *See* NRA 25484.

Birmingham CLP

The older records have been placed in the Social Sciences Department of Birmingham Public Library. The material includes minutes of Borough Party meetings 1919—1931, Delegate meetings 1933—1966, subcommittees 1933—1936, Executive Committee 1933—1967, Finance and General Purposes Committee 1933—1936, 1943—1964 and other related records 1959—1980. There are also minutes 1892—1912, of the Birmingham Labour Church.

Birmingham and District Co-operative Party

Central and branch records, 1918—76, are in the Social Sciences Department, Birmingham Reference Library.

Birmingham Deritend CLP

Minutes, 1930—34, are in the Social Sciences Department, Birmingham Reference Library.

Birmingham Northfield CLP

Records, 1963—80, are in the Social Sciences Department, Birmingham Reference Library.

Bishop Auckland CLP

Records, 1950—70, are in Durham Record Office.

Bradford Trades Council

Records, 1867–1960, have ben placed in Bradford Central Library.

Brighouse and Spenborough Labour Party

Some records have been deposited in the West Yorkshire Record Office (NRA 21210). The deposit includes General and Executive Committee minutes, 1951–62; some sub-committee and ward minutes for a similar period and records of Brighouse Borough Council Labour Group, 1933–46, *See also* under *Elland Labour Party* below.

Brighouse Trades Council

Minute books, 1917–73, have been placed in Calderdale Public Library. *See* NRA 25401.

Brighton Labour Party

The records in Brighton Reference Library include records of Brighton Hove and District Trades and Labour Council (minutes, 1919–76; accounts, 1890–1957; delegates book, 1921–50; 24 vols of annual reports etc). The collection is listed (NRA 21834).

Bristol Borough Labour Party

The records for the period 1921–71 are in Bristol Record Office. The Record Office also has recent records (1958–83) of Bristol West CLP.

Caernarvon Borough CLP

Correspondence and papers, 1924–1926, are in Gwynedd Record Office.

Caithness and Sutherland CLP

Minutes, 1945-date, are with the Constituency Secretary.

Cambridge Labour Party

Records, 1906–76 have been deposited in Cambridgeshire County Record Office (NRA 22966). The collection includes minutes from 1913, balance sheets, election addresses, ward minutes etc. Some very recent material is closed until 1985.

Cambridgeshire CLP

An important collection of papers has been deposited in Cambridgeshire County Record Office. This collection comprises records of the Cambridgeshire Trades Council and Divisional Labour Party (called from 1956 the Cambridgeshire Constituency Labour Party) from its foundation in 1918 to 1966 and the Cambridgeshire Federation of Labour Parties.

Cambridge University Labour Club

Minutes, 1920–28, are in Cambridge University Library.

Carlisle and District Trades Council

Minute books and papers, 1907–74, have been placed in Cumbria Record Office.

Carmarthenshire County Council Labour Group
Minute books, 1954, 1964–1969 have been placed in Dyfed Archives.

Castleford and District Trades Council
Records, 1950–70, are in West Yorkshire Record Office. *See* NRA 21207.

Cheltenham and District Trades Council
Minutes, registers and accounts, 1894–1968 are in Gloucestershire Record Office.

Chepstow Labour Party
Minute books, 1932–52, are in Monmouthshire Record Office.

Chigwell and Ongar CLP
Minute books, 1955–70, are in Essex Record Office.

Cleveland CLP
Minute books, 1928–52, are in Cleveland County Archives.

Colne Valley CLP
Minute books, etc., 1918–1945, are in Huddersfield Polytechnic Library.

Coventry Trades Council
An extensive set of records has been deposited in the Modern Records Centre, University of Warwick. The records include duplicated annual reports, minutes of Delegate Executive Committee meetings, attendance registers, accounts etc. There are also two notebooks, 1897 and 1901, believed to have been kept by John Chater, secretary of the Trades Council *c* 1900.

Dalkeith Labour Party
A minute book, 1935–1951, is in the National Library of Scotland.

Derby and District Trades Council
A minute book, 1913–26, is in Derby Public Library.

Derbyshire West CLP
A scrapbook of news cuttings, together with the first minute book of Matlock Labour Party (1924–36) is in Derbyshire Record Office. In addition, minute books of the Constituency Association, 1924–1947, have also been placed in Derbyshire Record Office. A list is available (NRA 25247)

Dewsbury Labour Party
Minute books etc., 1909–73 are in West Yorkshire Record Office.

Doncaster Labour Party
Records 1920–1957, have been transferred to Doncaster Metropolitan Borough Archives.

Dorchester Trades Council
Minutes and other papers, 1918–1974 are in Dorset Record Office.

Dundee CLP
Reference should be made to the collection of miscellaneous records in Dundee Public Library.

Dunfermline CLP
Minutes, 1954-date, are with the Constituency Secretary.

Eastbourne Trades Council
Minutes, 1937–49, are in Brighton Reference Library.

East Grinstead CLP
One file of minutes, 1918–20, is in BLPES (Coll Misc 498).

Edinburgh Labour Party
A minute book, 1911–14, is in the National Library of Scotland.

Edinburgh South Labour Party
Records 1922–1960, are in the National Library of Scotland (ref MS Dep 203).

Elland Labour Party
Five minute books of the Executive Committee and the Finance and Propaganda sub-committees, 1921–38, are with the West Yorkshire Record Office. *See* NRA 21210.

Epsom Labour Party
The records were deposited in Surrey Record Office in May 1977 (NRA 20754) Access to documents under 15 years old is restricted. The collection comprises minutes of AGMs, General Council meetings, General Management and Executive Committee meetings, 1937–66.

Farnworth Trades Council
Minutes, 1894–1917, are in Salford Archives Centre. Records of Farnworth and Worsley CLP, 1940–1979, are in Bolton Metropolitan Library.

Faversham Labour Party
Minute books since 1918 have been deposited in Transport House.

Flintshire East CLP
Records, 1955–1973, are in Clwyd Record Office, Hawarden.

Galloway CLP
Minutes, March 1957-date, are with the Constituency Party Secretary.

Glasgow Maryhill Ward Labour Party
Minutes, etc, 1917–1965 have been placed in the Mitchell Library, Glasgow.

Glasgow Woodside CLP
Minutes, 1960-date, are with the Constituency Secretary.

Gloucester CLP
Minute books from 1899 to 1946 are in Gloucestershire Record Office.

Greenwich CLP
Minutes, 1927–58, are in Greenwich Local History Library, Mycenae Road, Blackheath, London.

Guildford Trades Council
Records, 1913–62, are in Surrey Record Office. *See* NRA 25844.

Halifax CLP
Records, 1928–71, have been placed in Calderdale Metropolitan Borough Archives. A list is available (NRA 24676)

Halifax Trades Council
Records, 1866–1974, are in Calderdale Metropolitan Borough Archives, Halifax. *See* NRA 25447.

Hartlepool Trades Council
Minutes and other records, 1960–79, are in Cleveland Archives Department.

Haslingden Trades Council
Minutes, 1963–77, are in Lancashire County Record Office.

Hebden Bridge Trades Council
Minutes, 1957–1968, are in Calderdale Public Library.

Home Counties Labour Association
Some records are in the Garnsworthy papers (*q.v.*) at BLPES (ref Coll Misc 540).

Huddersfield CLP
Records, 1918–25 are in Huddersfield Polytechnic Library.

Hull Central Labour Party
Records, 1955 to 1966, are in the Brynmor Jones University Library, Hull.

Huyton CLP
Records are reported to be in Knowsley Central Library.

Inverness Trades Council
Minutes for May 1926 are in the National Library of Scotland.

Ipswich Labour Party
Correspondence and other papers, 1920–46, are in Suffolk Record Office, Ipswich Branch.

Knutsford Labour Party
Minutes, 1947–81, are in Cheshire Record Office.

Lanarkshire Labour Womens Advisory Council
Minutes, 1931–45, and accounts, 1921–41, are in the Mitchell Library, Glasgow.

Leamington Spa Trades Council and Labour Party
Records, 1921–32, are in Warwickshire Record Office.

Leeds City Labour Party
An extensive collection of MBs, accounts, ledgers, correspondence etc. has been deposited in Leeds Archives Department. Special permission is required to see material less then 30 years old (*see* NRA 20880).

Leeds Central CLP
Minute books and other material, January 1923 onwards, are in Leeds Archives Department.

Leeds North CLP
Minutes 1922–1925 and also other ward minutes are in Leeds Archives Department.

Leith CLP
Minute books, 1939–56, are deposited in the National Library of Scotland.

Lewes Labour Party
Minutes, papers, 1928–49, are in East Sussex Record Office.

Liverpool Region Cooperative Party
Minute books, 1923–63, are in Liverpool Record Office.

Liverpool Toxteth CLP
Minute books, 1956–62, are in Merseyside County Archives.

Manchester Ardwick CLP
Recent records, 1971–80, are in Manchester Central Library.

March and District Trades Council
Accounts, 1945–61, are in Cambridgeshire Record Office.

Motherwell and Wishaw CLP

Minutes of the Dalkeith Branch, 1935–51, are in the National Library of Scotland (ref MS Dep 200).

Newcastle CLP

Tyne and Wear Record Office has Newcastle Trades Council records (1949–74) (NRA 24939) and records of Newcastle City (1965–75) and Newcastle South CLP (1955–80).

Newport CLP

Minute books, 1912–57, papers and printed material are in the Library of Swansea University.

New Tredegar Trades Council

Minute books, 1938–65, are in the Library of Swansea University.

Northampton Trades Council

The records were placed in Northamptonshire Record Office in 1977. A list has been prepared (NRA 21332). The extensive deposit includes 4 Minute Books with Annual Reports of the Council 1895–1917; 1 Minute Book with press-cuttings 1928–30; 2 volumes of typescript of Council minutes for 1932–48; Council minutes 1948–50, 1955–67; 2 files of Executive Committee minutes, 1948–67; Minute Book of the May Day Committee, 1911–1914; Cash Book 1915–1940; Annual Reports 1923–1957. There are also *c* 105 correspondence files from 1936 onwards.

Northern Ireland Labour Party: Women's Section

Minute books, 1924–30, are in the Northern Ireland Public Record Office.

North Wales Labour Federation

A minute book, 1923–30, is in the Huw Edwards papers (*q.v.*), deposited in the National Library of Wales.

Northwich and District Labour Party

Minutes, 1948–69, are in Cheshire Record Office.

Nottingham Trades Council

Minute books 1883–1920 and 1925–1941 are in Nottingham University Library. Annual Reports from 1908 are in Nottingham Public Library.

Nuneaton CLP

The agent's correspondence, 1923–38, has been placed in Warwickshire Record Office.

Orkney and Shetland CLP

Manuscript minutes, January 1937 (formation) – October 1938 are retained by Mr. Peter Jamieson, 21 St Magnus Street, Lerwick.

Perth and District Trades Council
Minute books, 1897—1969, are in the Sandeman Public Library, Perth.

Preston Trades Council
A carbon copy out-letter book of the Secretary, 22 February 1892—12 June 1893, is in Lancashire County Record Office (ref DDX 1089/16—19).

Pudsey CLP
Records, 1948—76, are in Sheepscar Library, Leeds.

Redcar Trades Council
Minute books, 1942—67, are deposited in Cleveland Archives Department

Rothwell CLP
Records, 1958—76, are in Sheepscar Library, Leeds.

Sheffield Trades and Labour Council
Minutes and other records, 1941—75, are in Sheffield City Libraries.

Shoreditch and Finsbury CLP
Minute books, 1948—63, are in Hackney Borough Library.

Smethwick Cooperative Party
Minutes, 1952—74, are in the Social Science Department, Birmingham Reference Library.

Solihull CLP
Minutes, 1957—74, are in the Social Science Department, Birmingham Reference Library.

Southall Labour Party
Minute books and other records, 1920s—70s, of Uxbridge Labour Party and Southall and Norwood Trades Council have been deposited in the Greater London Record Office.

Southampton Trades Council
Minutes, 1929—53, are in Southampton Civic Record Office.

Southwark and Camberwell Trades Council
The records, 1953—77, are in Southwark Local Studies Library together with the records, 1919—38, of Southwark SE CLP. A list is available (NRA 26450).

Sowerby CLP
Records from 1907 to 1946 have been placed in Calderdale Public Library. NRA 25402.

Stalybridge and Hyde CLP
Minutes, correspondence etc., 1950–74, are in Tameside Metropolitan Borough Archive.

Stirling and Falkirk CLP
Records of the CLP and TC, some dating back to 1907, are in the Central Region Archives. *See* NRA 24621.

Stockport CLP
Minutes, 1896–1973, are in Stockport Central Library, which also has records of the Stockport Labour Fellowship.

Stockport Trades Council
The surviving records are in Stockport Central Library.

Sunderland CLP
Records, 1945–73, are in Tyne & Wear Record Office.

Sussex Federation of Trades Councils
The records, in Brighton Reference Library, contain minutes (incomplete), Annual Reports (incomplete) and correspondence with the Federation, all for the years 1950–1974, of the affiliated Trades Councils.

Swansea Labour Party
Minute books since 1916 were used by Kenneth O. Morgan in *Wales in British Politics.*

Swindon Trades Council
There is a full account based on material available locally in A. Tuckett: *Up with All That's Down: A History of the Swindon Trades Council 1891–1971* (Swindon, 1971).

Swinton & Pendlebury Trades Council & Labour Party
Minutes, 1948–58, are in Salford Archives Centre, Irlam, Manchester.

Thorne and District Trades Council
The records in Doncaster Archives Department comprise minutes, 1956–74 and correspondence, 1971–74. A list is available (NRA 23156).

Todmorden Trades Council
Minute books, 1892–1970, are in Calderdale Public Library. *See* NRA 25403.

Tottenham and Wood Green CLPs
Records, 1924–76, are in Haringey Public Library.

Uxbridge Labour Party
Minute books, 1920s–70s, are in the Greater London Record Office.

Walthamstow CLP
The records, 1926–65, are in Waltham Forest Library Local History Department.

Warwick and Leamington CLP
A full collection of records has been deposited in the Modern Records Centre, University of Warwick (ref MSS 133). The collection includes Executive Committee Minutes, 1919–29, 1940–54, 1956–73, GMC minutes, accounts, 1922–45, various subject files, 1950–76 and miscellaneous fairly recent correspondence.

Wick and District Trades Council
Minute books, 1944–67, are in Aberdeen University Library (ref MS 2677).

Wolverhampton CLP
The records in Wolverhampton Borough Archives (ref Acc 456) include minutes of Wolverhampton CLP, 1906–30, Wolverhampton West, 1930–48, and Wolverhampton Central, 1948–50. A list is available (NRA 26171).

Wrexham TC and CLP
Records, 1915–52, are in Clwyd Record Office.

York CLP
Minute books and other records, 1916–66, have been placed in York City Archives.

LADIES' NATIONAL SILK ASSOCIATION
Some papers, 1890–94, are in Manchester Central Library.

LAMBETH PALACE LIBRARY
Among the recent accessions to Lambeth, not reported in earlier volumes of *Sources* are minutes for 1908 of the Pan Anglican Congress (ref MSS 2449–50); minutes of the Commission on the Eastern Churches, 1909–12 (MSS 2412); minutes of the House of Bishops, China, 1912–41 (MSS 2447); minutes of the Bishops' War Committee, 1939–49 (MSS 2448); papers of the Baakleen Medical Mission, 1899–1916 (MSS 2608–10); papers of the Syria and Palestine Relief Fund, 1916–18 (MSS 2611–13); letters from Archbishop Lang to Wilfried Parker, 1908–45 (MSS 2881–84); minutes of the Eastern Churches Committee, 1924–32 (MSS 2926); minutes of the South African Education Fund, 1901–11 (MSS 2927–9); minutes of the Archbishop's Overseas Advisory Committee, 1931–47; minutes of the Association for the Furtherance of Christianity in Egypt, 1883–1904 (MSS 2539–40); papers of the Archbishop's Mission to the Assyrian Christians, 1879–1919; papers of Mrs Buxton on the German Church, 1932–41 (MSS 2651–55), minutes of the Central Church Reading Union, 1926–52 and minutes of the Parochial Mission Womens Association, 1883–86.

Readers Note
See also the entries for **Alan Campbell Don** and **Canon J. A. Douglas**. Readers should also note that the limitation on access to the papers of Archbishops Temple and Fisher was reduced from 40 to 30 years in January 1982.

LAW SOCIETY OF SCOTLAND

The records are held by the Scottish Record Office (ref GD 353). The collection consists of two minute books of the Joint Committee of Legal Societies in Scotland (1922–41), a minute book of the General Council of Solicitors in Scotland (1934–49) and another minute book of the Council's General Purposes Committee (1941–44); also twenty minute books of the Societies Council and Committees (1949–70). There is also a minute book of the Legal Aid Committee of the General Council of Solicitors in Scotland and of the Law Society of Scotland (1949–50). All these records are under closure for 100 years.

LEAGUE OF COLOURED PEOPLES

Although no central archive has been located, there is relevant material in the papers of Kathleen, Lady Simon, deposited in Rhodes House Library, Oxford (ref Brit Emp 525). The collection has been listed (NRA 9942). The material on the League includes newsletters, May 1941–March 1948 (37 items), annual reports, an envelope containing minutes of meetings and a file of correspondence dealing with the League.

LEAGUE OF LIBERALS AGAINST AGGRESSION AND MILITARISM

Although no central archive has been located, there is relevant material in the papers of Alexander MacCallum Scott, MP. These papers have now been deposited in Glasgow University Library.

LEAGUE OF LOYALTY AND ORDER

See **Church Reform League**

LEASEHOLDERS' ASSOCIATION OF GREAT BRITAIN

The Association's records are held by Mr. Richard Wiggs, Fairfield House, Biggleswade, Bedfordshire. They include the minutes of the Association, 1950–72, financial records and cashbook 1956–72, membership records 1961–74, an Annual Report 1972–3, a miscellaneous correspondence file 1970–6 and a general file 1974–5. The Association derives from the Deptford Leaseholders' Association, established July 1950, which became the London Leaseholders' Association in 1953.

LEFT BOOK CLUB

In addition to the information cited in *Sources* Vol. 1, p 145, some relevant material has come to light in the personal papers of Sir Victor Gollancz, in the Modern Records Centre, University of Warwick (ref MSS 157). In addition, the records of the Belfast Left Book Club have now been deposited in the Northern Ireland Public Record Office.

LIBERAL PARTY

Since the entry in *Sources* Vol. 1, pp 146–7 the records of the **National Liberal Club** (*q.v.*) have been placed in Bristol University Library, whilst other records e.g. the **Rainbow Circle** (*q.v.*) have also come to light. In addition the following information is available on regional and constituency records:

Beckenham and Penge Liberal Association

Records, 1910–38, have been placed in Bromley Public Library.

Berwickshire Liberal Association

Papers, correspondence and accounts, 1873–1920, have been deposited in the National Library of Scotland.

Blackpool Liberal Association

Records, 1901–70, are in Lancashire Record Office.

Bradford Manningham Liberal Club

Records, c 1870–79, are in Bradford Central Library.

Derbyshire North Liberal Registration Association

Treasurer's papers, 1879–81, are in Derbyshire County Record Office.

Exeter University Liberal Club

A minute book, 1948–56, of the then University College of the South West Liberal Club, is in Exeter University Library.

Glasgow Hillhead Liberal Association

Records, 1926–49, have been deposited in Strathclyde Regional Archives.

Harborough Liberal Association

Minute books, 1885–1963, have been deposited in Leicestershire Record Office.

Lancashire, Cheshire and North West Liberal Association

Records, 1908–44, are in Manchester Central Library (NRA 24632, 24633).

Leeds and County Liberal Club

Annual reports, 1897–1913, are in the privately-owned Leeds Library.

Leicester Liberal Club

Records, 1886–1922, are in Leicester Museum (now part of Leicestershire Record Office).

Lewisham North Liberal Association

Miscellaneous records, including minute books, 1950–1971, have been placed in Lewisham Local History Library, Manor House, Old Road, Lee, London, SE13.

Lewisham South Liberal Association
Minute books, 1966–71 only, in Lewisham Local History Library.

Lewisham West Liberal Association
Minute books, 1962–71, old membership records etc, in Lewisham Local History Library.

Liverpool City Council Liberal Group
Minutes of meetings, 1891–1901, are in Liverpool Record Office.

London Liberal Party
Minute books and other records, 1920s–70s, have been deposited in the Greater London Record Office. In addition, there is a minute book, 1890–95, of the Progressive Party, (the name of the Liberals on the L.C.C.).

Manchester Liberal Federation
Records of Manchester Progressive Association, 1911–15, and minute books of Manchester Liberal Womens Central Council, 1924–38, are in Manchester Central Library.

Manchester North-West Liberal Association
Minute books 1910–48, and statements of accounts, 1928–44, are in Manchester Central Library.

Manchester Rusholme Liberal Association
Minutes, 1931–32, are in Manchester Central Library.

Midlothian Liberal Association
Minute books, 1880–1912, together with a scrapbook of the 1879 campaign, are in St. Andrews University Library.

Newcastle-on-Tyne Liberal Club
Records, 1879–1960, are in Tyne and Wear County Archives. *See* NRA 26364.

Perthshire West Liberal Association
Minute books, 1885–87 are in Dundee District Archives. Other letters and papers, 1900–12, are in Perth and Kinross District Library.

Scottish Liberal Club
The minute books, 1879–1953, have now been placed in the National Library of Scotland.

Stockport Liberal Association
The records are in Stockport Central Library. They comprise minute books, newspaper cuttings, registers and lists of officials, 1868–1949.

Wakefield Liberal Association
Some records, *c* 1937, are in Wakefield Metropolitan Library.

Walsall Liberal Association
The records have been placed in Walsall Public Library. The collection includes Association minutes, 1907–42; Walsall Liberal League minute book, 1910; Walsall Young British Liberals Society minute book, 1906–07; Walsall Young Liberals League minute book, 1923–28; and electoral miscellanea, 1910, A list is available (NRA 23295).

Welsh Liberal Members Committee
A minute book, 1886–89, is in Newport Public Library.

Welsh National Liberal Council
A minute book, 1902–21, is in the University College of North Wales.

See also **Society of Certified and Associated Liberal Agents**

LIFE OFFICES' ASSOCIATION

The Association has retained its records at its head offices, Aldermary House, London EC4N 1TP. The Association was formed in 1889 to protect and advance ordinary life assurance, including negotiations on parliamentary legislation and taxation. The records include cash books, 1890–1956; circulars, 1890–1974; committee minutes, 1888–1974; correspondence, 1890–1974; and general meetings minutes, 1865–1921. There are also the committee minutes, 1923–56, of the Association of Life Assurance Offices in India.

LIVERPOOL COTTON ASSOCIATION

The records have been placed in Liverpool Public Library. The collection includes minute books, memoranda, reports and miscellaneous papers, 1842–1943.

LORDS' DAY OBSERVANCE SOCIETY

Since the entry in *Sources* Vol. 1, pp 158–9, the Society has moved its offices to Penge. It has retained its records.

MANAGEMENT RESEARCH GROUP

An archive has been deposited amongst the Ward papers with the Business History Unit, BLPES. The papers generally refer to Group 1 of the MRG but some papers relating to Groups 2 to 8 are also included. The collection consists of MRG bulletins (1932–59); the minutes of Directors' Dinner Discussions (1931–58); the papers of the Governing Council; Annual reports (1927–37) of MRG Groups 1–8 and one Annual report of Group 1 and one Annual report of Groups 2–8 together; the minutes and reports (1934–45) of individual Groups 2–9; the general papers (mainly reports) of the MRG headquarters research staff (1929–58) which comprise half the archive; the papers of Group 1 Executive Committee (1929–59) and the minutes of Group 1 General Meetings (1928–59); the minutes (1928–34) of eleven Group 1 sub-committees on a variety of topics, e.g. Budgetary Control, Insurance, Labour, Office Management, Organisation of Companies, fourteen 'subject' files of Group 1 on topics such as Civil Defence Insurance, Industrial Planning (4 files) and the TUC; the working papers of Groups 1–8 (1929–39) on various topics, and miscellaneous printed material and files of press cuttings and articles.

MANCHESTER COTTON ASSOCIATION

The records of the Association were transferred to the Central Library, Manchester, (ref M26) in September 1965, following the Association's dissolution. Some volumes are missing or damaged due to bombing in 1940. A list is available (NRA 11195).

Formed in 1894, the Manchester Cotton Association grew out of the Federation of Master Cotton Spinners' Association (Manchester). Its aim was to organise and regulate the importation of raw cotton (via the newly-opened Manchester Ship Canal) directly into Manchester. By the turn of the century it had also assumed the functions of classifying and marketing cotton goods and providing information on the trade. The contraction of the raw cotton trade, and the textile industry generally, led to the decision of a Special Board Meeting on 10 May 1965 that the Association should go into liquidation.

The records comprise Board Minute Books (1894–1917, 1926–49, 23 vols), Finance Committee Minutes (1937–54, 3 vols), Protection Committee Minutes (1905–34, 3 vols), a variety of sub-committee minutes, cash books, statistics on the cotton trade and material concerning the establishment of a central bureau for the sale of cotton in Manchester.

MANCHESTER TRANSVAAL COMMITTEE

Some relevant records have been deposited in the John Rylands University Library, Manchester. The collection consists of c 60 letters and papers including some printed items (1899–1900). There are 12 letters from C. P. Scott to L. T. Hobhouse, 5 sheets containing names of those in sympathy with the objects of a meeting exclusively for women, 13 June 1900, Queen's Hall, London, and other letters addressed to Scott and Hobhouse.

MASS OBSERVATION

The archives, described in *Sources* Vol. 1, p 163, have now been comprehensively listed (NRA 24301).

MECHANICS' INSTITUTES

Ashton and Dukinfield Mechanics' Institute
Records, 1825–1901, *see* NRA 0625.

Bacup Mechanics' Institute.
Records, 1861–1908, are in Lancashire Record Office.

Brighouse Mechanics' Institute
Records, 1853–1907, are in Calderdale Archives Department.

Cam Mechanics' Institute
Records, 1865–1964, are in Gloucestershire Record Office.

Cannock Mechanics' Institute
Papers relating to (1872) are in the Hatherton MSS (NRA 4022).

Chesterfield and Brampton Mechanics' Institute.
Minutes 1841–80 are in Derbyshire Record Office.

Cwmavon Mechanics' Institute
A list of members (1849–51) is in Glamorgan Record Office.

Derby Mechanics' Institute
Minute books, 1825–87, ledgers and correspondence are in Derby Public Library

Downpatrick Mechanics' Institute
Minute books, 1864–79, are in the Public Record Office of Northern Ireland.

Dumfries and Maxwelltown Mechanics' Institute
Miscellaneous records, 1825–1909, are in the Ewart Library, Dumfries.

Evesham Institute
Council minutes, 1837–97, are in Evesham Public Library.

Gateshead Mechanics' Institute
Minute books, 1836–1962, are in Gateshead Public Library.

Guildford Mechanics' Institute
Some early records are in Surrey Record Office.

Halifax Mechanics' Institute
The records have been placed in Halifax Public Library.

Haltwhistle Mechanics' Institute
Minutes, registers etc., 1920–48, are in Northumberland County Record Office.

Haslingden Mechanics' Institute
Subscription register (1846–60) is in Lancashire Record Office.

Horsforth Mechanics' Institute
Records, 1882–1917, are in Leeds Archives Department.

Ipswich Mechanics' Institute

The records are in Suffolk Record Office (Ipswich). The collection comprises minute books, 1824–1950, accounts, 1836–1961, annual reports, 1915–63, a membership register, 1929–59 and the records of Ipswich Working Mens College, 1862–95.

Keighley Mechanics' Institute

Minutes of committees, students' fee register, etc. 1829–1944, are in Keighley Library, which also has minutes of Oakworth Mechanics' Institute, 1920–35.

Kendal Mechanics' Institute

Minutes (1868–74) are in the Cumbria Record Office at Kendal.

Leeds Mechanics' Institute

Reports, minutes, files, etc. 1824–1940, including records of the Leeds Institute of Science, Art and Liberature are in Leeds City Library.

Leicester Mechanics' Institute

Minute Books (1833–70) of the Wellington St. Mechanics' Institute (NRA 6086).

Leighton Buzzard Working Men's Institute

Minute Books, correspondence and accounts, 1866–1904, are in Bedfordshire Record Office.

Llanelli Mechanics' Institute

The papers are in Dyfed Record Office.

Monkwearmouth Workmens' Club and Institute

Minutes, etc., 1910–58, are in Tyne and Wear Record Office, Newcastle.

Newcastle-on-Tyne Mechanics' Institute

Five minute books, (1834–79) are in Newcastle City Library.

North Shields Mechanics' Institute

Correspondence, etc., 1841–74 (North Tyneside Archives Department).

Sheffield Mechanics' Institute

Records, 1923–90, are in Sheffield City Library. The records of People's College, Sheffield, 1813–1912, including a manuscript history of the College by John Derby, are in Sheffield University Library.

Shelley (Huddersfield) Mechanics' Institute

Minute books, 1948–78, are in Huddersfield Public Library.

Shrewsbury Mechanics' Institute

A few early items are in Salop Record Office.

Smethwick Institute
Minutes, 1887–1928, are in Warley Public Library.

Stourbridge Mechanics' Institute
Papers concerning are in the Palfrey Collection (NRA 1501).

Sudbury (Staffs) Institute Club
Records, 1834-date (Sudbury 9945).

Swindon Mechanics' Institution
Records, 1848–1947, can be found in the British Transport Historical Records.

Wakefield Mechanics' Institute
Minutes of committee and council, 1841–1921, and minute books of various sub-committees, are in Wakefield Public Library.

Wolverhampton Athenaeum and Mechanics' Institute
Minutes and accounts, 1835–70, are in Wolverhampton Central Library.

Wrekenton Mechanics' Institute
Secretary's book 1897–1931 is in Gateshead Public Library.

Yorkshire Union of Mechanics' Institutes
Papers (1840–1921) are deposited in Leeds City Library.

MIDLAND BOLT, NUT, SCREW AND RIVET EMPLOYERS' ASSOCIATION

Relevant material can be found in the Modern Records Centre, University of Warwick (ref MSS 33). This includes a microfilm of the minutes of the Assocation, 1942–68, material on its history and a file *re.* agreements. The Association was founded in 1942 to deal with wages and working conditions and to establish a standard for general observation by employers in the trade. From January 1977 the Association became a section within the West Midlands Engineering Employers Federation.

MINERS' INTERNATIONAL FEDERATION

An extensive collection of records, covering the period 1890–1968, is in the International Institute of Social History, Amsterdam.

MISSION TO LONDON

The papers of the Mission, 1948–52, were given to Lambeth Palace Library by the Reverend Dr. G. Huelin in 1966 (ref MSS 1948–60). The Mission was launched by the Bishop of London in 1949 to restore the religious life of London after the Second World War. The collection includes minutes of the Mission's Executive

Committee; minutes, reports and papers of the Advisory Council; financial accounts, 1947–52; accounts of previous missions to London, in 1874 and 1883; a history of the Mission by the Reverend Frank Tyler, the organising secretary; monthly briefing letters for incumbents and local centre representatives; extensive records of rallies, meetings, conferences, etc; and collections of press cuttings.

MORAL WELFARE WORKERS' ASSOCIATION
The records are in Church House Record Centre. A list is available (NRA 24405).

NATIONAL ADVISORY CENTRE ON CAREERS FOR WOMEN
The records of this body (formerly the Women's Employment Federation) have been placed in the Fawcett Library, City of London Polytechnic. They cover the period 1918 to 1960.

NATIONAL ALLIANCE OF EMPLOYERS AND EMPLOYED
Some relevant records are in the Iron and Steel Confederation deposit in the Modern Records Centre, University of Warwick. The Alliance was founded in December 1916, and in July 1925 it merged with the Industrial League and Council to form the National Industrial Alliance. The material in the Modern Records Centre comprises minutes, reports, specimen lectures, some weekly notes and balance sheets, 1917–19.

NATIONAL AMALGAMATED FURNISHING TRADES' ASSOCIATION
Some records of the Association, and various predecessor organisations were placed in the National Library of Scotland (ref Acc 4056) on permanent loan from the Scottish Committee of the Society for the Study of Labour History in 1966, through the good offices of Ian MacDougall, Esq. The deposit comprises roll books (1854–70) and cashbooks (1846–54, 6 vols) of the Edinburgh Cabinetmakers' and Chairmakers' Society, minute books of the United Operative Cabinet and Chairmakers' Association of Scotland (1893–1902) and cashbooks of the National Amalgamated Furnishing Trades' Association (1910–32).

NATIONAL AMALGAMATED UNION OF LIFE ASSURANCE WORKERS (NAULAW)
Some records have been deposited at the Modern Records Centre, University of Warwick. The files deposited by M. A. Best, a former Vice-President and Acting President of the union include correspondence 1919–61; Insurance Unions' Consultative Committee minutes and related correspondence 1940–50; reports and correspondence re the London and Manchester Assurance Co Ltd, files re the Fabian Society Enquiry into commercial insurance and the possibility of nationalisation; and files on the conditions of work of insurance agents. S. P. Long, former secretary of the London District Council of the NAULAW has deposited a file of minutes, correspondence and papers on pensions 1960–75, deriving from his work with Retired Members Association.

NAULAW was established in 1884 as the National Union of Life Assurance Agents; in 1919 its title was changed to the National Amalgamated Union of Life Assurance Workers.

NATIONAL ASSOCIATION FOR MATERNAL AND CHILD WELFARE

The records of the Association, together with some records of predecessor organisations, have now been deposited in Liverpool University Library. An outline list is available (NRA 26460).

NATIONAL ASSOCIATION FOR THE CARE AND RESETTLEMENT OF OFFENDERS

Some records of the association – which was founded in 1966 – together with records of its predecessor, the Central Discharged Prisoners Aid Society, have been deposited in the Modern Records Centre, University of Warwick. A list is available (NRA 23021). The collection comprises annual reports, reports of regional groups, subject files, etc. The Modern Records Centre also has the files of Lord Donaldson of Kingsbridge relating to his work as chairman of NACRO, 1961–78.

NATIONAL ASSOCIATION OF CITIZENS' ADVICE BUREAUX

The records deposited at the Greater London Record Office consist of five series of files, c. 1940–1960. One series comprises subject files, another national statistics for the service. The remainder relate to closed and current bureaux, and are arranged either by name of the bureau or by geographical region.

In 1939 Citizens' Advice Bureaux were set up as local centres of a national voluntary service to provide free information on wartime problems, including evacuation and rationing. After the war the service offered advice on family and personal problems, in collaboration with social workers, the legal profession and other agencies. The National Citizens' Advice Bureaux Council (after 1973 the National Association of Citizens' Advice Bureaux) was responsible for the policy of the service, and for passing to the bureaux up-to-date information on legislative and other provisions affecting citizens.

NATIONAL ASSOCIATION OF DIVISIONAL EXECUTIVES FOR EDUCATION

An extensive collection of records (101 boxes), covering the period 1934–74 is in Southampton University Library (ref L18 WH1). The collection includes correspondence regarding the inaugural meeting and constitution of NADEE (1946–1969), the minutes of the Association (1947–1974) and miscellaneous correspondence (1947–51). There are numerous 'subject' files on the Association's activities covering such diverse topics as membership, election of officers, secondary education, religious education, staffing of schools and local government reorganisation, to name but a few. There are also numerous files of correspondence with particular organisations such as the Association of Education Committees, the Association of Municipal Corporations, the National Union of Teachers, the County Councils' Association and the British Institute of Adult Education, together with files of correspondence with various Education Authorities. Also in the collection are the minutes and correspondence of the Executive, General Purposes and Standing Orders Committees, and various sub-committees (1948–74) together with correspondence pertaining to conferences and resolutions, plus reports (1947–73). Financial correspondence (1947–73) is held. A number of Ministry memoranda, circulars, publications and press notices (1947–73) also comprise part of the collection.

Correspondence relating to the constitution and rules of the Federation of Part 3 authorities (1932–43), Executive Committee Minutes (1932–45), correspondence and records of expenses of the Executive Committee (1933–45); circulars (1933–45); minutes and related papers of Annual Meetings (1922–45); and Treasurer's statements, balance sheets and correspondence (1932–1945). There are 13 files of correspondence with various organisations e.g. the Association of Education Committees, the Association of Urban District Councils and several divisions of the Part 3 Authorities Federation, together with 69 'subject' files e.g. membership, post primary education, post-war planning and the autonomy of Part 3 education committees. Also in the collection are some miscellaneous papers of Dr. White.

NATIONAL ASSOCIATION OF LABOUR TEACHERS

Records of the Association, and of the later Socialist Educational Association, covering the period 1926–80, have been deposited in the Greater London Record Office. The collection includes minutes, financial and membership records, correspondence, publications and records relating to campaigns and enquiries.

The Association originated in 1926 when several members left a Teachers Labour League meeting, owing to the pro-Communist policy which had been developing in the League, and organised themselves under the name of the Association of Labour Teachers. In 1928 the National Association of Labour Teachers was formed to increase and organise support within the teaching profession for the principles and programme advocated by the Labour Party and to assist in the work of developing and formulating the education programme of the Labour Party. The Association was reorganised in 1961 and the more broadly-based Socialist Educational Association formed, open to all eligible for membership of the Labour Party. This aims to foster a socialist approach to education issues and promote a socialist education system in Britain.

NATIONAL ASSOCIATION OF SCHOOLMASTERS

The records of the Association were deposited in 1971 in the Modern Records Centre, University of Warwick (ref MSS 38A). A list has been prepared (NRA 21376). The Association was originally formed with the National Union of Teachers at the 1919 NUT Conference. In 1922 it decided to secede from the NUT. In 1970 the NAS entered a 'Joint Two Alliance' with the Union of Women Teachers and the two merged in 1975.

The collection includes the minute book of the Finance and General Purposes Committee (1923–25); miscellaneous Conference documents 1927–70; papers and minutes of the NAS special committee on representations to the Burnham Committee; Annual Reports and Yearbooks 1919–41; copies of *The New Schoolmaster* (the NAS journal) 1921–73; volume of copies of the NAS *Bulletin* 1939–44; 400 pamphlets and leaflets of the NAS (1928–70), and other printed material belonging to other bodies and local branches.

The collection also includes the minute books, rules, agenda, etc. of local School-masters Associations: London Schoolmasters' Association (1919–38); Leicester Certified Schoolmasters' Association (1920–26); Merseyside Federation of School-masters (1923–32) and Newcastle upon Tyne branch of the NAS.

NATIONAL ASSOCIATION OF SOCIAL WORKERS IN EDUCATION

The records of the Association have been deposited in the Modern Records Centre, University of Warwick. The Association was formerly known as the Education Welfare Officers National Association (EWONA). The collection includes National Council minutes, 1897–1961, Conference minute books, 1897–1907, Conference Journals, 1948–69 and two local minute books for Leeds, 1901–22, and for the Lancashire, Cheshire and North Wales Federation, 1905–13. A complete run of *Journals* is held for the years 1946–69 and various subject and correspondence files. This original deposit has been added to by important complementary deposits. These later deposits include School Attendance Officers' National Association NEC minutes, 1923–43; EWONA NEC minutes, 1943–8, 1961–73. Some correspondence files were included in this deposit, especially concerning the Children & Young Persons Bill, 1963, the Plowden Committee, 1968, the Seebohm Committee, 1970 and the Ingleby Committee, 1957. In a later deposit, the Modern Records Centre received minutes and reports, 1967–76, national account books, 1922–78, some national correspondence and other papers together with Liverpool branch minutes, 1936–59. In addition, Mr. R. Grimoldby, former President of EWONA, has deposited his personal papers, which supplement material already received from EWONA. Included are items relating to the Yorkshire and Lincolnshire Federation of EWONA, and a run of the *Education Welfare Officer*, 1960–75.

NATIONAL ASSOCIATION OF TEACHERS IN FURTHER AND HIGHER EDUCATION

The surviving records of the Association, and its two constituents, the Association of Teachers in Technical Institutions (ATTI) and the Association of Teachers in Colleges and Departments of Education (ATCDE) have been deposited in the Modern Records Centre, University of Warwick (ref MSS 176). The records of the Association of Teachers in Technical Institutions include Council minutes, 1904–67, with some Council papers, Executive Committee minutes 1904–1975, Finance Committee minutes, 1905–68, and the minutes of various special committees, as well as press-cuttings, 1920s–30s and 1950s–60s.

For the Association of Teachers in Colleges and Departments of Education the deposit includes minutes of the Training Colleges' Association, 1918–41, miscellaneous papers, 1918–40, and tenure cases, 1935–40; minutes of two teaching sections, and some papers of several joint committees of the TCA and the Council of Principals. Of the latter, minutes, memoranda and lists of members, 1929–42, have been deposited, as well as a minute book of the Group of Principals of Men's Training Colleges, 1925–9. Executive Committee minutes from the foundation of ATCDE in 1943 have been deposited, with other series of minutes, including Finance and General Purposes Committee, 1951–75, the Conditions of Service Committee, 1952–76, and the AGM, 1950–72. The deposit also includes extensive correspondence and subject files, and annual reports, 1944–57, the Association's *News Sheet*, 1952–62, and *Communiqué*, 1970–5, and pamphlets, 1968–74.

NATIONAL BIBLE SOCIETY OF SCOTLAND

Some records survive at the offices of the Society, 5 St Andrew Square, Edinburgh, EH2 2BL. Most of the correspondence files prior to 1939 were pulped during the war, but the postwar records include the correspondence of missionaries in the field and correspondence with other missionary societies, mainly concerning the translation and distribution of the Bible. Permission to consult the archives of the Society must be obtained in writing from the General Secretary.

NATIONAL BUSWORKERS' ASSOCIATION

The only known surviving material on this association can be found in correspondence in the administrative files of the National Union of Railwaymen, deposited in the Modern Records Centre, University of Warwick (ref MSS 127). The Association was founded in October 1950 and was centred on Hampshire and Dorset Motor Services Ltd.

NATIONAL CAMPAIGN FOR THE HOMELESS (SHELTER)

Launched in December 1966. Directed in its early years by Des Wilson. Played a major role in formulating new strategies and action to solve the housing crisis. The archives of Shelter are most easily available on a microfiche produced by Harvester Press. The microfiche publication includes unpublished minute books of the Board of Management, all Shelter pamphlets, research reports, press releases, bulletins, Annual Reports, etc.

NATIONAL COMMITTEE FOR RESCUE FROM NAZI TERROR

Certain records are in the Board of Deputies archive (*see Sources*, Vol. 1, pp 20–1). These include executive committee minutes and correspondence (1943–45), and further special files including minutes, bulletins, memoranda and correspondence (refs C11/7/7/3d/6; E1/74; E3/536). Also of relevance are the Joseph Leftwich papers, at the Central Zionist Archives.

NATIONAL COMMITTEE OF CONSTITUENCY LABOUR PARTIES

Some relevant records can be found in the Garnsworthy papers in BLPES (ref Coll Misc 540). The papers include correspondence with the Surrey Labour Federation, 1934–35; the Home Counties Labour Association, 1935–36; minutes, circulars, reports and correspondence of the National Committee, 1936–40; and a draft constitution of the National Committee from the late 1930s.

NATIONAL COUNCIL FOR CIVIL LIBERTIES

Since the entry in *Sources* Vol. 1, pp 172–3, further material has been deposited in the Brynmor Jones Library, University of Hull. This material includes pamphlets from 1934; Executive Committee minutes from 1944; Finance/Appeals Committee from 1943; Refugee and Aliens Sub-Committee, 1941–46; Overseas Sub-Committee, 1937–41 and 1944–54, Democratic Rights in Armed Services Sub-Committee, 1947; material on Anti-Semitism, 1938–45, and Public Order, 1931–37.

NATIONAL COUNCIL FOR THE ABOLITION OF THE DEATH PENALTY

Since the entry in *Sources* Vol. 1, p 169 some records have been located in the archives of the Howard League for Penal Reform in the Modern Records Centre, University of Warwick (ref MSS 16). The records consist of minute books, 1923–48, balance sheets, most annual reports and the journal.

NATIONAL COUNCIL FOR VOLUNTARY ORGANISATIONS (NCVO)

The Council (formerly the National Council of Social Service) was founded in 1919 to promote the systematic organisation of voluntary social work, both at national and local level. It adopted its present name in 1980. The Council has retained many records at its London headquarters, 26, Bedford Square, London WC1. The records include minutes, correspondence, and other papers dating back to the Council's foundation. The papers include material on the development of the Welfare State, unemployment in the 1930s, the National Health Service, the formation of Rural Community Councils and such specific projects as the International Year of the Disabled. Applications to see the papers should be addressed to the Head of Central Registry at the Council. A published history is also available, *Voluntary Social Action* by M. Brasnett (1969).

NATIONAL COUNCIL OF SOCIAL SERVICE

See **National Council for Voluntary Organisations**

NATIONAL FEDERATION OF BUILDING TRADES EMPLOYERS

In addition to the main archives, described in *Sources* Vol. 1, p 177 the records of a constituent organisation, the Central Association of Master Builders of London, have been deposited in the Greater London Record Office. These records, 1872–1950, include minutes, records of Conciliation Boards and membership records. Also deposited are records of the Builders Benevolent Institution 1847–1959 and Builders Clerks Benevolent Institution 1883–1963.

The Central Association was founded in 1872 with the object of promoting and protecting the interests of the building trade of London in general and of members of the Association in particular. The name was changed to the London Master Builders' Association in 1899. Between 1918 and 1922 it was known successively as the London Master Builders' and Aircraft Industries' Association and the London Master Builders' Association in 1922. It became the London Region of the National Federation of Building Trades Employers in 1928.

NATIONAL GRAPHICAL ASSOCIATION

The archive of the National Graphical Association in the Modern Records Centre, University of Warwick (*see* Sources Vol. 1, p 178) was added to in 1980 by the deposit from its Manchester offices of the records of the small but important National Union of Wallcoverings, Decorative and Allied Trades. This union, formed in 1975 when the Wallcoverings Staff Association amalgamated with the

Wallpaper Workers Union, transferred its engagements to the National Graphical Association in 1979.

The deposited records comprise Paper Stainers Union of General Workers minutes from 1897; Wallpaper Stainers' Trade Union Federation minutes, 1917–51; Wallpaper Workers' Union minutes, 1918–75, annual reports and balance sheets; Wallcoverings Staff Association minutes, 1970–5; extensive correspondence and papers. A list is available (NRA 24668). The Centre also has records since 1885 of the Society of Lithographic Artists, Designers, Engravers and Process Workers. The Society amalgamated with the NGA in 1982.

NATIONAL INSTITUTE OF INDUSTRIAL PSYCHOLOGY

The records have been deposited in BLPES. The collection of 20 volumes and 85 boxes includes Executive Committee minutes, 1921–53; Vocational Guidance Committee records, 1921–38; Finance and General Purposes Committee minutes, 1934–47, 1949–73; Women's Committee minutes, 1930–39; correspondence, 1933–37; staff files, 1933–77 (closed at present); internal papers *re* research projects etc.

NATIONAL LIBERAL CLUB

Since the entry in *Sources* Vol. 1, pp 182–183 the archive of the Club has been acquired by Bristol University Library. The collection mainly concerns the Club itself and not so much the political history of the Liberal Party. The detailed contents of the archive are membership registers (1882–1954) and General Committee minute books (1897–1968). There are also minute books of many other committees and sub-committees (details are available from the Librarian), and miscellaneous papers relating to the founding and early history of the Club.

The collection also includes the accounts and minute books (1943–1966) and miscellaneous papers of the Womens Liberal Federation, the Reports (1904–1965) and committee minutes (1914–1965) of the Liberal Social Council, General Election addresses (1892 to date), By-election addresses (1905–1910, 1911, 1913–1919) and London County Council election addresses (1889–1913).

See also Liberal Party.

NATIONAL MINORITY MOVEMENT

In addition to the material cited in *Sources* Vol. 1, p 184, some material is at the Modern Records Centre, University of Warwick (ref MSS 81). This includes copies of minutes of Coventry District Committee, 1925–30, and Midland Bureau, 1919–31, and a few related documents.

NATIONAL REFORM UNION ·

Some records of the Union are with the archives of the Cobden Club (*q.v.*), now deposited in West Sussex Record Office. The National Reform Union, with its head office in Manchester, was founded in 1864 by members of the committee of the Anti-Corn (Laws) League, its objects (as stated in 1914) being to support Liberal Party policies, with special emphasis on free trade. The Union was wound up in 1946 and its assets (and archives) transferred to the Free Trade Union. The material at the West Sussex Record Office comprises minutes of the Executive and other committees, February 1914 – December 1946, printed Annual Reports, 1926, 1927, and the resolution winding up the Union, 1946.

NATIONAL SAFETY FIRST ASSOCIATION

See **Royal Society for the Prevention of Accidents**

NATIONAL SOCIETY FOR CLEAN AIR

See **Environment and Planning.**

NATIONAL SOCIETY FOR THE PREVENTION OF VENEREAL DISEASE

A collection of letters, cuttings and pamphlets, 1937–44, has been deposited in the Wellcome Institute for the History of Medicine. A list is available (NRA 24909).

NATIONAL TITHEPAYERS' ASSOCIATION

Although no central records have been located, some important branch records are deposited in Dorset Record Office (NRA 20478). They include minutes, letter-books, tithe case papers of the Dorset branch (1937–42), Crewkerne branch (1934–35) and the Salisbury branch (1939–54).

NATIONAL TRACTION ENGINE OWNERS' AND USERS' ASSOCIATION

A collection of papers relating to the NTEOUA and its successor, the National Traction Engine and Tractor Association (NTETA), has been deposited with the Institute of Agricultural History and Museum of English Rural Life, University of Reading.

The collection consists of the minute books (1900–1946), annual reports (1903–44) and annual financial statements (1894–1900 and 1928–45) of the NTEOUA and *c.* 100 of its administrative files mostly from the 1930s and 1940s. There are the annual reports (1945–56), annual financial statements (1946–50) and 15 administrative files (1940s and 1950s) of the NTETA. The collection also includes papers of the related organisations, the Steam Cultivation Development Association (SCDA) and the Threshing Machine Owners Association (TMOA). These consist of the minute books (1915–26), annual reports (1916–38) annual financial statements (1924–41) and 5 administrative files (1920s and 1930s) of the SCDA, and two minute books of the TMOA, one for the Berkshire Branch (1940–54) and one for the Oxfordshire Branch (1940–54).

NATIONAL TRADE DEFENCE ASSOCIATION

An important collection of records of the Midland District, and of the Birmingham and Midland Counties Wholesale Brewers Association, has been deposited in Staffordshire County Record Office, (ref D3163). A list is available (NRA 22810). The papers of the Birmingham and Midland Counties Wholesale Brewers Association include 14 volumes of minutes of General and Committee Meetings (1891–1937), 15 volumes of 'appendices to Minutes', consisting of correspondence, papers considered at meetings, annual reports and statements of accounts (1895–1940).

There are 26 series of circulars sent out by the Association (1913–1939), plus 12 files on miscellaneous subjects, mainly consisting of general correspondence with individual breweries. Amongst the papers are the records of the National Trade Defence Association – Midland District, founded in 1891 as the Midland Counties Federated Brewers Association. This Association was formed to support the electoral scheme put forward by the National Trade Defence Fund. These records include 4 volumes of minutes of general and committee meetings (1891 to 1939), 5 volumes of minutes of the Birmingham and Aston Trade Committee (1891–1948), the minutes of agent's meetings (1 vol, 1891–92), the District Agents Annual Reports (1901–1939) and minutes of meetings of retail delegates 1901–1934.

Amongst miscellaneous files there is one relating to elections 1892–1910, correspondence relating to by-elections (1 file) 1929–1943, and a volume on the attitudes of Midland candidates to the Trade 1934–42.

There are also minutes of the Shropshire Wholesale Brewers Association (1 vol) 1948–1970, and Birmingham Cold Storage Ltd., (3 vols) 1899–1941.

NATIONAL UNION OF BANK EMPLOYEES
See Banking, Insurance and Finance Union

NATIONAL UNION OF HOSIERY AND KNITWEAR WORKERS

A collection of records has been deposited in Leicestershire Record Office. A list is available (NRA 21103). The collection is made up of two basic parts: the records of the Leicester and Leicestershire Trimmers Association, deposited by the Union, per Mr. R. W. Leach in June 1976; and the records of the Leicester Hosiery Union together with various Nottinghamshire branches, deposited by the Union in October 1976.

The papers of the Leicester and Leicestershire Trimmers Association consist of the Annual, Quarterly and Special meetings minutes, 1869–1934 (7 volumes). The Executive Committee minutes exist for 1892–1935 (9 volumes). There is a file of typescript minutes of General, Management Committee and Sectional Board meetings, 1935–41. There is an 'out letter-book', 1904–10; 22 files of correspondence and papers on various topics, 1897–1957; 5 contribution books, 1866–1913; and Balance Sheets for 1911–44.

The Leicester Hosiery Union records consist of 6 volumes of Executive Committee minutes, 1887–1931, and 2 volumes of trade and shop committee minutes, 1917–35.

The Hinckley Hosiery Union papers consist of Annual, General and Special meeting minutes (1 volume) for 1930–46, 11 volumes of Executive minutes 1918–44; and accounts 1897–1928. The collection also includes minutes of the meetings of the Nottingham Hosiery Union (3 volumes, 1912–25), the Nottingham & District Hosiery Finishers' Association (1 volume, 1919–21), the Ilkeston and District Hosiery Union (3 volumes, 1899–1944), the Loughborough Hosiery Union (2 volumes, 1923–48) and miscellaneous items. See also the study by Richard Gurnham, *200 Years: The Hosiery Unions, 1776–1976* (Leicester, 1976).

NATIONAL UNION OF JOURNALISTS

Since the entry in *Sources* Vol. 1, p 194, an extensive collection of records has been deposited in the Modern Records Centre, University of Warwick (ref MSS 86). The collection includes NEC minutes, Education, Finance and various sub-committee minutes, 1907–13, 1914–55; Annual Delegate Meetings (5 vols, 1909, 1912–16, 1917–18, 1926–32, 1933–37); Emergency Committee minutes, 1914–16; NUJ Approved Society, minutes, 1912–19; correspondence of the Training Department; War Distress Fund Committee minutes; two boxes of personal papers of J. S. Dean; and a file of papers relating to the NUJ's submission to the Royal Commission on the Press, 1961.

Among the branch records are material for Cambridge (2 vols of minutes, 1911–24), Central London (6 vols of minutes, 1910–35 and 2 folders of correspondence and papers), Hastings (1 vol of minutes, 1908–18) and two minute books covering the entire existence of the *Star* editorial chapel, 1936–60, with two files of correspondence and papers.

NATIONAL UNION OF LABOUR ORGANISERS AND ELECTION AGENTS

No details are available on the main records, but the minutes of the Exective Committee, 1959–63 as well as Midland District Committee minutes, 1941–53, are in the Social Science Department of Birmingham Reference Library.

NATIONAL UNION OF MINEWORKERS

Since the entry in *Sources* Vol. 1, p 195, considerable deposits of regional union records and relief funds have been made. They are outlined below, in alphabetical order:

Ashton, Haydock, Bolton, etc. Miners' Trade Union

One volume of printed district committee minutes for 1896 has been donated to the Modern Records Centre, University of Warwick.

Denbighshire and Flintshire Miners' Federation
See under **North Wales** (below)

Durham County Collier, Enginemens', Boiler Minders' and Fireman's Association

The records have been deposited in Durham County Record Office (ref D/EFB 1–92). The collection covers the period approximately 1872–1963, and includes minute books, financial records, day books, arbitration committee minutes, files of correspondence and some branch records.

Fife and Kinross Miners' Association
See under **Scotland** (p. 77)

Lanarkshire Miners' Union
See under **Scotland** (p. 77)

Lancashire and Cheshire Colliery Tradesmen and Kindred Workers' Association

The records are in Bolton Metropolitan Borough Library. The association became a constituent association of the National Union of Mineworkers (NUM Lancashire Tradesmen's Area) in 1945. In July 1968 it became the NUM North-Western Area.

The collection consists of Executive Committee Minutes 1921–1968, Monthly, Quarterly, Half-Yearly and Annual Reports and Accounts, 1920–34, 53 correspondence files (1951–78) on various subjects e.g. Wages Rates, National Insurance Acts, Branch Correspondence, Political Affiliations, etc. There are printed minutes (1920–1969) of the Executive and sub-committees of the Lancashire and Cheshire Miners' Federation (from 1945 the Lancashire Area of the NUM), together with reports and accounts, Minutes of the Lancashire and Cheshire Joint Committee and Miners' Welfare Committee (1924–33) and Annual Conference Reports 1951–68 of the National Federation of Colliery Enginemen, Boilermen and Mechanics (NUM Group 2) 1924–33. The correspondence files may not be consulted without the consent of the depositor.

Lancashire and Cheshire Miners' Federation

Certain records, 1912–49, have been deposited in Wigan Record Office.

Lancashire and Cheshire Miners' Permanent Relief Society

The records are in Wigan Record Office. They comprise minutes, 1874–1947, ledgers, 1899–1936, valuation books, 1908–1960 and other financial and legal records.

Larkhall Miners' Association
See under **Scotland** (p.77)

Midlands Area

Application to see these records, which consist of two minute books, 1928–1949, yearly rota for TUC, Labour Party Conference, Miners Federation Executive Committee delegates, and a photograph album, should be made to the Administrative Officer at the Midlands Area Office of the NUM, 12, Lichfield Road, Stafford, where the records are held.

North Staffordshire Area

A collection is held at the offices of the NUM, Park Road, Burslem, Stoke-on-Trent It covers the years 1892–1971 and includes minutes, records of expenditure, receipts, treasurer's reports, balance sheets, contribution records and branch membership numbers.

Northumberland and Durham Miners' Permanent Relief Fund

The records have been deposited in Tyne and Wear Record Office (ref Acc 919). A list is available (NRA 21125). The collection comprises 16 minute books of the General Committee, 1862–1921. There are also printed annual reports, 1862–1926; printed actuarial reports, 1877–1941 (with gaps); reports of the assets and liabilities of the Fund, 1862–83; and printed rules of the Fund, 1899.

Northumberland Colliery Mechanics' Association

The records are in Northumberland Record Office. They include minutes of committee 1888–1935, council 1928–48, annual conference 1905–17, delegate meetings 1894–1935, account books 1876–1957, record books of compensation cases 1900–42, superannuation fund accounts 1907–51, and branch contribution books 1906–26.

North Wales
The surviving records are held in the NUM Area Office at Wrexham. They have been listed by Clwyd Record Office. Clwyd Record Office holds the records of the Denbighshire and Flintshire Miners' Federation. These comprise minutes, correspondence and other papers, 1889–1982.

Scotland
The records of the former Lanarkshire Miners' Union and the NUM (Lanarkshire Area), covering the period 1887–1962, have been deposited in the National Library of Scotland (ref Dep 227). Also deposited in the National Library of Scotland are the NUM records for the Ayr region for the period 1938–67, as well as the three surviving minute books, 1890–94, of the Larkhall Miners' Association (ref 8023–5). These were kept by its Secretary, Robert Smillie. In 1980, the National Library of Scotland, also acquired the minutes, 1901–13, of the Fife and Kinross Miners' Association.

Warwickshire Miners' Association
The minutes of the Warwickshire Miners' Association, 1903–35, and a list of members, 1940–54, have been deposited in Warwickshire County Record Office.

NATIONAL UNION OF RAILWAYMEN
Since the entry in *Sources* Vol. 1, p 199, a very extensive collection of records has been deposited in the Modern Records Centre, University of Warwick (ref MSS 127). Virtually no records appear to have survived for two of the small constituent unions, the General Railway Workers Union and the United Pointsmen's and Signalmen's Society, but for the NUR and the ASRS an extensive series of records has been deposited. Material received to date includes legal correspondence and papers relating to both the Taff Vale and Osborne cases, amongst which are the minute books of the Men's Committee on the Taff Vale Railway, 1900–01, and the minute book of the Walthamstow branch of the ASRS, 1877–1905, as well as correspondence with ASRS branches and other unions. Other ASRS records deposited include ASRS proceedings and reports, 1892–1913, and branch balance sheets over a longer period.

The Railwaymen's Parliamentary Representation Association is represented by proceedings of its 1911 AGM, and the NUR's trusteeship of the Central Labour College is reflected in a box of records deposited in accordance with a decision taken in September 1929.

Full details of the various deposits of records are given in the *Guide* to the Modern Records Centre. Even since the Guide was prepared, other important records have been deposited e.g. NUR Political sub-committee minutes, 1920–34; Negotiating Committee minutes, 1936–45, administrative files, including an important series concerning relations with other unions for the inter-war period and material on the **National Busworkers Association** (*q.v.*); also five circulars, 1924–46; material on the 1921 miners dispute, the London Underground etc.

Note Printed catalogues of the Taff Vale and Osborne case papers are available from the Centre (Occasional Publications, 3 and 4).

NATIONAL UNION OF SEAMEN

Since the entry in *Sources* Vol. 1, p 200, a major deposit of the records of the Union has been made in the Modern Records Centre, University of Warwick. The collection includes Executive Council minutes, 1911–59; management committee, 1929–37; finance (and general purposes), 1911–53; minutes (various dates) of some 19 branches, including Hull Sailors' Mutual Association/Seamen and Marine Firemen's Amalgamated Association, 1884–95, Bristol, 1921–50, Sunderland, various dates between 1887 and 1968, and Malta, 1919–25. Some District Maritime Board minutes were included in the deposit, as well as some subject groups of papers, for example on the manning question. British Seafarers' Union records deposited include Finance Committee minutes, 1915–21, and Southampton branch minutes, 1911–21.

NATIONAL UNION OF STOVE GRATE WORKERS (NUSGW)

A collection of papers has been deposited on loan at the Brian O'Malley Central Library and Arts Centre, Rotherham. It includes two minute books, December 1894–November 1912 and a 'Round Robin', 1891. The archives of the Union (now the Union of Domestic Appliance and General Metal Workers) from 1912 are still at the Union headquarters in Imperial Chambers, High Street, Rotherham.

NATIONAL UNION OF VEHICLE BUILDERS

See **Transport and General Workers' Union**

NATIONAL UNION OF WALLCOVERINGS' DECORATIVE AND ALLIED TRADES

See **National Graphical Association**

NEVER AGAIN ASSOCIATION

No central archive has been located, but reference should be made to the Alan Graham papers, deposited in BLPES (see *Sources*, Vol. 3, pp 181–82). These contain a file of minutes and correspondence of the Never Again Association as well as correspondence with *Allies inside Germany*.

NEW BRITAIN MOVEMENT

It is reported that the archives, together with those of the New Europe Group, are with New Atlantis.

NEW ULSTER MOVEMENT

Minutes and correspondence, 1969–75, are in the Public Record Office of Northern Ireland.

NON-CONFORMIST UNIONIST ASSOCIATION

Letters and other papers of the Secretary, Dr. W. E. Ball, 1888–89, are in the Northern Ireland Public Record Office.

NORTH LANCASHIRE AND CUMBERLAND TEXTILE WORKERS' ASSOCIATION

The records of the predecessors of the union and other similar organisations have been placed in Lancashire Record Office (ref DDX 1078). A list is available (NRA 20343).

Among the important deposits that have been made are:

Blackburn and District Weavers', Warpers' and Winders' Association

The collection comprises minutes 1903–1949, reports and accounts 1915–49 and a receipt book 1948–66.

Darwen Weavers', Warpers' and Winders' Association

The collection comprises minutes 1888–1957, reports, journals and balance sheets 1886–1960, nomination book for death money 1897–1951, and rules, 1912.

General Union of Lancashire and Yorkshire Warp Dressers

The collection contains minutes, 26 May 1894–12 October 1918 and rules, 1919.

Nelson and District Association of Warp Dressers (Colne Branch)

The collection contains only minutes, January 1895–January 1898.

Nelson, Colne, and Darwen Chain Beamers' Association

The only deposited item would appear to be an unemployment register, 9 November 1914–30 December 1932.

Preston and District Weavers', Warpers' and Winders' Association

The extensive deposit comprises minutes, 1864–1959, membership records, 1866–1941, collection lists, 1902–35, cases and complaints books, 1904–64, correspondence 1860–1868, weekly accounts 1937–45, strike pay and stoppage books, 1887–1938, contribution books, 1895–1940, wages calculation books and papers, 1906–45, legal papers, 1894–1926, rules 1885, and miscellaneous, 1922–c. 1974.

Reference should also be made to the records of the Leeds and District Warp-dressers', Twisters' and Kindred Trades Association (*see* NRA 22817).

NORTHERN CARPET TRADE UNION

The surviving records, covering the period 1894–1975 have been deposited in Calderdale Public Library by Leslie Smith Esq, the Secretary of the NCTU. A list has been prepared (NRA 22941). The deposit would appear to include records of such predecessor unions as the Halifax Brussels Carpet Weavers' Association, the Northern Counties Power-Loom Carpet Weavers' Association and the Northern Counties Carpet Trades' Association.

The deposited records include a manuscript minute book of General and Committee Meetings 1892–1903 and 10 volumes of minutes of the NCTU and its predecessor. There is a minute book of H. Shed Brussels Weavers (1873–1892); 2 minute books of NCTU General Committee and other meetings (1904–21); 7 minute books of the NCTU Executive Committee and other meetings (1921–1966); NCTU Annual Reports and Balance Sheets (1894–1960); a file of duplicated NCTU minutes with various accounts and correspondence (1928–1962). Financial records comprise 3 cash books (1901–1953); 6 account books with branch and general monthly accounts (1916–1962); 12 contributions books (1892–1970). There is also a book of branch accounts 1956–67, used cheque books 1931–1950, an envelope containing miscellaneous financial papers, mainly referring to the Halifax Friendly and Trade Societies Club, and 4 account books listing the accounts of various branches 1892–1920.

Included in the correspondence is an 'out' letter book 1906–13, a large file of correspondence with branches 1909–1916; and a file of correspondence with the Board of Trade, Ministry of Labour, War Office and other Government departments 1912–1918.

There are 4 general correspondence files 1917–67; and 24 files of correspondence with various employers 1915–1966. 27 files of correspondence and material relating to various Industrial Councils for the carpet industry (1918–1975) exist, as do 10 files of correspondence with other organisations in the labour movement between 1919–1975 (these are mainly comprised of correspondence with the TUC). There are two National Affiliation of Carpet Trade Unions letter books 1917–1920.

Branch material, such as minutes, accounts books, cash books and contribution books, is available for numerous branches including Manchester, Rochdale, Halifax, Durham, Heckmondwike, Workington, etc.

NORTHERN FRIENDS PEACE BOARD

Records, including minutes, reports etc. from 1913 onwards are in Leeds Archives Department. A list is available (NRA 24585).

NORTHERN IRELAND CIVIL SERVICE ALLIANCE

A collection of minute books, correspondence etc. of the Alliance, together with records of the Civil Service Professional Officers' Association and the Ulster Public Officers' Association c 1922–70, are in the Public Record Office of Northern Ireland.

NORTHERN TEXTILE AND ALLIED WORKERS' UNION

The records of the Union were deposited in Lancashire County Record Office in December 1976 (ref DDX 1102) by C. Hopkinson Esq of the Textile Centre, Preston. The Union, established c 1860 as the North Lancashire Card, Blowing Room and Ring Spinners' Association, operated over an area which ultimately extended as far north as Carlisle. In 1961 its engagements were transferred to the Accrington Card Blowing Room and Ring Spinners' Association and the title Northern Textile and Allied Workers' Union adopted. The deposited records include minutes, 1913–65; accounts, 1900–66; contribution records, 1866–1968; registers of members,

1919–56; stoppage books, 1914–61; quarterly reports, 1902–53 and miscellaneous material, 1874–1968.

NORTHUMBERLAND AND DURHAM MINERS' PERMANENT RELIEF FUND

See **National Union of Mineworkers**

NOTTINGHAM AND DISTRICT HOSIERY FINISHERS' ASSOCIATION

The surviving records, 1874–1956, were deposited in Nottingham University Library by the Association's secretary in October 1957. A list has been prepared (NRA 7886). The collection comprises minutes, 1919–56 as well as minutes of the Basford and District Hosiery Trimmers and Finishers Association, 1874–1919, the Basford and District Bleaching, Dyeing, Scouring and Trimming Auxiliary Trades Association, 1913–27 and minutes of the Nottingham and District Hosiery Finishers Joint Council, 1927–46.

NUFFIELD SOCIAL RECONSTRUCTION SURVEY

The papers of the Survey, 1940–44, are in the Library of Nuffield College, Oxford, to whom enquiries should be addressed. *See also* **Nuffield Trust for Special Areas.**

NUFFIELD TRUST FOR SPECIAL AREAS

The papers of the Trust, *c.* 1935–39, are in the Library of Nuffield College, Oxford.

NURSERY SCHOOLS ASSOCIATION OF GREAT BRITAIN AND IRELAND

See **British Association for Early Childhood Education**

OVERSEAS BISHOPRICS FUND

The Fund, which was founded on 1 June 1841, was known prior to 1959 as the Colonial Bishoprics Fund. The first secretary was the Reverend E. Hawkins, Secretary of the Society for the Propagation of the Gospel. The records of the Fund are held at Church House, Dean's Yard, Westminster, London SW1, but are not open to the general public. Application for access must be made in writing to the Honorary Secretary. The records are of value for the changing status of the church, the problems of financing the church and obtaining the necessary letters patent for new sees from the Colonial Office.

PALESTINE POLICE OLD COMRADES' ASSOCIATION

The records have been assembled by the Association's Chairman, E. P. Horne Esq., 33 West Avenue, Hendon, London W4. Founded in 1948, the Association holds meetings and other activities to bring together veterans of the Palestine police force. By 1948, this force included some 5,000 British expatriates. The surviving records are described in detail in P. Jones: *Britain and Palestine: A Guide to Archive Sources for the British Mandate* (OUP 1979).

PALESTINE PROTEST COMMITTEE

Only a very few records appear to have survived. The Central Zionist Archives have a little material, 1930–31 (ref A241). This consists of minutes, correspondence and other papers donated by the Committee's secretary, Alexander Gordon. The Committee was formed in 1930 to protest against the Passfield White Paper and was particularly active in the Whitechapel by-election.

PALESTINE STATEHOOD COMMITTEE
See British League for a Free Palestine

PARLIAMENTARY ASSOCIATION FOR WORLD GOVERNMENT

An extensive collection of records of the association and of allied organisations was deposited in Sussex University Library in April 1977 by Mrs Catharine McAllister. A list is available (NRA 20887). The Parliamentary Group for World Government was founded in 1945 by Henry Osborne MP, to introduce federalist ideas into national politics. To finance secretarial help the Parliamentary Association for World Government was formed in 1950, and further financial aid came through the establishment of the One World Trust. In 1963 the Parliamentary Association dropped the word Parliamentary to become the Association for World Government. To pursue the aims of the Parliamentary Group, and to coordinate international federalist activities the World Association of Parliamentarians for World Government was created in 1952 at the second London Conference on World Government. In 1958 it changed its title to 'World Parliament Association'.

The collection, in 23 boxes, covers mainly the period 1952–64. There are numerous printed papers, accounts, minutes, reports, correspondence etc. of the Parliamentary Association for World Government. Amongst very many other items are annual reports and balance sheets of the World Association of Parliamentarians for World Government/World Parliament Association. There is a file on its inaugural meeting and 2 volumes of minute books (typescript) of general and executive meetings, 1952–59.

There is a file on the report by Clement Davies on the organisation and activities of the Association, 1957. In addition there are 4 files of correspondence and other papers regarding meetings of the World Parliament Association Executive and Council 1958, 1959 and 1964. There is also a file containing a report on the World Government Organisation for 1960.

Correspondence includes a file of general correspondence (1957–59) of the Director of PAWG about the executive's activities, and 3 files on miscellaneous subjects belonging to the Secretary-General WAPWG/WPA (1957–61). The papers are divided under subject matter such as members and membership, for which there is a Membership Book of the PAWG and 10 files of correspondence from the Secretary-General of WAPWG/WPA with members relating to membership 1953–62. There are 4 files relating to the organisation and finance of the PAWG, mainly consisting of correspondence of the Director and Assistant Director and there are seven files of correspondence belonging to the Secretary-General of WAPWG.

There are one or more files on each of the 12 conferences 1951–1963 originating in the first London Parliamentary Conference on World Government 1951.

PEN AND POCKET BLADE FORGERS' AND SMITHERS' PROTECTION SOCIETY

The papers are in Sheffield City Library. The collection includes minute books, accounts, registers of members, correspondence etc. covering the period 1859–1954.

PENWORKERS' FEDERATION

The surviving records of this small trade union, which transferred its engagements to the General and Municipal Workers Union in 1974, have been deposited in the Modern Records Centre, University of Warwick (ref MSS 42). The collection includes minutes, from foundation in 1919 to 1972, correspondence, 1968–73, annual reports, 1919–73, minutes of the Works Committee, M. Myers and Son Ltd, 1963–74 with correspondence, 1965–74.

PHARMACEUTICAL SOCIETY OF GREAT BRITAIN

The society has retained its records. These records, together with other material collected by the society, have recently been listed (NRA 26284).

PLAID CYMRU

In addition to the material cited in *Sources* Vol. 1, pp 212–13, there have been important additions to the Plaid Cymru material deposited in the National Library of Wales. These include records of the Bangor office, further records of the Executive Committee, 1932–50, the records of the Cardiff office, files on the 1943 University of Wales by-election, and much material on the various campaigns the party has waged. There are minute books for local areas and committees in Anglesey (1931), Caernarfon (1932–6), West Denbigh (1932–8), Merioneth (1934–43), East Glamorgan (1942, 1948–53) and Montgomery (1951–7).

PLUMBERS' TRADE UNION/UNITED OPERATIVE PLUMBERS ASSOCIATION

Since the entry in *Sources* Vol. 1, p 88 some records of the union have been deposited in the Modern Records Centre, University of Warwick (ref MSS 134). The collection includes minute books (including some National Executive Committee minutes), accounts and membership records, *c.* 1860–1900, for numerous local societies. There are subject files concerning, for example, the National Plumbers' Society, the National Union of Operative Heating and Domestic Engineers and General Metal Workers, and files concerning the Chemical Contractors Agreement, 1941–2. There are also some printed items issued by the union. In addition the Centre has some records of the East London Society of Operative Plumbers: minute books, 1874–89; balance sheets, 1881–8; cashbook, 1872–83; rulebook. *c.* 1880; together with registration books, 1865–1922, for the Scottish Plumbers.

POLITICAL AND ECONOMIC PLANNING

Since the entry in *Sources* Vol. 1, p 213, the extensive surviving records have been placed in BLPES.

POLITICAL STUDIES ASSOCIATION

Recent papers have been deposited in BLPES. They include six boxes of conference papers and correspondence, 1969–81. Special conditions of access exist.

POSTAL, TELEGRAPH AND TELEPHONE INTERNATIONAL

The archives, 1922–68, are reported to be in the International Institute of Social History in Amsterdam.

POST OFFICE ENGINEERING UNION

Since the entry in *Sources* Vol. 1, p 214, an extensive deposit of the Union's archives has been made in the Modern Records Centre, University of Warwick. The collection includes minutes of Council meetings of the Engineering and Stores Association, 1910–15; NEC minutes, 1905–15; branch minute books from Aylesbury, 1915–31, and Wimbledon 1915–23; Standard Wages and Reclassification Committee minutes and circulars, 1917–19; *Journal*, 1911–16. Some membership registers of the E & SA are also held. Reports of the Amalgamated Society of Telephone Employees are held, 1910–15, with a few items on transfer questions, 1911–15. Minutes of the National Joint Committee of Postal and Telegraph Associations are held for the years 1913–20.

From the POEU there are NEC minutes from 1921–29; Standing Joint Committee minutes, 1930–54; Experimental Changes of Practice minutes, 1928–39; Annual Leave Special Committee minutes, 1924–31; London Engineering District Whitley Council (POEU) minute books, 1920–32.

In addition, there are NEC circulars, correspondence relating to wage claims and extensive Whitley Council records. Also of relevance are the records accumulated by R. Leonard Fagg, a member of the POEU NEC from 1929–36. They are also at the Modern Records Centre.

POST OFFICE MANAGEMENT STAFFS' ASSOCIATION (POMSA)

Some records of the Association, since 1981 the Communication Managers Association, have been placed in the Modern Records Centre, University of Warwick. Among the older records are minutes of the Postal Inspectors' Association, 1895–1924.

POWER LOOM CARPET WEAVERS AND TEXTILE WORKERS ASSOCIATION

The records of the union were deposited in Hereford and Worcester Record Office,

Worcester, in 1978, by the General Secretary (ref 8211). A list has been prepared (NRA 21957). A condition of the deposit is that no document may be consulted without prior reference to the Association.

The collection consists of about 270 minute books, account books, letters, programmes, rule books, wage lists, printed matter and other papers. It includes 25 volumes of minutes of Association and Committee meetings (1866–1914), 30 various contributions ledgers (1886–1936), cashbooks (1873–1910), and 6 general account books (1867–1929). There are volumes of minutes belonging to the Kidderminster Trades Council and local Labour Party (1930–47) and Trades Council alone (1948–66), Bewdley local Labour Party (1953–55), and the National Affiliation of Carpet Trade Unions. There are 4 files of correspondence (1939–43) belonging to the latter body, and 8 files of correspondence belonging to the Carpet Weavers and Textile Workers Association (1936–69). A number of rule books, programmes of events and similar miscellanea also exists.

PRESERVATION OF THE RIGHTS OF PRISONERS (PROP)
Certain archives of the 'prisoners' trade union' are now being microfilmed by Harvester Press.

PRESSED GLASSMAKERS' SOCIETY OF GREAT BRITAIN
The surviving records, 1891–1966, have been placed in Tyne and Wear Record Office.

PRIMROSE LEAGUE
In addition to the material cited in *Sources* Vol. 1, p 215, a further collection of papers, belonging to Primrose Dame Mrs Tyson Amherst, may be found at BLPES (ref Coll Misc 569). The papers are in the form of correspondence, printed circulars, accounts and membership lists, and concern the Ladies Grand Council of the League, 1885–87.

PROGRESSIVE LEAGUE
In addition to the papers cited in *Sources*, Vol. 1, p 216, Washington University Library, St. Louis, Missouri, has purchased a small collection of Progressive League material, 1935–63, including correspondence between Ashton Burrall and Alec Craig and various British authors and political figures. The correspondence concerns readings and lectures for the League, Poetry Circle readings, and conferences. Amongst the correspondents are W. H. Auden, Cecil Day Lewis, Ernest Gombrich, and Sir Julian Huxley.

PROTESTANT REFORMATION SOCIETY
The surviving records of the Society are retained by the General Secretary, 1 Lawn Mansions, 7f High Street, Barnet, Hertfordshire. The Society was founded in 1827 as the British Society for Promoting the Principles of the Reformed Religion. The records would appear to consist only of minute books (1827–1926, 1956-date) and a very incomplete series of printed annual reports.

PUBLIC MORALITY COUNCIL

The records of the Council, 1899–1965, have been deposited in the Greater London Record Office. Scarcely any survive for the earliest period, the most useful series being annual reports, 1901–1913, and 1932–1953, with gaps. Council and various special committee minutes cover *c.* 1940–1965; some subject files are not yet fully listed.

The Council (originally known as the London Council for the Promotion of Public Morality) was founded in 1899 to combat vice and indecency in London, and to stimulate their repression by the legal means which were already available, but neglected. Its members included representatives of the Church of England, of the Roman Catholic and Non-conformist Churches, as well as of the Jewish faith, with leaders in education, doctors, and others concerned with these social problems. It continued until 1969, concentrating later on opposition to sex and pornography in general, as well as in the theatre, cinema, radio and television.

RAILWAY TELEGRAPH CLERKS' ASSOCIATION

See **Transport Salaried Staffs' Association**

RAINBOW CIRCLE

The records of this influential Liberal Party discussion group were deposited in BLPES in May 1978 (ref Coll Misc 575). The collection includes minute books (4 volumes, 1894–1924), membership lists, correspondence, and papers relating to its dissolution, 1929–66. The Circle was founded by William Clarke, J. A. Hobson, the Revd. Percy Dearmer, J. R. MacDonald, Herbert Burrows, etc.

RELEASE

The records of the Release Collective have been placed in the Modern Records Centre, University of Warwick. The Collective was founded in 1967 to provide legal advice to young persons who claimed harassment by the police. It has subsequently developed as a national alternative legal and welfare organisation, with a deep involvement in drug counselling. The initial deposit at the Modern Records Centre consisted of 11 boxes of records and documentation, including not only correspondence and case papers but also publications and material from a range of other alternative organisations. In a second deposit, a further group of administrative records, 1968–76, was placed in the Centre. This deposit included social psychiatric day books, 1973–76. Researchers should note that access to unpublished material is severely limited.

REVOLUTIONARY COMMUNIST PARTY

See **International Marxist Group**

ROAD HAULAGE ASSOCIATION

Since the entry in *Sources*, Vol. 1, p 233, the Association has placed its records in the Modern Records Centre, University of Warwick. The deposit includes selected non-current post-war files on such topics as nationalisation and denationalisation, dock work regulations, contracts of employment etc. Prior written permission is necessary to consult certain of this material.

ROSSENDALE UNION OF BOOT AND SHOE OPERATIVES

The surviving records of the Union were deposited in Lancashire Record Office (ref DDX 1160) by the Secretary, T. Whittaker Esq., in September 1977. A list has been prepared (NRA 21148). Records less than 30 years old, and company files of all dates, cannot be seen without the permission of the donor.

The collection includes 53 volumes of General Meeting and Committee minutes for the years 1895–1968. A volume of the Unity Committee Minutes, 1930–32 is included in the records, as are 8 volumes of Conciliation Board Minutes (1927–1962). The minutes and expenses of various departments and sub-committees from, in some cases, 1925 to 1969 exist. The Treasurers' cash books for 1895–1948 survive in 12 volumes, as do 17 volumes of the Secretaries' cash books (1895–1969). There are 23 bound volumes of contribution ledgers (1895–1932) and a further 43 volumes of unbound contribution ledgers (1932–1969). Two strike pay books (1910–1930) and 2 distress pay books (1920–22) are held.

Twenty-one files of shoemaking price lists and agreements ranging from 1899 to 1956 are included in the collection. There are copies of the magazine *Unity* from 1926 to 1970. Twenty-five files of correspondence with various companies between 1910 and 1973 belong to the collection, but cannot be seen without the depositor's permission.

Note Lancashire Record Office also possesses the records of the Lancashire Footwear Manufacturers' Association (ref DDX 1187) A list is available (NRA 21759).

ROYAL AERO CLUB

The records of the Club have been deposited in the Royal Air Force Museum, Hendon (refs AC 75/8, 75/21, 75/26).

ROYAL CENTRAL ASIAN SOCIETY

The archives housed by the Society at 12 Orange Street, Haymarket, London WC2, include texts of unpublished lectures, some of which would have political interest. Examples are Jon Kimche's lecture *The Arab-Israeli Conflict* (8 April 1947) òr *The future of British interests in China*, by Trevor Powell (15 October 1947). Application to see any item must be made in writing to the Secretary.

ROYAL ECONOMIC SOCIETY

The records of the Society were placed in December 1979 on indefinite loan in the BLPES (Acc No M1445), through the good offices of Professor Aubrey Silberston. The organisation was founded in 1890 as the British Economic Society and incorporated as the Royal Economic Society in 1902. The records (27 vols, 1890–1970) comprise minute books (7 vols, 1890–1970), cash books (7 vols, 1890–1961), ledgers (8 vols, 1890–1956), registers of members (4 vols, 1891, 1901–10, 1921–30, 1949–66), and a journal of income and expenditure (1937–74).

ROYAL SCOTTISH SOCIETY FOR THE PREVENTION OF CRUELTY TO CHILDREN

The surviving records covering the period 1884–1974 are in the Scottish Record Office.

ROYAL SOCIETY FOR THE PREVENTION OF ACCIDENTS

The records have been deposited in Liverpool University Archives (ref D 226). A list is available (NRA 25023). The Royal Society was formed in May 1940, but its antecedents included the London Safety First Council (1917) and the British Safety First Association (1918). These amalgamated in 1924 to form the National Safety First Association.

ROYAL STATISTICAL SOCIETY

The records have been retained by the Society. Enquiries concerning access should be addressed to the Secretary at 21 Bentinck Street, London W1. An unpublished list is available (NRA 14718). The Society's own records include minutes, registers of donations, ledger accounts and loan registers. In addition the archives also include a number of miscellaneous manuscripts of William Stanley Jevons (1835–1882) in a cardboard box and 3 folders. These include various charts, statistics and a paper given to the British Association 'On the Study of Periodic Commercial Fluctuations'.

Miscellaneous manuscripts belonging to William Newmarch (1820–1882) also exist, covering the years 1859–1882. These include letters and memoranda *re* meetings of the British Association and the Social Science Association, and lecture notes for lectures to the Political Economy Club.

ROYAL TOWN PLANNING INSTITUTE
See **Environment and Planning**

SAVE EUROPE NOW

Since the entry in *Sources*, Vol. 1, p 232, a collection of papers relating to the organisation has come to light in the Gollancz papers at the Modern Records Centre, University of Warwick (ref MSS 157/3/SEN).

The 4 files include a 1945 paper regarding the invitation and founding meeting, 8 October 1945 and administrative papers, circular letters of invitation, notes on the meeting and extracts from speeches, a typescript text of the Prime Minister's statement on the German situation, correspondence *re* the role of the USSR in Germany, and replies from MPs, Anglican Bishops, the London Union and the Fellowship of Reconciliation. A file of correspondence with Attlee on the proposed surrender of voluntary rations and other contributions to relieve European distress, together with critical replies from Attlee and the Ministry of Food. There are two files (157/3/SEN/3 and 4) of miscellaneous documents pertaining to a variety of aspects of the problem of distress in Europe and its relief.

SAW-MAKERS' PROTECTION SOCIETY

A number of the Society's minute books have been deposited at Sheffield Central Library by the Society. The collection consists of 8 Minute Books covering the years 1860 to 1975. Current books, and copies of agreed prices for 1923, 1926, 1930 and the 1940s onward are retained by the Secretary.

SCOTTISH AERONAUTICAL SOCIETY

The minutes for 1907–15 have been purchased by Strathclyde Regional Archives. *See* NRA 25613.

SCOTTISH AGRICULTURAL ORGANISATION SOCIETY

The society has retained its records, which have been listed. *See* NRA 24340.

SCOTTISH ALLIANCE OF EMPLOYERS IN THE PRINTING AND KINDRED TRADES

See **Society of Master Printers of Scotland**

SCOTTISH ASSOCIATION FOR MENTAL HEALTH

The records, covering the period 1921–76, were deposited in 1978 in the National Library of Scotland (ref Acc 7170). The records consist of organisational correspondence and other papers of the Association and predecessor bodies. The Association was established at a meeting in Glasgow in 1923, following on the experiences of several Special School teachers on a local Care Committee formed in Paisley *c.* 1920, and the title of the organisation was changed at the first AGM to 'The Scottish Association of Mental Welfare', representing an extension of the Association's aims from the care of mentally handicapped children to include more general mental health work.

In 1938 the SAMW amalgamated with the Scottish Child Guidance Council (established 1934) under the title 'Scottish Association for Mental Hygiene', renamed in 1949 the Scottish Association for Mental Health. Following a brief period in abeyance, the Association was re-organised on its present basis in 1976–7.

The papers have been arranged as follows: boxes 1–3, minutes and related papers; boxes 4–9, papers relating to affiliated local voluntary associations; boxes 10–11, correspondence with other voluntary associations; boxes 12–14, conference organisation; box 15, miscellaneous files; boxes 16–24, general office files; boxes 25–26, financial records; Vol. 1, photographs; Vols. 2–37, account books.

SCOTTISH CONVENTION

The National Library of Scotland has the minute books 1942–49, together with some papers relating to the Scottish Covenant Association. There is also relevant material in the records of the Scottish National Party also deposited in the National Library of Scotland.

SCOTTISH COUNCIL FOR AFRICAN QUESTIONS

The surviving records, 1952–76, have been placed in Edinburgh University Library.

SCOTTISH COUNCIL OF TENANTS' ASSOCIATIONS

Minutes of the Association, 1948–59, together with minutes of the Glasgow Council of Tenants' Associations, 1949–54 are in Glasgow University Library.

SCOTTISH ENGINEERING EMPLOYERS' ASSOCIATION

An extensive archive has been retained by the Association at its Glasgow offices. A list is available (NRA 19998). Apart from records of the Association itself, including minutes, letterbooks and accounting records, there are minutes of numerous other employers' associations in Scotland (e.g. East of Scotland, Dundee and District, Kilmarnock District). There are also minutes of such bodies as the West of Scotland Iron and Steel Founders' Association (1910–20), the Scottish Employers' Federation of Iron and Steel Founders (1908–20), the Scottish Sheet Metal Workers Employers' Association (1907–21) and the Scottish Coppersmiths Employers' Association (1911–19).

SCOTTISH IRON AND COAL MASTERS' ASSOCIATION

The records are in Glasgow University Library (ref UGD/49). A list is available (NRA 21848). The collection includes three minute books of the Scottish Manufacturing Iron Trade Conciliation and Arbitration Board, 1899–1919; and a box of minutes, 1898–1912; 10 letter books of the Board, 1916–52; 7 Agreement Books, 1906–46; 20 letter books of the Scottish Iron and Coal Masters' Association, 1910–57; and 3 letter books of the Scottish Steel Founders Wages Association. There are 21 boxes of miscellaneous committee minutes, reports and circulars, 1898–1956, including papers on the returns of rates and conditions. Some 47 boxes exist containing the records of the Coal Masters. These include files on railway rates, arbitration, legal actions and the Nationalisation Act, and cover the years 1896–1947.

SCOTTISH LACE AND WINDOW FURNISHERS' ASSOCIATION

The records have been deposited in Glasgow University Library. A list has been prepared (NRA 21414). The collection comprises two minute books of British Lace Furnishings Ltd 1942–74; 15 minute books of the Scottish Lace Manufacturers' Association (AGMs, members and committee meetings, 1931–77); 3 minute books of the Scottish Lace Furnishing Manufacturers (formerly The Lace Furnishing Manufacturers' Association, Scotland and Nottingham) 1946–49, 1951–77. There is also a volume of press cuttings, as well as minutes of Joint Board Meetings between Manufacturers' Associations and the Scottish Lace and Textile Workers' Union 1946–77, and of the Federation of British Lace Curtain and Curtain Net Manufacturers, 1938–39.

SCOTTISH LANDOWNERS' FEDERATION

The records were deposited in the Scottish Record Office in 1976. They have been listed and consist of 562 subject files, mainly dealing with legislation relating to landownership. The covering dates are 1906–61. All items are closed for 25 years from the date of the last paper.

SCOTTISH LICENSED TRADE ASSOCIATION

The records of the society (from its foundation in 1880) have been retained in its offices. A list is available (NRA 23660). The association maintained an active parliamentary lobby which is reflected in the 25 volumes of surviving minutes. The records of the South East of Scotland Licensed Trade Association (1874–1942) have survived in the Edinburgh office (*see* NRA 24929).

SCOTTISH LICENSED TRADE VETO DEFENCE FUND

A collection of papers has been deposited at the Mitchell Library, Glasgow. The collection of 12 boxes contains a large number of files on a wide range of topics relating to the licensing trade and the affairs of the Fund. The first two boxes contain 55 files on subjects such as the 'Monopolies Commission', 'Modernisation League of Greenock', 'Polls 1965, Share Copies, Circulars etc' and 'Miscellaneous reports, 1920–late 1960s'. Box 3 contains 29 files on American Prohibition, the 'New Zealand Campaign' and 'Scottish Temperance Associations', while Box 4 has 37 files on polls in various wards of Scotland e.g. 'Craigton Ward Glasgow – Local Veto Poll 1963', 'Greenock Poll File 1970' covering the years 1952–70. Boxes 5 and 6 contain 33 files mainly of news cuttings, pamphlets and handbills (1945–1960s) on the question of the veto together with miscellaneous material regarding polling organisation (1946–64). Box 7 contains various reports, memoranda and printed material on a number of topics (1913–67) together with correspondence and papers regarding polls in the Craigton Ward, Glasgow (1956). Box 8 holds miscellaneous posters, handbills and press cuttings and Box 9 other printed material including Parliamentary Papers on Licensing questions, Parliamentary election returns, Hansards, details of polls on the veto and lists of MPs active over the licensing question. Box 11 holds the Fund's Annual Reports 1973–77 and various articles and reports on licensing and Box 12 contains miscellaneous material.

SCOTTISH MOTOR TRADE ASSOCIATION

The association, which was formed in 1903, has retained its records. These include minute books since 1919. The archive has been listed (NRA 24920).

SCOTTISH SCHOOLMASTERS' ASSOCIATION

A collection of papers can be found amongst the James Fowler deposit in Aberdeen University Library (ref MS 2700). The collection comprises minutes, correspondence and other papers concerning the activities of the Scottish Schoolmasters' Association and other teachers' professional organisations, 1935–1963; an incomplete run of *The Scottish Schoolmaster*, 1935–1965; and pamphlets and periodicals issued by the association and kindred organisations, 1935–1959.

SCOTTISH TEMPERANCE ALLIANCE

See **Temperance**

SECONDARY HEADS' ASSOCIATION

See separate entries for **Head Masters' Association and Association of Head Mistresses**

SECULAR EDUCATION LEAGUE

Some surviving records of the League can be found in the archives of the Ethical Union (see *Sources*, Vol. 1, p 27). The material was used by Susan Budd in *Varieties of Unbelief.*

SERBIAN SOCIETY OF GREAT BRITAIN

Records of this society, as well as records of the Serbian Relief Fund, can be found in the Library of the School of Slavonic and East European Studies, University of London.

SHELTER

See **National Campaign for the Homeless**

SHIP AND BOAT BUILDERS' NATIONAL FEDERATION

The non-current records of the Federation have been deposited in the Modern Records Centre, University of Warwick (ref MSS 53). The Federation, which was founded in 1913 as the Boat and Yacht Builders' and Proprietors' and Allied Trades Protection Association, acts on behalf of firms engaged in the manufacture of small boats. The collection includes Executive Committee minutes, 1913–52, finance committee minutes, 1921–34, minutes relating to Admiralty tenders, 1937–41 and an early cash book and membership register.

SHIPBUILDERS' AND REPAIRERS' NATIONAL ASSOCIATION

The records were presented to the National Maritime Museum in 1977 on the dissolution of the Association. The collection is complete, except for a small number of files retained by the SRNA Dissolution Committee, a few passed on to the new state holding company, British Shipbuilders Ltd, and a similar number of the newly-formed Shipbuilders' and Shiprepairers' National Association, the group established by the remaining private firms in the industry. The records consist of the papers of the Shipbuilding Employers' Federation, 1889–1971 (*q.v.*) the Dry Dock Owners' and Repairers' Central Council, 1910–73; the Shipbuilding Conference, 1928–79; and the National Association of Marine Enginebuilders, 1939–77.

The records of the Dry Dock Owners' and Repairers' Central Council consist of minutes 1910–59; and circulars, 1910–56. A great number of files relate to different aspects of dry docking, and there is a series on the wartime Emergency Repairs Agreement, 1940–46.

The Shipbuilding Conference records include private minute books, 1928–45; circulars, 1928–69; and files on almost every aspect of the trading and commercial activities of the shipbuilding industry. There are also files on shipbuilding in other countries and a body of records relating to the Shipbuilding Corporation Ltd, a company established in the early years of the war to build ships on government account.

The records of the National Association of Marine Enginebuilders consist of minute books, 1939–44, with minutes of a later date concerned with material of a technical nature. There are also files on foreign competition, 1945–75; contract conditions, 1969–72; and submissions to the Geddes Shipbuilding Enquiry Committee, 1966.

In addition to these records, the following regional bodies have deposited their papers:

Clyde Shipbuilders' Association

The records have been deposited in Glasgow City Archives. The extensive collection includes minute books, 1914–68, 46 vols.; cash books and ledgers, 1897–1963; membership statistics, yard conference notes, wage rates for individual yards, Demarcation Committee minutes, correspondence, the problems of dilution, etc. There is also extensive material on wage rates, old company agreements, individual cases, etc. A list is available (NRA 18718).

Liverpool Shipowners' Association

Records, 1895–1960, are in Merseyside County Archives (NRA 25222). Also deposited are records of the Liverpool Steamship Owners' Association (NRA 26225).

Mersey Ship Repairers' Association

Minutes, 1911–79, are in the City Library, Liverpool Record Office.

North of England Shipowners' Association

The records, including minute books, 1871–1965; annual reports, 1893–1944; and press cuttings, 1882–91, have been deposited with Tyne and Wear County Archives. A list is available (NRA 22517).

North East Coast Shiprepairers' Association

The records, 1889–1977, have been deposited with Tyne and Wear County Archives. A list is available (NRA 21708).

South Coast Engineering and Shipbuilding Employers' Association

The records, 1902–78, have been deposited in Southampton City Record Office.

Tyne Shipbuilders' Association

The records, 1885–1965, including minute books, 1891–1965, and letter books, 1930–37, have been deposited with Tyne and Wear County Archives. A list is available (NRA 21710).

Wear Shipbuilders' Association

The records, 1853–1970, including minute books, 1853–1970, have been deposited with Tyne and Wear County Archives. A list is available (NRA 22558).

SHIPBUILDING EMPLOYERS' FEDERATION

The records were deposited in the National Maritime Museum in 1977 with those of the Shipbuilders' and Repairers' National Association. They include the minute book of the Executive Committee of the Federation of Shipbuilders and Engineers, 1889 to 1898; the SEF minute books, 1899 to 1965; a complete run of circulars, 1899 to 1965 and, slightly less complete, 1966 to 1967, the means by which the central body communicated to the local membership. The bulk of the collection, however, is to be found in the very large number of the SEF files which have survived. These start in the 1930s, although many contain papers gathered before this date. The files touch on every aspect of labour relations, including wages, bonus payments, piecework rates, nightshift working, allowances, demarcation, apprenticeship, training and safety. In the files are correspondence, memoranda, statistical returns, minutes of meetings and agreements. The SEF also prepared labour statistics on a weekly and monthly basis, and a quarterly return submitted to the Ministry of Labour on numbers employed. These have been retained, 1936 to 1960; and there are strike returns, 1959 to 1967, 1972 to 1976, and accident statistics, 1963 to 1971.

SIGN AND DISPLAY TRADES UNION

The records of the Union, which merged with NATSOPA in 1972 (see *Sources*, Vol. 1, p 189), have now been deposited in the Modern Records Centre, University of Warwick (ref MSS 106). The collection includes NEC minutes, 1917–72; miscellaneous financial statements, 1938–50, 1963–67; annual reports, 1929–55; *Newsletters*, 1939–72; delegate conference reports, 1956–72; and *Circulars*, 1970–72. The deposited subject files deal mostly with relations with particular employers, or employer associations, 1930s–1960s. Also included in the deposit are files of notes for speeches by A. C. Torode, former General Secretary of the Union.

SILK ASSOCIATION OF GREAT BRITAIN AND IRELAND

The records of the Association were deposited in Manchester Central Library (ref M197) in August 1974 by Peter Gaddum Esq of H. J. Gaddum & Co. Ltd., Macclesfield. A handlist has been prepared (NRA 18871). The Association grew out of a conference to promote the Silk Industries of the United Kingdom held at the Royal Jubilee Exhibition in Manchester in October 1887. In 1915 it became an Incorporated Association.

The collection comprises minutes (1897–1915, 4 vols), circulars, newspaper cuttings, some annual reports and correspondence. There are also four volumes of papers relating to the Board of Trade enquiry into the silk industry, September–November 1923, which consist of the papers of J. J. Farrell, President of the Silk Association, used in that enquiry and its Report. There are numerous other reports on various aspects of the industry and the activities of the Association.

SIMON COMMUNITY

Some material relating to the Simon Community has been deposited in the Modern Records Centre, University of Warwick (ref MSS 68) by Martin Wright, a former member of the National Executive and chairman of the Cambridge Cyrenians Ltd. The Simon movement itself was founded in 1963 to care for the rootless and socially isolated homeless. The material at the Modern Records Centre consists of Wright's correspondence with and concerning the Simon national organisation and with other local Cyrenian groups, 1964–74. The files include minutes, financial reports, etc. as well as Simon publications, including incomplete runs of *Simon Star*, 1964–

74 and *Social Action*, 1969–72. In a second deposit, the Modern Records Centre received additional minutes, reports, draft publicity, and correspondence, 1972–74. In addition, the correspondence, minutes, reports and other papers of the Cambridge Cyrenians, 1965–74, have been transferred to Cambridgeshire County Record Office.

SINN FEIN STANDING COMMITTEE

The minutes for the period 1919–22 are in the Public Record Office in Dublin.

SIX POINT GROUP

The surviving records (*c.* 1921–81), including minutes, conference papers, correspondence, newsletters etc. are in the Fawcett Library, City of London Polytechnic.

SOCIALIST COMMENTARY

Some records have been deposited with the Socialist Vanguard Group collection in the Modern Records Centre, University of Warwick (ref MSS 173). The collection includes minutes of business meetings, 1954–59, some workbooks of Dr. Rita Hinden as editor, some *Socialist Commentary* files concerning contacts with MPs, prominent authors, policy decisions etc. There are runs of the journal *Socialist Vanguard, Contact, Commentary* and *Socialist Commentary. See also* **Socialist Vanguard Group** and **Socialist Union.**

SOCIALIST EDUCATIONAL ASSOCIATION

See **National Association of Labour Teachers**

SOCIALIST REVIEW GROUP

Relevant material can be found in the Ken Tarbuck papers deposited in the Modern Records Centre, University of Warwick (ref MSS 75). A list is available (NRA 21336). The material comprises a MS National Committee minute book, 1950–53, a Birmingham branch minute book, 1950–53, some correspondence and an incomplete run of *Socialist Review*, 1950–61.

SOCIALIST UNION

Some records of this group, which replaced the Socialist Vanguard Group (SVG) in 1950 can be found in the Modern Records Centre, University of Warwick, among the SVG archive (ref MSS 173). The material comprises minutes and Management Committee minutes, 1951–9; AGM minutes, 1952–9; membership files; finance files, 1953–9; principles, rules and information sheets; and material *re* Democracy Study Group, schools and meetings.

SOCIALIST VANGUARD GROUP

Some records of this group were deposited in the Modern Records Centre, University of Warwick (ref MSS 173) by Dr Rene Saran, the daughter of Mary Saran, editor/joint editor of *Socialist Commentary*, 1941—55. A list is available (NRA 25816). The Group (SVG) was established in 1929 as the British Section of the Militant Socialist International (Internationalen Socialisten Kampf-Bundes, ISK) in Germany. The ISK had evolved in 1926 from the Internationaler Jugendbund, a small educational group of members of the main German Left parties led by the philosopher Leonard Nelson. The English Group was never large, but had an influence disproportionate to its size. In 1950 the SVG was replaced by the Socialist Union (*q.v.*) its journal, *Socialist Commentary* (*q.v.*) continued and provided a focus after the Socialist Union was formally dissolved.

The collection comprises applications for membership (*restricted*), Executive Committee minutes, 1943—8, Executive Committee correspondence, 1946—8, file of half-yearly reports, etc., from 1929 (*restricted*); administrative documents; a file *re* finances; subject files, including *re* Russia, aspects of army life, tea plantations etc; duplicated national letters, 1941—2, For the London branch there is a file of minutes, reports and correspondence, 1943—9 (*restricted*). There is also some material on the ISK. The main ISK archive is believed to be in Frankfurt. See Mary Saran's autobiography *Never give up* (London 1976) and Werner Link, *Die Geschichte des Internationalen Jugend-Bundes und des Internationalen Socialistischen Kampf-bundes* (Meisenheim, 1964).

SOCIALIST YOUTH INTERNATIONAL

Some surviving records, covering the period 1923—46, are in the International Institute of Social History, Amsterdam.

SOCIETY FOR CHECKING THE ABUSES OF PUBLIC ADVERTISING

The surviving records of the Society have been deposited in the Greater London Record Office. The Society was originally founded in 1893 by Richardson Evans to focus public opinion on the disfigurement caused by outdoor advertising. It later campaigned against the siteing of petrol filling stations and the litter problem. It lobbied busily concerning the Advertisement Regulation Acts of 1907, 1925 and 1948. It was eventually wound up in 1952—53. The records deposited include Executive Committee minute books, 1911—28, an agenda book 1932—51, an attendance book, 1932—51, a ledger 1931—50 and two account books, 1930—35, 1936—46.

See also Environment and Planning

SOCIETY FOR THE RELIEF OF DISTRESS

The records of the Society, 1860—1963, have been deposited in the Greater London Record Office. They include minutes, records of almoners, accounts and correspondence. The Society was founded in 1860 for the relief of distress in London and its suburbs. The relief was administered by accredited visitors later known as almoners. Records less than ten years old are not available for public inspection.

SOCIETY FOR THE SUPPRESSION OF THE OPIUM TRADE
See **Anti-Opium Society**

SOCIETY OF AUTHORS

The records of the Incorporated Society of Authors, Playwrights and Composers have been placed in the British Library (ref Add MSS 56575–57264). This very extensive archive of 690 volumes covers the period 1879–1967. It was purchased on 15 March 1969 and incorporated in June 1971. The collection is arranged as follows: A – Members' Files (Add MSS 56575–56862); B – Subject Files (Add MSS 56863–56898); C – Legal Files (Add MSS 56899–57001); D – General Correspondence (Add MSS 57002–57032); E – Miscellaneous (Add MSS 57033–57050); F – Letterbooks (Add MSS 57051–57264).

SOCIETY OF BRITISH GAS INDUSTRIES

The surviving records up to 1960 of this trade association have been placed in the Modern Records Centre, University of Warwick (ref MSS 231). The records include main minutes (from 1906), records of General Meetings and sections, and some financial records. Founded in 1905, the society was based in Leamington. A list is available (NRA 24977).

SOCIETY OF CERTIFIED AND ASSOCIATED LIBERAL AGENTS

In addition to the records in the Sheepscar Library, Leeds (*Sources*, Vol. 1, p 244), the records of the North West District are in Manchester Central Library. They include Executive Council minute books, 1903–51. A list is available (NRA 24631).

SOCIETY OF CIVIL AND PUBLIC SERVANTS

An extensive collection of records has been deposited in the Modern Records Centre, University of Warwick (ref MSS 232). A list is available (NRA 24976). The records include minutes, publications and files of several predecessor unions, the earliest dating to the 1890s.

SOCIETY OF LONDON BOOKBINDERS

The records of this Society were purchased by the British Library in April 1966 and incorporated in October 1972 (ref Add MSS 57562–57635). The papers were largely collected by John Jaffray and consist of 74 volumes, mainly minute books, for the period 1796–1919. For the history of the Society, see E. Howe and J. Child, *The Society of London Bookbinders, 1780–1951* (1952).

SOCIETY OF MASTER PRINTERS OF SCOTLAND

The records of the Society (*c*. 1920–70) are in the National Library of Scotland.

SOCIETY OF MEDICAL OFFICERS OF HEALTH

The records of this organisation, including correspondence and minute books, 1902–74, have been deposited in the Contemporary Medical Archives Centre at the Wellcome Institute. The Wellcome Institute also has the records of the Association of Medical Officers of Health for England and Wales. A list is available (NRA 25580).

SOCIETY OF POST OFFICE EXECUTIVES

A collection of papers has been deposited with the Modern Records Centre, University of Warwick, by Arthur Willitt, ex-President of the Society. The collection includes papers of the Society's predecessors, the Post Office Engineering Inspectors (1910–42), the Post Office Engineering Inspectorate (1942–47), the Society of Telecommunication Engineers (1947–1968) and the Association of Post Office Executives (1968–1972). The collection includes circular letters from these various bodies to Council (1937–75); Annual Conference agenda and minutes 1921–74, with some verbatim conference and EC reports; verbatim reports of joint meetings of SPOEI and the Society of Post Office Engineering Chief Inspectors 1941–42; circular letters from the SPOEI (1937–46) and STE (1947–52) to branch secretaries. There are PO Engineering Departmental Whitley Council circular letters to Staff Side and some subject files, particularly on senior staff salary negotiations (1972–75) and finance (1963–65) are held. A large number of papers, pertaining to the Wales and Border Counties Engineering Whitley Committee, exist in the form of SPOEI/STE minutes of meetings, with correspondence and reports 1939–70. There are also Engineering Labour Force Sub-Committee minutes and related papers, 1959–63, subject files on promotion, accommodation, staff transfers, substitution and reorganisation of the Chester telephone area (1950s–60s). The North Wales branch records (1939–45) include minutes, attendance books and branch correspondence. The Willitt deposit is complemented by a collection of SPOE papers including verbatim reports of Executive Committee meetings 1930–47, Executive Committee minutes 1920–36, conference reports 1920–36 and records of the SPOEI amalgamation 1940–42. SPOE publications held include the *Post Office Engineering Inspector* (1914–29) and the *Review* (1938–73). There are volumes of the *Post Office Electrical Engineers' Journal* (1927–75). Papers, (including conference papers 1965–72 and reports on activities 1963–74) are held pertaining to the Postal, Telegraph and Telephone International (*q.v.*).

SOCIETY OF THE SACRED MISSION

The records, covering the period from 1890 to the present, have been retained at Willen Priory, Milton Keynes. A list is available (NRA 26270).

SOUND CURRENCY ASSOCIATION

Thirty volumes of press cuttings (1911–38) of David Mason (1865–1945), the founder and Chairman of the Association are in the House of Lords Record Office.

SPARTACUS LEAGUE

See International Marxist Group.

STATE CHILDREN'S AID ASSOCIATION

Minutes of the Executive Committee, 1897–1900, together with correspondence and minutes of the British Hospitals Contributory Scheme Association, are in BLPES.

STUDENT CHRISTIAN ASSOCIATION

Since the entry in *Sources*, Vol. 1, p 290, the papers have reportedly been moved from the Bodleian Library to Selly Oak College, Birmingham.

SUGAR ASSOCIATION OF LIVERPOOL

The records, from the foundation in 1882 up to 1981, when the Association ceased business, are in Merseyside County Archives. A list is available.

TAILORS' AND GARMENT CUTTERS' UNION

The minutes, 1883–1911, were deposited in Nottingham Public Library in 1968. They comprise four volumes, 1883–93, 1893–1905, 1905 and 1906–11.

TELECOMMUNICATIONS STAFF ASSOCIATION

A small deposit can be found in the Modern Records Centre, University of Warwick (ref MSS 190). The TSA was formed in 1970 following the resignation of the Executive Committee of the National Guild of Telephonists and the box of records received on deposit relates to applications and appeals, 1972–4, by the TSA, members and officials under the Industrial Relations Act, 1971, for recognition as a sole bargaining agent and in respect of its activities as a registered trade union.

TEMPERANCE

In addition to the material cited in *Sources*, Vol. 1, pp 253–257, the following additional records have been reported:

British League of Juvenile Abstainers
Two registers (1847–51, *c* 1885–94) are in the Campbell papers (*see* NRA 13863).

Colne and District Temperance Society
Minutes, 1890–1935, are in Lancashire County Record Office.

Doncaster Temperance Society
Minutes, 1848–60 and minutes of the Doncaster and District United Temperance Council, 1946–56, are in Doncaster Museum (*see* NRA 12415).

Glasgow Abstainers' Union
The records are in Strathclyde Regional Archives. A list is available (NRA 22005).

Huddersfield Temperance Society
The records are in the Archives Department, Huddersfield Central Library.

Lancashire and Cheshire Band of Hope and Temperance Union
Minute books, etc., 1866–1945, are in Manchester Public Library. A list is available (NRA 21589).

Leeds Temperance Society
Minute books are in the Crosfield Collection, Leeds Central Library.

Manchester and Salford Women's Christian Temperance Association
Minutes, 1880–1966, are in Manchester Public Library.

Newport Temperance Society
The records, 1885–1963, have been deposited. *See* NRA 12535.

North Wales Temperance Union
Correspondence and papers, 1908–12, are in Caernarvonshire Record Office.

Rochdale Temperance Society
The minute books are in Rochdale Public Library.

Scottish Temperance Alliance
The records, 1846–1934, have been deposited in Glasgow University Archives.

South Wales Women's Temperance Union
The records, 1901–65, have been deposited in the National Library of Wales.

Ulster Women's Christian Temperance Union
Minute books and other papers, 1921–69, have been placed in the Public Record Office of Northern Ireland.

TEXTILE TRADES' FEDERATIONS
The Lancashire Record Office holds the following collections:

Darwen Textile Manufacturing Trades' Federation
Minutes, 1909–14 (ref DDX 1078/3).

North Lancashire Textile Employers' Association
(Ref DDX 1116.) The records consist of minutes 1836–1961 of annual, members, executive and committee meetings, annual and committee reports, 1911–55; letter books, 1853–1962; correspondence files, 1910–61; Preston Guild files, 1802–1932; cash books 1913–65; levy ledgers and cash books, 1908–61; and Annual Statements of Accounts, 1897–1966. Copies of the rules for various branches of the Association, price lists and agreements, handbooks and miscellaneous material are held. The minutes, correspondence, rules and papers, 1914–63, of the Chorley Cotton Manufacturers' Association are also held.

North East Lancashire Textile Manufacturers' Association
(Ref DDX 1145.) The records were deposited by I. Cooke Esq of Nelson. Items under 30 years old cannot be produced without permission of the depositor. The collection includes the minutes 1894–1963; ledgers, 1912–63; and cash book, 1945–60, of Burnley Master Cotton Spinners' and Manufacturers' Association; the minutes,

1888–1963, ledgers, 1920–63, and cash books, 1948–61 of Colne and District Coloured Goods Manufacturers' Association; the minutes, 1891–1963, letter books, 1938–63, ledgers, 1916–63, and cash book, 1925–63, of Nelson and District Manufacturers' Association; the minutes, 1890–1963, ledgers, 1890–1963, and cash book, 1922–61, of Padiham Master Cotton Spinners' and Manufacturers' Association; and various printed rule books, price lists and miscellanea.

Preston and District Trades Federation
(Ref DDX 1089/19.) There are minutes and attendance registers, 1907–63; together with circulars regarding the 1945 General Election and correspondence, 1961–65.

Additional note: The Calderdale Public Library holds the papers of the Todmorden Textile Federation, whilst the records of the Bolton Master Cotton Spinners' and Textile Employers' Association, 1893–1961, are in Bolton Metropolitan Borough Library.

TRANSPORT AND GENERAL WORKERS' UNION

Since the entry in *Sources*, Vol. 1, p 263, the extensive records of the union, together with many of its constituent unions, have been deposited in instalments in the Modern Records Centre, University of Warwick (ref MSS 126). A detailed list of the material deposited is contained in the *Guide* to the Modern Records Centre. The following description is intended to give an outline of the range and variety of deposited material. This includes: Dock, Wharf, Riverside and General Workers' Union: annual reports and minutes of delegate meetings, 1890–1920; *Dockers' Record*, 1901–21; National Union of Docks, Wharves and Shipping Staffs: Quayside and Office, 1919–21; Amalgamated Society of Watermen and Lightermen: reports and accounts, 1893–1921; Amalgamated Association of Tramway and Hackney Carriage Employees: quarterly and annual reports, 1892–1919, agenda and reports of proceedings of annual delegate meetings, 1911–1919; souvenirs, rulebook, 1891; *Tramway and Vehicle Worker*, 1905; London and Provincial Union of Licensed Vehicle Workers (previously the London Cab Drivers' Trade Union): *Cab Trade Record*, 1897–1908, annual reports and reports of delegate meetings, 1916–19, *Licensed Vehicle Trades Record*, 1913–19; United Vehicle Workers: various publications; Workers' Union: annual reports, 1905–26, *Record*, 1913–29; National Amalgamated Union of Enginemen, Firemen, Mechanics and Electrical Workers: quarterly reports and balance sheets, 1895–1926; National Transport Workers' Federation: reports, 1911–27; National Federation of General Workers: reports, 1918–22; National Sailors' and Firemen's Union: reports of annual general meetings, 1912–16; National Association of Operative Plasterers: reports of conferences with the National Association of Master Builders, 1899 and 1904, auditors' (from 1905 known as annual) reports, 1873–1967, monthly reports, 1886–1932, quarterly reports, 1932–65, half yearly reports, 1965–7; Scottish Plasterers' Union: minute books, 1916–68, with one correspondence book.

From the T&GWU itself, Annual Reports are held, 1922–74; Biennial Delegate Conference Reports, 1923–75; Rules Conference Reports, 1950–74, and GEC minutes, 1923–74.

Notes
(a) *The Bevin Papers*

The Transport and General Workers' Union papers of Ernest Bevin are also included in the T&GWU deposit. The Bevin papers, which derive from his work as a union official between the wars, principally as General Secretary of the T&GWU from its foundation, include numerous groups of papers relating to committees on which he served. Amongst these the Committee on Inland Waterways and the Standing Committee on Mineral Transport bulk large in terms of documentation. Other committees and organisations, such as the Society for Socialist Inquiry and Propaganda, are also represented, as well as the Union itself.

(b) *The National Union of Vehicle Builders*

Until 1980, the records of this union, founded as the United Kingdom Society of Coachmakers in 1834, were separately preserved in the NUVB Museum, Holyhead Road, Coventry. It was proposed to move them to the T&GWU Regional Offices in West Bromwich. This collection includes not only records of the National Union of Vehicle Builders (NUVB), but also records of the United Kingdom Society of Coachmakers (UKS), the London and Provincial Society of Coachmakers (L&P), the Amalgamated Society of Wheelwrights, Smiths & Kindred Trades (ASW) and the Amalgamated Society of Wheelwrights, Smiths and Motor Body Makers (ASWSMBM). The collection includes Quarterly Reports and Journals: UKS (1848–1919), NUVB (1919–1972); Executive Minutes UKS, 4 vols, (1907–1918); Executive Minutes NUVB, 4 vols, (1919–1947); Executive Minutes, L&P, 1 vol, (1911–1916); Executive Minutes, ASW, 3 vols, (1896–1924); Executive Minutes, ASWSMBM, 1 vol, (1912–1924); Rules and Delegate Conference Notes, NUVB, (1924–1946)

(c) *North Wales Quarrymen's Union*

Contrary to the information cited in *Sources*, Vol. 1, pp. 264–265, the records are now in Caernarvon Area Record Office, not the National Library of Wales. The collection comprises minute books, 1891–1933, cash books, 1885–1914 and other records, including the papers of the Secretary, R. W. Williams (1903–57).

In addition to the central archives of the Union, information is also available on certain important regional deposits of the T&GWU.

(i) *Manchester Region*

Records for the period 1923–65 are deposited in Manchester Central Library (ref M86).

(ii) *Newcastle Area*

The records have been deposited in Tyne and Wear Record Office (ref Acc 673). A list is available (NRA 20933). The collection includes minutes and reports of the Area Committee (4 bundles) 1921–43, minutes of the General Workers Trade Group National Committee (4 bundles) 1933–70, minutes and records of the Statutory Quarterly meeting of the Docks National Committee, 1952–69 (2 bundles), 1 bundle of minutes of the Waterways National Committee, 1952–69 and the minutes of various affiliated trade committees, e.g. Agricultural District Committee, Docks and Waterways Committee. There are 22 such bundles of minutes, 1921–69.

Five bundles of general correspondence exist (1923–52) and a further five bundles on organisational matters. There are six bundles on specific subjects, e.g. industrial disputes, election of delegates to 3rd Rules Conference (1936–62).

41 volumes of the annual record of the T&GWU (1928–69) are part of the collection, together with General Council's Reports to the annual TUC (1960–63, 1966, 1967–70). There are 7 volumes and 3 bundles of documents containing the reports of Special Conferences of the TUC Executive, 1940–69.

TRANSPORT SALARIED STAFFS' ASSOCIATION

Further details are now available of the collection which has been deposited at the Modern Records Centre, University of Warwick (ref MSS 55) (see also *Sources*, Vol. 1, p 266). The collection includes the minutes of the Executive Committee (1900–06, 1913–50), Annual Reports (1908–25), Conference Proceedings (1899–1928), General Secretary' Circulars (1938–59); two files on the relations with the railway unions – the RCA Treasurer's file concerning agreements with the railway companies (1920s) and a file of RCA memoranda (1914–1930s). Branch minutes are held for Accrington (1944–64), Liverpool Street Station (1915–21), Middlesbrough No. 1 branch (1907–53), Nottingham (1897–1900) and Wisbech (1908–19, 1933–55) plus the branch accounts for Nottingham (1898–1903) and Sheffield (1900–07). Publications include the TSSA *Journal* 1947–67, the *Railway Herald* 1896–9, and the *Railway Clerk* 1908–23. The TSSA deposit has now been added to by the addition of certain early items of the Railway Telegraph Clerks' Association.

TRAVELLERS' AID SOCIETY

Some records of the society, covering the period 1885–1952, are with the Fawcett Library, now deposited in the City of London Polytechnic.

UNION OF BOOKMAKERS' EMPLOYEES

Records of this small union are in the Modern Records Centre, University of Warwick (NRA 24620).

UNION OF CONSTRUCTION, ALLIED TRADES AND TECHNICIANS

Since the entry in *Sources*, Vol. 1, p 267, an important series of records has been deposited in the Modern Records Centre, University of Warwick (ref MSS 78). This extensive archive includes records of many of the constituent unions of UCATT. However, holdings are not comprehensive for all of these parts for all periods. Because of the volume and complexity of records held, the following list is only a very provisional outline of the material in the Centre.

(1) Building Trades Unions. Among records held of UCATT constituent unions are:

(a) Operative Bricklayers' Society
Annual reports, 1862–1920; monthly reports, 1861–1910; yearly returns of members' payments, 1879–1920; circulars, from 1915–20. Various branch minute books have also survived.

(b) Operative Stonemasons' Society
The collection includes the minute book of delegates to the Building Trades Conference 1858–59, admission of members records, 1886–1911, and a bank book for 1864–67. There are 98 volumes of fortnightly Return Sheets, 1834–1910, and copies of the Journal of the Operative Stonemasons' Society (which replaced the Return Sheets) for the years 1911–21. There are 4 rule books from the period 1881–95, miscellaneous printed items, and several publications by other societies, as well as the records of some sixteen branches.

(c) Manchester Unity of Operative Bricklayers

Monthly reports and trade journals, 1869–1912; contributions books and ledgers, 1897–1913; report of an arbitration on hours of labour, 1923; and a file re disposal of funds on amalgamation, 1920s.

(d) Amalgamated Union of Building Trade Workers (AUBTW)

Formed from the three above organisations. Within this deposit are the O.B.S. continuation minutes, 1921–65, as well as minutes, AUBTW, No. 1 Divisional Council, 1930s; No. 2 (later No. 3) Divisional Council, 1919–51; minutes of the proposed amalgamation with other building workers' unions, 1920s and 1930s. The AUBTW archive also includes membership records, account books, quarterly and monthly reports.

(e) Association of Building Technicians

Formed in 1919 as the Architects' and Surveyors' Assistants Professional Union. Minutes of Executive and General Councils between 1919 and 1969 (incomplete) with Emergency E.C. minutes, 1938–39.

(f) Building and Monumental Workers' Association (Scotland)

The deposited records are mainly financial, consisting of a register of members, 1884–1941; a general roll of members of the granite section, 1880–1940; 2 general cash books 1938–42; a general ledger, 1936–42; an expenditure and an income ledger for 1938–42; Branch receipts and committee expenses and accounts. There are also volumes of the Building and Monumental Workers' *Trade Journal* for 1924–35 and 1939–41.

(g) National Building Labourers and Constructional Workers' Society

Annual reports, 1923–50.

(h) National Federation of Building Trade Operatives

The main records of the union have been placed in the Civil Engineering Library of the University of Manchester Institute of Science and Technology (UMIST). The duplicate material at the Modern Records Centre includes: membership registers, 1863–1904; cash and account books, 1920s–1940s; executive committee minutes, 1951–65; a run of *Operative Builder*, 1947–60. From UCATT's London regional office have come NFBTO annual conference proceedings, 1939, 1942, 1945, 1950–65; and NFBTO London Regional Council minutes (various series), 1922–69.

(i) Amalgamated Slaters, Tilers and Roofers' Provident Society

Minute books, 1926–65; account books and ledgers, 1920s–30s; also correspondence files especially on Labour-Only sub-contracting, *c.* 1964–7; and the transfer of engagements of the AS & T to the AUBTW, 1966–69; the *Slate Trade Gazette*, 1904, 1907, 1908, 1910–14. (*See* NRA 23738 for further details).

(2) Woodworkers Unions

(a) *Amalgamated Society of Carpenters and Joiners*

The records include three volumes of minutes of the Executive Committee 1915–21, three volumes of minutes of the General Council 1871–1921, and a volume of minutes of meetings with the General Union regarding amalgamation in 1920. There are 26 branch admission of members books, 1895–1920; and 13 branch registration books, 1901–21, providing details of membership. Some 187 files, mostly of printed circulars, exist regarding organisational matters in the years

1906–20, including files on topics such as Labour Representation–Parliamentary Fund 1906, the attack on trade unionism in Dublin (1913) and the 1913 Trade Union Act. Eight volumes of printed reports including monthly, annual and financial reports cover the years 1860–1920, and there are 14 items relating to branch and management committee activities, including some branch minutes for the years 1863–1945.

For the Associated Carpenters and Joiners of Scotland there are annual and other reports, 1863–1911.

(b) General Union of Carpenters and Joiners

Two Executive Committee minute books survive, 1918–20, as well as the minutes of the sub-committee to consider the amalgamation of the GUC&J and the ASC&J, 1920; various reports, rulebooks and registers, 1866–1920.

(c) Amalgamated Society of Woodworkers

An amalgamation of the two above organisations. Minute books re amalgamation, General Council minute books, 1922–66 (5 vols.); annual and monthly reports, 1937–65; reports of annual delegate conferences, 1947–64; and a run of letter-books, 1916–65, and cash books, 1930s–50s. Non-current correspondence files have been accepted, covering regional and local organisation, and various subject files, especially re industrial accidents. Notable within the ASW deposit are records from the predecessors of the Belfast 12th Branch of the ASW, including a minute book of the Journeyman Cabinet Makers of Belfast, with a membership list dating from 1788–1810. Annual reports of the Association of Carpenters and Joiners of Scotland run from 1863–1910 and the minutes of the joint committee of Glasgow and district branches are also held, 1876–87. From UCATT's London Office have come records of the ASW Southwark Progressive Branch (originally GUCJ Southwark Progressive Lodge) minutes, 1890–1945, 1960–64.

(3) Decorators and Painters Unions

(a) Amalgamated Society of House Decorators and Painters

The original society arose from the desire for amalgamation. In 1865 several local London societies formed a loose federation, the 'General Council' but dissatisfaction with the Council led to the formation of the General Association of Amalgamated House Painters in 1866. The two merged to form the ASHDP in 1868. This failed due to financial difficulties, but a second society emerged in 1872. This took over the East London Painters' Union and the Universal Federation of Painters (of Bermondsey) in 1900. In 1904 it amalgamated with the National Amalgamated Society of Operative House Painters and Decorators to form the National Amalgamated Society of Operative House and Ship Painters and Decorators (NASOHSPD) (q.v.). The deposited papers include the minutes of the Executive Council, Oct 1903–Nov 1906, three registration books, 1873–1900; and the Annual Reports, 1872–1900.

(b) National Amalgamated Society of Operative House and Ship Painters and Decorators

Records deposited include minute books, 1880–1920; Reports, 1921–63; Journal, 1928–40; quarterly and annual reports of delegate meetings, etc. There is also some similar material for the Manchester Alliance of Operative House Painters (General Alliance).

UNION OF DOMESTIC APPLIANCE AND GENERAL METALWORKERS

See **National Union of Stove Grate Workers**

UNION OF JEWISH WOMEN

Anglo-Jewish Archives at the Mocatta Library, University College, London, hold minute books and reports of meetings (1902–62) and annual reports (1903–44, 1944–61). The collection (ref AJ/73) also includes reports (1949) to the International Council of Jewish Women (ref AJ/188). The Union was founded in 1902 as the representative body of Jewish women working for the welfare of educated women and girls.

UNION OF JUTE, FLAX AND KINDRED TEXTILE OPERATIVES

The records of the union, 1906–66, have been placed in Dundee District Archives, along with the records of the Jute Sack and Bag Manufacturers' Association.

UNION OF POST OFFICE WORKERS

Since the entry in *Sources*, Vol. 1, p 270, some records have been deposited at the Modern Records Centre, University of Warwick. The deposit includes Executive Committee minutes 1919–60; General Purposes Committee minutes 1919–57 and 1965; Post Office Departmental Whitley Council, Staff Side minutes 1920–28; Sussex District UPW minutes 1920–57; Annual delegate conferences, minutes and agenda 1960s–1970s; and UPW wage claims and evidence 1926–7 and 1938. Journals include *From UPW House* (1940–55), *Whitley Bulletins* (1957–75), *The Post* (1890–93, 1899, 1954–66), *Postman's Gazette* (1895–96, 1907–18), *The Postal Clerks Herald* (1906–14), *the Telegraphist* (1883–88), *Telegraph Journal* (1899–93) and the *Postal and Telegraph Record* (1915–19). Subject files and research papers are held on various topics including the cost of living (1935–64) branch circulars (1953–70) and a UPW pamphlet collection and 2 boxes of papers on equal pay. Access to unpublished material is only allowed with the prior approval of the Union.

NB. The main archive has been retained by the Union.

UNION OF SHOP DISTRIBUTIVE AND ALLIED WORKERS

The Union still retains its records, but reference should be made to the Hallsworth papers deposited in the Modern Records Centre, University of Warwick.

UNIONIST SOCIETY

The records of the Northern Ireland-based Unionist Society have been deposited in the Public Record Office of Northern Ireland. The records, in seven volumes covering the period 1942–1977, include minute books, attendance registers and correspondence files.

UNITED CECIL CLUB

The records of the Club and its predecessors were deposited, in August 1976 and April 1977, in Kent Archives Office by H. J. F. Crum Ewing, Vice-Chairman of the Club. A list is available (NRA 20727). The United Cecil Club came into existence in 1949 on the merging of the United Club and the Cecil Club. The Cecil Club was originally formed in 1882 to organise publication of the *National Review*. The United Club, founded in 1887, absorbed the Constitutional Union (established 1881) in 1891.

The collection includes minutes of the *National Review* Organising Committee 1882–83, of the Cecil Club committee 1883–1905, of general meetings 1884–1905, balance sheets 1887–1905, press cuttings, agenda etc. There is similar material for 1923–1940. The collection also includes minutes of the Constitutional Union, its Executive Committee 1881–1890; its general meetings 1882–1890; joint meetings of Constitutional Union and United Club committees 1890–91, the United Club General Meeting 1891; and minutes of the United Club Executive Committee 1891–96.

Six minute books contain the minutes of United Club General Meetings 1887–1949; United Club Executive Committee Meetings 1896–1949; United and Cecil Club General Meetings 1949 to 1961, United and Cecil Club Executive Committee, 1949 to 1974, the annual accounts of the United and Cecil Club 1949 to 1961 and minutes of United Club sub-committees 1904–09.

There is also an agenda book for General and Committee meetings 1937–61, an attendance book and notices of agenda and committee minutes (4 files) for 1956–1975 etc.

UNITED COMMERCIAL TRAVELLERS' ASSOCIATION

The records have been deposited in the Modern Records Centre, University of Warwick.

UNITED IRISH LEAGUE

The minutes of the Standing Committee of the National Directory, 1902–06, are in the Library of Trinity College, Dublin.

UNITED LAW CLERKS' SOCIETY

Minute books and other records, 1832–1969, have been placed in the Greater London Record Office.

UNITED OPERATIVE PLUMBERS' ASSOCIATION

See **Plumbers' Trade Union**

UNITED SERVICE CLUB

The records, 1815–1970, have been deposited in the National Army Museum.

UNITED SOCIETY OF ENGRAVERS

An important collection of records of the Society and its predecessors has been placed in the John Rylands University Library of Manchester. Among the bound volumes of minutes are: Union of Engravers to Calico Printers and Paper Stainers, minute books, (1889–1907, 5 vols); Amalgamated Union of Engravers to Calico Printers and Paper Stainers, minute books (1907–28, 2 vols); AUE Rough Minute Book (1905–19); AUE Scottish Branch, minute book (1912–26); Scottish United Engravers' Society, minute book, (1888–98); Scottish Union of Engravers to Calico Printers and Paper Stainers, minute book (1898–1912); English and Scottish Engravers to Calico Printers and Paper Stainers Trade Union Federation, minute book (1904–09), United Society of Engravers, minute books, (1929–50, 3 vols).

In addition there are bound volumes of branch minutes for Accrington, (1928–39) and Dinting (1909–59), contributions books; Union of Engravers to Calico Printers and Paper Stainers (later AUE and USE), (1900–60, 15 vols); Scottish Members' Contributions (1898–1930, 2 vols); Funeral Benefit Levy Scheme, Accounts, (1924–42); Entrance Fee Books, (1894–1946 and 1895–1908, 2 vols); Apprentice Register (1899–1972); Census of Members, with Ages, (1924); and a Deceased Members Book (1956–73). The collection is completed by numerous files of Wallpaper Industry Agreements, 1940–72, Textiles and Job Shops Agreements, 1932–73, printed annual reports, rule books, etc.

VOLUNTARY EUTHANASIA SOCIETY

Since the entry in *Sources*, Vol. 1, p 274, the records have been deposited in the Contemporary Medical Archives Centre at the Wellcome Institute. The collection covers the period 1931–77. A list is available (NRA 25587).

WEAVING TRADE UNIONS

Accrington and District, and Church and Ostwaldtwistle Weavers' Association

A collection has been deposited at the Lancashire Record Office (ref DDX 1138). It covers the years 1890–1969 and includes minutes and financial records. Items less than 30 years old can only be produced with the permission of the depositor, Mrs. M. Lampitt. A list is available (NRA 20863).

Burnley and District Textile Workers' Unions

A collection has been deposited in the Lancashire Record Office (ref DDX 1274). It includes minutes for predecessor organisations and various committees, 1872–1962; correspondence and memoranda, 1885–1969; financial records, 1884–1963; publications and reports, 1914–64; papers on wage agreements, health and safety of workers, etc. and miscellaneous papers. Records less than 30 years old may not be produced without authority. A list is available (NRA 23236).

Haslingden Operative Spinners' Association

A collection has been deposited at Lancashire Record Office (ref DDX 1134). It includes minutes, 1868–1963; Contribution Books, 1876–1950; Account Books, 1886–1959; annual balance sheets, 1920–66; correspondence, 1867–1976; and miscellaneous rule books. A list is available (NRA 20862).

Amalgamated Association of Beamers, Twisters and Drawers (Hand and Machine)

A collection has been deposited at the Lancashire Record Office (ref DDX 1269). The collection includes minute books, 1917–68; Rule Books, Annual Reports, 1965–69; newspaper cuttings, 1895–1942; records of the Heywood Branch, 1933–60; the Nelson Branch, 1939–72; the Preston Branch, 1870–1973; and various other material. A list is available (NRA 23239).

WELSH MEMBERS COMMITTEE

The minute books of this influential committee of Liberal MPs (1886–89) are in Newport Central Library.

WEST INDIA COMMITTEE

Since the entry in *Sources* Vol. 1, p 276, the archives have been purchased by the Government of Trinidad in 1981 and were given to the Library of the University of the West Indies at St Augustine. A list is available (NRA 25250). A microfilm is available in the Institute of Commonwealth Studies, London. The collection also includes some records, 1887–90, of the Anti-Bounty Association.

WEST MIDLAND GROUP ON POST WAR RECONSTRUCTION AND PLANNING

The archives of the group, formerly in the office of the Bournville Village Trust, were placed in Birmingham University Library in February 1967. The Group was formed in 1941 and, over the next decade, was to exercise a considerable influence in local and regional affairs. The collection, which includes minutes, correspondence etc. is listed.

WOMEN'S EMPLOYMENT FEDERATION

See **National Advisory Centre on Careers for Women**

WOMEN'S FORUM

Records, including minute books, reports, correspondence files etc. for the period 1935–76 are in the Fawcett Library, City of London Polytechnic.

WOMEN'S GROUP ON PUBLIC AFFAIRS

See **Women's Forum**

WOMEN'S INTERNATIONAL LEAGUE FOR PEACE AND FREEDOM

Since the entry in *Sources*, Vol. 1, pp 278–9, the BLPES has received an additional deposit of material. This consists of the papers acquired by Mary Nuthall, President of the WILPF and has relevant material on the British section of the movement.

WOMEN'S SUFFRAGE GROUPS

In addition to the information cited in *Sources*, Vol. 1, pp 279–84, some important local and regional deposits have been made. The records of the Glasgow and West of Scotland Association for Women's Suffrage have now been deposited with the Mitchell Library, Glasgow by Miss M. J. Buchanan. The collection includes the minute books (1902–33) and letter books (1913–18) of the Executive Committee, the minute book of the Hospitals Committee (1915–19), the minute book of the Glasgow Women's Suffrage Society Organising Committee (1918–24), the minute book of the Scottish Women's Hospitals (1916–17), the minute book of the 'Exchange for Voluntary Workers' Committee (1916), the minute book of the Women's Local Representation Joint Committee (1919–22) and 19 printed articles relating to women's suffrage.

In South Wales, the Glamorgan Record Office has the records of the Cardiff and District Women's Suffrage Society 1910–56.

In East Anglia, Cambridgeshire Record Office has the reports of the Cambridge Women's Suffrage Association, 1886–1918.

WORKERS' INTERNATIONAL LEAGUE

See **International Marxist Group**

WORKERS' TRAVEL ASSOCIATION

The records of the organisation are reported to be in Kent County Record Office. This organisation was founded in 1921 to promote travel for working people. The collection includes minutes, correspondence, financial accounts etc. since its foundation.

WORKERS' UNION

Since the entry in *Sources*, Vol. 1, p 264, a valuable collection of material accumulated by Dr. Richard Hyman for his study of the Workers' Union (1971) has been deposited in the Modern Records Centre, University of Warwick (ref MSS 63). The collection includes minute books from Brierley Hill, Lincoln and Newark, Braintree, Bocking and Calvert for the 1920s, as well as publications of the Union such as rulebooks, conference documents and the first and second general statements of account, 1898–1900. The collection also comprises subject files, notably on the Mid-Cornwall china clay workers' strike of 1913.

WORLD JEWISH CONGRESS (British Section)

The Institute of Jewish Affairs at 55 New Cavendish Street, London W1 holds a considerable archive, mainly covering World War II and the organisation's intensive work on behalf of refugees, etc. There are minutes and reports of the British section and of the European executive. The pre-war records are sparse and in poor condition, but in 1940 the organisation transferred much of its business from Paris to London. The wartime and later papers include a large number collected by A. L. Easterman as an officer of the Congress, and the material in date order includes *aide mémoires*, representations and correspondence. Other relevant material of the parent body is held in New York and at the Central Zionist Archives in Jerusalem.

The World Jewish Congress was set up in Geneva in 1936 to combat Nazism and to co-ordinate the policies and activities of Jewish communities throughout the world on questions of common interest and common concern.

The British Section, also formed in 1936, maintained branches in Birmingham, Glasgow and Manchester.

WORLD UNION OF JEWISH STUDENTS

There appear to be few records prior to 1958 of the World Union, which was founded in 1924. The British office at 247 Grays Inn Road, London WC1 holds only reports to the WUJS Conference (1946) by Jewish students in Palestine, Bulgarian students etc., on conditions in their countries, whilst the World University Service at Geneva holds material on the WUJS's 1933 opposition to student conferences in Germany.

WORLD ZIONIST ORGANISATION

The Central Zionist Archives at Jerusalem hold the records of the various Zionist bodies, including papers of the World Zionist Organisation based in London, Zionist congresses and the executive (ref Z1-6, S1-40, Lk1-14 etc). The organisation was founded at the first Zionist Congress in August 1897. The organisation aimed to secure for the Jewish people a home in Palestine guaranteed by public law. The Basle Congress of 1897 adopted a constitution providing for a self governing World Organisation with the Zionist Congress as the supreme body. From World War I until 1948, the World Zionist Organisation had its headquarters in London.

YOUNG MEN'S CHRISTIAN ASSOCIATION

In addition to the records cited in *Sources*, Vol. 1, p 290, the Scottish National Council also has retained its records. Their collection includes the minutes of various committees, 1874–1975; Annual Reports, 1898–1974; copies of the YMCA Magazine, 1874–1930; material relating to individual YMCAs, and various other papers. A list is available (NRA 23273).

YOUNG WOMEN'S CHRISTIAN ASSOCIATION

Contrary to the information cited in *Sources*, Vol. 1, p 291, the association has in fact decided to retain its records rather than deposit them in the Modern Records Centre. The records retained include minutes, etc, of the following councils and committees: National Council, 1884–1960; United Central Council, 1885–96; British National Council Standing Committee, 1898–1913; Executive Committee, 1913–63; various financial committees from 1906–1940's; various training committees; Employment Committee, between 1888 and 1913; Industrial Law Committee, 1897–1913, 1919–35; Industrial Law Indemnity, 1900–20; Industrial Law Committee enquiries and complaints, 1898–1908, 1908–10; Public Affairs Committee, 1933–53; Girls Work Committee, 1930–9; Unemployment Committee, 1933–9; various overseas and international committees; Religious committees since 1914; Relief Abroad, 1944–6; Rural Group, 1945–9; Survey and Extension Committee, 1928–41; Hostel and Canteen Group, 1939–45; Employment, 1888–9, 1902–7, 13–19; and finally Training and Personnel Committee, 1914–57.

YOUTH MOVEMENTS

Since the entry in *Sources*, Vol. 1, pp 287–292, the Youth Movement Archive has been transferred from University College Cardiff to BLPES. Among the organisations whose records are included in the transfer are the Woodcraft Folk, the Kibbo Kift Kindred and the Greenshirts. There are published handlists available for the Kibbo Kift Kindred and the Woodcraft Folk.

PART II

A Guide to the Personal Papers of Private Individuals

ABRAHAM, Louis Arnold (1893–)

Principal Clerk of Committees, House of Commons, 1952–58.

A substantial collection of personal papers, mostly relating to his detailed research on parliamentary procedure, has been deposited in the House of Lords Record Office.

ABRAHAM, Major-General William Ernest Victor (1897–1980)

Commander, Upper Burma Battalion, Burma Auxiliary Force, 1932–37. Service in World War II in Greece, Middle East and Burma.

A microfilm of his papers is in the Cambridge Centre for South Asian Studies. The microfilm includes details of a tour made in Burma in March 1942 as liaison officer to General Alexander in Rangoon, various papers concerning the defence of Burma, India Budget papers 1943–44 and miscellaneous other Indian papers.

ABRAHAMS, Abraham (1898–1955)

Anglo-Jewish Zionist Revisionist. Journalist. British delegate, World Revisionist Congress, 1929. Editor, *Jewish Standard*, 1940–48.

The Jabotinsky Institute in Israel has acquired the papers.

ABRAMSKY, Chimen (1917–)

Goldsmid Professor of Hebrew and Jewish Studies, University College, London.

Professor Abramsky possesses some letters of importance to Harold Laski, relating to the Passfield White Paper of 1929, written to him by Arthur Henderson and other members of MacDonald's Cabinet as well as some minor letters relating to Hovevei Zion in the 1890s.

ADAM, Charles Fox Frederick (1852–1913)

Diplomat. Secretary of Embassy, Washington 1897. Chargé d'Affaires, Madrid, 1899–1904.

Some of his papers survive among the Adam family correspondence and papers (NRA 9954). There is some personal correspondence and newspaper cuttings but only a little material relating to diplomatic affairs.

ADAMS, Sir Walter (1906–1975)

Academic. Director, London School of Economics, 1967–74. Secretary, Academic Assistance Council, 1933–38. Deputy Head, British Political Warfare Mission, USA, 1942–44. Assistant Deputy Director General, Political Intelligence Department, Foreign Office, 1945. Secretary, Inter-University Council for Higher Education Overseas, 1946–55, Principal, University College of Rhodesia and Nyasaland, 1955–67.

The papers, which are closed, have been deposited in BLPES, to whom enquiries should be addressed.

ADDIS, Sir Charles Stewart (1861–1945)

Financier and banker. Director, Bank of England, 1918–32.

Since the entry in *Sources*, Vol. 5, p 2, the surviving papers have been placed in the Library of the School of Oriental and African Studies. The collection of diaries, letters and papers covers the period 1881–1945.

ADLER, Elkan Nathan (1861–1946)

Author and publicist. Pioneer English Zionist. Member of the English Hovevei Zion.

The Jewish Theological Seminary in New York has a collection of his personal papers which contain a variety of relevant materials, e.g. travel journals of visits to Palestine (undated); reports, minutes, correspondence and miscellaneous material of the Anglo-Jewish Association (1888–1921) and reports of institutions in Palestine supported by the Association; correspondence between Adler and the Conjoint Foreign Committee of the Board of Deputies of British Jews (1903–1920); reports, financial statements, legal contracts, correspondence and other miscellaneous material,

ADLER, Rabbi Hermann Naphtali (1839–1911)

British Chief Rabbi, 1891–1911. Principal, Jews' College. Anti-Zionist.

Enquiries should be directed to Mr. A. Shischa, 10 The Ridgeway, London NW11, who has relevant papers.

AGNEW, Patrick (fl 1950s)

Trade unionist in Ulster; Stormont MP (Lab), Armagh South, 1938–44.

His papers have been placed in the Public Record Office of Northern Ireland (ref D 1676). The collection includes two personal diaries, 1955–56, correspondence and two minute books of the Armagh branch of the Northern Ireland Labour Party, 1933, 1946–47.

AGNEW, Sir Patrick Dalreagle (1868–1925)

Indian Civil Service. Deputy Commissioner of the Punjab 1898. Managing Director and Vice Chairman, Central Prisoners of War Committee 1916–19.

His family correspondence and papers, 1900–09, were acquired by the India Office Library in 1959.

ALDERSON, Lieutenant-General Sir Edwin Alfred Hervey (1859–1927)

Commander in Mashonaland, 1896; Commanded Mounted Infantry in South Africa 1900–01. Brigadier-General commanding 2nd Infantry Brigade Aldershot 1903–07. Served World War I.

Papers and newspaper cuttings, with part of a staff diary for 1896 are in the National Archives of Zimbabwe.

ALDRED, Guy Alfred (1886–1963)

Socialist journalist and propagandist.

Since the entry in *Sources*, Vol. 5, p 2, the records have been transferred from Baillie's Library to the Mitchell Library, Glasgow.

ALEXANDER, Major-General Edward Currie (1875–1964)

Served North West Frontier 1897, Mahsud Waziri operations 1902, Mohmand Expedition 1908, Kurdistan 1919, Iraq 1920.

Papers covering his service in the Indian Army, 1902–34, including letters from Lieutenant-General Sir George MacMunn are in the Imperial War Museum.

ALEXANDER, Horace (fl 1930s–1940s)

Missionary in India. Close confidant of Nationalist leaders.

His papers, including correspondence with Nehru etc. are in the Nehru Memorial Library, Delhi.

ALISON, General Sir Archibald (1826–1907)

Military career, including C-in-C, Egypt 1882–83. Commanded Aldershot Division, 1883–89. Adjutant-General 1888. Member, Council of India 1889–99.

His letter-books and journals, 1849–1916, have been placed in the Bodleian Library.

ALLENBY, 1st Vt
Field Marshal Sir Edmund Henry Hynman Allenby (1861–1936)

C-in-C, Egyptian Expeditionary Force 1917–19. High Commissioner for Egypt, 1919–25.

A collection of papers covering his career has now been placed in the Liddell Hart Centre for Military Archives. The papers include Boer War letters, letters from the Western Front, Palestine and Egypt 1914–22, photographs and material collected by Wavell for his biography.

ALLFREY, Lieutenant-General Sir Charles Walter (1895–1964)

Served European War 1914–18. Commander, V Corps, North Africa and Italy 1942–44. GOC, British troops in Egypt 1944–48.

The papers, now at the Liddell Hart Centre for Military Archives, King's College London include diaries, microfilms of photograph albums and other papers concerning his command of 43 Division and V Corps in the Tunisian and Italian campaigns, 1943–44.

ALVERSTONE, 1st Vt
Sir Richard Everard Webster, 1st Bt (1842–1915)

Attorney General, 1885–Feb 1886; Aug 1886–92; 1895–1900.

Since the negative entry in *Sources*, Vol. 3, p 10, the British Library has purchased three volumes of letters written to him 1865–1918.

ANDERSON, Brigadier-General Austin Thomas (d 1949)

Army career. Served with Tochi Field Force 1897 and Tirah Expeditionary Force 1897–98. Comptroller and Assistant Military Officer to Governor General of Australia 1939–44.

Three volumes of his diary, 1914–18, when he commanded RA 62nd Division in France are in the Royal Artillery Institution.

ANDERSON, Professor James Norman Dalrymple (1908–   )

Lawyer and academic. Professor of Islamic Law, University of London. Arab specialist. Arab Liaison Officer, Libyan Arab Force, World War II.

The papers have been placed in the Library of the School of Oriental and African Studies, to which enquiries should be adressed.

ARCHDALE, Lieutenant-Colonel O. A.

Army career. Liaison Officer to Lord Gort, 1940.

The Imperial War Museum has his diary which he kept when in France, May-June 1940. The diary clearly reveals the collapse of the will to resist in the French High Command.

ARCHER, Admiral Sir Ernest Russell (1891—1958)

Naval career.

Certain letters and papers are in the Imperial War Museum.

ARCHIBALD, Major-General S. C. M. (1890—1973)

Served World War I, Ypres, Somme, Messines etc. Commanded 11th Anti-aircraft Division 1941—43. Adviser to Canada on anti-aircraft defence.

His memoirs, 1909—50, are in the Imperial War Museum. They include much descriptive material on trench warfare and tactics in World War I.

ARMOUR, Reverend James Brown (1842—1928)

Educationalist and Protestant Home Rule supporter.

A collection of papers, 1860—1928, is in the Public Record Office of Northern Ireland.

ARMSTRONG, Sir William (1915—1980)

Civil servant. Head of the Home Civil Service, 1968—74, previously Joint Permanent Secretary to the Treasury, 1962—68.

Certain papers concerning economic policy are at the Public Record Office (BA/6).

ARNETT, Edward John (1876—1940)

Colonial civil servant. Served Nigeria etc.

The papers are in Rhodes House Library, Oxford. The collection includes correspondence, reports, memoranda etc. concerning Northern Nigeria, Sokoto 1902—40 (ref MSS Afr S 952).

ARNOT, R. Page (b 1890)

Historian of the Labour movement.

His papers have been deposited in the Brynmor Jones Library, Hull University. They include files of correspondence, 1917—74; files *re* writings and lectures, 1931—74: general files, 1916—74; and a file on his experiences as a conscientious objector, 1917—18.

ARTHUR, Sir Oswald Raynor (1905—1973)

Colonial service. Governor, Falkland Islands, 1954—56.

His letters home as Governor of the Falklands are in Rhodes House Library.

ASHBURNHAM, Sir Cromer (1831—1917)

Military career. Commanded 3rd Battalion Rifles, Eastern Sudan Campaign, 1884 and during Boer War. Governor of Suakim.

Some papers concerning Uganda are in the archives of the Royal Geographical Society.

ASHBY, Dame Margaret Corbett (1882—1981)

Feminist. Secretary, National Union of Women's Suffrage Societies.

Since the entry in *Sources*, Vol. 5, p 6, the papers have been acquired by the Fawcett Library, City of London Polytechnic.

ASHLEY, Francis Noel (1884—1976)

Colonial civil servant.

Papers as Commissioner for the Solomon Islands, 1931—1938 and as Chief Out Island Commissioner for the Bahamas are in Rhodes House Library.

ASKINS, Jack (fl 1950s)

Trade union activist. Joint Secretary of the British Campaign for Peace in Vietnam.

The Modern Records Centre, University of Warwick, has acquired his papers relating to the British movement against the Vietnam War (ref. MSS 189). The accession also includes papers relating to his work organising Manchester Corporation busmen, 1954—56, including copies of the *Busmen's Clarion*, 1954—55. A list is available (NRA 22696).

ATCHERLEY, Air Marshal Sir Richard (1904—1970)

OC, 219 Fighter Squadron 1939—40. AOC 211 Group, Desert Air Force 1943. Commander, Central Fighter Establishment 1945.

His papers, 1923—67, are with the Royal Air Force Museum (ref AC 73/6). The collection includes log books, photographs, press-cuttings, correspondence and other papers.

ATKIN, 1st B
James Richard Atkin (1867—1944)

Legal career. Chairman, War Cabinet Committee on Women in Industry, 1918—19. Chairman of Termination of the War Committee, 1918. Served on numerous other public bodies. President, Medico-Legal Society, 1923—29.

Miscellaneous papers relating to his legal practice and other interests have been placed in the House of Lords Record Office.

ATTLEE, 1st E
Clement Richard Attlee (1883—1967)

MP (Lab) Limehouse, 1922—50; Walthamstow West, 1950—55. Parliamentary Under-Secretary for War, 1924. Chancellor of the Duchy of Lancaster, 1930—31. Postmaster General, 1931. Lord Privy Seal, 1940—42. Secretary of State, Dominion Affairs, 1942—43. Lord President of the Council, 1943—45. Deputy Prime Minister, 1942—45. Prime Minister, 1945—51.

Since the entry in *Sources*, Vol. 3 p 19, all the papers formerly in University College, Oxford, have been transferred to the Bodleian Library.

AWBERY, Stanley Steven (1888—1969)

M.P. (Lab) Bristol Central, 1946—64.

The deposited records have now been listed by Glamorgan Archives Service. *See* NRA 26546.

BADER, Group Captain Douglas Robert Steuart (b 1910)

World War II fighter pilot. Commanded First RAF Canadian Fighter Squadron (242).

His unlisted papers, 1939—70, are in the Royal Air Force Museum (ref AC 72/6).

BAIER, Otto

Positivist.

Some papers are in the Brynmor Jones Library, University of Hull. The collection comprises correspondence, notes, addresses delivered and miscellaneous items relating to the positivist teachings of Auguste Comte and the Temple of Humanity in Liverpool, 1854—1939.

BAINES, Sir Jervoise (1847—1925)

Indian Civil Service. Census Commissioner in India, 1889—93. Secretary, Royal Commission on Opium 1894—95. President, Royal Statistical Society 1909—10.

His papers, 1870—1929, have been deposited in the Bodleian Library (Dep b141—7 c283—92 d231—6 e88—91).

BAKER, Harry (1871—1928)

English Zionist pioneer. Co-founder, Glasgow Zionist Society.

The Central Zionist Archives in Jerusalem hold the papers (ref A 51).

BAKER, Colonel John Slade (d 1966)

Military service. *Sunday Times* correspondent.

The Middle East Centre, St. Antony's College, Oxford, has his papers. The collection includes Palestine press cuttings, 1940, notes for lectures; interviews with King Hussein; and diaries (1952—65) covering service for the *Sunday Times* in the Middle East.

BAKER, Philip J. Noel- (1889—1982)

MP (Lab) Coventry, 1929—31; Derby, 1936—50; Derby South, 1950—70. Parliamentary Secretary, Ministry of War Transport, 1942—4. Minister of State, Foreign Office, 1945—6. Secretary of State for Air, 1946—7; Commonwealth Relations, 1947—50. Minister of Fuel and Power, 1950—1.

The papers, cited in *Sources*, Vol. 3, p 22, have now been deposited in Churchill College, Cambridge. The collection comprises 730 boxes of papers, 1918—78, covering most aspects of his political career. There is material on the political offices he held, his constituency work, League of Nations affairs, disarmament and the Olympic Games. A detailed list is available (NRA 24828).

BALFOUR, Lieutenant-Colonel Francis Cecil Campbell (1884–1965)

Military Governor of Baghdad 1919–20. Deputy Governor, Red Sea Province, Sudan 1926–27; Governor 1927–28. Governor, Mongalla Province 1929–30.

Various papers concerning Iraq, the Sudan, Syria and Arabia c1900–53 are in the Sudan Archive, Durham University Library. Topics covered include the Al-Najaf disturbances, March–June 1918, the revolt of Faqi Ali in the Nuba Mountains 1915–16, letters to his mother and papers concerning the visit of the Prince of Wales to Mongalla Province, March–April 1930.

BALLARD, Brigadier-General Colin Robert (1868–1941)

Military career. Served World War I. Military Attaché, Romania, 1917–18. President, Allied Police Commission, Constantinople, 1920–23.

The papers were given to the Liddell Hart Centre for Military Archives in 1968 by his nephew, Brigadier J. A. W. Ballard of Whitchurch, Salop. The papers consist of letters relating to Flanders and France as well as family matters. There is no material later than 1915.

BALLARD, Admiral George Alexander (1862–1948)

Served in Boxer uprising. Admiral of Patrols, East Coast, World War I. Admiral Commanding, Malta. Director, Operations Division, Admiralty War Staff.

The papers have been acquired by the National Maritime Museum.

BANTING, Air Vice-Marshal George Gaywood (1898–1973)

Served World War II. Air Officer Commanding Rhodesian Air Training Group, 1946–49. Air Officer Commanding No. 21 Group, Flying Training Command, 1949–51.

Various papers concerning his air force career, mainly World War II are in the Imperial War Museum.

BARBOUR, Nevill (d 1974)

Arab propagandist. Served Middle East, World War II.

The Middle East Centre, St. Antony's College, Oxford has his papers on Arab affairs and North Africa, with correspondence concerning Palestine (1936–40). There are also articles on Zionism; articles, memoranda and letters on Palestine (1937–60) and press cuttings on Palestine.

BARCLAY, Sir Colville Adrian de Rune (1869–1929)

Minister, Washington, 1918; Sweden, 1919–24; Hungary, 1924–28. Ambassador, Portugal, 1928–29.

Since the entry in *Sources*, Vol. 2, p 10, some papers have been presented to BLPES, to whom enquiries should be addressed.

BARKER, Ambrose

Early anarchist.

His unpublished autobiography was used in Quail *The Slow Burning Fuse*. No further details are available.

BARKER, Colin (fl 1960s—1970s)

International Socialist.

A substantial group of papers has been deposited by Colin Barker in the Modern Records Centre, University of Warwick (ref MSS 152). Access to unpublished material must have the depositor's prior approval. The collection of papers of the International Socialism group (known as the Socialist Workers' Party after 1 January 1977) includes duplicated papers and minutes 1964—73, internal bulletins, 1969—71, conference material and branch papers for Manchester and Oxford. There is correspondence on editorial matters of *International Socialism*. In addition to numerous rank-and-file publications, there are fairly complete runs of *The Worker*, 1972—75, *News and Letters* 1968—70 and such American and French publications as *Workers Power* and *Voix Ouvrière*. Some earlier material donated to Colin Barker by a former Revolutionary Socialist League member is also deposited in the Modern Records Centre. It consists of duplicated bulletins of the Left Faction of the Revolutionary Socialist League, 1938—43 and papers relating to the question of fusion with the Workers' International League.

BARKER, Henry (1858—1940)

Builder and Labour activist.

The surviving papers, including material relating to the Labour Union, are in the archives of the Labour Party.

BARNARDO, Dr Thomas (1845—1905)

Philanthropist

His surviving correspondence, papers, sermons etc., as well as the papers on his homes and charities, are deposited in Liverpool University Archives. A list is available (NRA 22753).

BARNBY, 2nd B
Hon. Francis Vernon Willey (b 1884)

MP (Con) Bradford South, 1918—22.

Since the entry in *Sources*, Vol. 3, p 28, his papers have been acquired by the Centre for South African Studies, University of York. A list is available (NRA 21884).

BARNES, Ernest William (1874—1953)

Bishop of Birmingham.

The papers which were used in the biography by his son, *Ahead of His Age: Bishop Barnes of Birmingham* (Collins, 1979), have now been deposited in Birmingham University Library. A list is available (NRA 26562).

BARNES, Sir Hugh Shakespear (1853—1940)

Foreign Secretary, Government of India, 1900—03. Lieutentant-Governor, Burma, 1903—05. Member, Council of India, 1905—13.

Since the entry in *Sources*, Vol. 2, p 12, further papers have been deposited at the Bodleian Library (ref Mss. Eng hist c 253-61). The collection includes memoranda, letters and dispatches relating to the North-West Frontier (1880—1908); correspondence and papers relating to the Nushki railway, North-West Frontier (1899—

1922) including letters from Austen Chamberlain and Curzon to the Council of India (1905–13), to the Burmah Oil Company, Standard Oil Co., Shell Transport and Trading Co. and Asiatic Petroleum Co. (1904); and to the Burma Railway (1902–04). There are miscellaneous printed speeches, letters and memoranda (1876–9) plus various official papers and printed memoranda (1899–1905).

BARNES, Leonard John (1895–1977)

Writer, philosopher and poet. Critic of British colonial policy. Author of *Caliban in Africa* (1930), *The Duty of Empire* (1935), *Empire or Democracy* (1939) etc. Secretary of the Delegacy for Social Training, Oxford University, 1947–62.

In addition to the information cited in *Sources*, Vol. 5, p 8, further papers are held by the School of Oriental and African Studies (ref PP MS 9). The collection includes 15 published books written or jointly written by Barnes or in which he is mentioned; 6 articles by Barnes, notebooks and rough notes for books, notes on African visits and writings (mainly 1960s), bound manuscripts relating to West and Central Africa (1966–69) and a collection of bound and unbound manuscripts on general topics (1940s–1970s). There are also 4 reports in which Barnes was involved (1945–1951) on Youth Service and on Malay Education. His correspondence includes 3 folders dealing with his books and professional affairs (1959–77) his correspondence with Colin Knight-Adams (1965–71) and correspondence and diaries of Dr. L. N. Tackson (1960–71). There is a folder of biographical information on Barnes.

BARNES, Sir William Lethbridge Gorell (1909–   )

Diplomatic service, 1932–39. Offices of War Cabinet, 1939–45. Treasury, 1945–46. Colonial Office, 1948–63. Personal Assistant to Prime Minister, 1946–48. Deputy Under-Secretary, Colonial Office, 1959–63.

Sir William has retained his papers. These are believed to include notebooks containing the notes which he took in pencil of the various cabinet committees of which he was secretary during the period 1939–45; flimsy copies of virtually everything which he personally wrote during the period 1946–48; and a certain number of personal papers for the period whilst in the Colonial Office.

BAROU, Dr. Noah (1889–1955)

Member, Board of Deputies. Chairman, European Executive, World Jewish Congress, in London.

The Institute of Jewish Affairs, 13–16 Jacob's Well Mews, George Street, London W1, has the papers. The collection includes a little material on Palestine and Zionism in relation to displaced persons and the 'Exodus' Incident. His office files are in the World Jewish Congress Archives.

BARRACLOUGH, Brigadier Sir John

Army career.

Some papers have been acquired by the Imperial War Museum.

BARROW, General Sir Edmund (George) (1852–1934)

Served Indian Army, Tirah expedition etc. Chief of Staff, China Expeditionary Force 1900. Secretary, Government of India, Military Department 1901–03. Military Secretary, India Office 1914–17. Member, Council of India, 1917–24.

His official and semi-official papers on army administration, and on the Mesopotamia Commission (1916), together with personal correspondence, diaries etc., 1877—1930, are in the India Office Records. There is also correspondence in the Hardinge papers at Cambridge University Library, including his note on the defence of Mesopotamia, 16 March 1915, and a note on action to be taken in the event of war with Persia.

BARTHOLOMEW, General Sir William Henry (1877—1962)

Director of Recruiting and Organisation, War Office, 1927—28. Commandant, Imperial Defence College 1929—31. Chief of General Staff, India 1934—37. GO C-in-C Northern Command York 1937—40.

One box of his papers has been deposited in the Liddell Hart Centre for Military Archives. It includes papers relating to operations in Palestine, especially the third Battle of Gaza 1917—18, miscellaneous correspondence, including letters from Chetwode to Wigram, India 1935 and Northern Command and Civil Defence papers. A list is available (NRA 23061).

BARTON, Robert Childers (b 1881)

MP (Sinn Fein), Wicklow West, 1918—22.

Since the entry in *Sources*, Vol 3, p 31, some papers have been acquired by the Public Record Office of Ireland, Dublin. The collection mainly concerns the Anglo-Irish Treaty negotiations.

BATTERSHILL, Sir William Denis (1896—1959)

Colonial administrator.

Since the entry in *Sources*, Vol. 2, p 13, an important collection of papers has been deposited in Rhodes House Library (ref Brit Emp s 467). A list is available of the 14 boxes of material (NRA 26072).

BAXTER, Charles William (1895—1969)

Minister, Iceland, 1947—50.

Since the entry in *Sources*, Vol. 2, p 13, a few surviving papers have now been deposited in the Imperial War Museum. These relate only to his early career as a young officer.

BEATTY, 1st E
Admiral of the Fleet Sir David Beatty (1871—1936)

Distinguished naval career. C-in-C, Grand Fleet, 1916—19. 1st Sea Lord, 1919—27.

Since the entry in *Sources*, Vol. 2, p 13, the extensive surviving papers have been placed in the National Maritime Museum.

BEAUMONT, Sir Henry Hamond Dawson (1867—1949)

Chargé d'affaires, Montenegro, 1909—10. Counsellor, Constantinople, 1914; Rome, 1915—16. Minister, Venezuela, 1916—23.

Since the entry in *Sources*, Vol. 2, p 14, a microfilm of the autobiography, covering the period 1867—1942, is now in the Imperial War Museum. The autobiography is of particular value for his service at St. Petersburg, Constantinople and in Venezuela.

BEDDINGTON, Brigadier Sir Edward (1884–1966)

Military career. Staff Officer to General Gough during World War I.

One box of his papers is deposited in the Liddell Hart Centre for Military Archives. It includes his memoirs, 1884–1959 which contain an account of the Curragh incident, 1914.

BEHRENS, Sir Leonard (1890–1978)

Liberal Party activist. President, Liberal Party Organisation, 1955–57.

His correspondence and papers have been acquired by the John Rylands University Library of Manchester.

BELCHEM, Major-General Ronald Frederick King (b 1911)

Military career. Chief of Staff to Field Marshal Viscount Montgomery, 1948–50.

His papers are reported to be at the Royal Artillery Institution. His memoirs were published in *All in the Day's March* (Collins, 1978).

BELFIELD, Lieutenant-General Sir Herbert Eversley (1857–1934)

Military career. Director of Prisoners of War, 1914–1920. Responsible for negotiating welfare of British prisoners of war and internees in enemy lands.

The papers relating to the 1st World War have been purchased at Sotheby's by the Imperial War Museum. The collection includes his personal diaries describing conferences on prisoner of war matters held at the Hague and Berne in 1917 and a small folder of correspondence with the Duke and Duchess of Connaught from 1917 and 1918 on the subject of aid to prisoners of war in enemy lands.

BELGRAVE, Sir Charles Dalrymple (1894–1969)

Financial Adviser, Government of Bahrein, 1926–57.

His diaries, mainly relevant to events in Bahrein, 1915–61, have been placed in the Cambridge Middle East Centre, Sidgwick Avenue, Cambridge.

BELL, Sir Gawain Westray (1909–   )

Colonial service, Middle East, Sudan, Palestine, 1938. Lieutenant Colonel, Arab Legion. 1942–45. Secretary General, South Pacific Commission, 1966–70.

Further information is now available since the entry in *Sources*, Vol. 2, p 15. The letters and papers have been promised to Rhodes House Library. There are, for example, about 1000 letters written to his parents (1931–44) and miscellaneous papers relating to Palestine and the Arab Legion (1938–44). Other papers deal with Nigeria and the Sudan.
   The Imperial War Museum has copies of papers given by Bell to the Jordanian National Memorial Museum. These are a series of Orders issued to Arab Legion Officers (*c* 1940–43) which reflect social relations and educational standards etc. in the Legion. Sir Gawain Bell retains photograph albums.

BELL, Gertrude Margaret Lowthian (1868–1926)

Oriental scholar; archaeologist and government official. Oriental Secretary to the High Commissioner of Iraq from 1920.

In addition to the material cited in *Sources*, Vol. 5, p 14, the Royal Geographical Society holds 13 volumes of her notebooks.

BENNETT, Arnold (Enoch) (1867–1931)

Novelist, playwright and man of letters.

The most important collection of his journals is in New York Public Library. Other material can be found in the British Library (ref BM Add Mss 59841), Keele University Library and the Arnold Bennett Museum, Corbridge. The Library of University College, London has four manuscripts of his works, notebooks, correspondence with his agent J. B. Pinker, together with other letters and papers, *c* 1902–31.

BENYON, Major-General Sir William (1866–1955)

Indian army career.

His papers have been deposited in the India Office Library (ref MSS Eur D 830). The collection includes letters, diaries, press-cuttings etc., relating mainly to service on the North-West Frontier and covering the period 1888–1955.

BERKELEY, Sir Ernest James Lennox (1857–1932)

Administrator of the British East Africa Company's Territories, 1891–92. Commissioner and Consul-General, Uganda, 1895–99. Consul-General, Tunis, 1899–1920.

Two lengthy letters to Sir Percy Anderson, 1896, are in the library of the Royal Commonwealth Society. They comment frankly on administrative, political and religious problems in Uganda.

BERKELEY, G. F. (fl 1920s)

Secretary, Peace with Ireland Council.

Miscellaneous papers are in the National Library of Ireland (Ms 10922).

BERNAL, Eileen (fl 1950s–70s)

Pacifist.

Some papers have been deposited in the BLPES (ref Coll Misc 537). They include papers on the history of peace councils, 1950–72, and contain material such as the Dorking Peace Council Annual Report, 1972; Reading and District CND scrapbooks of minutes, press cuttings, etc., 1950–67; Reading Peace Council correspondence, 1972; and correspondence, reminiscences and reports by individuals involved with various local peace councils. The minute book of the London Federation of Peace Councils, 1938–40, and related material is held, as are reminiscences etc. by members of national peace councils in Greece, Guyana, South Africa, New Zealand and Vietnam.

BERNAL, John Desmond (1901–71)

Scientist; writer on science and society; Marxist publicist. Fellow of The Royal Society. Professor of Physics, Birkbeck College, University of London, 1937–63; Professor of Crystallography, 1963–8. Foreign member, Academy of Sciences, USSR, 1958. Awarded Lenin Peace Prize, 1953. Author of *The Social Function of Science* (1939), *Marx and Science* (1952), *Science in History* (1954), etc.

Since the entry in *Sources*, Vol. 5, p 16, the papers cited as being at Birkbeck College, were transferred during 1979 to Cambridge University Library on permanent loan.

BERNARD, Sir Charles Edward (1837—1901)

Indian Civil Service. Commissioner, Central Provinces, 1874—77. Chief Commissioner, Burma, 1880—87. Secretary, Revenue, Statistics and Commerce Department, India Office, 1888—1901.

His letter book 1880—85, as Chief Commissioner of British Burma, is in the India Office Library (ref Mss Eur D 912). It consists of semi-official correspondence *re* commercial relations with the Court of King Thibaw.

BEST, Captain Sigismund Payne (fl 1930s)

British Intelligence Officer at centre of the Venlo incident (1939).

The material at the Imperial War Museum comprises reports on the 1939 Venlo incident, his subsequent imprisonment at Buchenwald and Dachau and post-war correspondence with Generals Halder and von Falkenhausen. Other material is believed to be at the Intelligence Corps Museum, Ashford, Kent.

BICKFORD, Colonel Wilfred Annesley (d 1978)

Army career.

Some papers are in the Imperial War Museum. The collection includes an account of the British Mission to Czechoslovakia in 1938 to observe the enforcement of the Munich agreement and papers relating to his subsequent service in Burma.

BIGGER, F. J. (0000—00)

Irish Nationalist.

Some papers are in the National Library of Ireland. These include letters received from Casement, Stopford Green, Sean Rooney, Dorothy Stopford, etc. *c.* 1910—27.

BILNEY, Air Vice-Marshal Christopher Neil Hope (1898—   )

Served World I, 1914—18; North Sea and Middle East; India, 1925—30; Air Ministry, World War II. Air Officer in Charge of Administration, Headquarters Maintenance Command, 1949—51. Director-General, Technical Service, Air Ministry, 1951—52. President, Ordnance Board, Ministry of Supply, 1953—54.

The papers at the Imperial War Museum, cited in *Sources*, Vol. 2, p 18, are in fact copies, not the originals.

BINNEY, Sir George (1900—1972)

Commercial Attaché, Stockholm, World War II.

Certain papers, including material on blockade busting collected by his biographer, Ralph Barker, are in Churchill College, Cambridge. A list is available (NRA 25825).

BINNEY, Admiral Sir Thomas Hugh (1883—1953)

Deputy Director, Plans Division, Admiralty, 1925—27. Commanded HMS *Hood* 1932—33. ADC to King George V, 1934. Commandant, Imperial Defence College,

1939. Admiral Commanding Orkneys and Shetlands, 1939–42. Governor of Tasmania, 1945–51.

The Imperial War Museum has his papers concerning his service in the Royal Navy, 1899–1943, including material on the role of HMS *Queen Elizabeth* in the Dardanelles campaign (1915); the Peace and War Complements Committee, 1935–36, and the Royal Navy during the Second World War, 1939–42.

BLACKALL, Sir Henry William Butler (1889–   )

Legal career in colonial service. Attorney General, Cyprus, Gold Coast etc. Chief Justice of Trinidad and Tobago 1943–46. Chief Justice of Hong Kong 1946–48. President, West African Court of Appeal, 1948–51.

Some papers are in Rhodes House Library, Oxford. They include correspondence and memoranda on legal matters for the period 1919–50. Access to some of the material is restricted.

BLACKBURNE, Sir Kenneth William (1907–1980)

Colonial service. Director of Information, Colonial Office, 1947–50. Governor, Leeward Islands, Jamaica.

Since the entry in *Sources*, Vol. 2, p 20, his papers have been placed in Rhodes House Library (ref MSS Brit Emp s 460). A list is available (NRA 26249).

BLACKETT, Lord
Patrick Maynard Stuart Blackett (1897–1974)

Scientist and Public Servant.

Since the entry in *Sources*, Vol. 5, p 17, an extensive collection of papers has now been deposited in the Library of the Royal Society by Lady Blackett, the Royal Society and Professor H. Elliot. A list is available (NRA 22627). Lady Blackett retains his diaries of naval service, press cuttings, photographs etc.

Section A of the deposited collection relates to biographical and personal material (106 boxes); Sections B and C to his work as a nuclear physicist. Section D deals with his wartime activities and work on Government committees, 1936–73, and includes files on bombing policy, 1941–46; the anti-U-boat campaign; the Chiefs of Staff Sub-Committee on future weapons and its successors; the Advisory Committee on Atomic Energy and various other committees. Section E relates to Blackett's political activities and includes 10 files on the Gaitskell Group and 12 files on his miscellaneous socialist and Labour Party activities, 1956–64, e.g. with the Fabian Society Science Group, the Labour Party Science and Industry Sub-Committee etc. 13 files cover his work on the Advisory Council on Technology and as Scientific Advisor to the Ministry of Technology, 1963–72. 8 files relate to his appearances before various Labour Party and official committees, e.g. PLP Science Group, 1960–62; Fulton Committee on the Civil Service, 1966–67. 2 folders of press cuttings and printed matter relate to Labour, science and the 1964 General Election. Section F holds 85 files on his science-related interests, assembling notes and working papers, lectures, broadcasts, publications and correspondence. Section G (126 files) deals with his overseas activities relating to science, defence and economic development. Section H (157 files) deals with lectures, broadcasts, publications, 1934–73, by Blackett which are not included in the special subject sections and Section I consists of correspondence not included in other sections.

BLACKETT, Sir Basil Phillott (1882–1935)

Civil servant, specialist on finance and Treasury affairs. Finance Member, Viceroy's Executive Council, India, 1922–28. Director, Bank of England.

Since the entry in *Sources* Vol. 2, p 20, when certain papers could not be traced, an important collection of papers has now been deposited in the India Office Library. The letters and correspondence mainly relate to his period as Finance Member of the Viceroy's Executive Council, 1922–28.

BLENKINSOP, F. W. G. (d 1946)

Colonial civil servant. District Commissioner, Beersheba and Galilee.

The Middle East Centre, St. Antony's College, Oxford has a private memorandum (1944) on the Arab-Jewish conflict in Palestine, which was circulated privately.

BLUNDELL, Sir Michael (1907–   )

Farmer and Politician in Kenya.

The papers have been deposited in Rhodes House Library, Oxford. A list is available (NRA 22652). Among the papers, which cover the period 1948–76 are 7 files (Boxes 25–27) on the Kenya Constitutional Conferences of 1960 and 1962; 10 files (Boxes 28–29) on political and economic affairs in Kenya (1948–72); and 29 files (Boxes 30–33) of press cuttings, 1954–62.

BLYTH, Right Revd. George Francis Popham (d 1914)

Bishop in Jerusalem, 1887–1914.

His papers are in Lambeth Palace Library (ref MSS 2227-37). The collection comprises notes by his daughter for a proposed biography; an index of correspondents; correspondence with successive Archbishops of Canterbury; papers concerning the Church Missionary Society and his dispute with it; and records of the Jerusalem and the East Mission. The main archives of the Jerusalem and the East Mission at the Middle East Centre, St. Antony's College, Oxford, include further papers of Bishop Popham Blyth.

BLYTHE, Ernest (b 1889)

MP (Sinn Fein) Monaghan North, 1918–22. Minister in the 1st and 2nd Dail.

Since the entry in *Sources* Vol. 3, p 48, an extensive collection of his papers has been placed in the Archives Department, University College, Dublin (ref P24). The material relates to a number of Blythe's activities including those in the Irish Volunteers *viz*. agenda for meetings and letters from the secretary (1914–15); the deportation order relating to Blythe (1915); electoral leaflets (1918); and letters he received in gaol (1918–19). Relating to his time in office there are reports, procedures and memoranda of the 1st Dail (Jan–Aug 1921) and the 2nd Dail (Aug 1921–Aug 1922); minutes, reports and correspondence of the Provisional Government (Aug 1922); and correspondence, reports and memoranda submitted by government departments for meetings of the Executive Council of the Cumann na nGaedheal government (1922–32). Correspondence, reports and memoranda on a number of topics are held including the League of Nations (1923–28), the Constitution (Amendment) Committee 1926, the Army Enquiry Committee (1924), the Economic Committee (1928–29); the Imperial Conference (1926) and sub-conferences (1929), and the status of the Governor General (1932). There are papers regarding the organisation and electoral policies of Cumann na nGaedheal and Fine Gael (1927–66); on the Army Comrades' Association (1932–33); the National Guard (1933); the Young Ireland Association (1933); League of Youth (1933–35); on economic and social policy (1932–35); on Ailtiri no hAiseirghe (1942–43); and the Irish Electoral System Reform Society (1968). Personal correspondence (1919–36) received by Blythe as a member of the Dail and Senate is held. A large number of papers relate to his interest in Drama and the Irish language and very full papers relating to the administration of the National Theatre Society Ltd (Abbey Theatre) exist. There are also drafts of his published writings and research notes plus various published journals and press cuttings.

BOOTHBY, Commander Frederick Lewis Maitland (1881–1940)

Pioneer airplane and balloon pilot. Sent on mission to Somaliland to report on feasability of air operations against the Mullah 1914–15. Commanded armoured cars, and concerned with the introduction of the tank.

His papers, 1909–25, not at present listed, are in the Royal Air Force Museum (ref AC 70/1).

BOOTMAN, Air Chief Marshal Sir John Nelson (1901–1957)

Air Officer Commanding Air HQ Iraq 1948–50. Controller of Supplies (Air), Ministry of Supply 1950–53. AO C-in-C, Coastal Command 1953–56.

His unlisted papers, 1922–42 are in the Royal Air Force Museum (ref AC 72/14).

BOURNE, Sir Frederick Chalmers (1891–1977)

Indian Civil Service from 1920. Governor, Central Provinces and Berar, 1946–47; East Bengal, 1947–50.

Since the entry in *Sources*, Vol. 2, p 23, the papers covering the period 1933–71 have now been deposited in the India Office Library (ref Mss Eur E 364). The collection, which includes the papers of Frances, Lady Bourne, includes correspondence, service documents, one volume of a travel journal and press cuttings.

BOWEN, Dr. Edward George (1911–   )

Scientist. Involved in development of radar.

Eleven boxes of his papers on the development of radar (1935–78) have been placed in Churchill College, Cambridge.

BOWRA, Cecil Arthur Verner (1869–1947)

Officiating Inspector-General of Chinese Customs, 1913, 1918–20, 1923. Commander, Newchwang Volunteer Force, South Manchuria, during Boxer Rebellion.

His papers covering both his official career and family matters, are in the Library of the School of Oriental and African Studies. The papers include genealogical material of the Bowra family and a 4-page memorandum of service with the Chinese Maritime Customs, 1923. A list is available (NRA 16588).

BOYD, Lachlan Macpherson (1904–   )

Colonial civil servant. Resident, Buganda, 1947–51. Minister of Local Government, Uganda, 1955–60.

Certain material is available at Rhodes House Library. The collection includes a diary when Resident in Buganda during the 1949 disturbances and a memorandum on these disturbances.

BOYD, Thomas J. L. Stirling (1886—1973)

Lawyer, Chief Justice of Sarawak, 1930—39. Author of *The Laws of Sarawak* (1936).

Various papers covering the years 1918—71 are held by Rhodes House Library. The collection includes account books, correspondence, an unpublished manuscript on the 1939 Sarawak crisis, etc. A list is available (NRA 19633).

BOYLE, Marshal of the Royal Air Force, Sir Dermot Alexander (1904—)

Director-General of Personnel, Air Ministry, 1948—49, Director-General of Manning, Air Ministry, 1949—51; AO C-in-C, Fighter Command, 1953—55. Chief of Air Staff, 1956—59.

The papers have been promised to the Royal Air Force Museum, Hendon.

BOYLE, Sir Edward (1878—1945)

Chairman, Balkan Committee. Hon Treasurer, Serbian Relief Fund, 1914. Acting British Commissioner for Serbia, 1915.

Some papers have been presented to the Brotherton Library, University of Leeds, by Lord Boyle of Handsworth. The collection includes the correspondence of Mary Edith Durham (1863—1944) with Sir Edward Boyle on Balkan affairs (202 items), together with various related papers, 1923—45.

BRABAZON OF TARA, 1st B
John Theodore Cuthbert Moore-Brabazon (1884—1964)

MP (Con) Chatham, 1918—29; Wallasey, 1931—42. Parliamentary Secretary, Ministry of Transport, 1923—4, and 1924—7. Minister of Transport, 1940—1. Minister of Aircraft Production, 1941—2.

Since the entry in *Sources*, Vol. 3, p 54, the papers have been deposited in the Royal Air Force Museum, Hendon (ref AC 71/3, 76/41).

BRADWELL, 1st B
Thomas Edward Neil Driberg (1905—1976)

MP (Ind, then Lab) Maldon, 1942—55; Barking, 1959—74.

His papers, diaries etc are in the Library of Christ Church, Oxford.

BRAND, 1st B
Robert Henry Brand (1878—1963)

Served South Africa, 1902—09. Deputy Chairman, British Mission in Washington, 1917—18. Financial Adviser to Lord Robert Cecil, Paris, 1919; to German Government, 1922. Financial Representative of South Africa, Genoa Conference, 1922. Member of Macmillan Committee on Finance and Industry, 1930—31. Head of British Food Mission, Washington, 1941—44. Treasury Representative in Washington, 1944—46. Chairman, British Supply Council in North America, 1942, 1945—46. United Kingdom Delegate, Bretton Woods and Savannah Conferences.

Since the entry in *Sources*, Vol. 2, p 27, the papers have been deposited at the Bodleian Library, Oxford. The collection consists of the business papers of the Hon. R. H. Brand and covers his activities from his employment in South Africa, on coming down from Oxford, to his death. There are 182 files held in the same order as Brand himself used, together with additional files of material which Brand did not catalogue.

BRAUND, Sir Henry Benedict Linthwaite (1893—1969)

Indian judicial career. Chairman, enquiry into Burma Riots, 1938—39. Regional Food Commission, Eastern Region, India, 1943—44.

His papers have been placed in the India Office Library (ref Mss Eur D 792). The material includes a volume of press cuttings on the 1938 Burma riots, a transcript copy of Braund's report of the 1943 famine in East India and thee letters from Sir Archibald Cochrane, Governor of Burma, 1936—41, on Indian immigration into Burma.

BRAYNE, Frank Lugard (1882—1952)

Entered Indian Civil Service 1905. Assistant Commissioner in the Punjab 1905—14. Deputy Chief Political Officer, Aleppo, 1918—20. Various posts as Deputy Commissioner etc. in the Punjab. Organiser of 'Gurgaon experiment'. Author and lecturer.

An extensive collection of his papers, comprising diaries, letters, correspondence and printed material, 1900—52, has been deposited in the India Office Library (MSS Eur F 152). The collection numbers 49 boxes and is strongest for the period 1920—46. As well as his books, pamphlets and articles there is important correspondence with Geoffrey Dawson, Lord Ismay, the Military Secretary to Lord Willingdon and with Brayne's uncle, Lord Lugard.

BRENNAN, Joseph (b 1887)

Irish Nationalist. Secretary, Department of Finance, 1923—27.

The papers have been deposited in the National Library of Ireland, but they have not yet been arranged and listed. They consist of a large collection dealing with Brennan's career in the Irish administration from the years prior to 1922 until the late 1950s.

BRIDGEMAN, 1st Vt
William Clive Bridgeman (1864 1935)

Conservative politician and Cabinet Minister. Secretary of State for Home Affairs, 1922—24. 1st Lord of the Admiralty, 1924—29.

Since the entry in *Sources*, Vol. 3, p 58, his personal and political papers, diaries, newscuttings and books, together with papers of his wife, have been placed in Shropshire Record Office.

BRIGGS, Major-General Raymond (1895—   )

Army career. Commander, 2nd Armoured Brigade. GOC I Armoured Division. Director, Royal Armoured Corps, War Office, 1943—47. Member, Tank Board, 1943—46.

The Imperial War Museum holds his diaries, covering his period in command of the 2nd Armoured Brigade, and the 1st British Armoured Division in North Africa, and as Director of the Royal Armoured Corps, 1943–45.

BRISCOE, Robert (d 1969)

Irish politician. Fianna Fail member of Dail, 1927–65. Lord Mayor of Dublin, 1956–57, 1961–62. Jewish Communal Leader, active Revisionist, member of the New Zionist organisation executive.

The National Library of Ireland has a very large collection which includes material on relations between Ireland and Zionist organisations and Israel in the 1940s. His autobiography *For the Life of Me* appeared in 1959. In addition, ten files of his papers are in the Jabotinsky Institute in Israel.

BROADHURST, Brigadier Ronald Joseph Callender (1906–   )

Army career. Deputy Commander, Arab Legion, 1939–47. Equerry to King Abdullah.

The Brigadier has retained relevant papers concerning service in the Arab Legion etc.

BROADWOOD, Lieutenant-General Robert George (1862–1917)

Army career. Brigadier-General, commanding Orange River Colony, 1904–06. Commander, troops in South China, 1906. ADC to the King.

His letters and papers were acquired in 1975 by the National Army Museum.

BROCKWAY, Baron
Archibald Fenner Brockway (1888–   )

Labour politician.

In addition to the material cited in *Sources*, Vol. 3, p 60, Churchill College, Cambridge has acquired further papers.

BROMHEAD, Sir Benjamin Denis Gonville (1900–1981)

Indian career. Political Agent, North Waziristan, 1945–47.

A small collection was given to the India Office Records by his widow (ref MSS Eur D 1005).

BROWN, Brigadier-General E. Craig (fl 1914–1918)

Military career.

The Imperial War Museum has some papers, 1893–1923, including detailed letters and diaries from the Western Front, 1914–17.

BROWN, Vice-Admiral Francis Clifton (1874–1963)

Naval career. Head of Naval Mission to Greece, 1917–19.

The papers were presented to the National Maritime Museum by Mrs. Clifton Brown in 1963. They consist of a continuous run of logs, 1890–1900; diaries, 1890 to 1902; notebooks and loose papers, including some relating to his period as naval attaché in Greece between 1917 and 1919. There are also some comprehensive photograph albums, 1890–1911, but no papers for Brown's World War I service.

BROWNE, Edward Granville (1862–1926)

Professor of Arabic at Cambridge 1902–26. Co-founder of Persia Committee in October 1908 to change the British Government's policy towards Persia and to force Russia to respect the independence of Persia. His co-founder was the traveller and businessman H. F. B. Lynch.

The surviving papers formerly with his son, Sir Patrick Browne, have been deposited in Cambridge University Library. The papers were used by D. McLean in 'English Radicals, Russia and the fate of Persia 1907–13' (*English Historical Review*, vol XCIII April 1978).

BROWNING, Oscar (1837–1923)

Historian, author and teacher.

Since the entry in *Sources*, Vol. 5, p 27, the biography by Ian Anstruther (London, 1983) gives Eastbourne Central Library as the location for these papers.

BRUCE, Admiral Sir Henry Harvey (1862–1948)

Naval career. Commodore and Admiral-Superintendent, HM Dockyard, Rosyth, 1915–20. Promoted Vice-Admiral 1922; Admiral 1926.

Eight volumes of his diaries 1915–20, are in the Naval Historical Library.

BRUCE, Richard Isaac (1840–1924)

Indian civil servant. British Commissioner, Afghan-Waziristan Delimitation Commission, 1894; Waziristan, 1894–95. Author of *The Forward Policy, and its Results*.

His correspondence and papers, 1865–1924, have been acquired by the India Office Library (ref Mss Eur F 163). Most of the papers later than 1900 are those of his son Charles Edward Bruce (1876–1950), of the Indian Political Service. These papers, mainly on the North West Frontier, consist of private and official correspondence, miscellaneous reports, newspaper cuttings, etc.

BRUNDRETT, Sir Frederick (1894–1974)

Scientific Adviser, Ministry of Defence. Chairman, Defence Research Policy Committee, 1954–59.

Two boxes of his papers and lectures were deposited in Churchill College, Cambridge in September 1979. They are concerned mainly with science and defence, 1951–72.

BRUNSKILL, Brigadier George Stephen (1891–   )

Military service, World Wars I and II. Temporary Brigadier and Colonel in Charge of Administration, Palestine.

Copies of his memoirs are in the Imperial War Museum.

BRUNTON, Captain Chisholm Dunbar (1887–   )

Military service. Raised nucleus for the subsequent Arab Legion, 1920. Second Commissioner, Palestine-Syria Boundary Commission, 1921. Liaison Officer to High Commissioner, Palestine and GOC Egypt, 1920–22.

The Middle East Centre, St. Antony's College, Oxford, has copies of his reports on disturbances in Palestine and Jordan, intelligence data and suggestions. He retains copies of the articles he wrote about Palestine.

BUCHANAN, Sir George Seaton (1869–1936)

Senior Medical Officer, Ministry of Health.

Some papers, 1859–1908, are in the Public Record Office (MH113). They include reports on sanitary arrangements in ships, lodging houses and private dwellings and investigations into outbreaks of infectious diseases.

BUCHER, General Sir Roy (1895–1980)

Indian army career. GOC-in-C, Eastern Command, 1946–47. Chief of Staff, India, 1947. C-in-C, Army of India, 1948–49.

Since the entry in *Sources*, Vol. 2, p 32, an important collection of papers has been deposited in the National Army Museum (ref Acc 7901–87). A list is available (NRA 23387). The collection includes papers and correspondence relating to his career in the Indian Army and Army of India, 1945–49, and his post-retirement activities, to 1977. Papers relating to his active service include correspondence, maps, reports, etc. including a typescript 'Report on the Disturbances in Calcutta commencing 16 August 1946', a typescript Army HQ India Operation Instructions, etc. *re* Kashmir, 1947–48, correspondence with Attlee *re* Kashmir, 1949–50; secret correspondence, orders and reports *re* situation in Hyderabad Mar- Sept 1948. Correspondence files 1948–72 include letters from Nehru (1949–64), Philip Noel-Baker MP (1949–65), Lord Slim (1949–58) and Sardar Patel, Nehru's Deputy (1949–70). Post-retirement papers include material on Bucher's work in the British Legion, 1968–77.

BUCKNALL, Lieutenant-General G. C. (fl 1939–1945)

Military career.

An important collection of papers in the possession of his children has been photocopied by the Imperial War Museum. The collection includes the private diary which he kept when in command of the 5th Division in Sicily and Italy in 1943 and of XXX Corps in England and Normandy from January to August 1944 and a set of XXX Corps intelligence summaries for the first vital weeks of the Normandy campaign. Among his papers there are also letters from Field Marshal Montgomery and Generals Browning and Horrocks about Bucknall's controversial removal from the command of XXX Corps in August 1944.

BULL, Sir William James, 1st Bt (1863–1931)

MP (Con) Hammersmith, 1900–18; Hammersmith South, 1918–29.

Further to *Sources*, Vol. 3, pp 67–8, Churchill College, Cambridge has now acquired a collection of correspondence and papers. *See* NRA 26806.

BULLARD, Sir Reader William (1885–1976)

Levant Consular Service, from 1906. Military Governor, Baghdad, 1920. Minister, Saudi Arabia, 1936–39; Iran, 1939–44. Ambassador, Iran, 1944–46.

Since the entry in *Sources*, Vol. 2, p 32, the Middle East Centre, St. Antony's College, Oxford has acquired his notes on the method of recruitment to the Levant Consular Service, and an account of a meeting between Ibn Saud and Lord Belhaven in a letter of 19 Jan 1938.

BURNETT, Admiral Sir Robert Lindsay (1887—1959)

Naval career.

The surviving papers have been photocopied by the Imperial War Museum, through the good offices of his niece, Mrs. A. Boglan. The collection includes an unpublished memoir covering the Admiral's life up to the outbreak of war in 1914, but its strength lies in the records of his commands of the Home Fleet Destroyer Flotillas and then the 10th Cruiser Squadron in defence of convoys to North Russia between September 1942 and December 1943. There are a number of particularly interesting documents, including war correspondents' despatches and letters from fellow officers, relating to the passage of Convoy PQ18 to Russia, the action with the German pocket battleship *Hipper* on 31 December 1942 and the sinking of the *Scharnhorst*, when Vice-Admiral Burnett was flying his flag in HMS *Belfast*, off the North Cape on 26 December 1943.

BUSCARLET, Air Vice-Marshal Sir Willett Amalric Bowen- (1898—1967)

Air career. Air Commodore, 1943. Retired with rank of Air Vice-Marshal, 1946.

An unlisted collection of his papers covering the period 1916 to 1963 is in the Royal Air Force Museum (ref AC75/12).

BUSTEED, Air Commodore H.R. (1887—1965)

Air force career.

An unlisted collection of papers, covering the period 1912 to 1964 is in the Royal Air Force Museum, Hendon (ref AC 73/16-17).

BUTLER OF SAFFRON WALDEN, Baron
Richard Austen Butler (1902—1982)

MP (Con) Saffron Walden, 1929—65. Parliamentary Under-Secretary, India Office, 1932—37. Parliamentary Secretary, Ministry of Labour, 1937—38. Parliamentary Under-Secretary of State, Foreign Office, 1938—41. President of the Board (later Minister) of Education, 1941—45. Minister of Labour, 1945. Chancellor of the Exchequer, 1951—55. Lord Privy Seal, 1955—59. Secretary of State for Home Affairs, 1957—62. 1st Secretary of State and Deputy Prime Minister, 1962—63. Secretary of State for Foreign Affairs, 1963—64.

The papers, cited in *Sources*, Vol. 3, p 71, have now been placed in the Wren Library, Trinity College, Cambridge, to whom enquiries should be addressed.

BUTLER, Major-General Stephen Seymour (1880—1964)

Military career. Head of Naval Intelligence, Constantinople, 1919—20; Military attaché, Bucharest, 1923—26. GOC, 48th Division, Territorial Army, 1935—39. Head of Military Mission to Turkey, 1939—40; Ethiopia, 1941—43.

In addition to the papers described in *Sources*, Vol. 2, p 35, the Imperial War Museum now holds a microfilm of his memoirs. These cover his service as an intelligence officer at Gallipoli and in France, 1915—18; with naval intelligence at Constantinople, 1919—20, as head of the British Military Mission to Turkey, 1939—40 and as a liaison officer in Africa, 1941—45.

BUTTERFIELD, Sir Herbert (1900–1979)

Historian.

His correspondence and papers have been acquired by Cambridge University Library.

BUXTON, Clarence Edward Victor (1892–1967)

Colonial administrator. Assistant District Commissioner, East Africa, 1919. District Officer, Kenya, 1922. Acting District Commissioner, Palestine, 1938–40.

The collection in eight boxes at Rhodes House, Oxford, relates mainly to Kenya and Zanzibar, although there is some material on Palestine about the rebellion in the Gaza-Beersheba division at the time of the Munich Conference (September 1938), the changing attitude of the people since then and the counter-revolutionary movement.

BUZZARD, Rear-Admiral Sir Anthony Wass (1902–1972)

Naval career. Director of Naval Intelligence, 1951–54.

A collection of papers, not at present available, has been deposited in Churchill College, Cambridge. The collection (64 boxes) comprises conference papers on deterrents and disarmament (1960s) and one file of his early naval papers.

CAINE, Sir Sydney (1902–   )

Assistant Under-Secretary, Colonial Office, 1944–47; Deputy Under-Secretary, 1947–48. Third Secretary, Treasury, 1948. Head of UK Treasury and Supply Delegation, Washington, 1949–51. Director, London School of Economics, 1957–67.

Sir Sydney has retained his papers. No details are available.

CALLWELL, General Sir Charles Edward (1859–1928)

Served Afghan, Turko-Greek and Boer Wars. Director of Military Operations, War Office, 1914–15.

George Cassar states in *Kitchener, Architect of Victory* that Callwell's papers could not be traced. His letters to Kitchener, 1915–16, are in the Public Record Office.

CAMINADA, Jerome Charles (fl 1940s–1950s)

Journalist. *The Times* correspondent, with special service in Palestine, 1946, South Africa, etc.

The Times archive holds various papers including press cuttings, correspondence, a file on Palestine (1945–48) and other material on South Africa, Egypt and *The Times* foreign department.

CAMPBELL, Vice-Admiral Gordon (1886–1953)

MP (Con) Burnley, 1931–5.

Since the entry in *Sources*, Vol. 3, p 76, a number of records bearing on service in Q-ships in World War I have been placed in the Imperial War Museum.

CAMPBELL, James Duncan (1833—1907)

Commissioner of Chinese Customs.

Over 1400 items of his correspondence are with the Sir Robert Hart papers in the Library of the School of Oriental and African Studies.

CAMPION, 1st B
Gilbert Francis Montriou Campion (1882—1958)

Clerk of the House of Commons, 1937—48. Clerk of the Consultative Assembly, Council of Europe, 1949. Editor of *May's Parliamentary Practice* (14th and 15th editions).

His papers are in the House of Lords Record Office (ref Hist Coll 259). The collection, in 20 boxes, covers the period 1906—58. It includes his papers as secretary to the Bryce Conference on Reform of the House of Lords, 1917 and Speaker Lowther's Conference on Devolution 1919, notes and drafts for his publications, parliamentary diaries, diary and papers of an official tour of the Commonwealth Parliaments 1948—9 and papers of his secretaryship at the Council of Europe. There are also copies of Lord Campion's articles and lectures and some papers relating to the Inter-Parliamentary Union and the History of Parliament Trust. The collection was deposited by T. R. Chester, Esq, attorney to Lady Campion, in 1978.

CARADON, 1st B
Sir Hugh Mackintosh Foot (1907—   )

Diplomatic career. Assistant British Resident, Transjordan, 1939—42. Served British Military Administration, Cyrenaica, 1943. Colonial Secretary, Cyprus, 1943—45; Jamaica, 1945—47. Chief Secretary, Nigeria, 1947—51. Governor, Jamaica, 1951—57; Cyprus, 1957—60. Ambassador, United Nations, 1961—62. Minister of State for Foreign and Commonwealth Affairs and UK Permanent Representative, United Nations, 1964—70.

Rhodes House Library, Oxford, holds a tape-recording and transcript of an interview with Lord Caradon, relating to his colonial service including the period in Palestine. He retains no papers, but his memoirs *A Start in Freedom* appeared in 1964.

CAROE, Sir Olaf Kirkpatrick (1892—1981)

Indian Civil Servant. Foreign Secretary, Government of India. Governor, North West Frontier Province, 1946—47.

His papers including material relating to his Governorship of the North West Frontier Province, 1946—47, have been acquired by the India Office Records.

CARR, Sir Frederick Bernard (b 1893)

Colonial civil servant. Chief Commander, Eastern Provinces, Nigeria, 1943. Chief Secretary, Eritrea, 1949—50.

Reminiscences of his service covering the period 1919—49 in Nigeria, are in Rhodes House Library, Oxford.

CARR SAUNDERS, Sir Alexander (1886—1966)

Social scientist and academic. Director, London School of Economics.

A small collection of his papers, consisting of engagement diaries, address books and notebooks, 1945—65, has been deposited with the BLPES (ref Coll Misc 549).

CARTER, Air Commodore David William Frederick Bonham- (1901—)

Air career. Officer Commanding, No. 45 Wing, RAF Dorval, PQ, Canada. AOC, RAF, Hong Kong, 1951—53. Retired, 1953.

An unlisted collection of papers, covering the period 1885 to 1971 is in the Royal Air Force Museum, Hendon (ref. AC 74/13, 75/6). The collection covers his service with the Royal Canadian Air Force, 1940—43 and with No 5 (Bomber) Group, 1943—45.

CARTER, Sir Edgar Bonham- (1870—1956)

Legal Secretary, Sudan, 1899—1917. Senior Judicial Officer, Baghdad, 1917. Judicial Adviser, Mesopotamia, 1919—21.

The Middle East Centre, St. Antony's College, Oxford, has a file of Bonham-Carter's official memoranda, and notes etc., relating to Palestine and Mesopotamia (1919—21). The Sudan Archive, School of Oriental Studies, University of Durham, has some papers about Bonham-Carter's service in the Sudan.

CARTER, Sir Maurice Bonham- (1880—1960)

Private Secretary to Asquith, 1910—16. Assistant Secretary, Ministry of Reconstruction, 1917; Air Ministry, 1918.

Family correspondence and other papers for the period 1890—1955, are reported to be at Hampshire Record Office.

CARTER, Sir Richard Henry Archibald (1887—1958)

Private Secretary to Secretary of State for India, 1924—27. Assistant Secretary, Indian Statutory Commission, 1927—30. Secretary-General, Round Table Conference, 1930—31. Assistant Under-Secretary, India Office, 1936. Permanent Secretary, Admiralty, 1936—40. Chairman, Board of Customs and Excise, 1942—47. Permanent Under-Secretary, India, 1947. Joint Permanent Under-Secretary, Commonwealth Relations, 1948. Chairman, Monopolies and Restrictive Practices Commission, 1949—53.

Since the entry in *Sources*, Vol. 2, p 40, some papers have been located in the India Office Library (ref MSS Eur C 200). The material, acquired in 1967, appears to consist mainly of notes on the powers of the Secretary of State for India and the Council of India.

CASEMENT, Sir Roger David (1864—1916)*

Consular official and Irish patriot. Entered the British consular service in 1892. Member of the Irish National Volunteers, 1913. Visited Berlin as a propagandist for Irish nationalism, 1914. Executed for treason by the British Government, 1916.

In addition to the information cited in *Sources*, Vol. 5, p 34, his letters to Fritz Pincus (1896—1915) have been acquired by Trinity College, Dublin.

*Casement's knighthood was withdrawn in 1916.

CASSELL, Sir Ernest Joseph (1852—1921)

Banker, financier and philanthropist.

One box of xerox material and a microfilm of his correspondence with Churchill and Haldane, 1909—13, is in Churchill College, Cambridge. Special conditions of access apply.

CAVE, 1st Vt
Sir George Cave (1856—1928)

Cabinet minister. Secretary of State for Home Affairs, 1916—19. Lord Chancellor, 1922—24, 1924—28.

Reference should now be made to the 62 volumes of correspondence and papers, covering the period 1859—1932 in the British Library (Add MSS 62455-62516).

CAWSTON, George

Imperialist. Confidant of Cecil Rhodes.

A collection of papers has been acquired by Rhodes House Library.

CECIL, Lord Edward (1867—1918)

Served diplomatic mission to Abyssinia 1897. Military Governor of the Transvaal. Agent General, Sudan Government. Director of Intelligence, Cairo. Financial Adviser to the Egyptian Government, 1912—18.

Many of his papers disappeared in Cairo after his death. However, an important collection of his family and official papers can be found with the Cecil-Maxse papers deposited in Kent Archives Office. His service in Egypt, particularly during the period between Kitchener's suspension and the appointment of Sir Henry McMahon as High Commissioner, is the best documented of his activities. Very little material survives among the Cecil family archives at Hatfield House, except for some family letters and two volumes of papers concerning the siege of Mafeking.

CHAMBERLAIN, George Digby (1898—   )

Colonial civil servant. Assistant Chief Secretary, Northern Rhodesia, 1939. Colonial Secretary, The Gambia, 1943—47; Acting Governor, 1943—44. Chief Secretary, Western Pacific High Commission, 1947—52.

His papers as Chief Secretary of the Western Pacific High Commission were acquired by Rhodes House Library in 1968.

CHAPLIN, Sir (Francis) Drummond (1866—1933)

Correspondent of *The Times* at Johannesburg 1897—98, for *Morning Post* at St Petersburg 1899—1900. Administrator of Southern Rhodesia 1914—23, Northern Rhodesia 1921—23. Director of the British South Africa Company.

An extensive collection of his papers is housed in the National Archives of Zimbabwe. His general correspondence, 1896—1932, consisting of 3433 folios, deals mainly with political affairs in South Africa and Rhodesia. Correspondents include Sir Walter Hely-Hutchinson, C. D. Rudd, Sir Gilbert Parker, Rudyard Kipling, Sir Percy Fitzpatrick, Baron Ampthill, Lord Selborne, Col. Sir Charles Crewe, Sir L. Wallace, Sir Philip Wrey, V. Stent, Lord Buxton, Sir Charles Coghlan, General Jan Smuts, Sir James McDonald and Sir John Chancellor. Chaplin's correspondence with

Major the Hon. W. L. Bagot (1906—25), 216 folios, covers labour on the Rand, the Maritz Rebellion, comments on Britain during the War, the extent of German financial interests in wartime South Africa etc. Other major series of correspondence can be found with Viscount Buxton, G. G. Dawson, Sir George Farrar, P. L. Gell, etc.

CHAPMAN, Air Chief Marshal Sir Ronald Ivelaw (1899—   )

AOC No. 38 Group, 1945—46. C-in-C, Indian Air Force, 1950—51. AOC-in-C, Home Command, 1952. Deputy Chief of the Air Staff, 1952—53; Vice-Chief of the Air Staff, 1953—57.

Photocopies of his papers are available at the Imperial War Museum. They include a 45-page transcript extract from his memoirs covering his service in the RFC in France, 1914—18; in the RAF in the inter-war years, including the period in Afghanistan; and his experience as a POW in Germany during World War II.

CHARLES, Major-General Sir Richard Henry Havelock (1858—1934)

Medical career. President, Medical Board. Medical Adviser to Secretary of State for India.

His 1885 diary, whilst with the Afghan Boundary Commission, is at the Wellcome Institute Library (ref MS 1551).

CHATER, Major-General Arthur Reginald (1896—1979)

Served European War, 1914—18. Senior Royal Marines Officer, East Indies, 1931—33; Home Fleet, 1935—36. Commander, Sudan Camel Corps, 1927—30; Somaliland Camel Corps, 1937—40. Military Governor and Commander, British Somaliland, 1941—43. Director of Combined Operations, India and South East Asia, 1944—45.

The remaining papers in private hands, cited in *Sources*, Vol. 2, p 43, were given on the General's death to the Liddell Hart Centre for Military Archives, King's College, London. Most of this material related to Somaliland and the Sudan, 1928—77.

CHESHIRE, Air Chief Marshal Sir Walter (Graemes) (1907—1978)

Air force career. AOC, French Indo-China, 1945—46. AOC, Gibraltar, 1950—52. AOC, RAF Malta, and Deputy C-in-C, (Air) Allied Forces, Mediterranean. Air Member for Personnel, Ministry of Defence, 1964—65.

His memoir of the Allied Disarmament Mission in Saigon in 1945, entitled *The Gremlin Task Force*, was acquired by Churchill College, Cambridge in April 1979.

CHILDERS, (Robert) Erskine (1870—1922)

Author and Irish politician. Author of works on military affairs and on Home Rule. Secretary to the Irish delegation at the Treaty negotiations, 1921.

In addition to the material in the National Library of Ireland, cited in *Sources*, Vol. 5, p 36, the Imperial War Museum has acquired his World War I diaries, through the good offices of Andrew Boyle. The first four of the eight diaries describe in vivid detail the problems of early naval aviation.

CHILTON, Lieutenant-General Sir Maurice Somerville (1898—1956)

Served European War, 1916—18, and War of 1939—45. Chief of Staff, 2nd Army, and Deputy Adjutant-General, 21 Army Group, British Liberation Army, 1944—46. Director of Air, War Office, 1946—48. COC-in-C, Anti-Aircraft Command, 1953—55. Quartermaster-General. 1955—56.

Since the entry in *Sources*, Vol. 2, p 45, Lady Chilton has deposited in the Imperial War Museum the official accounts of operations in 2nd Army and 21 Army Group, 1944—45. Lady Chilton had earlier reported no surviving papers.

CHRISTISON, General Sir Alexander Frank Philip, 4th Bt (1893—   )

C-in-C, Allied Land Forces, South East Asia, 1945. Allied Commander, Netherlands East Indies, 1945—46.

In addition to *Sources*, Vol. 2, p 46, the Imperial War Museum also has a typescript copy (217 pp) of his memoirs, written in 1980. A further copy of this is held in Churchill College, Cambridge.

CILCENNIN, 1st Vt
James Purdon Lewes Thomas (1906—1960)

MP (Con) Hereford, 1931—55. 1st Lord of the Admiralty, 1951—56.

Since the entry in *Sources*, Vol. 3, p 89, some papers, *c* 1950—59 have been placed in Dyfed Record Office (Carmarthen). A list is available (NRA 24422).

CLARK, C. D. Le Gros

Colonial civil servant.

His correspondence as Chief Secretary, Sarawak, for the period 1941—59, covering such questions as internment and murder, is in Rhodes House Library.

CLARK, Sir Ernest (1864—1951)

Assistant Under-Secretary, Ireland, 1920—31. Secretary, Northern Ireland Treasury, 1921—25. Member, Australian Economic Mission, 1928—29; Joint Exchequer Board, Great Britain and Northern Ireland, 1930. Governor, Tasmania, 1933—45.

In addition to the information given in *Sources*, Vol. 2, p 46, some papers are with the Royal Society of Tasmania. The papers fall into two groups. Sir Ernest's personal papers, covering the period 1927—1945, consisting of letters, speeches and notices of appointment; and his notes and primary sources which he accumulated because of his interest in Tasmanian history. Applications to use these papers should be sent to the Council of the Royal Society of Tasmania.

CLARK, Sir George (1890—1979)

Historian. President of the British Academy.

His papers relating to *De Werwelwind* were presented to the British Library by Sir George in 1976 (Add Mss 59779). *De Werwelwind* was a monthly wartime magazine edited by Sir George of which 23 numbers were issued and dropped by the RAF over the Netherlands. The main collection of papers is reported to be in the Bodleian Library, Oxford.

CLARK, Sir William Henry (1876–1952)

High Commissioner for Basutoland, Bechuanaland and Swaziland 1934–39.

Correspondence, papers, despatches and memoranda are in the National Archives of Zimbabwe. His correspondence (109 folios, 1934–39) deals mainly with the administration of the High Commission territories. His memoranda include 'Progress in the High Commission territories, January 1935 to January 1940' and 'Notes on the negotiations for transfer to the Union Government of the High Commission territories'.

CLARKE, Major-General Sir Edward Montagu Campbell (1885–1971)

Director of Artillery, 1938–42; Director-General, 1942–45.

In addition to his own papers at the Imperial War Museum, cited in *Sources*, Vol. 2, p 47, an extensive private correspondence from 1937 onwards can be found in the papers of Brigadier G. MacLeod Ross, also held by the Imperial War Museum.

CLARKE, Sir Percy Selwyn Selwyn (1893–1976)

Colonial administrator and civil servant.

Since the entry in *Sources*, Vol. 2, p 47, Rhodes House Library has acquired an important collection of papers. A list is available (NRA 26286).

CLAUSON, Sir Gerard Leslie Makins (1891–1974)

Colonial Office service. Assistant Under-Secretary, Colonial Office, 1940–51.

Some World War II diaries (in shorthand) are reported to remain with Mr. Oliver Clauson (son), Nafferton Lodge, 12 High Road, Loughton, Essex. Other official papers were returned to the Foreign and Commonwealth Office.

CLAYTON, Brigadier Sir Iltyd Nicholl (1886–1955)

Military career. Adviser on Arab Affairs, Minister of State, Cairo, 1943–45. Head of British Middle East Office, 1945–48. Minister, Cairo, 1947–48.

Some papers, formerly with his daughter, Mrs. J. C. B. Gosling, of North Court, Abingdon, have now been deposited with the Middle East Centre, St. Antony's College, Oxford.

CLEARY, John H. (fl 1920s)

Irish Nationalist.

His papers, including correspondence of Eamon de Valera, Eamon Donnelly and others concerning the organisation of Cumann na Poblachta and Sinn Fein, 1922–23, are in the Public Record Office of Ireland, Dublin.

CLITHEROW, Lieutenant-Colonel John Bourchier Stracey (1853–1931)

Army career. Took part in the Jameson Raid.

His journal of the Jameson Raid, August 1895–February 1896, is in the National Army Museum (*see* NRA 18641).

CLOW, Sir Andrew (1890—1957)

Indian Civil Service. Deputy Secretary, Government of India, 1936—38. Governor of Assam, 1942—47. UK representative on UN Economic Commission for Asia and Far East, 1947—48. Member, Royal Commission on Labour in India. 1929—31.

The material at the Cambridge Centre for South Asian Studies includes a personal and detailed transcript diary kept while on the Royal Commission on Labour in India, 1929—30. Access to the collection is restricted.

CLWYD, 1st B
Sir John Herbert Roberts, 1st Bt (1863—1955)

MP (Lib) Denbighshire West, 1892—1918.

Since the information in *Sources*, Vol. 3, pp 93—4, certain papers for the period 1878—1918, mainly concerning temperance, have been deposited in Clwyd Record Office.

COAD, Major-General Basil Aubrey (1906—1980)

Army career. Commanded 130 Infantry Brigade, 1944—46; formed and commanded 27 Infantry Brigade, 1948—51.

The Imperial War Museum has some papers, relating to his commands in North-West Europe, 1944—45, and in Korea 1950—51.

COEN, Sir Terence Creagh (1903—1970)

Indian Civil Service, 1927—47.

Some letters home from Sir Terence, for the years 1928—30, have been presented to the India Office Library by Mrs. Y. C. Snell (ref MSS Eur D 845). They contain candid and amusing comments on his experiences as a District Officer in the Punjab. Also included are two typescript copies of his book *The Indian Political Service: a study in indirect rule* (London 1971).

COGHILL, Sir (Marmaduke Nevill) Patrick Somerville, 6th Bt (1896—   )

Military service. World War I, Iraq and Turkey; World War II, in Middle East. Colonel, Arab Legion, Jordan, 1952—56.

Sir Patrick has given his papers to the Imperial War Museum and the Middle East Centre at St. Antony's College, Oxford. The Middle East Centre has copies of his unpublished autobiography *Before I Forget*; diary and notes, 1941—45; and two volumes of *Middle East Wartime Jottings*. The Imperial War Museum has copies of the two diaries *Before I Forget* and *The War Diary of Lt. Col. Sir Patrick Coghill, Bt., R.A., August 1941—July 1945*.

COHEN OF BIRKENHEAD, 1st B
Henry Cohen (1922—1977)

Professor of Medicine, University of Liverpool, 1934—65. Public servant. Chairman, Central Health Service Council, etc.

A collection of his papers has been deposited with the University Archives, Senate House, Liverpool, by Professor A. B. Semple (ref D 200). The papers, in the first consignment, include publications and reports by Lord Cohen and by other people

(1932–71) largely relating to Liverpool University; miscellaneous biographical material, 1957–70; miscellaneous correspondence, 1930–40; correspondence relating to the Medical Advisory Committee, 1942–43; Lectureships, 1969–72; the Chair of Medicine at Liverpool, (1934, 1965) and press cuttings. A later consignment contains much personal material relating to Lord Cohen's various honours, peerage, etc.

COHEN, R. A. Kelf- (1895–)

Under-Secretary, Ministry of Fuel and Power, 1946–55.

His unpublished autobiography is in BLPES (ref Coll Misc 677).

COLLIER, Air Marshal Sir Alfred Conrad (1895–)

Air attaché USSR, 1934–37. Head of British Military Mission, 1941.

His papers have been acquired by the Liddell Hart Centre for Military Archives, King's College, London.

COLLINS, Jesse (1831–1920)

MP (Lib) Ipswich 1880–86; (Lib Un) Birmingham Bordesley, 1886–1918. Parliamentary Secretary, Local Government Board, 1886; Parliamentary Under-Secretary of State, Home Office, 1895–1902.

In addition to the information cited in *Sources*, Vol. 3, p 98, his journal of a tour in India, September 1901–January 1902, is in the British Library (Add Mss 58773).

COLLINS, Michael (1890–1922)

Irish Republican leader. MP (Sinn Fein) Cork South, 1918–22.

In addition to the material cited in *Sources*, Vol. 3, p 98, 3 boxes of papers can be found in University College, Dublin (ref P7). The collection includes files of correspondence (1922) with staff at general headquarters and with brigade commands as well as files of correspondence with contacts in England and Scotland mainly in relation to the purchase of arms (1919–22).

COLVILLE, Sir John (1915–)

Private Secretary to Winston Churchill, 1940–1941, 1943–45. Principal Private Secretary to the Prime Minister, 1951–55.

Since the entry in *Sources*, Vol. 2. p 50, his diaries and notebooks, 1939–50, have been placed in Churchill College, Cambridge. These include his very important wartime diaries and the notebook of the 1953 Bermuda Conference.

COLVIN, Sir Elliot (1861–1940)

Agent to the Governor-General in Rajputana; Chief Commissioner Ajmer-Merwara.

His memoirs, together with miscellaneous papers, 1873–1939, are in the India Office Library.

COMERFORD, James (1855–1931)

Pioneer Socialist. Active in Lanarkshire Miners' Union and the ILP.

The National Library of Scotland has a microfilm of a notebook containing his poems *c.* 1920 on miners' life and work (ref Acc 4870). According to MacDougall, *Labour Records in Scotland* (p. 438), no other papers are known to have survived.

CONGREVE, General Sir Walter Norris (1862–1927)

Military career. C-in-C, Southern Command, 1923–24. Governor and C-in-C, Malta, 1924–27.

Since the entry in *Sources*, Vol. 2, p 50, the papers have been placed with the family archives in Staffordshire Record Office.

COOPER, Professor James (1846–1922)

Church historian. Moderator, General Assembly of the Church of Scotland.

His diaries have been deposited in Aberdeen University Library (ref MSS 2283/1-44). A list is available (NRA 22900). The collection comprises 44 volumes of diary for the years 1867 to 1922, some of which contain enclosures. Volumes 39 and 40 cover his term as Moderator of the General Assembly of the Church of Scotland, May 1917–May 1918. The diaries were used by H. J. Wotherspoon in *James Cooper, a memoir* (London, 1926).

COOPER, Selina Jane (1868–1946)

Suffragist. Active in the women's movement in Lancashire and the North West.

A collection of papers has been acquired by Lancashire County Record Office (ref DDX 1137). A list is available (NRA 20902). The collection, which was used by Jill Liddington in *One Hand Tied Behind Us*, includes material on the Clitheroe branch of the National Union of Womens Suffrage Societies, printed reports and pamphlets, correspondence, photographs, certificates and press cuttings. The correspondents include W. H. Beveridge, Maurice Bonham Carter, Millicent Garrett Fawcett, A. V. Greenwood, J. Keir Hardie, Ramsay MacDonald, J. S. Middleton, the Pankhursts, Pethick Lawrence, Marion Phillips, Hannen Swaffer etc.

COOPER, Sir William Mansfield- (b 1903)

Academic. Professor of Industrial Law, University of Manchester. Vice-Chancellor, 1956–1970. President, Council of Europe Committee of Higher Education and Research, 1966–67. Author of *Outlines of Industrial Law* (1947).

His papers are in the John Rylands University Library of Manchester. A list is available (NRA 20286). The collection consists of numerous minutes, agenda, printed papers, reports etc. of the many public committees and sub-committees on which Sir William served (e.g. Fulbright Commission, Independent Television Association Educational Advisory Council, Western European Union, Council of Europe, etc.).

COPEMAN, F. B. (fl 1930s)

Commander, British Battalion, International Brigade in Spain.

Some material has been loaned to the Imperial War Museum. It includes lists of members of the British Battalion together with diary accounts of the main actions in which he was involved.

CORBETT, Sir Vincent Edwin Henry (1861–1936)

Financial adviser, Egyptian Government 1904–07. Minister Resident, Venezuela, 1907–10; Bavaria and Württemberg 1910–14.

His letter-book, September 1892–October 1893, when Second Secretary in Constantinople is in the Public Record Office (PRO 30/26/124).

CORFIELD, Sir Conrad Laurence (1893–1980)

Indian Political Service, 1925–47. Political Adviser to the Viceroy, as Crown Representative, 1945–47.

The papers were presented by Sir Conrad to the India Office Library (ref Mss Eur D 850). The collection, covering the period 1939–72 comprises three boxes of semi-official correspondence, memoirs, and articles and other papers relating to his interests in Central African affairs.

COURTNEY, Air Chief Marshal Sir Christopher (1890–   )

Air force career.

His letters and papers, covering the period 1907–64, have been placed in the Royal Air Force Museum, Hendon. (ref AC 77/2H, 77/31).

COWLEY, Lieutenant-General Sir John Guise (1905–   )

Military career.

Churchill College, Cambridge has acquired a collection of papers for the period 1935–80. A list is available (NRA 23365). Earlier, the College acquired his memoir of the 1956 Suez operation (NRA 18561).

COX, Sir Christopher (William Machell) (1899–   )

Educational adviser, Secretary of State for the Colonies, 1940–61; Ministry of Overseas Development after 1964.

The papers, which were listed by the Bodleian Library, have been deposited in the Public Record Office.

COX, Major-General Sir Percy Zachariah (1864–1937)

Consul and Political Agent, Muscat, Bushire etc. Foreign Secretary, Government of India, 1914. Acting Minister, Persia, 1918–20. High Commissioner, Mesopotamia, 1920–23.

In addition to the information given in *Sources*, Vol. 2, p 54, there are two of his journals in the archives of the Royal Geographical Society. Both are concerned with Somaliland, where Cox paid visits in 1894 and 1898–99.

CRAWFORD, Colonel Fred (fl 1890s–1910s)

Ulster gun-runner.

Relevant papers are in the Northern Ireland Public Record Office. The collection includes diaries of his visits to New York in 1886, to Cairo in 1890 and to Melbourne in 1892, together with a diary kept during the Boer War whilst serving with the Donegal Artillery, 1900–1; an out-letter book 1906–11 which includes letters to Lord Ranfurley, Benny Spiro and Frank Hall; a letter from Craig to Crawford in 1918 concerning the purchase of the *Mountjoy*; typescript copies of descriptions of the UUF gun-running at Larne, 1914, by Crawford and Captain Agnew; circulars, letters, memoranda, etc. on Unionist affairs, gun-running, etc. 1881–1937.

147

CRAWFORD, Major-General John Scott (1889–1978)

Deputy Director-General of Armaments Production, 1943–45.

Nine boxes of his papers, memoirs, diaries and photographs were acquired by Churchill College, Cambridge, in March 1979. A list is available (NRA 24344).

CRAWFORD, Sir (Walter) Ferguson (1894–1978)

Political Service, Iraq and Sudan. Governor, Northern Province, Sudan 1942–44. Palestine Government, Liaison Officer, 1944–46. Head, British Foreign Office, Middle East Development Division, 1946–60. Director-General, Middle East Association, 1960–64.

The papers (1930–1936) have been placed in the Sudan Archive, University of Durham.

CRAWFURD, Helen

Suffragette and Communist.

Her unpublished autobiography is with the archives of the Communist Party, retained at their head Offices.

CREAGH, Major-General Sir Michael O'Moore (1892–1970)

Military career, World War II. Served UNRRA, 1944–46. Deputy Chief of Greece Mission.

A collection of papers has been given to the Liddell Hart Centre for Military Archives, Kings College, London by Mrs. D. Crichton-Maitland. The collection consists of reports, dispatches and correspondence concerning the involvement of the 7th Armoured Division, 4th Armoured Brigade and XII Corps in North Africa during World War II.

CRESWELL, Captain John (fl 1912–1979)

Naval career.

Four boxes of his naval papers, 1912–70, are in Churchill College, Cambridge. A list is available (NRA 18561).

CRICK, Wilfred

Economic Adviser, Midland Bank. Member, Anglo-American Committee of Enquiry on Palestine, 1946.

The Midland Bank's Archives, c/o The Secretary's Offices, Head Office, Poultry, London EC2P 2BX, contain a large collection of Crick's papers. In addition, there are papers at the Public Record Office (PRO 30/78) relating to the Anglo-American Committee of Enquiry on Palestine, 1946. The unpublished papers comprise the minutes of hearings at Washington DC, Jan–Mar 1946 (PRO 30/78/1-16) and at Jerusalem, March 1946 (PRO 30/78/17-26). A list is available (NRA 23636). Certain private papers are still retained by him.

CRILLY, Daniel (1857–1923)

MP (Irish Nat), Mayo North, 1885–1900. Editor, *United Irishman*; editorial staff, *The Nation* (Dublin).

The papers are in the National Library of Ireland (ref MSS 5937).

CROFT, Sir William Dawson (1892–1964)

Chief Civil Assistant to Minister of State in Cairo, 1943–45. Chairman, Board of Customs and Excise, 1947–55.

In addition to the information given in *Sources*, Vol. 2, p 56, his papers on the economic aspects of Pakistan, 1943, and on the case of the Nawab of Balanpur, 1946, are in the India Office Library.

CROSSMAN, Richard Howard Stafford (1907–1974)

MP (Lab) Coventry East, 1945–Feb 1974. Minister of Housing and Local Government, 1964–6. Lord President of the Council and Leader of the House of Lords, 1966–8. Secretary of State for Social Services, 1968–70. Editor, *New Statesman*, 1970–2.

Since the compilation of the entry in *Sources*, Vol. 3, p 113, the full transcripts of the diaries which he kept as a Cabinet Minister (published in three volumes, 1975, 1976, 1977) have been deposited in the Modern Records Centre, University of Warwick Library. (The transcripts are the primary source, since Crossman had the practice of re-using his tapes.) Transcripts of the earlier diaries which he kept as a backbencher are being edited by Dr. Janet Morgan for selective publication; they will in due course be deposited in the Modern Records Centre. The Centre also holds some miscellaneous political and constituency papers, including a series of press cuttings of articles by Crossman.

CROWE, Sir Colin Tradescant (1913–   )

Diplomat. Chargé d'affaires, Cairo, 1959–61. Deputy UK Representative to the UN 1961–63. Ambassador, Saudi Arabia, 1963–64. High Commissioner, Canada, 1968–70. UK Permanent Representative to UN, 1970–73.

An account (1957–61) of the restoration of relations between Britain and Egypt after the Suez episode is in the Middle East Centre, St. Antony's College, Oxford.

CULLEY, Group Captain Stuart Douglas (1896–1975)

Inspector, Royal Iraq Air Force; British Military Mission to Iraq 1937–40. OC, RAF Palestine and Transjordan 1940–41. Air Ministry 1941–42. Subsequent service in North Africa and Italy 1943–44 and India 1945.

His papers, 1918–74, not at present listed, are in the Royal Air Force Museum (ref AC 74/11, 74/233, 75/17).

CURREY, Admiral Bernard (d 1936)

Naval career. ADC, King George V, 1910–11. Rear Admiral, Home Fleets, Portsmouth, 1913. Senior Naval Officer in Charge, Gibraltar, 1915.

Three volumes of his diaries, 1885–1914, are in the National Maritime Museum.

CURREY, Rear-Admiral H. S. (fl 1914–1918)

Naval career.

His diary account of the visit of the Grand Fleet to the BEF in 1915 is in the Imperial War Museum.

DALE, Sir Henry Hallett (1875–1968)

Fullerian Professor of Chemistry, 1942–46. Member, Scientific Advisory Committee to War Cabinet, Advisory Committee on Atomic Energy etc. Secretary and President, Royal Society.

The Public Record Office has his private office papers (ref CAB 123/213-238) concerning the work of the Scientific Advisory Committee, 1940–1948.

DALLEY, F. W.

Guild Socialist.

A microfilm of his papers has been acquired by Hull University Library. The material on microfilm includes correspondence with G. D. H. Cole, A. R. Orage, S. G. Hobson, H. B. Brougham and W. Laud. There are also papers on the National Guild League, minutes of the National Guild Council, a variety of papers on the producer guilds etc. There is also material on later organisations for workers control, such as the Workers Control League.

DALRYMPLE, Sir Charles, 1st Bt (1839–1916)

MP (Con) Bute, 1868–85; Ipswich, 1886–1906.

Since the entry in *Sources*, Vol 3, p 117, the papers have been deposited in the National Library of Scotland (ref Acc 7228[233-303, 317-324]). The deposit also includes his diaries, 1856–1916.

DANNREUTHER, Tristan (c. 1872–1963)

Naval career. Served Dongola expedition, 1896. Various commands, including the *Intrepid* 1911, the *Mars* 1914–15 and the *Kinfauns Castle* 1915. An Assistant Director of Naval Intelligence 1919–21.

His papers were presented to the National Maritime Museum in 1963 by Rear-Admiral H. E. Dannreuther, except for the letters from Captain Dannreuther to his mother which were presented by Captain H. M. Dannreuther in 1973. The papers include logs, 1887 to 1891, night order books, 1911–17, notebooks 1890–91, diaries 1887–1958 and remark books, 1893–1912. There are numerous letters from Dannreuther to his mother written between 1885 and 1919, except for the years 1909–1914, and official documents relating to the ships under his command.

DANSON, Sir Francis Chatillon (1855–1926)

Businessman and public servant. Chairman, Birkenhead Conservative Association, 1896–1904. President, Liverpool Chamber of Commerce.

His papers are amongst the Danson Family Archives deposited with Merseyside County Archives. They include 11 wet-copy letter-books (1884–1911, 1925–1926), and over 6,000 letters received, 1897–1926, including letters from a number of eminent academics.

D'ARCY, Lieutenant-General John Conyers (1894–1966)

Military service. Officer Commanding, 9th Armoured Division, 1942–44; General Officer Commanding, Palestine, 1944–46.

Mr. C. V. R. D'Arcy (son), Rodings, Bucks Hill, Kings Langley, Herts WD4 9AP, has a collection of letters, which include some relating to service in the Middle

East. Some letters relating to Palestine have been copied by the Middle East Centre, St. Antony's College, Oxford.

DARLING, Ernest William (1905–   )

Leading member, Communist Party of Great Britain.

Four boxes of papers are in the Hoover Institution on War, Revolution and Peace, Stanford University, California. The collection includes writings, correspondence, memoranda, reports, leaflets and clippings, 1920–60, relating to the communist movement, political conditions, labour and housing in Great Britain.

DARLING, General Sir Kenneth Thomas (1909–   )

Military career.

His records of commands in Java (1946) and Cyprus (1958–60) have been placed in the Imperial War Museum. The Museum expects to acquire further papers.

DASH, Sir Arthur (Jules), (1887–1974)

Indian Civil Service. Political Agent, Tripura 1919–27; Secretary to the Government of Bengal in the Education Department 1928–31. Chairman, Public Service Commission, East Pakistan 1947–51.

Some of his papers are in the India Office Library (one file, 285 folios, covering the period 1918–26). Further instalments of his papers and memoirs have also been promised. Other papers and memoirs are in the Cambridge South Asia Archive.

DAVEY, Peter Christmas (fl 1938–1946)

Colonial civil servant. Political Officer, Aden, 1938–46 etc.

Some papers, given to the Middle East Centre, St. Antony's College, Oxford, have been placed on loan in Rhodes House Library (ref MSS Ind Ocn s 214). The collection includes 11 volumes of diaries (with photographs), October 1932–November 1946 concerning Aden and the Red Sea area. There are further desk diaries.

DAVIDSON, Air Vice-Marshal Sir Alexander Paul (1894–1971)

Air Attaché, Poland, Lithuania, Latvia and Estonia 1939–40. Bomber Command 1940–41; HQ Levant 1942. HQ Middle East 1942–43. AOC Iraq and Persia 1944–45.

His papers, not at present listed, are in the Royal Air Force Museum, Hendon (ref AC71/25). They cover the period 1916 to 1954.

DAVIES, Ellis William (1871–1939)

MP (Lib) Caernarvonshire South, 1906–18; Denbigh, 1923–9.

Contrary to the information cited in *Sources*, Vol. 3, p 121, the National Library of Wales does not hold a corpus of his papers, but there are a few of his letters scattered in various collections held by the Library.

DAVIES, Major-General Henry Rudolph (1865–1955)

Commanded 3rd Brigade, 1915–16; 33rd Brigade, 1917; 11th Division, 1917–19; 49th Division, 1919–23.

In addition to the papers cited in *Sources*, Vol. 2, p 62, his travel journals (15 vols. 1887–99) with the Siam Boundary Commission are with the Royal Geographical Society.

DAVIES, Major-General Llewelyn Alberic Emilius Price- (1878–1965)

Served South Africa, 1899–1902, European War, 1914–18. President, Standing Committee of Enquiry regarding Prisoners of War, 1918–19. Assistant Adjutant-General, Aldershot Command, 1920–24. Commanding 145th Infantry Brigade, 1924–27. Assistant Adjutant and Quartermaster-General, Gibraltar, 1927–30.

Since the entry in *Sources*, Vol. 2, p 62, a collection of several hundred letters written to his wife during World War I are in the Imperial War Museum. The collection provides an almost daily commentary on his own career and on the progress of the war. There is material on the battles of the Somme and Third Ypres.

DAVIS, Admiral Sir William Wellclose (1901–   )

Naval career. Director of Under-Water Weapons, 1945–46. Naval Secretary, Admiralty, 1950–52. Vice-Chief of Naval Staff, 1954–57. C-in-C, Home Fleet, and Eastern Atlantic (NATO), 1958–60.

Since the entry in *Sources*, Vol. 2, p 63, his unpublished autobiography (8 vols) has now been placed in Churchill College, Cambridge.

DAVITT, Michael (1846–1906)

Irish nationalist. Founder, Irish Land League.

Since the entry in *Sources*, Vol. 5, p 54, the papers have been placed in Trinity College, Dublin. The papers include a minute book of the Irish Parliamentary Party, 1880–86.

DAVY, Major Anthony Edward Gains (1908–   )

Indian Political Service 1935–47. Political Agent in Bhopal, 1947. Political Adviser to the Nawab of Bhopal, 1947–49.

Certain papers, containing the Nawab's views on relations between India and Pakistan and Davy's assessment of the international strategic position are in the India Office Records (MSS Eur D 1006).

DAWSON, (George) Geoffrey
Geoffrey Robinson (1874–1944)

Journalist. Editor, *The Times*.

The large collection of papers in the care of the family, cited in *Sources*, Vol. 5, p 54, was acquired by the Bodleian Library, Oxford in August 1980. A list is available (NRA 25619). The collection includes correspondence, diaries and other papers for the years 1893 onwards.

DE BUNSEN, Sir Bernard (1907–   )

Educationalist. Director of Education, Palestine, 1946–48. Chancellor, University of East Africa.

Sir Bernard has retained his papers. A description of the material concerning the final days of the British mandate in Palestine is given in Philip Jones *Britain and Palestine 1914–1948* (OUP 1979).

DE BUNSEN, Sir Maurice William Ernest (1852–1932)

Minister, Paris, 1902–05; Portugal, 1905. Ambassador, Spain, 1906–13; Austria-Hungary, 1913–14. Special Ambassador, South America, 1918.

Since the entry in *Sources*, Vol. 2, p 64, important further information is available on his papers. The family papers are in the care of Lady Salisbury-Jones, Mill Down, Hambledon, Portsmouth, Hampshire and have now been listed (NRA 20352). The family papers cover the period *c*. 1826–1945. The papers of most relevance to Sir Maurice are his letters to his family (1857–1931), professional papers (1877–1930), private papers (1852–1934) and letters from diplomatic colleagues and friends (*c*. 1888–1920). There are also the papers of his wife (née Bertha Lowry-Corry) *c*. 1890–1945 and those of her uncle, William Lowry-Corry, Baron Rowton, who was Disraeli's Private Secretary, 1866–81. The Rowton papers cover the period *c*. 1877–1903.

DELANY, Gerald (1885–1974)

Reuters Chief Correspondent, Middle East, 1915–40.

His papers as a correspondent in Cairo are in the Middle East Centre, St. Antony's College, Oxford. The papers include his notes on Egyptian politicians.

DELL, Robert (1865–1940)

Journalist and author. Paris correspondent, *Manchester Guardian*. Subsequently based in Geneva, 1920–21, Berlin, 1922–24, Paris, 1925–32 and Geneva, 1932–37.

Six boxes of his surviving papers have been deposited in BLPES, by his younger daughter Sylvia Blellock (Acc M735). Since Dell died in New York, few papers have survived. The BLPES collection consists mainly of his letters to his daughters on political as well as family affairs, especially for the period of the 1st World War and the early 1920s. There are cuttings and manuscripts and a little other correspondence.

DENHAM, Lady Gertrude Mary

Director, Women's Land Army, 1939–46.

The papers, which are in private hands, have been copied by the Liddell Hart Centre for Military Archives, King's College, London.

DENHAM, Captain Henry Mangles (1897–   )

Naval attaché, Stockholm, 1940–45.

His memoirs and papers relating to service in Stockholm are in Churchill College, Cambridge. A list is available (NRA 25826).

DENING, Lieutenant-General Sir Lewis (1849–1911)

Indian army career.

Papers covering the period 1899–1910 are in the National Army Museum.

DE SALIS, Captain Antony Fane (1897–1976)

Naval service, World Wars I and II.

153

The Imperial War Museum has papers, letters and memoranda *re* the fighting efficiency of destroyers, and covering his naval career (1913–47), including service at Jutland and in China (1930s) and Palestine (1947).

DESCH, Cecil Henry (1874–1958)

Positivist and metallurgist.

A collection of papers has been acquired by Sheffield University Library. A list is available (NRA 17354). The collection includes correspondence, diaries and other papers for the period 1886–1958. There are notebooks of his school and university days and material on visits abroad. Of most political interest is the correspondence (over 1600 items) dealing with Positivism and the history and organisation of science and society.

DEUTSCHER, Isaac (1907–1967)

Polish-born Communist. Expelled after active career in Communist Party of Poland. On staff of *The Economist* and *The Observer* in London. Historian, whose most famous writings include *Stalin: A Political Biography, The Unfinished Revolution: Russia 1917–67* and the three-volume biography of Leon Trotsky.

The papers were acquired in 1977 by the International Institute of Social History, Amsterdam, from his widow, Mrs. Tamara Deutscher of Hampstead, London. The collection contains a comprehensive correspondence with many scholars and politicians, including Heinrich Brandler, E. H. Carr, Pierre Frank, Daniel Guérin, Bertrand Russell and Natalya Sedova-Trotsky. There are also numerous manuscripts of Deutscher's works.

DEVERELL, Field-Marshal Sir Cyril John (1874–1947)

Distinguished military career. Senior commands, World War I, India, etc., Chief of the Imperial General Staff, 1936–37.

Since the entry in *Sources*, Vol. 2, p 67, the Imperial War Museum has acquired his notebook whilst commanding 20th Infantry Brigade in 1916.

DICKENS, Admiral Sir Gerald Charles (1879–1962)

Naval career; active service, World War I. Deputy Director, Plans Division, Admiralty, 1920–22. Director of Naval Intelligence Division, 1932–35. Commander, Reserve Fleet, 1935–37. Naval Attaché, The Hague, 1940. Principal Liaison Officer with Allied Navies, 1940. Flag Officer, Tunisia, 1943–45; Netherlands, 1945–46.

Since the entry in *Sources*, Vol. 2, p 68, the Imperial War Museum now has copies of records of his command of HMS *Harpy* in the Mediterranean, 1914–15.

DICKSON, Rear-Admiral Robert Kirk (1898–1952)

Naval career. Naval Assistant, First Sea Lord, 1933–36. Deputy Director of Plans, Naval Staff, 1943–44. Chief of Naval Information, 1944–46. Commanded aircraft-carrier HMS *Theseus* 1946–48. Head of British Naval Mission to Greece, 1949–51.

Correspondence and other papers have been acquired by the National Library of Scotland (ref MSS 13501–588). The collection of family correspondence, diaries and naval papers includes descriptions of the battles of the Falkland Islands, 1914, Gallipoli, 1915, and Jutland, 1916; life at the Admiralty 1939–40; active service,

1940–42; meeting with Sir Winston Churchill, 1943; and social and diplomatic life in Athens, 1949–51. In addition, his autobiographical notes are in the Scottish United Services Museum.

DILL, Field-Marshal Sir John Greer (1881–1944)

Served South Africa, 1901–02; European War, 1914–18. Director of Military Operations and Intelligence, War Office, 1934–36. Commander, British Forces in Palestine, 1936–37. GOC-in-C, Aldershot Command, 1937–39. Commander, 1st Army Corps in France, 1939–40. Chief of Imperial General Staff, 1940–41. Head of British Joint Staff Mission, United States, 1941–44.

Since the entry in *Sources*, Vol. 2, p 68, certain papers have been placed in the Liddell Hart Centre for Military Archives. The collection consists of World War I official correspondence and reports, staff college notes and lectures, maps, newspaper cuttings, photographs and family correspondence. There are also letters of condolence written to the family after Dill's death and some World War II papers of the Field-Marshal's son, Colonel J. de G. Dill. The Montgomery-Massingberg collection in the Centre also contains some Second World War correspondence from the Field-Marshal whilst the papers of Major Sir Reginald Macdonald-Buchanan (also at the Centre) have relevant material.
  More recently, the Public Record Office revealed that it housed Dill's personal and official correspondence as GOC, Palestine, as Chief of the Imperial General Staff etc. (WO/282).

DIXON, Sir Charles (1888–1976)

Assistant Under-Secretary of State, Commonwealth Office.

His memoirs (1969) are in Dundee University Library.

DOBB, Maurice Herbert (1900–1976)

Economist.

His papers are in the Library of Trinity College, Cambridge.

DON, Reverend Alan Campbell (1885–1966)

Anglican. Chaplain to the Archbishop of Canterbury.

His diaries, 1931–46, are in Lambeth Palace Library (ref MSS 2861–71).

DONALDSON, Arthur (fl 1946–1972)

Scottish Nationalist. Chairman of the Scottish National Party, 1960–69. Journalist. Editor, *Scots Independent*.

His papers, covering the period 1946–72, have been presented to the National Library of Scotland (ref Acc 6038). The collection includes minutes, reports and correspondence relating to the Scottish National Party (10 boxes, 1924–72), together with 17 boxes of miscellaneous nationalist pamphlets and printed matter; 14 vols of press cuttings; and files of *Scots Independent* 1926–35.

DONNELLY, Desmond Louis (1920–1974)

MP (Lab) Pembroke, 1950–68; (Ind) 1968–70.

Since the entry in *Sources*, Vol. 3, p 132, a collection of his papers has now been deposited with the National Library of Wales. The collection cannot be consulted without the consent of the depositor, Mrs. Rosemary Donnelly, of Fishguard.

This substantial collection incudes a large number of correspondence files on specific subjects including Parliamentary Elections in Pembrokeshire, 1949–70; Cyprus, 1958–60; Donnelly's expulsion from the Labour Party, 1968; steel nationalisation, 1964–65; administration of the Democratic Party, 1969–70. Correspondents include leading contemporary political figures. The 17 files of general correspondence, 1950–74, include amongst the correspondents prime ministers and cabinet ministers of the period. 5 files contain correspondence and papers of Sir Anthony Eden, 1956–72; Dean Acheson, 1960–71; and Sir Roy Welensky, 1967–74. There are 2 files of diary notes, Feb 1963–Oct 1967, and part of a draft autobiography by Donnelly. Numerous files of speeches, articles, addresses and reports are held, together with a massive collection of press cuttings, 1940–74.

DORMER, 14th B
Charles Joseph Thaddeus Dormer (1864–1922)

Naval career. Naval attaché, Tokyo, 1906–08. Gentleman Usher to the King, 1919.

His letters and papers, 1882–1914, are among the Dormer family papers (NRA 11084). Most of the papers would appear to relate to his naval service on such ships as HMS *Surprise*, 1887–89 and the *Iron Duke*.

DORRIEN, General Sir Horace Lockwood Smith- (1858–1930)

Distinguished military career. Commander, 2nd Army Corps and 2nd Army, 1914–15. Governor, Gibraltar, 1918–23.

In addition to *Sources* Vol. 2, p 70, the Imperial War Museum also holds a typescript copy (328pp) of the diary he kept from August 1914–May 1915.

DOUGLAS, Canon John Albert (d 1956)

Honorary General Secretary, Church of England Council on Foreign Relations, 1933–45.

His personal papers, (93 vols) covering the period 1911–54, have been deposited in Lambeth Palace Library.

DOW, Sir Hugh (1886–1978)

Indian Civil Servant. Governor of Bind, Dihar, etc.

His papers, 1919–55, have been deposited in the India Office Records.

DOWBIGGIN, Sir Herbert Layard (1880–1966)

Colonial police career. Inspector General, Ceylon Police, 1913–37. Special duties, Palestine Police Force, 1930.

A diary and other papers, covering the period 1901–37, are in Rhodes House Library, Oxford.

DRAKE, Sir Eugen (John Henry Vanderstegen) Millington- (1889–1972)

Minister, Uruguay, 1934–41. Chief Representative, British Council in Spanish America, 1942–46.

The papers described in *Sources*, Vol. 2, p 72, have now been placed in Churchill College, Cambridge. The collection comprises 66 boxes of papers on diplomatic and British Council affairs in Argentina and Uruguay. Churchill College also possesses the diaries of his early diplomatic career in Russia and South America.

DREYER, Admiral Sir Frederic Charles (1878—1956)

Naval career. Assistant Director, Anti-Submarine Division, Admiralty, 1916—17. Director of Naval Ordnance, 1917—18. Director of Naval Artillery, 1918—19. Assistant Chief of Naval Staff, 1924—27; Deputy Chief, 1930—33. C-in-C, China Station, 1933—36. Inspector of Merchant Navy Gunnery, 1941—42. Chief of Naval Air Services, 1942—43.

In addition to the information cited in *Sources* Vol. 2, p 72, twelve boxes of his personal and naval papers, covering the period 1878—1956, were acquired by Churchill College, Cambridge in March 1979.

DRUMMOND, Sir Victor Arthur Wellington (1833—1907)

Diplomat. Minister Resident, Munich and Stuttgart, 1890—1903.

Some material can be found among the Drummond (Cadbury) Mss in Hampshire Record Office. Although the collection includes correspondence, diaries and autograph volumes, most of the material would appear to be household and family papers. The collection is listed (NRA 14022).

DRURY, Sir Frank Gavan (1852—1936)

Legal career. Justice of the High Court of Australia, 1913—31. Chief Justice, Commonwealth of Australia, 1931—35.

His papers have been acquired by the National Library of Ireland.

DUMAS, Admiral Philip Wylie (1868—1948)

Naval career from 1881. Naval Attaché, Germany, Denmark and Netherlands, 1906—08. Assistant Director, Torpedoes, at Admiralty, 1914.

Since the entry in *Sources*, Vol. 2, p 74, the papers cited have now been placed on loan to Peter Liddle at Sunderland Polytechnic. A microfilm copy is available at the Imperial War Museum.

DUNCAN, Joseph Forbes (1879—1964)

Founder and Secretary, Scottish Farm Servants' Union, 1912—45. President, International Landworkers Federation, 1924—50; Scottish Trades Union Congress, 1926. Chairman, Scottish Agricultural Improvement Council, 1951—60.

The papers have been acquired by the National Library of Scotland (ref Acc 5490/ 5601). The collection includes one file of letters to his wife, 1905—08, with descriptions of his union and political activities, together with seven files of further correspondence and papers, 1914—63.

DUNCAN-SANDYS, Baron
Duncan Edwin Sandys (1908—   )

MP (Con) Norwood, 1935—45; Streatham, 1950-Feb 1974. Financial Secretary, War Office, 1941—43. Parliamentary Secretary, Ministry of Supply, 1942—44. Minister of Works, 1944—45. Minister of Supply, 1951—54. Minister of Housing and Local Government, 1954–57. Minister of Defence, 1957–59; Aviation, 1959–60. Secretary of State for Commonwealth Relations, 1960–64. Secretary of State for the Colonies, 1962–64.

Since the entry in *Sources*, Vol. 3, p 139, the papers have been deposited in Churchill College, Cambridge.

DUNNE, James Heyworth- (fl 1919–1949)

Arabist. Reader in Arabic, University of London.

Six boxes of his papers, 1919–49, are in the Hoover Institution on War, Revolution and Peace, Stanford University, California. The collection includes studies, notes, photostats, manuscripts, correspondence, etc. dealing with history, philosophy, literature, education and religion in Egypt, the Arab world, and Turkey.

DURAND, Sir Edward (Law) (1845–1920)

Indian Civil Service. Assistant Commissioner, Afghan Boundary Commission, 1884–86. Resident, Nepal, 1888–93.

His papers (1884–86) whilst serving as Assistant Commissioner to the Afghan Boundary Commission are in the India Office Library.

DURNFORD, Vice-Admiral John Walter (1891–1967)

Naval career. Chief Staff Officer, Malta, 1937–39. Commanded HMS *Suffolk*, 1939–40. Served Australian Commonwealth Naval Board, 1941–42. Commanded HMS *Resolution* 1942–43. Director of Naval Training, Admiralty, 1945–47.

An unpublished autobiography, together with other papers covering his career, 1904–48, has been acquired by the Imperial War Museum. The collection includes naval correspondence, 1924–49, personal correspondence, 1926–63 and miscellaneous naval papers.

EASSIE, Major-General William James Fitzpatrick (1900–1974)

Military career. Served World War II, Sicily, North-West Europe. Director of Supplies and Transport, Far East Land Forces, 1949–51.

The papers were deposited in the Imperial War Museum in 1975. The collection includes reports on the administration of the Second Army during the campaign in North-West Europe and associated reports on supply and transport problems.

EASTERMAN, Alexander Levvey (1890–)

Journalist and Zionist. Chief foreign correspondent, *Daily Herald*. Foreign Editor, *Daily Express*. London Political Secretary, World Jewish Congress.

The Institute of Jewish Affairs has certain of his papers, mainly concerning his work for the World Jewish Congress and for Zionism. Nineteen of his letters (1921–45) to Weizmann are in the Weizmann Institute. In addition, the Board of Deputies' archives hold records (ref C14) of the Palestine Committee (1940s) including Easterman's correspondence and memoranda.

EDER, Dr. Montague David (d 1936)

Psychoanalyist, Zionist and author. Member, Socialist League, 1889. Council of Jewish Territorial Organisation, from 1905; Zionist Commission, Palestine, 1918; President, Zionist Federation of Great Britain and Ireland, 1931–36.

A collection of papers can be found in the Central Zionist Archives. In addition, an extensive correspondence with Weizmann is in the Weizmann Institute.

EDWARDES, Harold Stanley Whitfield (1879–1963)

Assistant Resident, Northern Nigeria, 1905–15, 1921–24.

His papers are in Rhodes House Library, Oxford.

EDWARDS, Huw Thomas (fl. 1920–1970)

Trade union leader, politician, man of letters.

A collection of his papers has been deposited in the National Library of Wales. It includes correspondence, 1929–70, reflecting his involvement with such bodies as the Council of Wales, the Welsh Tourist Board, the Welsh Gas Board, Welsh Economic Council and the TGWU. There are printed reports and articles both by Edwards and others, and a collection of press cuttings, 1932–67, relating to his activities. The collection includes a lot of interesting miscellaneous material, such as a minute book of the North Wales Labour Federation, 1923–30; a memo on post-war development in Wales; a report on South Wales Ports, 1954; papers relating to re-organisation of local government in Wales; the constitution of the Council of Wales; the Welsh language; television in Wales, and other topics related to Edwards' many activities and interests.

EGERTON, Sir Alfred (1886–1959)

Expert on energy. Member, Science Advisory Committee, War Cabinet. Chairman, Scientific Advisory Committee, Ministry of Fuel and Power 1948–53. Secretary, Royal Society, 1938–48.

Ten boxes of his papers, covering the period 1908–34 are in the Imperial College of Science and Technology. Further personal papers have been placed by his widow in the Royal Society.

EGERTON, Major-General Granville (George Algernon) (1859–1951)

Served Tel-el-Kebir, occupation of Crete 1897 and Sudan Campaigns. Inspector of Infantry 1916.

One box of his letters and papers is in the Scottish United Services Museum.

ELLIOT, Walter Elliot (1888–1958)

MP (Con) Lanark, 1918–23; Kelvingrove, 1924–45 and 1950–8; Scottish Universities, 1946–50. Parliamentary Secretary and Minister of Health for Scotland, 1923–4 and 1924–6. Parliamentary Under-Secretary of State, Scotland, 1926–9. Financial Secretary, Treasury, 1931–2. Minister of Agriculture and Fisheries, 1932–6. Secretary of State for Scotland, 1936–8. Minister of Health, 1938–40.

Since the entry in *Sources*, Vol. 3, p 146, the papers have been presented to the National Library of Scotland by Baroness Elliot of Harwood (ref Acc 6721). The deposit comprises 10 boxes and 38 cuttings albums. A list is available in the Library.

ELLIOT, Air Chief Marshal Sir William (1896–1971)

Served European War, 1914–18; South Russia, 1919. Assistant Secretary, Committee of Imperial Defence, 1937–39; War Cabinet, 1939–41. Director of Plans, Air Ministry, 1942–44. Air Officer Commanding, Gibraltar, 1944; Balkan Air

Force, 1944–45. Assistant Chief Executive, Ministry of Aircraft Production, 1945–46. Assistant Chief of Air Staff (Policy), 1946–47. C-in-C, Fighter Command, 1947–49. Chief Staff Officer to Minister of Defence and Deputy Secretary (Military) to Cabinet, 1949–51. Chairman, British Joint Services Mission, Washington, and U.K. Representative, NATO, 1952–54.

Since the entry in *Sources*, Vol. 2, p 79, his surviving papers have been deposited in the Liddell Hart Centre for Military Archives, King's College, London. Very few papers remain concerning his RAF and Cabinet appointments and the majority of the papers are from the post-war period and after his retirement from military service. During his career he made a wide circle of friends, particularly in the USA, and the surviving correspondence reflects these contacts. Although many series are incomplete, some contain interesting retrospective comments on events and personalities during the Second World War and many shed light on Anglo-American relations, American politics, and defence in the post-war period. Elliot never kept a diary or retained any official or semi-official papers connected with his military appointments. A list of the collection is available (NRA 23649).

ELLIOTT, Major-General J. G. (fl 1939–1945)

Military career.

A valuable unpublished account of the Battle of Keren in Eritrea, February-March 1941, is in the Imperial War Museum.

ELLIS, Captain Robert Meyrick (1901–)

Naval career.

His papers are in Churchill College, Cambridge. The material includes naval papers (1933–43) and his autobiography, 1917–48. A list is available (NRA 21108).

ELSTON, David Courtenay (d 1971)

Journalist, *Palestine Post; The Times* correspondent, Jerusalem, 1949–58.

The Times archive holds a substantial file of Elston's correspondence, from 1949.

ENSOR, Sir Robert Charles Kirkwood (1877–1958)

Historian, journalist and author.

The extensive collection of papers, cited in *Sources*, Vol. 3, p 63, has now been moved to the Bodleian Library, Oxford.

ERRINGTON, Sir George (1839–1920)

MP 1874–85. Special mission to the Vatican, 1881–85. Created Baronet for services in Rome, 1885.

His correspondence concerning the special mission to the Vatican, 1881–85, is in the Public Record Office (FO 800/235-239).

ESSEX, Sir (Richard) Walter (1857–1941)

MP (Lib) Cirencester, 1906-Jan 1910; Stafford, Dec 1910–18.

The papers cited in *Sources*, Vol. 3, p 150, are still held in private hands, but the address is now White Oaks, Station Road, Woldingham, Caterham, Surrey.

ETHERIDGE, Richard (Dick) Albert (1909–)

Trade unionist activist. Joined AEU, 1940. Senior Shop Steward, Austin Works, Longbridge.

The collection of papers in the Modern Records Centre, University of Warwick, provides a useful insight into a leading figure in the shop stewards' movement. The material consists of daily working notes, shop stewards minutes, some relevant correspondence as well as pamphlets and other material accumlated by Etheridge during over 30 years in the shop stewards movement.

EVANS, Lieutenant-General Sir Geoffrey Charles (1901–)

Served War of 1939–45. GOC, 5th and 7th Indian Division, Burma, 1944–45; Allied Land Forces, Siam, 1945–46; 42nd (Lancashire) Division and North West District, 1947–48; 40th Division, Hong Kong, 1949–51. Director of Military Training, War Office, 1948–49. Temporary Commander, British Forces, Hong Kong, 1951–52. Assistant Chief of Staff (Organisation and Training), Supreme Headquarters Allied Powers Europe, 1952–53. GOC-in-C, Northern Command, 1953–57.

Since the entry in *Sources*, Vol. 2, p 82, the papers have now been deposited in the Imperial War Museum.

EVANS, Gwynfor (1912–)

Welsh Nationalist. MP (Plaid Cymru), Carmarthen, 1966–70; Oct 74–79. Hon Sec Heddychwyr Cymru (Welsh Pacifist Movement), 1939–45. President, Plaid Cymru, since 1945. Chairman, Union of Welsh Independents, 1954. Publications include *Plaid Cymru and Wales* (1950), *Wales can Win* (1973), etc.

His papers have been acquired by the National Library of Wales, to whom enquiries should be addressed.

EVANS, John Emrys (1853–1931)

Transvaal politician. Controller of the Treasury and Auditor General in the Transvaal.

Correspondence and papers covering the period 1894–1923 are in the British Library (Add MSS 60319–60331).

EVERETT, Colonel Sir William (1844–1908)

Army career. Vice-Consul, Erzerum, 1879. Consul, Kurdistan, 1882–88. Professor of Military Topography, Staff College, 1888.

His papers (c 1879–1885) on service as a military consul at Erzerum, together with maps etc. have been copied by St. Antony's College, Oxford.

EVERSLEY, 1st B
George John Shaw-Lefevre (1831–1928)

MP (Lib) Reading 1863–85; Bradford Central 1886–95. Secretary to the Admiralty 1871–74. First Commissioner of Works 1880–83, 1892–94. Postmaster-General 1883. President of the Local Government Board 1894–95.

His political and family correspondence and papers, 1876–1928 are among the papers of the Earls of Aberdeen (Haddo House MSS) owned by the Haddo Trustees

(NRA 9758). The papers include correspondence on Hungarian-Croatian affairs, his study of the Turkish Empire, the Irish question, proportional representation 1917–24, the Commons and Footpaths Preservation Society 1921–27, local taxation of judicial rents etc.

EWBANK, Sir Robert Benson (1883–1967)

Indian Civil Service.

Some material was placed in Cumbria Record Office (Kendal) by Archdeacon W. F. Ewbank in July 1977. The collection includes two scrapbooks, a photograph album and a memoir entitled *Lively Years in India: the Indian Civil Service 1907–1936*.

FAIREY, Sir (Charles) Richard (1887–1956)

Aircraft pioneer.

Reference should be made to the papers in the Royal Air Force Museum, Hendon (ref AC 76/30, 76/46).

FALLS, Sir Charles Fausett (1890–1936)

MP (Ulster Un) Fermanagh and Tyrone, 1924–29.

Since the entry in *Sources*, Vol. 3, p 154, a collection of papers has been located in the Public Record Office of Northern Ireland (ref D 1390). The papers, for the period 1909–35, relate to the activities of the Orange Order, Ulster Volunteer Force etc. in County Fermanagh.

FARQUHARSON, Robert (1836–1918)

MP (Lib) Aberdeenshire West, 1880–1906.

His correspondence, diaries and other papers are part of the A. Farquharson papers surveyed by NRA (Scotland). Of most political interest is a 15-volume diary which consists of a useful record of parliamentary and political events, constituency business and Farquharson's social life. The papers have been listed (NRA 20361).

FAUSSETT, Captain Sir Bryan Godfrey- (1863–1945)

Equerry to George V, 1901–36. Extra Equerry to Edward VIII, 1936, and subsequently to George VI, 1936–45.

The papers (32 boxes and 17 albums) have been placed in Churchill College, Cambridge. The collection includes diaries, photographs and correspondence. A list is available (NRA 23857).

FAWCETT, Commander H. W. (fl 1939–1945)

Naval career. Anti-submarine warfare division, Naval Staff, 1939–45.

Six boxes of his papers concerning anti-submarine warfare have been placed in Churchill College, Cambridge. The collection also includes photographs of the Battle of Jutland.

FAY, Sir Sam (1856–1953)

Director of Movements, War Office January 1917–March 1918. Director General of Movements and Railways, War Office, and Member of Army Council 1918–19.

No papers have been located. Reference should be made to his book *The War Office at War* (1937) which contains quotations from his diary.

FELL, Douglas Yates (1910–   )

Indian Civil Service.
Papers, 1947–56, mainly relating to the state of Kalat's accession to Pakistan are in the India Office Library.

FERGUSSON, Sir James, 6th Bt, (1832–1907)

MP (Con) Ayrshire, 1854–68; Manchester N.E., 1885–1906. Parliamentary Under-Secretary, India, 1860–7; Home Affairs, 1867–8; Foreign Office, 1886–91. Post-master General, 1891–2. Governor and C-in-C, South Australia, 1868–73; New Zealand, 1873–5. Governor, Bombay, 1880–5.

In addition to the information cited in *Sources*, Vol. 3, p 156, four volumes of his correspondence as Under-Secretary for Foreign Affairs, 1886–91, are in the Public Record Office (ref FO 800/25-28).

FERRYMAN, Brigadier E. E. Mockler- (fl 1939–1945)

Military career. Served as Colonel MI 3 (German Intelligence). Commanded SOE section controlling resistance forces in Western Europe, World War II.

Copies of his privately-published memoirs are available at the Liddell Hart Centre for Military Archives, the Imperial War Museum and the Royal Artillery Institution.

FIELDEN, Air Vice-Marshal Sir Edward Hedley (1903–1976)

Air Force career.

His papers, 1933–75, are in the Royal Air Force Museum (ref AC 73/12, 77/12). The collection includes flying log books, correspondence, drawings and photographs.

FINDLAY, Sir Mansfeldt de Cardonnel (1861–1932)

Diplomat. Counsellor, Cairo Embassy.

Further to the information cited in *Sources*, Vol. 2, p 86, his correspondence as Counsellor in charge of the Cairo Embassy, mainly for the years 1902–05, is in the British Library (Add MSS 62124-125).

FISHER OF KILVERSTONE, 1st Lord
Admiral of the Fleet John Arbuthnot Fisher (1841–1920)

Naval career. Director, Naval Ordnance, 1886–91. Controller of the Navy, 1892–97, C-in-C, North America and West Indies, 1897–99. C-in-C., Mediterranean, 1899–1902. 2nd Sea Lord, 1902–03. C-in-C, Portsmouth, 1903–04. 1st Sea Lord, 1904–10, 1914–15.

Since the entry in *Sources*, Vol. 2, p 86, the papers have been placed in Churchill College, Cambridge. The very extensive collection (*c.* 150 boxes) includes papers and correspondence covering most of his career.

FITZGERALD, Lieutenant-Colonel Brinsley J. H. (1859–1931)

Military career. Private Secretary to Sir John French during World War I.

A microfilm of his diary and letters as Private Secretary to Sir John French has now been deposited in the Imperial War Museum.

FITZGERALD, Sir William Gerald Seymour Vesey (1841–1910)

Political A.D.C. to the Secretary of State for India, 1874–1900.

Six boxes of his correspondence and papers, 1876–1900 are in the India Office Library (MSS Eur F 119).

FLANNERY, Sir James Fortescue, 1st Bt (1851–1943)

MP (Con) Shipley, 1895–1906; Maldon, Jan 1910–22.

Since the entry in *Sources*, Vol. 3, p 160 his surviving papers have now been deposited in Essex Record Office.

FLOUD, Sir Francis Lewis Castle (1875–1965)

Permanent Secretary, Ministry of Agriculture, 1920–27; High Commisioner in Canada, 1934–38.

Since the entry in *Sources*, Vol. 2, pp 87–8, his papers, speeches and press cuttings have been acquired by Churchill College, Cambridge. *See* NRA 26808.

FOGARTY, Michael (1859–1955)

Bishop of Killaloe.

A small collection of his political papers is in the Killaloe Diocesan Archives. The papers were used in David Fitzpatrick *Politics and Irish life*.

FOOT, Sir Dingle Mackintosh (1905–1978)

MP (Lib) Dundee, 1931–45; (Lab) Ipswich, 1957–70. Parliamentary Secretary, Ministry of Economic Warfare, 1940–5. Solicitor-General, 1964–7.

Since the entry in *Sources*, Vol. 3, p 162, 28 boxes of his political and legal papers have been placed in Churchill College, Cambridge. The remainder of the papers, mainly typescripts and printed material relating to his legal work, have been placed in the Institute of Advanced Legal Studies.

FORREST, Sir George William David Starck (1845–1926)

Historian of India. Director, Imperial Record Office, Calcutta 1891–1900. Edited Indian state papers.

Letters to him, mainly about Indian history, from the 5th Marquess of Lansdowne, Earl Roberts and Marquess Curzon of Kedleston 1892–1916 are in the Bodleian Library (MSS Eng lett *c* 291 fols 238–342, e 133 fols 137–226).

FOSTER, Air Chief Marshal Sir Robert (1898–1974)

Air Force career.

Reference should be made to the papers in the Royal Air Force Museum, Hendon (ref AC 75/34).

FOULKES, Major-General Charles Howard (1875–1969)

Military career.

Since the entry in *Sources*, Vol. 2, p 89, a collection of papers and photographs, including diaries (1901–15) is in the Liddell Hart Centre for Military Archives, King's College, London. The papers mainly concern the development of gas warfare and photographic reconnaisance in World War I.

FRASER OF NORTH CAPE, 1st B
Admiral of the Fleet Sir Bruce Austin Fraser (1888–1981)

Naval career. First Sea Lord and Chief of Naval Staff, 1948–51.

Since the entry in *Sources*, Vol. 2, p 90, the papers have been acquired by the National Maritime Museum.

FREEMAN, Edward Bothamley (1838–1921)

Diplomat. Vice-Consul, Mostar, 1876; Consul, Sarajevo 1879; Consul-General Bosnia and the Herzegovina, 1891–1905.

His diary (1878) describing the Austrian occupation of Sarajevo is in the British Library (Add MS 57470). Further papers and journals, 1858–1921, were acquired in 1976 (*see* Add MSS 59746-59770).

FRENCH, Captain Godfrey Alexander (1900–   )

Naval career.

Four boxes of his naval papers, 1937–48, have been placed in Churchill College, Cambridge.

FRY, Sir Geoffrey (1888–1960)

Civil Servant. Successively Private Secretary to Bonar Law and to Stanley Baldwin.

Miscellaneous letters and papers, 1939, were acquired by Cambridge University Library in 1954.

FRY, Sir Leslie Alfred Charles (1908–1976)

Indian Army and Indian political service, 1928–1947. Diplomatic career. Ambassador to Hungary.

His papers including official and other correspondence, photographs, newspaper cuttings and memoirs, have been presented to the India Office Records by his widow (ref MSS Eur F 199). The collection includes material on Hungary.

FRYER, Sir Frederick William Richards (1845–1922)

Financial Commissioner, Burma 1888; Additional Member, Viceroy of India's Council, 1894–95; Chief Commissioner, Burma, 1895–97. Lieutenant-Governor, Burma, 1897–1903.

His papers, covering the period 1860–1922 have been acquired by the India Office Library (ref MSS Eur E 355). The collection, in three boxes, includes diaries and demi-official correspondence, mainly with the Viceroy.

FULLER, Sir John Michael Fleetwood (1864–1915)

MP (Lib) Westbury, 1900–1911. Junior Lord of the Treasury, 1906. Vice-Chamberlain, H. M. Household, 1907. Governor of Victoria, 1911–14.

The papers, cited in *Sources*, Vol. 3, p 167, have now been placed in Wiltshire

County Record Office. Although some of his papers have not survived, the collection includes both political and private correspondence. The political papers include correspondence, circulars, tracts and pamphlets, 1892–1911, dealing primarily with his work as an MP. Many of the papers relate to the two election campaigns of 1910. There are no papers (except for a few press cuttings) for his period as Governor of Victoria. The collection also includes some personal and private correspondence between Fuller and members of his family. A list is available (NRA 20416).

FURNESS, Sir Robert Allason (1883–1954)

Egyptian civil servant.

The papers have been acquired by the Middle East Centre, St Antony's College, Oxford. They concern publicity censorship in Egypt, 1940–44.

GAFFIKIN, T. Q. (fl 1940s)

Chief Police Officer, Perak. Senior Assistant Commisioner of Administration.

The papers have been placed in Rhodes House Library, Oxford (Ms Ind Ocn s 178). The collection includes material on the emergency in Malaya.

GAGE, Conolly Hugh
His Honour Judge Gage (1905–   )

MP (Ulster Un) Belfast South, 1945–52.

The political papers, cited in *Sources*, Vol. 3, p 168, covering the period 1945 to 1969, have now been placed in the Public Record Office of Northern Ireland.

GAITSKELL, Hugh Todd Naylor (1906–1963)

MP (Lab) Leeds South, 1945–63. Parliamentary Under-Secretary, Ministry of Fuel and Power, 1946–47. Minister of Fuel and Power, 1947–50. Minister of State for Economic Affairs, 1950. Chancellor of the Exchequer, 1950–51. Leader of the Labour Party.

Since the entry in *Sources*, Vol. 3, p 168, the papers have been acquired by the Library of University College, London. The extensive collection of his correspondence and papers (181 boxes) is not at present open. Enquires should be directed to the archivist.

GALLIGAN, Peter Paul (fl 1920s)

MP (Sinn Fein) Cavan West, 1918–22.

Since the entry in *Sources*, Vol. 3, p 169, his papers have been acquired by the Archives Department, University College, Dublin (ref P25). The collection consists of agenda, motions and memoranda on the Anglo-Irish Treaty, plus correspondence from his constituency, the Army Council and anti-Treaty groups regarding its ratification (1921–22). There is also some correspondence regarding the repayment of deposits lodged in the 1918 and 1921 elections and some notes compiled by Galligan while in Lewes prison (1917).

GALLOWAY, Lieutenant-General Sir Alexander (1899–1977)

Military career. GOC-in-C, Malaya, 1946–47. High Commissioner and C-in-C, British Troops in Austria, 1947–50.

Since the entry in *Sources*, Vol. 2, p 93, one box of his papers has been acquired by Churchill College, Cambridge. The correspondence, mainly 1960s–70s, includes letters from Montgomery.

GAME, Air Vice-Marshal Sir Philip Woolcott (1876–1961)

Served South Africa, 1901–02; European War, 1914–18. Director of Training and Organisation, Air Ministry, 1919–22. Air Member for Personnel, 1923–28. Governor, New South Wales, 1930–35. Commissioner, Metropolitan Police, 1939–45.

Since the entry in *Sources*, Vol. 2, p 93, the World War I material has been microfilmed by the Imperial War Museum.

GARNETT, William James (1878–1965)

Diplomatic service.

A collection of his papers has been deposited in Lancashire Record Office (ref DDQ). The collection includes 13 boxes of Garnett's correspondence from, and pertaining to, Constantinople, St. Petersburg, Persia, Tangiers, Morocco, Bulgaria, and Buenos Aires (1904–1922), together with diaries, descriptive accounts, narrative accounts, reports and photographs relating to his visits to those countries. There is also a box of correspondence with the Foreign Office, 1912–20, and a box of correspondence regarding public life in Britain, 1929–38. There is a box of private correspondence, 1909–22.

GARNSWORTHY, 1st B
Charles James Garnsworthy (1906–1974)

Labour activist. Involved in Constituency Movement.

A small collection of correspondence (6 folders), mainly relating to the National Committee of Constituency Labour Parties and the Home Counties Labour Associations has been placed on loan in BLPES by his widow (ref M 1372). The collection covers the period 1934–40. *See* NRA 15880.

GARRAWAY, Sir Edward Charles Frederick (1862–1931)

Medical officer and administrator in Southern Africa. Military Secretary to Governor-General and High Commissioner, South Africa, 1910–13; Resident Commissioner, Bechuanaland, 1916–17; Resident Commissioner and Commander, Mounted Police, Basutoland, 1917–26.

An extensive collection of his papers has been deposited in Rhodes House Library, Oxford. A list has been prepared (NRA 22526). The collection consists of correspondence, diaries and other papers.

GEORGE-BROWN, Baron
George Alfred Brown (1914–)

MP (Lab) Belper, 1945–70. Labour Cabinet Minister.

Since the entry in *Sources*, Vol. 3, p 172, the papers have been placed in the Bodleian Library, Oxford.

GIBB, Colonel John Hassard Stewart (1859–1933)

Army career. Served first Sudan Campaign 1885–86. Served Uganda Commission 1893–94, Boer War and World War I.

His papers were presented to the National Army Museum by the Worcestershire

Regiment Museum in 1974. The collection includes diaries 1885—86, 1893—95 (3 vols), letters relating to the Uganda Commission 1893—96 and miscellaneous maps and plans.

GIBBS, Air Marshal Sir Gerald Ernest (1896—)

Air Force career.

Papers, mainly relating to the development of air power, 1916—63, have been placed in the Liddell Hart Centre for Military Archives, Kings's College, London.

GIBSON, Charles William (1889—1977)

MP (Lab) Kennington 1945—50; Clapham 1950—59.

Since the entry in *Sources*, Vol. 3, p 173, the papers have been deposited in Sussex University Library. A list is available (NRA 21355). The collection consists of notebooks, texts or notes for speeches, press cuttings, correspondence and the draft of an autobiography, *Memoirs of a Cockney MP*. The correspondents include Herbert Morrison and Douglas Houghton. The collection throws light on his education, his early career as a union official and his work as a constituency MP.

GIBSON, T. H.

Scottish Nationalist.

The papers were presented to the National Library of Scotland (ref Acc 6058). The correspondence and papers relate to the Scottish Home Rule Association, the Scots National League and the Scottish National Party.

GILMOUR, Sir John, 2nd Bt (1876—1940)

Conservative politician. Cabinet Minister. Secretary of State for Home Affairs, 1932—35. Minister of Shipping, 1939—40.

The papers cited in *Sources*, Vol. 3, p 174, have now been placed in the Scottish Record Office.

GIROUARD, Colonel Sir (Edouard) Percy Cranwill (1867—1932)

Military and colonial career. Director of Railways, South Africa, 1899—1902. Governor, Northern Nigeria, 1908—09. Governor and C-in-C, East Africa Protectorate, 1909—12. Director-General of Munitions Supply, 1915.

George Cassar, *Kitchener, Architect of Victory*, states that the papers have not survived.

GLASIER, John Bruce (1859—1920)

Socialist propagandist.

Since the entry in *Sources*, Vol. 5, p 77, the papers formerly in private hands have now been deposited in the Sydney Jones Library, Liverpool University. The papers, with those of Katherine Glaisier, comprise some 2000 items of correspondence, diaries 1892—1919 etc. A list is available (NRA 25263).

GODDARD, Air Marshal Sir Robert Victor (1897—)

Air Force career. Air Officer in Charge of Administration, South East Asia Air Command, 1943—46. RAF Representative, Washington, 1946—48. Air Member for Technical Services, Air Council, 1948—51.

The material described in *Sources*, Vol. 2, p 97, has now been placed in the Liddell Hart Centre for Military Archives, King's College, London. It includes the typescript of *Epic Violet* concerning the antecedents of World War II, the phoney war and the evacuation of Dunkirk. A list is available (NRA 23069).

GODFREY, Admiral John Henry (1888—1971)

Naval career. Director of Naval Intelligence, 1939—42. Flag Officer Commanding, Royal Indian Navy, 1943—46.

In addition to the information cited in *Sources*, Vol. 2, p 97, some papers have been acquired by the National Maritime Museum.

GODLEY, General Sir Alexander John (1867—1957)

Military career; served European War, 1914—18. Military Secretary to Secretary of State for War, 1920—22. Commander-in-Chief, Army of the Rhine, 1922—24. GOC-in-C., Southern Command, 1924—28. Governor, Gibraltar, 1928—33.

In addition to the information in *Sources*, Vol. 2, p 98, an 1896 diary of the Sinoia patrol is in the National Archives of Zimbabwe.

GOLDBLOOM, Rabbi Jacob Koppep (1872—1961)

Zionist leader. Member, Zionist General Council from 1901. London Vice President, Zionist Federation, 1916—17; Chairman of Executive, 1920—40. Chairman, World Federation of General Zionists, 1936—38.

The papers have been deposited in the Central Zionist Archives, Jerusalem (ref A61). An extensive correspondence (*c.* 1917—49) with Weizmann is in the Weizmann Archives.

GOLDIE, Sir George Dashwood Taubman (1846—1925)

Imperialist, known as the 'founder of Nigeria'. Attended Berlin Conference, 1884—85, as expert on Niger question. Served Royal Commission on the South African War, 1902—03. President, National Defence Association 1905—1914, 1915—20.

According to J. E. Flint, *Sir George Goldie and the Making of Nigeria*, before his death Goldie systematically destroyed his papers and forbade his children even to write about him. Reference should be made to letters from Goldie to the Earl of Scarbrough (with the present Earl) and to the records of the Niger Company, presented to Rhodes House Library by the Earl of Scarbrough. A further important source is the extensive archive of John Holt and Co. of Liverpool.

GOLDSMID, Colonel Albert Edward Williamson (1846—1904)

Military career. Founder, Jewish Lads' Brigade and closely involved with Jewish Colonisation Association.

The Middle East Centre at St. Antony's College, Oxford, holds his log book (1903) of activities with the 1903 Commission to Sinai concerning the El-Arish colony scheme.

GOLLANCZ, Sir Victor (1893—1967)

Publisher. Launched Left Book Club, 1936. Reformer.

In addition to the material cited in *Sources*, Vol. 5, p 78, in September 1983 the

Modern Records Centre, University of Warwick, received the gift of a recently dis-
covered box of 1930s personal papers of Victor Gollancz. These form an important
supplement to the main series (given to the Centre in 1977), which commences in
the 1940s. The 1983 accession includes some items relevant to the history of the
publishing house, as well as correspondence relating to Gollancz's political and
humanitarian concerns and his social and family life.

Subjects of individual files include: Edmond Fleg, the Jewish writer; Gollancz's
purchase of the Favil Press Ltd and its business; the purchase of Brimpton Lodge
and maintenance of its garden; the appointment of a personal political secretary in
1938; political organisations, including the Labour Party (*but not the Left Book
Club*).

GOODMAN, Paul (1875—1949)

Historian and Zionist publicist.

In addition to the papers in the Central Zionist Archives, cited in *Sources*, Vol. 5,
p 79, Cyril Goodman (son), Tideways, Creeksea, Burnham-on-Crouch, Essex, has
other papers, including a Zionist Federation minute book. These are believed to be
closed.

GORDON, Lieutenant Commander Harry Pirie (1883—1969)
13th Laird of Buthlaw.

Served, World War I, Royal Naval Volunteer Reserve and on political mission to
Palestine; *The Times* foreign department, 1911—14 and 1919—39; Palestine, 1929;
World War II, in Admiralty Intelligence.

In addition to the material cited in *Sources*, Vol. 5, p 79, Mr Christopher Pirie-
Gordon CMG OBE (son), Via Palestro 3, Florence, Italy, has his father's other
papers, but no details are available.

GORDON-WALKER, Baron
Patrick Chrestien Gordon Walker (1907—1980)

MP (Lab) Smethwick, 1945—64; Leyton 1966—Feb 1974. Labour Cabinet Minister.

Since the entry in *Sources*, Vol. 3, p 179, the papers were given by his son, Robin
Walker, to Churchill College, Cambridge in May 1981. The collection includes the
diaries kept throughout his political career. A list is available (NRA 24835).

GORRINGE, Lieutenant-General Sir George Frederick (1868—1945)

Military career

His Boer War diaries (1900—01) are in the National Army Museum.

GOSSE, Sir Edmund William (1849—1928)

Librarian, House of Lords, 1904—14. Author and man of letters.

His unpublished diary, 1904—06, with material of political interest, is in the House
of Lords Record Office. There is further material, 1867—1928, consisting mainly of
letters to him, in the Brotherton Library, Leeds.

GOSSELIN, Sir Martin Le Marchant Hadsley (1847—1905)

Diplomat. Assistant Under-Secretary, Foreign Office, 1899—1902. Minister, Portugal, 1902—05.

His correspondence and papers, 1847–1905, are in Hertfordshire Record Office. Some miscellaneous correspondence and papers can also be found in the Milner papers (NRA 20313).

GOWER, Arthur Leveson (1851–1923)

Diplomat. Secretary of the Legation, The Hague, 1898–1905.

His diaries 1870–1922 and other family diaries and papers are in Surrey Record Office, to whom enquiries concerning access should be addressed.

GRACEY, General Sir Douglas David (1894–1964)

Military career.

Some papers relating to Burma and Indo-China, 1941–47, have been deposited in the Liddell Hart Centre for Military Archives, King's College, London by Lady Gracey, through the good offices of Colonel P. Dunn of the USAF.

GRAHAM, Major-General F. C. C. (fl 1939–1945)

Military career, World War II.

The Imperial War Museum has his short account of the allied evacuation from Crete in 1941. It gives a detailed picture of the growing chaos among the beleaguered forces.

GRANET, Sir William Guy (1867–1943)

Railway administrator. Director General of Movements and Railways, World War I.

A collection of his papers has been deposited by his grand-daughter in the Modern Records Centre, University of Warwick. A list is available (NRA 22556). The collection comprises one box of miscellaneous correspondence 1897–1943, and files relating to his work as Director General of Movements and Railways in the Great War. Amongst the correspondence are letters from Asquith, Rufus Isaacs and Montagu Norman.

GRANT, Sir Charles (d.1903)

Indian Civil Service. Served North West Frontier etc. Foreign Secretary, Government of India.

His papers are in the India Office Library (ref Mss Eur E 308). All the material is prior to 1900.

GRAVES, Richard Massie (1880–1960)

Levant Consular Service. Served Constantinople, Salonica, Uskub, Alexandria, etc. Served Egyptian Civil Service. Director, Department of Labour, Palestine Government, 1942–46. Adviser on Social Affairs, International Administration, Tangier, 1949–51.

In addition to the information cited in *Sources*, Vol. 5, p 80, a draft of the opening chapters of his autobiography is in the Middle East Centre, St. Antony's College, Oxford. The main collection of papers is with the Central Zionist Archives in Jerusalem.

GREEN, Archbishop Charles (1864—1944)

Archbishop of Wales.

His papers are in the St Deiniols Library, Hawarden. *See* NRA 24327.

GREENWOOD OF ROSSENDALE, Baron
Arthur William James Greenwood (Anthony Greenwood) (1911—)

MP (Lab) Heywood and Radcliffe, 1946—50; Rossendale, 1950—70. Secretary of State for Colonial Affairs, 1964—65. Minister of Overseas Development, 1965—66. Minister of Housing and Local Government, 1966—70.

Since the entry in *Sources*, Vol. 3, p 186, the papers of Lord Greenwood, together with those of Arthur Greenwood, have been placed in the Bodleian Library, Oxford.

GREENWOOD, Arthur (1880—1954)

MP (Lab) Nelson and Colne, 1922—31; Wakefield, 1932—54. Labour Cabinet Minister.

Since the entry in *Sources*, Vol. 3, p 186, the papers have been placed in the Bodleian Library, Oxford.

GRENFELL, Captain Russell

Writer on naval affairs.

His papers (3 boxes) have been deposited in Churchill College, Cambridge. The collection comprises correspondence and drafts for books on naval history, 1947—53.

GRETTON, Vice-Admiral Sir Peter (1912—)

Naval career.

His autobiographical papers are in Churchill College, Cambridge. *See* NRA 18561.

GREY, 4th E
Sir Albert Henry George Grey (1851—1917)

Administrator in Rhodesia, 1896—7; Director, British South Africa Company, 1894—1904. Governor-General of Canada, 1904—11. MP (Lib) Northumberland 1880—5; Tyneside 1885—6.

Since the entry in *Sources*, Vol. 2, p 103, further details are available concerning Grey's papers. The collection at Durham University consists mainly of photcopies; the originals were transferred to the Public Archives of Canada in Ottawa, in 1955. The collection comprises correspondence with Sir Wilfrid Laurier, 1904—11 (5 vols); correspondence relating to Canadian-American relations, mainly with James Bryce (British Ambassador in Washington), 1906—11, subjects include fisheries, commercial reciprocity, political situation in Canada (5 vols); private correspondence with Secretaries of State for the Colonies, 1904—11 (6 vols); correspondence with the Royal Family, 1905—11 (2 vols); miscellaneous correspondence, 1906—11 (copies), with such people as Joseph Chamberlain, Sir Edward Grey and Lord Strathcona (1 vol); correspondence relating to Newfoundland, 1906—11 (2 vols), and to the formation of the provinces of Alberta and Saskatchewan, 1905 (1 vol); miscellaneous Canadian correspondence, 1902—16: correspondents include Laurier, Strathcona, Rider Haggard and the Duke of Connaught. There are also notes by

Grey on members of the Senate and House of Commons (9 vols), as well as printed reports and articles.

GREY, Colonel Sir Raleigh (1860—1936)

Commander, Bechuanaland Border Police, Matebele War, 1893. Accompanied Jamieson into the Transvaal, 1896.

His Rhodesia papers, 1899—1931, have been deposited in Northumberland Record Office.

GROHMAN, Vice-Admiral Harold Tom Baillie- (1888—1978)

Naval career from 1902; served World War I (Grand Fleet, Dover Patrol in destroyers and minesweepers). Head of British Naval Mission to China, 1931—33. Commanded 1st Destroyer Flotilla, Mediterranean, 1934—36. Attached to HQ Mid-East in Cairo, 1941. Commanded HMS *Ramillies*, 1939—40. Rear-Admiral, Combined Operations, 1942. Flag Officer in Charge, Harwich, 1944; Kiel and Schleswig-Holstein, 1945—46.

In addition to the material cited in *Sources*, Vol. 2, p 104, a copy of his three-volume autobiography is also available in the Imperial War Museum.

GROVES, Brigadier-General Percy Robert Clifford (d1959)

Served France, Dardanelles, Middle East. Director of Flying Operations, Air Ministry 1918. British Air Representative, Peace Conference 1919.

Seven boxes of his papers, 1916—44, have been deposited in the Liddell Hart Centre for Military Archives, King's College. The collection consists mainly of memoranda and minutes of the Paris Peace Conference, Air Section, 1919—21. Further letters and papers concerning the Air Ministry and the British Delegation to the Paris Peace Conference are in the Imperial War Museum.

GROVES, Reg (1908—)

Journalist and historian. Pioneer member of the British Section of the International Left Opposition.

A collection of papers has been acquired by the Modern Records Centre, University of Warwick (ref MSS 172). The material on the British Left Opposition essentially comprises sources for Groves' *The Balham Group: How British Trotskyism Began* (London, 1974). It includes: CPGB Nine Elms Rail Group minutes, 1931—32; CPGB Balham Group minutes, 1932; correspondence, including some with the *Daily Worker* and the CPGB, 1929—32, and with the Communist League of America (Opposition), 1931—33. There are also various pamphlets and periodicals, including, *The Communist* (BLO bulletin); *Red Flag* (BLO monthly); and *The Jogger* (CP paper for Railway Clearing House clerks). There is also material regarding his various Labour candidatures — at Aylesbury in 1938 and 1945, at Eastbourne in 1950, Saffron Walden in 1951 and Ilford North in 1955. In each case (except for Ilford, where only 5 items have been deposited) there is correspondence, leaflets, press cuttings, etc.

GUEDALLA, Philip (1889—1944)

Historian and essayist. Liberal Parliamentary candidate. Secretary, Flax Control Board, 1917—20.

Since the entry in *Sources*, Vol. 5, p 84, his papers have been deposited in the Bodleian

Library, Oxford. The 28 boxes in the collection cover the period 1911 to 1944 and include correspondence with his publishers (Boxes 4, 5 and 24) relating to the years 1927–36; correspondence regarding visits to the USA (1927–38) and Canada (1933); the cinema and the Joint Committee on Films (Boxes 15–18); and the Ibero-American Institute and Ibero-American Committee of the British Council, 1933–44 (Boxes 19–21). Box 25 contains letters reacting to Guedella's role in the Campaign of British Intellectuals against Fascism. There are several boxes of material pertaining to lectures and articles by Guedella, together with press reviews of his work. Two files in Box 17 contain correspondence over control of overseas newsreel propaganda April-October 1940. Typescript transcripts and first editions of a number of Guedella's works, including *The Hundred Years*, were also deposited.

GULLAND, John William (1864–1920)

MP (Lib) Dumfries Burghs, 1906–18. Junior Lord of the Treasury, 1909–15. Joint Parliamentary Secretary to the Treasury and Government Chief Whip, 1915–16.

In addition to the information cited in *Sources*, Vol. 3, p 192, some sixty letters concerning Scottish Liberal organisation, 1894–1927, are in the National Library of Scotland.

GWYNNE, Bishop Llewellyn Henry (1863–1957)

Missionary. Bishop in Egypt and Sudan.

A collection of diaries, correspondence and other papers, 1884–1955, is in the archives of the Church Missionary Society deposited in Birmingham University Library.

HACKETT, General Sir John Winthrop (1910–   )

Officer Commanding, Transjordan Frontier Force, 1947-51. Deputy Chief of General Staff, 1964–66. Commander in Chief, British Army of the Rhine, and Commander, Northern Army Group, 1966–68. Principal, King's College, London, 1968–75.

Certain papers have been placed in the Liddell Hart Centre for Military Archives, King's College, London. A list is available (NRA 23070).

HADEN-GUEST, 1st B
Leslie Haden Haden-Guest (1877–1960)

MP (Lab) Southwark North, 1923–7; Islington North, 1937–50. Lord in Waiting, 1951.

Since the entry in *Sources*, Vol. 3, p 193, the papers have now been deposited in the House of Lords Record Office by the executors of Lady Haden-Guest. The collection consists chiefly of Haden-Guest's accounts of his visits to Russia and other European countries, and articles written by him on health conditions and famine relief work there, booklets and newspapers, in English and Russian, and some correspondence, 1919–36. There are also accounts of visits of the Medical Priority Committee to Austria, Italy, Malta and India, 1946, Scotland, 1950, West Germany, 1950 and of the National Medical Manpower Committee to Malta, 1954.

HAGGARD, Sir Godfrey Digby Napier (1884–1969)

Diplomat. Consul, Paris, 1932–38; New York, 1938–44. Director, American Forces Liaison Division, Ministry of Information, 1944–45.

Enquiries concerning the papers cited in *Sources*, Vol. 2, p 105, should now be directed to his daughter, Mme V. Lerens, 93B rue Groestenberg, Brussels, 1180 Belgium.

HAGGARD, John George (1850—1908)

Colonial service. Consul, Kenya, Zanzibar, Madagascar.

His papers, 1881—1908, are in Rhodes House Library, Oxford.

HAIG, 1st E
Field Marshal Sir Douglas Haig (1861—1928)

Distinguished military career. Commander, 1st Army, 1914—15. C-in-C, Expeditionary Force in France and Flanders, 1915—19; Forces in Great Britain, 1919—20.

The papers cited in *Sources*, Vol. 2, pp 105—6, have now been bought by the National Library of Scotland. The papers cover the whole of Haig's military career and include his World War I diary.

HAILES, 1st B
Patrick George Thomas Buchan-Hepburn (1901—1974)

MP (Con) Liverpool East Toxteth, 1931—50; Beckenham, 1950—7. Junior Lord of the Treasury, 1939 and 1944. Parliamentary Secretary, Treasury and Government Chief Whip, 1951—5. Minister of Works, 1955—7. Governor-General and C-in-C, West Indies, 1958—62.

Since the entry in *Sources*, Vol. 3, pp 193—4, the papers have been deposited in Churchill College, Cambridge. The collection comprises 50 boxes of papers, correspondence and newspaper cuttings. A detailed list is available (NRA 24830).

HAILSHAM OF SAINT MARYLEBONE, Baron
Quintin McGarel Hogg, 2nd Vt Hailsham (1907—)

MP (Con) Oxford, 1938—50; St. Marylebone, 1963—70. Joint Parliamentary Under-Secretary, Air Ministry, 1945. 1st Lord of the Admiralty, 1956—7. Minister of Education, 1957. Deputy Leader, House of Lords, 1957—60, and Leader, 1960—3. Lord Privy Seal, 1959—60. Lord President of the Council, 1957—9 and 1960—4. Minister for Science and Technology, 1959—64. Minister with special responsibility for Sport, 1962—4; unemployment in the North East, 1963—4; Higher Education, 1963—4. Secretary of State for Education and Science, 1964. Lord Chancellor 1970—4, 1979— .

Since the entry in *Sources*, Vol. 3, p 194, the papers have been placed in Churchill College, Cambridge. The very extensive collection (*c.* 600 boxes) consists of papers, correspondence and diaries. There are restrictions on access.

HAINING, General Sir Robert Hadden (1882—1959)

Director of Military Operations and Intelligence, War Office, 1936—38. GOC, British Forces in Palestine and Transjordan, 1938—39. GOC-in-C, Western Command, 1939—40. Vice Chief, Imperial General Staff, 1940—41. Lieutenant-General, Middle East, 1941—42.

In addition to the material cited in *Sources*, Vol. 2, p 106, a file covering his service as Intendant-General in the Middle East is in the Imperial War Museum.

175

HAKING, General Sir Richard Cyril Byrne (1862—1945)

Military career. Chief of the British Section, Armistice Commission, 1918—19. Commander, British Military Missions, Russia and Baltic Province, 1919. Commander, Allied Troops Plebiscite Area, East Prussia and Danzig, 1920. High Commissioner, League of Nations, 1921—23.

His war diary, 1918—20, and dispatches as Chief of the British Delegation to the Inter-Allied Armistice Commission are in the Public Record Office (WO 144).

HALAHAN, Air Vice-Marshal Frederick Crosby (d1965)

Air Force career. Director of Aeronautical Inspection, 1922—23. Director of Technical Development, Air Ministry, 1924—26. Promoted Air Vice-Marshal, 1927. Commandant, RAF Cadet College, Cranwell, 1926—29.

Correspondence, papers, photographs and publications, covering the period 1893 to 1952 are in the Royal Air Force Museum, Hendon (ref AC76/17—18, 37).

HALDANE, General Sir James Aylmer Lowthorpe (1862—1950)

Served India; South Africa, 1899—1900; European War, 1914—19. Military Attaché with Japanese Army, 1904—05. COC-in-C, Mesopotamia, 1920—22.

In addition to the material in the National Library of Scotland, cited in *Sources*, Vol. 2, p 106, the Imperial War Museum has his 1912—14 diary as a Brigade Commander.

HALDANE, Sir William Stowell (1864—1951)

Crown Agent for Scotland, 1905—17.

One box of his papers covering the period 1896—1916 is in the National Library of Scotland (ref Acc 7185). The deposit consists of letters (7, 1906—16) from Richard Bundon Haldane, Viscount Haldane; 2 bundles of papers relating to the Scottish Prison Commission, *c*. 1905—17; 1 bundle of Crown Office papers, 1909, and a memo *re* trawling legislation, 1905; 1 bundle of general correspondence, 1905—16; a copy of Crown Office *Regulations for Criminal and Other Investigations*, 1896.

HAMILTON, Admiral Sir Louis Henry Keppel (1890—1957)

Naval career; served World Wars I and II. 1st Naval Member and Chief of Naval Staff, Commonwealth Naval Board, 1945—48.

In addition to the papers in the National Maritime Museum, cited in *Sources*, Vol. 2, p 110, a few of his World War I letters can be found in the papers of his brother, Captain H. Hamilton, RN, deposited in the Imperial War Museum.

HAMPTON, 4th B
Major Herbert Stuart Pakington (1883—1962)

Military career.

The diary at the Imperial War Museum, cited in *Sources*, Vol. 2, p 110, is a copy, not the original.

HANS, Nicholas (fl1930—60s)

Educationalist.

The papers have been deposited in the University of London Institute of Education Library. The large collection, in five filing boxes, covers all the periods of his career from his earliest appointment in 1917. The correspondence is most concentrated for the 1950s and 1960s. The majority of the papers consist of manuscript or type-script notes, extracts and texts of his articles and publications. The correspondence comprises several hundred letters.

HARBER, Denzil D. (1909—1966)

Trotskyist activist, first in the Militant Group. Subsequently Secretary, Revolutionary Socialist League.

The papers have been placed in the Modern Records Centre, University of Warwick through the good offices of Julian Harber and his brothers (ref MSS 151). The collection includes files concerning the Left Opposition in Britain, especially the ILP and the activities of the Balham Group, 1932—38. There are also miscellaneous circulars and transcript Central Committee minutes, 1940—43, of the Revolutionary Socialist League, with some correspondence between the International Secretariat of the Fourth International and the Revolutionary Socialist League, and additional correspondence concerning factional activity and fusion with the Workers' International League. In addition to further files on the Revolutionary Communist Party and the Workers' International League, there is the draft of a novel written by Harber and a volume of press cuttings. Xerox copies of some of the files mentioned are available in the Brynmor Jones Library at Hull University.

HARCOURT, Admiral Sir Cecil Halliday Jepson (1892—1959)

Naval career. C-in-C, Hong Kong, 1945—46. Second Sea Lord, 1948—50. C-in-C, The Nore, 1950—52.

Since the entry in *Sources*, Vol. 2, p 110, the Imperial War Museum has acquired diaries and other papers covering his service career, 1941—48.

HARDIE, Frank Martin (fl 1920s—1970s)

Author.

His letters received, June 1926 to April 1977, were bought by the Bodleian Library from Winifred A. Myers Ltd. in 1978 (ref MSS Eng lett c 458—60, d 448). The collection, on literary and political topics, includes material on the Oxford Union 'King and Country' debate of 1933.

HARE, Major General Sir Steuart Welwood (1867—1952)

Military career.

Diaries and other records of his commands at Gallipoli and in Palestine, 1915—19, are in the Imperial War Museum.

HARPER, Captain Geoffrey Coleridge (1894—1962)

Naval career.

Three boxes of his papers, including diaries 1914—20, are in Churchill College, Cambridge.

HARPER, Vice-Admiral John Ernest Troyte (1874—1949)

Naval career. Director of Navigation, Admiralty, 1919—21.

In addition to the material cited in *Sources* Vol. 2, p 112, other papers are in Churchill College, Cambridge.

HARRINGTON, Timothy Charles (1851—1910)

MP (Irish Nat) Westmeath, 1883—5; Dublin Harbour, 1885—June 1910.

In addition to the papers in the National Library of Ireland (see *Sources*, Vol. 3, p 205), a collection of his letters to John Dillon, 1888—1910, is in Trinity College, Dublin.

HARRIS, 4th B
George Robert Canning Harris (fl 1930s—1940s)

Under-Secretary for India 1885—86. Under-Secretary for War 1886—89. Governor of Bombay 1890—95. Lord-in-Waiting to Queen Victoria 1895—1900. ADC to King Edward VII and King George V.

His correspondence as Governor of Bombay, March 1890 to January 1894 was deposited on permanent loan in the India Office Library by the 5th Baron Harris in 1960 (ref MSS Eur E 256). It consists of two bundles (916 folios). Important correspondents include the 9th Earl of Elgin, Viceroy and Governor-General of India, and the 1st Viscount Cross and the 1st Earl of Kimberley, Secretaries of State for India.

HARRIS, Lucien

Zionist activist. President, Zionist Youth Council, 1933—43.

His papers are in Manchester Central Library (ref M350). A list is available (NRA 23565). The collection includes papers and correspondence on the establishment of a Jewish homeland in Palestine, anti-semitism, refugees and education. There are numerous articles by Harris, 1935—39, miscellaneous correspondence and newspaper cuttings, 1933—38.

HARRISON, Brigadier Harold Cecil (d1940)

General Staff Officer, British Troops in China, 1933—37. Officer Commanding, 14th Infantry Brigade, Palestine, 1937—39.

Mrs E. Law, c/o Lloyds Bank Ltd, 38 Blue Boar Row, Salisbury, Wilts, has some private papers. The letters written by Harrison from Palestine in 1938 have been copied for the Middle East Centre, St. Antony's College, Oxford.

HART, Ernest (1875—1928)

Indian Civil Service 1918—28. Assistant Commissioner, Nicobar Islands, Andaman Commission 1921—28.

His papers, 1921—28, are in the India Office Library (MSS Eur D 738). Although the papers consist mainly of literary material, there is material on the problems of forming an administration in the Nicobar Islands and the medical and educational needs of the Islands.

178

HART, Sir Robert (1835—1911)

Entered Chinese Consular Service 1854. Joined Chinese Imperial Maritime Customs Service 1859. Inspector-General of Customs in China 1863—1906.

Fourteen volumes of family correspondence and miscellaneous papers, 1866—1908, are in the Bodleian Library Oxford. They include letters from his parents, brothers and sisters, letters to his wife and children, letters from officers in Peking etc. The collection was purchased in 1972. In addition, an autograph manuscript entitled 'The Peking Legations: a national uprising and international episode' (by Sir Robert) was presented to the British Library (Add MS 46499) by the Inspector-General of Chinese Maritime Customs in 1948.

A very extensive correspondence with his personal representative, James Duncan Campbell, *c* 1500 items, 1868—1906 is in the School of Oriental and African Studies (NRA 10511). It includes important series of letters from Campbell to Hart, some marked 'private', others 'semi-official'. A further 223 letters to Sir Francis Aglen, 1888—1911, are also in the School of Oriental and African Studies.

HASTED, Major-General William Freke (1897—1978)

Military career. Controller of Development, Kuwait, Persian Gulf, 1952—54.

Four boxes of his papers concerning the 14th Army and Kuwait are in Churchill College, Cambridge.

HAUGHTON, Major-General Henry Lawrence (1883—1955)

Career in Indian Army. Commandant, 11th Sikh Regiment, 1927. Military Secretary, Army Headquarters, India, 1931—33. Commander, Kohat District, 1936.

His diaries (5 vols, 541 folios) covering the period January 1907 to June 1912, are in the India Office Library (MSS Eur D 531).

HAVELOCK, Sir Arthur Elibank (1844—1908)

Colonial Service. Governor of West African settlements, 1881. Governor of Natal 1886—89; Ceylon 1890—95; Madras 1895—1901; Tasmania 1901—04.

His letter-books as Governor of Madras, March 1896-November 1900 (2 vols, 285 folios) are in the India Office Library (MSS Eur D 699). They include copies of letters to the Secretary of State for India, Lord George Hamilton, 1896—99 and copies of letters to the Viceroys, Lord Elgin and Lord Curzon, 1896—1900.

HAY, Lieutenant-Colonel Sir William Rupert (1893—1962)

Indian Political Service. Political Agent, Malakand, 1931—33. Counsellor, British Legation, Kabul, 1933. Resident, Waziristan, 1940—41. Resident, Persian Gulf, 1946—53.

His papers and correspondence, together with four diaries, 1911—56, are in St. Antony's College, Oxford.

HAYDON, Major-General Joseph C. (1899—1970)

Army career. Military Assistant to Hore-Belisha, 1938—39. Commander, Special Service Brigade of Commandos, 1940—42. Vice-Chief of Combined Operations, 1942—43.

The papers have been placed on permanent loan in the Imperial War Museum by his daughter, Miss M. A. Haydon. The papers cover the entire span of his life, but are most important for his periods as Military Assistant to Hore-Belisha, 1938—39, his command of the Special Service Brigade of Commandos, 1940—42, his spell as Vice-Chief of Combined Operations, 1942—43 and his command of the 1st Guards Brigade in Italy in 1944. The collection consists of diary extracts, official reports, letters from fellow officers, photographs and press cuttings.

HAYTER, Louis Henry (d1953)

Conservative Party organiser; activist in early years of the London County Council; agent for Westminster.

The surviving papers were placed in Leeds University Library by Lord Boyle, the university's then Vice-Chancellor in February 1976. The collection of c. 135 letters bound into a guard-book, includes correspondence, 1884—97 from Randolph Churchill, Goschen, Balfour, Lionel Raleigh Holland, the 1st Earl of Iddesleigh, Austen Chamberlain and Curzon. Many concern local politics in London and Hayter's work as a Conservative agent.

HAYWARD, Sir Maurice Henry Weston (1868—1964)

Indian Civil Service.

Eight volumes of memoirs, dating from 1944, are in the India Office Library (ref Mss Eur D 839). There is also a typescript entitled *Malayan Letters from Rangoon 1945* by Maurice John Hayward (b1906) of the Malayan Civil Service.

HEADLAM, Major-General Sir John (1864—1946)

Military career.

Some papers, covering the period 1860—1919 are in the Library of the Royal Artillery Institution (ref MD/183).

HEATH, Lieutenant-General Sir Lewis Macclesfield (1885—1954)

Military career.

His papers concerning the command of III Indian Corps, Malaya, in 1941—42, together with post-war correspondence concerning the Official History of the War in the Far East are in the Imperial War Museum.

HECTOR, Gordon Matthews (1918—   )

Acting Governor of the Seychelles 1953. Deputy Resident Commissioner and Government Secretary, Basutoland 1956. Chief Secretary, Basutoland 1964. Secretary, Basutoland Constitutional Commission 1957—58.

The papers are in Rhodes House Library. They include memoranda and other papers concerned with wartime service in Abyssinia and Madagascar and colonial service in the Seychelles and Basutoland, 1941—67.

HEMMING, (Arthur) Francis (1893—1964)

Civil servant. Secretary, International Council for non-intervention in Spain.

The papers at Corpus Christi College, Oxford, cited in *Sources*, Vol. 2, p 115, have now been moved to the Bodleian Library, Oxford.

HENDERSON, Alderman James Frederick (1867–1957)

Labour activist and pioneer.

A collection of papers was deposited in Norfolk Record Office in 1964 (ref MS 21525). A list is available (NRA 20672). The collection consists of 24 bundles of papers. These include bundles of correspondence on a variety of topics including 'socialist activities on Clarion campaign', 1914–15; the disaffiliation of the ILP from the Labour Party and the formation of the Socialist League 1932; letters from various socialists, many of them Fabians, 1893–1956; several bundles regarding his own publications, notes on lectures, and a bundle of press clippings, pamphlets etc. relating to his political activities.

HENDERSON, Lieutenant-Colonel Kenneth (1875–1955)

Military career; Indian Army, served World War I.

The papers at the Imperial War Museum, cited in *Sources*, Vol. 2, p 116, are in fact copies of originals still in private hands.

HENDERSON, Kenneth David (1903–   )

Sudan Political Service. Governor, Darfur Province, Sudan, 1949–53. Historian of the Sudan.

The Sudan Archive, University of Durham, has his diaries and papers, 1926–53.

HENDERSON, Major-General Patrick Hagart (1876–1968)

Military career. Served with 7th Division, France, 1914–15; 28th Division, Egypt and Macedonia, 1915–17; 27th Division, Macedonia, South Russia and Trans-Caspia, 1917–18.

A collection of albums, notes, official papers and diaries of his service in the RAMC is held by the Imperial War Museum.

HENDERSON, Captain R. A. (fl 1930s)

Naval career.

One box of his papers, relating to the Invergordon Mutiny, 1931, is in Churchill College, Cambridge.

HENEAGE, Sir Arthur Pelham (1881–1971)

MP (Con) Louth, 1924–45.

Since the entry in *Sources*, Vol. 3, p 216, his papers, 1911–58, have now been placed with the family archives in Lincolnshire Archives Office.

HERBERT, Sir Alfred Edward (1866–1957)

Businessman and industrialist. Controller of Machine Tools, Ministry of Munitions, World War I.

An important collection of personal papers is in the possession of Ian Hollick Esq., Wills Pastures, Wormleighton, Nr. Leamington Spa. For further details, see Joan Lane, *Register of business records of Coventry and related areas* (1977).

HERBERT, Sir Michael Henry (1857—1903)

Diplomat. Chargé d'affaires, Washington, 1888—89. Secretary of Legation Washington, 1892—93; The Hague 1893—94; Constantinople 1894—97; Rome 1897—98; Paris 1898—1902. Ambassador to the United States 1902—03.

Further details are now available of the papers owned by the Earl of Pembroke at Wilton House, Salisbury. The collection includes three boxes of diplomatic correspondence and papers, 1879—1903 with such figures as Salisbury, Rosebery, Lansdowne, Roosevelt and Laurier. There is also one box of correspondence with his brothers, the 13th and 14th Earls of Pembroke and one box of correspondence (1888—1903) with his wife. There is also one box of press cuttings relating to his career, 1888—1903, drawn from British and American newspapers.

HEREN, Louis Philip (1919—   )

Journalist. The Times foreign correspondent from 1947 in Israel and Middle East, 1948—50. Deputy Editor and Foreign Editor, The Times.

The Times archive holds papers which include material on the Middle East (1948—50), such as letters and cables from Tel Aviv.

HERVEY, Dudley Francis Amelius (1849—1911)

Entered Straits Settlements Civil Service 1867. British Resident, Malacca 1882—93. Member, Executive and Legislative Councils, Straits Settlements.

His correspondence and papers, chiefly relating to the regions he administered are in the National Archives of Malaysia.

HEYWOOD, Major-General Thomas George Gordon (1886—1943)

Military attaché, Paris, 1932—36; Commander, 7th Anti-Aircraft Division, 1939. Army representative, British Military Mission to Russia, August 1939. Command, military mission to Holland, 1940 and to Greece, 1940—41.

The papers have survived in private hands, in the possession of Mrs. Joan Heywood. Further details were not available.

HIGENBOTTAM, Sam (fl 1900s)

Pioneer Socialist.

A few letters to Higenbottam are in the Local Collection in Blackburn Central Library. The collection contains 4 letters from Philip Snowden, 3 from Ramsay MacDonald, 2 from Keir Hardie and single letters from Ben Tillett and J. Bruce Glasier.

HIGGINS, John Comyn (1882—1952)

Indian Political Service. Political Agent, Manipur State, 1917—33. Political Officer, Kuki Punitive Operations, 1917—19. Commissioner, Assam Valley, 1934. Chairman, Assam Public Service Commission, 1944—45.

The papers have been placed in the Library of the School of Oriental and African Studies.

HILDRED, Sir William Percival (1893—   )

Director-General, Civil Aviation, 1941—46.

Since the entry in *Sources*, Vol. 2, p 118, copies of his World War I diaries and letters have been placed in the Imperial War Museum.

HILKEN, Captain Thomas John Norman (1901—1969)

Naval career. Cammanded HM Escort Carrier *Emperor*, 1943—44. Naval air staff, SEAC 1945. Commanded HMS *Mauritius* (Flag Ship, East Indies Fleet), 1949—50. Deputy Director of Naval Intelligence, 1951—53.

Some material can be found in the Imperial War Museum. This includes his journal as commander of HMAS *Sydney*, January 1939—December 1940, his participation in Operation Tungsten against the *Tirpitz*, material on the invasion of southern France and his period as Military Governor of Penang, August-September 1945.

HINDE, Major-General Sir William Robert (Norris) (1900—1981)

Military career. Deputy Military Governor, British Section, Berlin, 1945—48. Deputy Director of Operations, Kenya, 1953—56.

His letters and correspondence (13 files, 1953—61) as Deputy Director of Operations during the Mau Mau Emergency in Kenya, are in Rhodes House Library.

HINSLEY, Cardinal Arthur (1865—1943)

Roman Catholic Archbishop of Westminster.

His correspondence, texts of speeches, photographs etc., together with his official files, are retained by the Westminster Diocesan Archives.

HINTON OF BANKSIDE, 1st B
Sir Christopher Hinton (1901—1983)

Scientist and adviser to Government.

Five boxes of his papers, including personal diaries, have been placed in Churchill College, Cambridge.

HOARE, Geoffrey Spencer (fl 1930s—1940s)

The Times correspondent; Cairo, 1936—41; Deputy War Correspondent, Egypt, 1941, and special correspondent, Middle East.

The Times archive holds a few papers by and concerning Hoare, relating to service in Athens, Crete, Jerusalem and Cairo during World War II.

HOBHOUSE, Sir Charles Edward Henry, 4th Bt (1862—1941)

MP (Lib) Devizes, 1892—5; Bristol East, 1900—18. Parliamentary Under-Secretary, India Office, 1907—8. Financial Secretary, Treasury, 1908—11. Chancellor of the Duchy of Lancaster, 1911—14. Postmaster General, 1914—15.

Since the entry in *Sources*, Vol. 3, p 224, his journals have been located in the British Library (Add Mss 60504—60507). Apart from the journal of a world tour (1890—91) and other travels (1889—1907), there are three volumes of journals, 1893—1915, of political importance. Almost the whole content of these has been published in E. David (ed) *Inside Asquith's Cabinet: from the Diaries of Charles Hobhouse* (1977).

HOBLEY, Charles William (1867–1947)

Colonial administrator. Chief Political Officer to Expeditionary Force, German East Africa, 1914–15.

His diaries of service in Africa, 1890–97 are in Rhodes House Library.

HODESS, Jacob (1885–1961)

Anglo-Jewish journalist. Acting Secretary, Zionist Executive, London, 1929–39.

The Central Zionist Archives (A194) hold papers, 1920–48, in English, including correspondence with Weizmann and speeches he wrote for Weizmann; and correspondence with Ben-Gurion on the British administration in Palestine.

HODSON, Sir Arnold Wienholt (1881–1944)

Colonial service. Consul, Southern Abyssinia, 1914–26. Governor, Falkland Islands, 1926–30; Sierra Leone, 1930–36. Governor and C-in-C, Gold Coast, 1934–41.

In addition to the information cited in *Sources*, Vol. 2, p 120, his papers relating to travel in North Africa are held by the Royal Geographical Society.

HOGAN, Hon. Sir Michael Joseph Patrick (1908–   )

Chief Magistrate, Palestine, 1936. Crown Counsel, 1937. Attorney General, Aden, 1945. Solicitor General, Palestine, 1947–48.

He has retained his unsorted papers, but these are not available.

HOGARTH, David George (1862–1927)

Traveller. Keeper of Ashmolean Museum, Oxford. Director of Arab Bureau, Cairo, 1916–18.

In addition to the material at the Middle East Centre, cited in *Sources*, Vol. 5, p 101, his diaries remain with Mrs. John Barron (grandniece) c/o Bedford College, Regents Park, London, NW1. Details are not available.

HOLLAND, Sir Robert (Erskine) (1873–1965)

Indian Civil Service. Political Agent, Muscat, Rajputana etc. Deputy Secretary, Government of India, 1914. Member, India Council, 1925–31. Judicial Adviser to Siamese Government, 1933–36.

The draft chapters of his work *The Indian States*, bound in two volumes, are housed in the Cambridge Centre for South Asian Studies.

HOLTBY, Winifred (1898–1935)

Novelist and author. Director of *Time and Tide* from 1926.

In addition to the material cited in *Sources*, Vol. 5, p 102, further papers can be found in Fisk University Library (See NUC 76-1447).

HOME, Brigadier-General Sir Archibald (1874–1953)

Military career.

The World War I diaries and other papers have been donated to the Imperial War Museum by his daughter, Lady Briscoe OBE. The diaries include first-hand accounts of most major battles in Belgium and France, and useful material on the employment of cavalry in trench warfare, relations with the French Army and the qualities of senior officers of the BEF.

HOOD, Lieutenant-General Sir Alexander (1888–1980)

Army medical service, World Wars I and II. Deputy Director of Medical Services, Palestine and Transjordan. Director General, Army Medical Services, 1941–48. Governor, Bermuda, 1949–55.

All his papers, including an unpublished autobiography, are held in the Library of the Royal Army Medical Corps.

HOPE, Sir Theodore Cracaft (1831–1915)

Indian administrator. Secretary to the Government of India Financial and Commercial Department, 1881–82. Member of the Governor-General's Council, 1882–87.

His papers (10 vols and one box) are in the India Office Library (ref Mss Eur D 705). The papers were transferred from the official archives in 1966. No papers appear to be dated later than 1890.

HORGAN, John

Redmondite; prominent Irish Nationalist.

A microfilm of his political correspondence is held in the National Library of Ireland.

HORNE, 1st B
General Henry Sinclair Horne (1861–1929)

Military career. Served South Africa. Commanded 2nd Division, 1915; 15 Corps in France, 1916; 1st Army in France, 1916. GOC-in-C, Eastern Command, 1919–23.

Maps, some letters and operation orders covering his command of the 1st Army in France, 1916–19 are in the Imperial War Museum.

HORNIMAN, Lieutenant-Colonel William Dartnell (1905–1973)

Military service. Officer Commanding, Palestine Command, Signals Regiment, 1944–47.

The Imperial War Museum has microfilms of extracts from his diaries (1920–72), including two volumes (1944–47) covering service in Palestine. The entries provide comment on the inter-racial conflicts, predominantly pro-Arab and anti-Jewish, and details of terrorist activities.

HORNSBY, Sir Bertram (d1943)

Governor, National Bank of Egypt. Military service, World War I.

His papers are deposited in St. Antony's College, Oxford. The material includes papers on economic and financial matters in Egypt, 1922–23, negotiations with the Egyptian Government for the renewal of the charter of the National Bank of Egypt in 1939, papers on the Maadi Company, a few papers on the Sudan, Palestine etc.

HORSFALL, Thomas Coghlan (1841–1932)

Educationalist and propagandist. Author of *Reforms Needed in Our System of Elementary Education, The example of Germany, The relation of National Service to the Welfare of the Community*, etc.

The papers in Manchester Central Library comprise 424 letters to him on education, physical training, military service, social reform and religion, 1878–1928, from politicians and economists including Winston Churchill, A. J. Balfour and Joseph Chamberlain.

HOSIE, Sir Alexander (1853–1925)

Diplomat and Chinese explorer. Consul General, Szechuen, 1902; Tientsin 1908–12. British Delegate, Shanghai International Opium Commission, 1909. Various publications on China.

His 1912 diary of his Manchurian travels is in the Royal Geographical Society.

HOWARD OF PENRITH, 1st B
Sir Esme William Howard (1863–1939)

Consul-General, Hungary, 1908–11. Minister, Switzerland, 1911–13; Sweden, 1913–19. Ambassador, Spain, 1919–24; United States, 1924–30.

Since the entry in *Sources*, Vol. 2, p 123, his diaries, correspondence and political files, 1882–1944, have been placed in Cumbria Record Office (ref DHW). The collection includes his diaries, 1891–1927; personal correspondence, which includes letters from leading public figures such as Curzon, Grey, Eden (1908–47); personal family correspondence (1898–1939); official correspondence (1885–1930); official despatches between Esme and the Foreign Office (1889–1919); personal and semi-official correspondence (1902–34); purely personal correspondence of Sir Esme (1906–36); literary works by Sir Esme (1891–1936); printed material, including pamphlets, circulars and Command Papers (1879–1939); financial (1884–1936); and other miscellaneous papers. A list is available (NRA 23774).

HUGESSON, Sir Hughe Montgomery Knatchbull- (1886–1971)

Minister, Baltic States, 1930–34; Persia, 1934–36. Ambassador, China, 1936–37; Turkey, 1939–44; Belgium (and Minister, Luxembourg), 1944–47.

The papers described in *Sources*, Vol. 2, p 125, were given to Churchill College, Cambridge in November 1976 by Lady Knatchbull-Hugesson. The collection includes 17 volumes of diaries, ranging from 1915 to 1952, and 137 letters, mainly for the period 1935–1937. Almost nothing exists for his time as Ambassador to Turkey.

HUGHES, Edward (1856–1925)

Welsh miners' leader. General Secretary, North Wales Miners, 1897. Permanent agent, 1898–1925.

The papers, which originally formed part of the records of the NUM North Wales Area records, are held at the Miners' Offices, Bradley Road, Wrexham. The collection includes 17 diaries, draft committee minutes, a manuscript of recollections (*c.* 1920), a manuscript biography (mainly Welsh), 1919 and some correspondence. The collection constitutes an almost complete autobiographical record of a trade union activist. A list is available (NRA 21135).

HUGHES, Brigadier (Hugh) (Llewelyn) Glyn (1892–1975)

First Medical Officer to see German Concentration Camp at Belsen. Vice-Director, BAOR, Medical Services, 1945.

Four large box files of correspondence, photographs, reports, etc., are in the Royal Army Medical College Library.

HUGHES, Professor John David Ivor (1885–1969)

Lawyer. Professor of Law, University of Leeds, 1919–51. President, Society of Public Teachers of Law, 1931–32. Member, Lord Chancellor's Committee on Legal Education.

A collection of his papers was deposited in the Brotherton Library, University of Leeds, in 1978 (ref MS 428). A list is available (NRA 22573). The collection mainly comprises notebooks kept while a student at Aberystwyth (1904) and Oxford (1911–15). The greater part of the material is on Roman Law, and includes notes taken at the lectures of Professor W. J. Brown at Aberystwyth and Professor H. Goudy and P. Vinogradoff at Oxford. There are 8 notebooks from his student days at Aberystwyth and London, 1904–10, and 16 from his Oxford days, 1911–15. There are 4 books of notes from his period at Leeds, 1919–51.

HUME, Colonel A. H. B. (fl 1930s)

Army career. Closely involved with Indian affairs.

His papers have been presented to the Cambridge Centre for South Asian Studies by Mrs. Lee-Warner. The collection includes correspondence relating to the Indian Defence League, the India White Paper and the Indian Empire Society. There is correspondence and occasional letters from Lord Fermoy, Sir Samuel Hoare, Lord Lymington, Louis Stuart etc., for the period 1931–36. Other letters deal with the Civil Disobedience movement, Civil Service examination papers, etc.

HUMPHREYS, Alderman Hubert (1878–1967)

Labour politician. Lord Mayor of Birmingham, 1949–50.

His personal correspondence is in the Social Sciences Department, Birmingham Reference Library.

HUNTER, Dorothy (1881–1977)

Conservationist and feminist.

The papers have been acquired by Surrey County Record Office. The collection includes letters relating to her work in politics, for such causes as women's suffrage and free trade, material on the National Trust and the Commons and Footpaths Preservation Society. Correspondents include Millicent Fawcett and other prominent women campaigners, as well as family letters. The collection also includes lecture notes, press cuttings, sketches and drawings, photographs and printed papers. A list is available (NRA 21232). The papers of Sir Robert Hunter are also at Surrey County Record Office and include letters to him from Octavia Hill, Canon Rawnsley and others concerning conservation.

HUNTER, Sir Robert (1844–1913)

Co-founder, National Trust.

See **Hunter, Dorothy**

HURD, Sir Archibald (1869–1959)

Naval correspondent.

Five boxes of papers, letters, newscuttings and scrapbooks were deposited in Churchill College, Cambridge in March 1980. A list is available (NRA 23856).

HUTCHINGS, Sir Robert Howell (1897–)

Indian Civil Servant. Secretary, Government of India Food Department, 1943. Member, Governor-General's Executive Council, India, 1946.

A microfilm of his papers is in the Centre for South Asian Studies, Cambridge. It includes a transcript report on the evacuation from Burma. Access to the material is subject to restrictions.

HUTT, George Allen (fl 1930–1950)

Communist journalist and author.

See **Proudfoot, David**

HUTTON, Lieutenant-General Sir Thomas Jacob (1890–)

GOC, Burma; and CGS, India, 1941–42.

Some material is in the Liddell Hart Centre for Military Archives, King's College, London. A list is available (NRA 23071). The deposit would appear to consist of his typescript 97pp. account of the campaign in Burma, December 1941–March 1942, entitled *Rangoon 1941–42: A Personal Record.* Two appendices to the typescript contain letters by Hutton, General Smyth and Brigadier Roberts *re. The Times Literary Supplement*, 1969.

HYAMSON, Albert Montefiore (1875–1954)

Anglo-Jewish literary figure. Director, Jewish Propaganda, Department of Information, 1917. Director of Immigration and Controller of Labour, Palestine, till 1934. Editor, *Zionist View*, 1917–19.

Anglo-Jewish Archives at the Mocatta Library, University College, London (ref AJ/77) has a collection of press cuttings. Most of Hyamson's correspondence and other papers were destroyed shortly after his death.

HYDE, Douglas (1860–1949)

Irish literary figure. President, Gaelic League, 1893–1915. President of Ireland, 1938–45.

His correspondence, together with literary manuscripts, covering the period 1890–1920, is in the National Library of Ireland.

IM THURN, Sir Everard (1852–1932)

Colonial service. Served Venezuelan Boundary Commission, 1897–99. Lieutenant-Governor and Colonial Secretary, Ceylon, 1901–04. Governor of Fiji and High Commissioner of the Western Pacific, 1904–10. President, Royal Anthropological Institute, 1919–20.

His anthropological and other papers are in the Royal Anthropological Institute, London.

INGLEBY, Holcombe (1854–1926)

MP (Con) Kings Lynn, Dec. 1910–18.

In addition to the information cited in *Sources*, Vol. 3, p 242, his First World War letters to his son have been presented to the Imperial War Museum by his grand-daughter, Mrs. S. Stevenson. The letters provide an insight into the life of a prosperous backbench MP during the war.

INGRAMS, William Harold (1897–1973)

Political Officer, Aden, 1934. Acting Governor, Aden, 1940. Resident Adviser, Hadramout States and British Agent, East Aden Protectorate, 1942–45. Assistant Secretary, Allied Control Commission for Germany (British Section) 1945–47. Chief Commissioner, Northern Territories, Gold Coast, 1947–48.

His papers on Aden *c.* 1914–62 have been given to the Middle East Centre, St. Antony's College, Oxford. Churchill College, Cambridge, has his papers for the Allied Control Commission in Germany (NRA 24345).

INVERCHAPEL, 1st B
Sir Archibald John Kerr Clark Kerr (1882–1951)

Minister, Central America, 1925–28; Chile, 1928–30; Sweden, 1931–35. Ambassador, Iraq, 1935–38; China, 1938–42; USSR, 1942–46; United States, 1946–48.

Since the entry in *Sources*, Vol. 2, p 128, the papers have been placed in the Bodleian Library, Oxford. They include papers and correspondence from the early 1900s to the 1940s, other papers of various dates and photographs.

IRWIN, Lieutenant-General Noel Mackintosh Stuart (1892–   )

Army career. Commander, 6th Infantry Brigade, 1939–43. Commands in India, West Africa, etc.

Some of his papers are in the Imperial War Museum. There are papers relating to the Dakar operation, 1940, and the Arakan campaign. There are reports, notes, orders and letters, including some from Wavell and Mountbatten.

JACKSON, Charles Lionel Atkins Ward- (1869–1930)

MP (Con) Leominster, 1918–22.

Since the entry in *Sources*, Vol. 3, p 244, the Imperial War Museum has acquired a copy of his World War I letters.

JACKSON, Major-General Sir Herbert William (1861–1931)

Served Nile, Dongola expeditions etc. Commander of forces at Fashoda during the Marchand Mission. Governor, Berber Province 1899–1900. Lieutenant Governor and Civil Secretary, Sudan 1900–02.

An eleven page typescript account of the Fashoda incident, 1898, is in the Sudan Archive, Oriental Section, University of Durham.

JACKSON, Commander Sir Robert Gillman Allen (1911–   )

Director General, Middle East Supply Centre and Principal Assistant to UK Minister of State, Cairo, 1942–45. Senior Deputy Director-General, UNRRA, 1945–47. United Nations service.

Sir Robert Jackson has retained some papers on the Middle East Supply Centre (1941–45) and on the work of the Minister of State (1942–44). These were used by Professor Martin Wilmington for his book, *The Middle East Supply Centre* (ed L. Evans) (1972).

JAMES, Vice-Admiral Thomas Norman (1878–1965)

Naval career. Various commands, e.g. HMS *Cardiff* 1919–21; HMS *President* 1921–23. Rear-Admiral in charge and Admiral Superintendent, Gibraltar, 1931–33.

His papers, including those as an eye-witness observer of such World War I naval engagements as Jutland, are at the Imperial War Museum. There is correspondence concerning the war at sea and also papers concerning the evacuation of Russian refugees, 1920. The collection was not listed at the time of writing.

JENKINS, Sir John Lewis (1857–1912)

Indian Civil Service. Assistant Commissioner, Sind, 1889–93. Commissioner of Customs, Bombay. Ordinary Member, Executive Council, Governor-General of India. 1910–12.

His papers (44 folios) have been acquired by the India Office Records (ref Mss Eur C 255). Included in the collection are letters from the Viceroy, Lord Hardinge, 1911–12.

JERRAM, Rear-Admiral Sir R. C. (fl 1906–1960)

Naval career.

His journals and papers. 1906–60, have been placed in the National Maritime Museum.

JERSEY, 7th Earl of
Victor Albert George Child Villiers (1845–1915)

Governor of New South Wales, 1890–93.

Some letters relating to his period as Governor of New South Wales are in the National Library of Australia (MS 2896). The correspondents include Henry Parkes, George Dibbs, Lord Derby, William Knox, S. W. Griffith, Lord Ripon and Rupert Leigh.

JOCHELMAN, Dr. David S. (1868–1941)

Zionist pioneer. Co-founder, Jewish Territorial Organisation, Chairman, Federation of Relief Organisations of Great Britain. Executive Member, Jewish Board of Deputies.

The Jabotinsky Institute in Israel has his papers (ref. P105).

JOHNES, Sir James Hills- (1833–1919)

Military career.

His 1900 journal of the Boer War is in the National Library of Wales.

JOHNSON, Sir Frank William Frederick (1866–1943)

Commanded Pioneer Corps, Rhodesia 1890. Chief Staff Office, Langberg Rebellion

1896. Commanded troops in Lahore, 1919. Member, Legislative Assembly, Southern Rhodesia, 1927–28.

His out letter-books, 1895–1905, are in the National Archives of Zimbabwe.

JOHNSON, Hewlett (1874–1966)

Left-wing Anglican clergyman. Popularly known as the 'Red Dean'.

Since the entry in *Sources*, Vol. 5, p 110, the papers are reported to have been deposited in the Library of the University of Kent.

JOHNSTON, Sir Harry Hamilton (1858–1927)

Colonial administrator and explorer. Vice-Consul, Niger Delta, 1885. Consul, Portuguese East Africa 1889. Commissioner for South Central Africa 1891–96. Special Commissioner, Uganda, 1899–1901.

His papers are in the National Archives of Zimbabwe. The collection includes correspondence and papers, 1871–1927, relating to his explorations and administrative posts (*c.* 900 folios). There are also 8 volumes of diaries and journals, 1878–89 and photographs and sketches *c.* 1880–1901.

JONES, Aubrey (1911–   )

MP (Con) Birmingham Hall Green, 1950–65. Minister of Fuel and Power, 1955–57. Minister of Supply, 1957–59, Chairman, National Board for Prices and Incomes, 1965–70.

Since the entry in *Sources*, Vol. 3, p 252, the papers have been placed in Churchill College, Cambridge. *See* NRA 18561.

JONES, Barbara Whittingham- (fl 1939–1945)

Author and journalist. Specialist in South-East Asian affairs.

A collection of 11 folders of transcripts of letters and papers concerning Indonesia, Malaya and Thailand during World War II was deposited in the Library of the School of Oriental and African Studies in 1961 (ref MS 145982).

JONES, Sir (Bennett) Melvill (1887–1975)

Mond Professor of Aeronautical Engineering, 1919–52. Chairman, Aeronautical Research Council, 1943–47. Attached Ministry of Aircraft Production, 1939–45.

His papers have been deposited in the Royal Air Force Museum, Hendon, through the Contemporary Science Archives Centre at Oxford. The collection (ref AC 76/6) includes lectures, notes, correspondence, diaries and other papers, 1905–69.

JONES, (H) Francis (1874–1949)

Welsh Nationalist. Treasurer of Plaid Cymru. Lecturer in Welsh History.

The papers are in the National Library of Wales. The collection consists mainly of letters relating to various aspects of his public life, including his work as a lecturer in Welsh History under the Workers' Educational Association, as Treasurer of Plaid Cymru, as Vice-Chairman of the 1947 National Eisteddfod held at Colwyn Bay, as organiser of the Urdd National Eisteddfod in Colwyn Bay in 1934, and as the author of a feature entitled 'Welsh Causerie' in the *North Wales Weekly News*.

The collection also contains correspondence dated 1899–1900 between H. Francis Jones and Miss Ann Ellen Williams, his future wife; letters inviting him to address various societies and institutions throughout the country; drafts of articles, essays and lecture notes mainly relating to various aspects of Welsh history and literature.

JONES, John Harry (1881–1973)

Economist. Expert on the coal industry. Professor of Economics, University of Leeds 1919–46.

His papers (83 items) on the coal industry in Britain and overseas, mid-1930s, are in the University of Leeds. They were given in December 1976 by Professor J. R. Crossley of the School of Economic Studies.

KABERRY, Phyllis Mary (1910–   )

Anthropologist.

The papers have been deposited in BLPES by Dr. Rowlands of University College, London. The papers, notes, photographs etc. are of most interest for her work in New Guinea. There are revealing notebooks on the Kalaba, etc.

KARSLAKE, Lieutenant-General Sir Henry (1879–1942)

Army career. GSOI, British Army on the Rhine, 1919. Served Peshawar, Southern Command etc. GOC, France, May–June 1940.

An important short report, published only in edited form, is in the Imperial War Museum. It covers operations south of the Somme, May–June 1940, with special reference to the lines of communication.

KELL, Major-General Sir Vernon George Waldegrave (1873–1942)

Served European War, 1914–18; War Office (MI5 etc.).

The papers, cited in *Sources*, Vol. 2, p 133, have now been loaned to the Imperial War Museum for copying. The collection includes documents concerning counter-espionage work, a journal covering service in the Boxer uprising, 1900–01, pocket diaries, 1939–41 and a biography by his wife, Constance.

KELLOCK, Thomas Oslaf (1923–   )

Colonial legal career. Director, Legal Division, Commonwealth Secretariat, 1969–72. Constitutional Adviser, HM Sultan of Brunei, 1975–76. Chairman, Anti-Apartheid Movement, 1963–65.

Some papers have been placed with the Centre for South African Studies, University of York. The collection includes papers relating to the Devlin Commission of Enquiry, Nyasaland, 1959, miscellaneous papers on South Africa, political trials in Malawi, the Boycott Movement of March 1964, the Riviona Trials and the World Campaign for the Release of South African Political Prisoners. A list is available (NRA 19618).

KELLY, Herbert (1860–1950)

Theologian, writer and historian. Director, Society of the Sacred Mission, 1893–1910. Professor, Theological College, Ikebukuro, Tokyo, 1913–19.

Miscellaneous papers are with the archives of the Society of the Sacred Mission at

Milton Keynes. Reference should be made to C. Kitching, *The Central Records of the Church of England*. Miscellaneous correspondence, including his letters to the Church Quarterly Review, are in Lambeth Palace Library.

KEMBELL, Major-General Sir George Vero (1859—1941)

Army career. Served North West Frontier and West Africa. Commanded Kano Sokoto expedition, 1903. Assistant Director and Director, War Office, 1909—13. Divisional Commander, India, 1917—19.

The Army Museums Ogilby Trust acquired 33 of his letters relating to the Mesopotamia Commission of Enquiry and service in India in 1964.

KENNEDY, Sir Charles Malcolm (1831—1908)

Head of Commercial Department, Foreign Office 1872—93. Plenipotentiary for the Treaty of The Hague 1882. Lecturer on International Law, Bristol, 1895—1902.

His correspondence relating to the Commercial Department, 1872—94, including correspondence as Commissioner at Paris 1874—75 is in the Public Record Office (FO 800/4—5).

KENNEDY, Hugh (1879—1936)

Chief Justice of Eire.

His legal and official papers, 1922—24, are in the Archives Department, University College, Dublin (ref P4). The papers (29 boxes) cover the period 1899—1936. The collection includes files concerning the legal functions of the office of Attorney General, particularly with reference to contemporary legislation, constitutional negotiations with the British government (1922—24), Constitution Committee (1922), Judiciary Committee (1922—23), the Boundary Commission (1922—24), the League of Nations and Imperial Conferences (1922—29). There is also material on the office of Chief Justice.

KENRICK, George Harry Blair (d1952)

Lawyer. Member, Legislative Council of Viceroy of India, 1910—16. Advocate General of Bengal.

One box of his papers, 1908—14, mainly relating to terrorism in Bengal is in the India Office Library.

KINCH, E. A. (fl 1896—1958)

Arab expert. Political adviser, Mosul.

Some papers are at the Middle East Centre, St. Antony's College, Oxford. The collection comprises copies of autobiographical notes, 1896—1958, and correspondence as Political Adviser, Mosul, with Cornwallis and others, 1941—44. There is material on the Kurdish situation and British policy towards the Kurds.

KING, Sir Norman (1880—1963)

Consular Service from 1907. Chargé d'Affaires, Mexico, 1925. Consul-General, Barcelona, 1926—38; Marseilles, 1938—40.

Since the entry in *Sources*, Vol. 2, p 137, a copy of his World War I diary is now available in the Imperial War Museum. The diary gives a detailed coverage of his service, 1914–16, mainly as a Political Officer attached to the British East Africa Expedition. It includes material on the disastrous British attack on Tanga and of the bombardment of Dar-el-Salaam by HMS *Goliath*.

KINTORE, 10th E of
Sir Algernon Hawkins Thomond (1852–1930)

Conservative Whip in House of Lords, 1885. Lieutenant-Governor of South Australia 1889–93. Deputy Speaker, House of Lords, 1913.

His papers are with the present Earl of Kintore, Inverurie, Aberdeenshire, Scotland (NRA 10210). His papers include one bundle of correspondence relating to his period in South Australia. Correspondents include Lords Carrington, Dufferin, Lansdowne, Ripon, Rosebery and Salisbury.

KIRBY, Sir Arthur Frank (1899–   )

Railway administrator in Middle East and Africa. General Manager, Palestine Railways. Director General, Hejaz Railway, 1942–4.

The papers at the Middle East Centre, St. Antony's College, Oxford, cover Palestine, Arabia, Persia and the Middle East generally. There is relevant material on the last days of the British mandate in Palestine and the handover to the United Nations prior to evacuation. Also there are articles on railways in Palestine and the Middle East.

KIRK, Sir John (1832–1922)

Chief Officer on Livingstone's expedition to Africa 1853–64. Agent and Consul General, Zanzibar. Plenipotentiary to Brussels African Conference 1889–90. Special Commissioner to the Niger Coast 1895. Foreign Secretary, Royal Geographical Society.

His papers are in the possession of Mrs. D. Foskett, 'Bishop's House', Brathay, Ambleside, Westmorland. The collection includes diaries, notebooks, telegrams, correspondence concerning the slave trade 1873, Zanzibar correspondence 1868–72, papers relating to the Brussels anti-slavery conference 1889–90, papers relating to Bibi Saimeh, letters relating to the Uganda Railway 1897–1920 and further political and miscellaneous correspondence. Much of the material has been published by R. Foskett (e.g. *The Zambesi journal and letters of Dr. John Kirk*, (2 volumes). In addition, some 17 letters to Kirk, from Rosebery, Jo Chamberlain, Sir H. M. Stanley etc. are in the National Library of Scotland (Acc 4084).

KIRKE, General Sir Walter Mervyn St. George (1877–1949)

Military career from 1896. Served Waziristan Campaign, 1901–02; European War, 1914–18. Deputy Director of Military Operations, 1918–22. Head of Naval, Military and Air Force Mission to Finland, 1924–25. Deputy Chief of General Staff, India 1926–29. Commander 5th Division and Catterick Area, 1929–31. GOC-in-C Western Command, 1933–36. Director-General, Territorial Army, 1936–39. Inspector-General, Home Defences, 1939. C-in-C, Home Forces, 1939–40.

In addition to the material cited in *Sources*, Vol. 2, p 138, further papers (1921–22) are housed in the Royal Artillery Institution (ref MD/576). In addition, in 1981, the Imperial War Museum received on loan from his son the diaries and other records of his command of M1 1b, the clandestine intelligence section at GHQ France, 1914–17. These papers shed interesting light on the problems of the effective gathering of military intelligence in World War I. His letters home supplement the diaries in giving his views on the general progress of the war. His papers as Deputy Chief of General Staff, India, 1926–29, are in the India Office Library.

KISCH, Brigadier Frederick Hermann (1888–1943)

Military career. British Delegation, Versailles Peace Conference 1919. Chairman, Palestine-British Trade Association. Head of the Palestine Executive, Jewish Agency, 1929–31.

The Israel State Archives (ref S25) hold his diary (1920s–30s), and over 1,000 letters exchanged with Weizmann (1921–1940) survive in the Weizmann Archives. Further papers and photographs remain with Michael Kisch (son) in Israel. His *Palestine Diary* appeared in 1938.

KITCHIN, Frederick Harcourt (1867–1932)

Journalist. Assistant Manager, *The Times*, 1908–09. Editor, *Glasgow Herald*, 1909–17.

Some papers can be found in the archives of *The Times*.

KNOWLES, Sir James Thomas (1831–1908)

Founder and Editor of the *Nineteenth Century*.

The papers formerly in the possession of Miss Irene Skilbeck are now in Westminster Central Reference Library.

LACK, Sir Henry Reader (1831–1908)

Civil servant and diplomat. Secretary to Commissioners, Commercial Treaty with France, 1860. Comptroller-General, Patent Office, 1884–97.

Papers relating to his work in the Board of Trade are in the Public Record Office (BT 191).

LAMBE, Admiral of the Fleet Sir Charles Edward (1900–1960)

Assistant Chief of Naval Staff (Air) 1945–46. C-in-C Far East Station, 1953–54. Second Sea Lord 1955–57. C-in-C. Mediterranean and NATO C-in-C Allied Forces Mediterranean 1957–59. Lord Commissioner of the Admiralty, First Sea Lord and Chief of Naval Staff 1959–60.

The papers, which remain in the possession of Lady Lambe, have now been listed (NRA 24919).

LANDAU, Rom (1899–1974)

Author, Sculptor, art critic and Middle Eastern traveller. Member of Executive, World Council of Faiths, London, 1936–44. Senior Specialist, Middle East Division of Ministry of Information, 1941. Member of Arab Committee, Political Intelligence Department of Foreign Office, 1941–44.

The Rom Landau Collection at the Carnegie Library, Syracuse University, Syracuse, New York, includes wartime material on the Middle East collected whilst in official service (1942–45)

LANDMAN, Samuel (Shemuel) (d 1967)

Lawyer and Zionist leader in Britain.

In addition to the material cited in *Sources*, Vol. 5, p 117, further papers are in the Jabotinsky Institute in Israel (ref P247). The British Library has Landman's pamphlet on the extent of Jewish pressure in bringing the United States into World War II.

LANE, Hugh Thompson (1914—   )

Indian Civil Service, United Provinces, 1937—47. Regional Food Controller, Meerut, 1943—45.

His papers, covering the period 1937—47, have been placed in the India Office Library & Records (ref Mss Eur D 827).

LARKCOM, Colonel E. H. Jacobs- (fl 1939—1945)

Military career. Served British Military Mission to China, 1943—45.

His papers, including his diaries of the British military mission to China in World War II are in the Liddell Hart Centre for Military Archives, King's College, London.

LARKING, Dennis Augustus Hugo (1876—1970)

Naval career. Served Mediterranean, West Indian and China Stations. Naval attaché, Rome, 1915—19, Balkans 1939—41.

The papers (1 box) were purchased by the National Maritime Museum from Messrs Francis Edwards in 1974. They consist of private letters to Larking from Admiral of the Fleet Earl Beatty and from Lady Beatty. The letters from Earl Beatty, 1914—28 date mostly from the war.

LAUGHTON, Sir John Knox (1830—1915)

Naval historian.

His correspondence and other notes are in the National Maritime Museum.

LAWRENCE, Sir Henry Staveley (1870—1949)

Indian Civil Servant. Commissioner, Sind, 1916—20. Acting Governor of Bombay, 1926. Author of *The Indian White Paper* (1934) and *Freedom from Fear and Want*.

One volume of miscellaneous papers (1932) was acquired by the India Office Library in 1972.

LEDDEN, James (fl 1914—1918)

Irish Nationalist and hunger striker.

His diary is in Limerick City Library.

LEE, Major-General Alec Wilfred (1896—1973)

Military career. Deputy Commander, British Army Staff, Washington, 1944—47.

A collection of papers has been presented to the Imperial War Museum by his widow. It consists of over 150 letters written by Lee to his parents, 1915—1946. The letters cover all his appointments and are particularly rich on Egypt and Palestine (Lee was the first officer sent from Cairo to Palestine in 1929 after the Arab rising) and as Deputy Commander of the British Army Staff in Washington, 1944—46. A number of his other letters are with the archives of the Staffordshire Regiment at Lichfield.

LESLIE, Sir Norman Alexander (1870—1945)

Civil servant.

His papers relating to the convoy system in 1917 are in Churchill College, Cambridge. *See* NRA 18561.

LESLIE, Sir Shane (1885—1971)

Irish Nationalist. Supporter of Gaelic revival. Contested Derry, 1911. Toured USA to raise funds. Editor, *Dublin Review*, 1916. Subsequent literary career.

The National Library of Ireland has acquired a large collection of his papers, mainly letters to him on Irish historical, literary and political matters but including some of his literary manuscripts. Listing of these papers has been completed.

LESTER, Muriel

Pacifist and social reformer.

Relevant material can be found in the records of the International Fellowship of Reconciliation, in the Sigmund Schultze archive, Soest, West Germany.

LEVER, Captain George Harold (1892—1973)

Captain with British Military Mission to Russia, 1919—20. Served under General Strickland in Ireland, 1920—21. Writer for *Manchester Guardian*.

The papers were deposited in 1973 in the Liddell Hart Centre for Military Archives, King's College, London. A list has been prepared (NRA 23072). The collection consists of papers relating to his service in the German South West Africa campaign 1914—15, as a member of the South African Defence Force, photographs of the campaign and other miscellaneous photographs. There is Lever's diary 1919—20 kept while serving with the British Military Mission to Russia, and photographs relating to it. Finally there are a few miscellaneous papers relating to Lever's service 1914—22.

LEWIS, Colonel David Francis (1855—1927)

Military service. In command at action of Rosaires. *The Times* correspondent with the French Army, Morocco, 1907, and Spanish Army, Melilla, 1909.

His journal of the 2nd Sudan War, 1898, is in the National Army Museum.

LEWIS, Major-General Sir Richard (1895—1965)

Military career. Served AFHQ, 1942—44. Deputy Director General, Finance and Administration, European Regional Office, UNRRA.

The papers were deposited by his daughters, Mrs. Palamountain and Mrs. Lomer at the Liddell Hart Centre for Military Archives, King's College, London, between 1975 and 1977. Additional material is expected. A list has been prepared (NRA 23073). The collection consists of four basic sections, relating to the various periods of Lewis's career. There is miscellaneous material, largely relating to the Advanced Mechanical Course at the Military College of Science, Woolwich (1932—

33). There are several reports for DCIGS (1938–41) on organisation of the War Office, organisation of the General Staff, the services required from the RAF for the Army in the field etc. There are five files pertaining to AFHQ on topics such as 'First Army Maintenance Project', 'Organisation in Italy after move of AFHQ', 'Staff Tables Br. formations' for the period 1942–44. 13 items exist relating to Lewis's work as Deputy Director General for Finance and Administration, UNRRA, including some printed booklets, files on 'British Armed forces – currency losses' and the contribution of the Department of Finance and Administration to UNRRA's work, general notes on UNRRA and several reports on UNRRA's activities.

LILLICRAP, Sir Charles Swift (1887–1966)

Assistant Director of Naval Construction 1936, Deputy Director, 1941. Director of Naval Construction, 1944–51.

The papers were presented to the National Maritime Museum in 1970 by his widow. There are memoranda and letters relating to the reorganisation of the Royal Naval Corps of Constructors, 1945–47, appointment diaries 1951–52, invitations, photographs, etc.

LINDSAY, Major-General George Mackintosh (1880–1956)

Served South Africa, 1900–02; European War, 1914–18. Inspector, Royal Tank Corps, War Office, 1925–29. Member, Mechanical Warfare Board, 1926–29. Service in Egypt and India. Commissioner of British Red Cross, etc., North West Europe, 1944–46.

In addition to the information cited in *Sources*, Vol. 2, p 146, a significant collection of Lindsay's papers was placed in the Centre for Military Archives, King's College, London, with the papers of Captain Sir Basil Liddell Hart. This collection, which relates almost entirely to the development of tanks between 1924 and 1944, was originally lent to Liddell Hart when he was engaged in writing *The Tanks, The History of the Royal Tank Regiment*, 1959. A further substantial collection is in the keeping of the General's family with whom the Centre is in contact.

LISTOWEL, 5th E of
William Francis Hare, Vt Ennismore (1906–)

Parliamentary Under-Secretary, India Office, 1944–5. Postmaster General, 1945–7. Secretary of State for India and Burma, 1947–8. Minister of State, Colonial Office, 1948–50. Parliamentary Secretary, Ministry of Agriculture and Fisheries, 1950–1. Governor-General, Ghana, 1957–60.

Since the entry in *Sources*, Vol. 4, p 16, his correspondence with Mountbatten, April to August 1947, on the transfer of power in India and related problems has been presented to the India Office Records (ref MSS Eur C 357).

LITHGOW, Sir James (1883–1952)

Industrialist. Seconded to Admiralty as Director of Shipbuilding Production, 1917. Controller of Merchant Shipbuilding and Repairs and a Member of the Board of Admiralty, 1940–46.

Since the entry in *Sources*, Vol. 2, p 147, the papers and other correspondence, 1891–1952, have been placed in Glasgow University Library.

LLOYD, Lieutenant-General Sir Francis (1853–1926)

Military career. Commanded 1st Guards Brigade, 1904–08; Welsh Division, Territorial Forces, 1909–13; London District, 1913–19. Food Commissioner, London and Home Counties, 1919–20.

In addition to the papers in Essex Record Office, cited in *Sources*, Vol. 2, p 148, a collection of *c.* 150 letters to him and his wife from Grenadier Guardsmen and officers serving in South Africa, 1899–1902, is in the National Army Museum. A list is available (NRA 23379).

LLOYD, Major-General Francis Thomas (1838–1912)

Military career. Served Egypt, Sudan etc. Governor, Royal Military Academy, Woolwich, 1897–1901. Colonel Commandant, Royal Artillery, 1909.

Some papers, covering the period 1884–1901, are in the Library of the Royal Artillery Institution, Woolwich.

LLOYD, Air Chief Marshal Sir Hugh Pughe (1894–1981)

Served European War, 1914–18; War of 1939–45. Air Officer Commanding, Malta, 1941–42. Commander, Allied Coastal Air Forces, Mediterranean, 1943–44; Commonwealth Bomber Force, Okinawa, 1944–45, C-in-C, Air Command Far East, 1947–49. Air Officer C-in-C, Bomber Command, 1950–53.

Since the entry in *Sources*, Vol. 2, p 148, the papers have been acquired by the Royal Air Force Museum, Hendon.

LOCKER, Berl (1887–1972)

Executive Member, World Zionist Organisation, 1931–48. Representative, Jewish Agency in London. Chairman, Jewish Agency Executive, 1948–56.

The Central Zionist Archives have Locker's papers (1948–56) as executive member of the Jewish Agency, and his papers relating to the Department of Public Relations (ref S41) together with a smaller personal collection (ref A263).

Some other material survives in the Archives of the Jewish Labour Movement (Histadrut Archives). The Hebrew transcripts of interviews given by Locker, amounting to 127 pages, are held by the Oral History Project, Institute of Contemporary History, at the Hebrew University. The Board of Deputies' Archive also holds some of his correspondence (1934–5) concerning Palestine and the Jewish Agency (ref C 14/10).

LONG, 1st Vt
Walter Hume Long (1854–1924)

MP (Con) Wiltshire North, 1880–5; Devizes, 1885–92; Liverpool West Derby, 1893–1900; Bristol South, 1900–6; Dublin County South, 1906–Jan 1910; Strand, Jan 1910–18; Westminster St George's, 1918–21. Parliamentary Secretary, Local Government Board, 1886–92. President of the Board of Agriculture, 1895–1900. President of the Local Government Board, 1900–5 and 1915–16. Chief Secretary for Ireland, 1905. Secretary of State for Colonial Affairs, 1916–19. 1st Lord of the Admiralty, 1919–21.

Since the entry in *Sources*, Vol. 4, p 20, some 41 volumes of correspondence and papers, 1859–1932, have been acquired by the British Library (Add MSS 62403–62443).

LORAINE, Sir Percy Lyham, 12th Bt (1880—1961)

High Commissioner, Egypt and Sudan, 1929—33. Ambassador, Turkey, 1933—39; Italy, 1939—40.

Since the entry in *Sources*, Vol. 2, p 150, his demi-official and family papers have been acquired by the Public Record Office (FO/1011). There is material on the Middle East, Italy and the Paris Peace Conference.

LOWIS, Cecil Champain (1866—1948)

Indian Civil Servant. Deputy Commissioner, Officiating Chief Secretary, Burma, 1903—04. Director-General of Egyptian Census, 1906—08.

His diary (1889) is in the India Office Library. In 1889 Lowis was Assistant Commissioner at Paungbyin in the Upper Chindwin District of Burma. The diary gives an interesting insight into the life of an administrator in an isolated up-country station.

LOWNDES, Sir George Rivers (1862—1943)

Lawyer and judge. Legal Member, Viceroy of India's Executive Council.

A collection of his papers, 1915—34 (57 items), was purchased in 1967 by Duke University Library (NUC 68—1577). It consists of letters received by Lowndes on political and judicial matters in which he was involved.

LOWTHER, Sir William (fl 1924—1965)

Trade unionist.

A collection of papers has been deposited in Tyne and Wear Record Office (ref ACC 1170). A list is available (NRA 23329). The collection includes papers concerning his political and trade union career (1924—65) mainly in the form of printed material, press cuttings (1922—60) and miscellaneous personal material.

LUDLOW, Brigadier-General Sir Walter Robert (1857—1941)

Military career. Commanded 184th Infantry Brigade, 1915—16. Area Commandant, BEF, Flanders, 1917—18.

Some material can be found in the Imperial War Museum, including a diary of his service as an Area Commandant in the Ypres sallent, 1917—18.

LUMBY, Christopher Ditmar Rawson (1888—1946)

Times service, including correspondent, Middle East (Cairo), 1931—37 and 1940.

The Times archive holds Lumby's correspondence from 1913, including letters and papers concerning his period based at Cairo and visits to Palestine, 1933 and July 1937. The correspondents include Deakin and Graves.

LUND, Lieutenant-General Sir Otto Marling (1891—1956)

Military career. Military Assistant to Chief of Imperial General Staff, 1934—36. Deputy Director of Operations, War Office, September 1939. Major-General, Royal Artillery, Home Forces, 1940—44. Director of Royal Artillery, 1944—46. GOC-in-C, Anti-Aircraft Command, 1946—48.

Since the entry in *Sources*, Vol. 2, p 152, the papers relating to his mission to Turkey in 1939, and his visits to France in 1940 are now in the Liddell Hart Centre for Military Archives. Mr. Anthony Lund, the General's son, has a collection of photograph albums and a diary concerning North Russia which he wishes to keep.

LYON, Major-General David Murray- (fl 1911–1970)

Army career. Commander, 11th Division, Malaya, 1941–42.

His papers, *c.* 1911–70 are in the National Library of Scotland (Dep 233). The papers include reports, correspondence, photographs and other documents relating to his service career in France and India and his command of the 11th Indian Division in Malaya 1941–42.

LYTTON, 2nd E of
Victor Alexander George Robert Lytton (1876–1947)

Civil Lord of the Admiralty 1916, 1919–20. Parliamentary Secretary (Additional) to the Admiralty, 1916–19. Under-Secretary of State for India, 1920–22. Governor of Bengal, 1922–27; Viceroy and Acting Governor-General of India, 10 April – 9 August 1925. Chairman, League of Nations Mission to Manchuria, 1932.

Since the entry in *Sources*, Vol. 2, p 153, the papers (10 boxes) have been placed in the India Office Records (ref MSS Eur F 160). *See* NRA 25554.

MACASKIE, Brigadier Charles Frederick Cunningham (1888–1969)

Chief Justice and Deputy Governor, North Borneo, 1934–45. Chief Civil Affairs Officer, British Borneo, 1945–46.

His papers have been deposited in Rhodes House Library, Oxford (MSS Pac s 71). The collection, contained in one box, consists of files of personal and semi-official correspondence concerning his post-war work in Borneo. There is also a typescript, dated 1964, of his unpublished autobiography. The collection was opened for inspection in 1980. A handlist is available (NRA 12998).

McCALL, Major A. G. (fl 1928–1976)

Indian career. Superintendant, Lushai Hills.

His papers, covering the period 1928–76, have been placed in the India Office Library.

McCARTAN, Michael (1851–1902)

MP (Irish Nat) Down South, 1886–1902.

Since the entry in *Sources*, Vol. 3, p 29, some papers have been acquired by the Archives Department, University College, Dublin (ref P11/B). The material (737pp, 1882–1900) consists of a letter-book containing accounts of the solicitors firm of Clarke and McCartan, Belfast and 300 letters written by McCartan to Timothy Harrington, J. F. Small, Joseph Biggar, Charles S. Parnell, John Dillon, Timothy M. Healy and John Morley among others, in relation to electoral and constituency affairs and to the political interests of the Irish Parliamentary Party.

McCLINTOCK, Vice-Admiral John William Leopold (1874–1929)

Naval career from 1887. Commanded HMS *Lord Nelson, Dreadnought, King*

George V and *Conqueror*. Director, Mobilisation Department, Cruiser Squadron, 1924–26.

The papers were presented to the Imperial War Museum by his daughter. The collection includes letters to his family describing the Gallipoli campaign, when McClintock commanded the battleship *Lord Nelson*. There is a detailed description of the bombardments of February and March 1915 of the Turkish forts at the entrance to the Dardanelles and the sinking of the *Irresistible* and the *Ocean*.

McCOY, William Frederick (1885–1976)

Northern Ireland lawyer and politician. MP (Unionist), Stormont Parliament, 1945–65.

The papers have been acquired by the Public Record Office of Northern Ireland. It is a full collection, comprising papers, pamphlets, correspondence, speeches, press cuttings etc. There is material on the question of Dominion status, parliamentary business at Stormont and representations on behalf of his constituents. The constituency material, which is sometimes fairly intimate, is closed for 75 years. The papers are less detailed on the Unionist Party machine and the Orange Order. A list is available (NRA 21973).

McCREERY, General Sir Richard Loudon (1898–1967)

Military career. Served World Wars I and II. Chief of General Staff, Middle East, 1942. Commanded 8th Army in Italy, 1944–45. GOC-in-C., British Occupation Forces in Austria, 1945–46; British Army of the Rhine, 1946–48.

A copy of the unpublished biography, cited in *Sources*, Vol. 2, p 154, is now at the Imperial War Museum.

McCRINDLE, John Ronald (1894–1977)

Managing Director, British Airways.

His papers (1917–45) are at the Royal Air Force Museum, Hendon. The collection comprises diaries, correspondence and other papers.

McDERMOT, Frank Charles (1886–1975)

Irish political activist, involved in Blueshirts etc.

The papers in the Public Record Office of Ireland, Dublin, include correspondence (1927–72) with some material concerning the Blueshirts.

MACDONALD, Major-General Sir James Ronald Leslie (1862–1927)

Army career. Chief Engineer, Uganda Railway, 1891–92. Commissioner, Uganda Protectorate, 1893. Commander, Juba Expedition, 1898–99, Tibet operations, 1903–04, Mauritius, 1909–12.

His diary notebooks relating to the Uganda Railway Survey (1891–92) are in Rhodes House Library.

MACDONALD, Malcolm John (1901–1981)

MP (Lab) Bassetlaw, 1929–31; (National Lab) 1931–5; (National) Ross and Cromarty, 1936–45. Parliamentary Under-Secretary, Dominions Office, 1931–5. Secretary of State, Dominion Affairs 1935–8 and 1938–9; Colonies, 1935 and 1938–40.

Minister of Health, 1940–1. High Commissioner, Canada, 1941–6; India, 1955–60; Kenya, 1964–5. Governor-General, Malayan Union and Singapore, 1946; Malaya, Singapore and British Borneo, 1946–8; Kenya (Governor, 1963), 1963–4. British Commissioner-General, South East Asia, 1948–55. British special representative in Africa, 1966–9.

Since the entry in *Sources*, Vol. 4, p 32, the papers have been deposited temporarily in the Library of the Royal Commonwealth Society by his family and will eventually be transferred to the Library of the University of Durham.

The papers cover in varying detail all periods of his career in Britain, Canada, South East Asia, India and Africa. They consist of official and private correspondence, memoranda and reports, diaries, scripts of speeches, drafts of books, articles and short stories. When cataloguing is completed the papers will be available for a limited period in the Library of the Royal Commonwealth Society in London for consultation by *bona fide* scholars, subject to any necessary restriction on confidential material, before transfer to Durham University. Anyone wanting permission to consult the papers when this work is completed should apply to the Librarian, Royal Commonwealth Society, 18 Northumberland Avenue, London. WC2 N5BJ, indicating the material required and the nature of their research.

MACDONALD, Margaret Ethel (d1911)

Wife of Ramsay MacDonald.

Five volumes of her papers are in BLPES. Covering the period 1895–1911, they relate to such social issues as the employment of women, factory and shop legislation, housing and the 1901–02 Licensing Bill.

McEVOY, Air Chief Marshal Sir Theodore (1904–   )

Air Force career.

A transcript of *The Development of Air Fighting*, covering from World War I to after the end of World War II, with appendices on firepower, performance, roles for combat etc. is in the Royal Air Force Museum (ref DC 73/30).

MacEWEN, Sir Alexander (1875–1941)

Author.

The papers, covering the period 1931–40, have been placed in the National Library of Scotland (Acc 6113). The collection includes corrected typescripts of addresses and broadcast talks and manuscripts together with drafts of an unpublished work on nationalism and political systems.

MACGARRITY, Joseph (fl 1916–1940)

Irish Republican.

His papers, covering the period 1916–40, are in the National Library of Ireland.

McGILLIGAN, Patrick (fl 1919–1972)

Irish politician and lawyer. Secretary to Irish High Commissioner in London, 1923; Minister for Industry and Commerce, 1924–32. Minister for External Affairs, 1927-32. Minister for Finance, 1948–51. Attorney General, 1954–57. Professor of Constitutional Law, University College Dublin.

An extensive collection of his papers (86 boxes, 1919–72) is in University College,

Dublin (ref P35). There is material on the Imperial Conferences, League of Nations (1923–32); Anglo-Irish relations (1921–22), Irish relations with Northern Ireland (1923–31), and the boundary question (1922–26).

McGOWAN, Seamus

Irish republican activist.

Some of his papers concerning the Irish Citizen Army can be found in the Cowan McGowan papers in University College, Dublin.

McGRIGOR, Admiral Sir Roderick (1893–1959)

Naval career. Chief of Staff to C-in-C China Station. Assistant Chief of Naval Staff, 1941–43; Vice Chief, 1945–47. First Sea Lord and Chief of Naval Staff, 1951–55.

The papers were presented to the National Maritime Museum in 1978 by Miss McGrigor. They consist of a chart used at the Dardanelles in 1915 by HMS *Foxhound*; letters concerned with proceedings on a 'North Spanish patrol', 1937; papers relating to the sinking of the Spanish Nationalist cruiser *Baleares*, 1938; and the China Station, 1940; miscellaneous papers, 1938 and 1943–45; press cuttings, 1949; and photographs, mainly 2nd World War but also some family photographs.

MacINNES, Professor Charles Malcolm (1891–1972)

Academic. Professor of Imperial History, University of Bristol, 1943–57. Author of *The British Empire and the War* (1941) etc.

The papers, relating to his war work, have been placed in Bristol Record Office.

McINTOSH, Alastair James (1913–1973)

Colonial service.

Four volumes of diaries as Protectorate Secretary and Chief Adviser to the High Commissioner of Aden (1948–1963) are available in Rhodes House Library, Oxford.

MACKAY, Ronald William Gordon (1902–1960)

MP (Lab) Hull NW, 1945–50; Reading North 1950–1.

In addition to the papers at BLPES, cited in *Sources*, Vol. 4, p 35, a collection of his personal papers has been deposited in Sussex University Library. The collection complements the archives of Federal Union (q.v.).

McLEOD, General Sir Roderick William (1905–1980)

Military career. Commanded Special Air Services Brigade, 1944–45. Director of Military Operations, India, 1945–46; London, 1951–54. GOC, 6th Armoured Division, 1955–56. Deputy Chief of Defence Staff, 1957–60. Commander, British Forces in Hong Kong, 1960–61. GOC-in-C, Eastern Command, 1962–64.

In addition to the material cited in *Sources*, Vol. 2, p 158, his lectures and notes concerning the founding of the Special Air Service have been given by the General to the Liddell Hart Centre for Military Archives.

MACLYSAGHT, Edward

Irish Nationalist.

A collection of papers is in the National Library of Ireland.

McMAHON, Sir (Arthur) Henry (1862—1949)

Served in India. Political agent in Zhob, Thulchotiali etc. Political Officer with Durand mission to Kabul, 1893. Foreign Secretary to the Government of India, 1911—14. British Plenipotentiary for Treaty with Tibet, 1913—14. First High Commissioner for Egypt, 1914—16.

Letters, 1897—1902, to Major-General Sir Thomas Perrott (1851—1919) from McMahon are in the India Office Library, together with further correspondence and papers.

MACNEILL, John (Eoin) (1867—1945)

MP (Sinn Fein) Londonderry City, 1918—22. (Also elected in 1918 for the National University of Ireland).

In addition to the information in *Sources*, Vol. 4, p 40, some 4,000 items of his papers and correspondence are in the National Library of Ireland.

McPARTLIN, Thomas (fl 1877—1923)

Irish trade unionist. President, Trade Union Congress.

One box of his papers, 1877—1923, is in the Archives Department, University College, Dublin (ref P19). The collection includes correspondence with members of the trade union movement including Louie Bennett, Thomas Farren, Thomas Johnson and William O'Brien, mainly with reference to the contemporary trade union movement in Ireland. There is correspondence in relation to Labour Party affairs (1913—33), and also some letters concerning the Lockout (1913) and others to O'Brien in Frongoch prison, Wales (1916).

McQUEEN, Lieutenant-General Sir John Withers (1836—1909)

Army career. Commander, Punjab Frontier Force, 1886—90.

His papers were presented to the National Army Museum by Mrs. M. McQueen in 1968. They include notebooks, despatches and reports relating to the Hazara Field Force 1888, a volume of copy letters to General Roberts discussing the organisation of troops on the North West Frontier and a notebook (1879) relating to the tribes of the North West Frontier.

McSWEENEY, Terence (fl 1918—1922)

MP (Sinn Fein), Mid Cork, 1918—22.

Since the entry in *Sources*, Vol. 4, p 42, reference should be made to the papers of his sister, Mary McSweeney, which have been acquired by University College, Dublin (ref P48). There is a substantial amount of material relating to him, his imprisonment and his death, possibly amounting to 5 boxes. The collection has not beeen processed but the material relating to his work is largely correspondence, notes and photographs. These papers, together with the papers of Lily O'Brennan and Maire Comerford have much information on Cumman na mBan.

MADIN, Joseph (1892–1967)

Socialist and Trade Unionist leader in Sheffield.

A collection of his papers, books and pamphlets has been acquired by Sheffield University Library. The papers have extensive material on the Labour College and the AEU. There is biographical material, literary notes and press cuttings. A detailed list is available (NRA 20789).

MALCOLM, Donald Wingfield (1907–   )

Colonial administrator.

The papers have been acquired by Rhodes House Library through the Oxford Colonial Records Project. The collection consists of 16 boxes of material. It includes a diary (and photographs) when Malcolm accompanied Lord Hailey around Africa south of the Sahara. Another companion on this trip (the scientist Dr. D. B. Worthington) has also placed his papers at Rhodes House Library (MSS Afr s 1425). Among other papers of Malcolm are a box of papers as Assistant District Officer at Mwanza, papers on Hailey's African Survey and material on land tenure and land utilisation. A list is available (NRA 17814).

MALET, Sir Edward Baldwin (1837–1908)

Minister Plenipotentiary, Constantinople, 1878–79, Cairo 1882. British Representative, African Conference at Berlin. Ambassador to Germany, 1884–95. Member, International Court of Arbitration at The Hague, 1900–06.

His private correspondence (13 vols) while Ambassador to the German Court 1884–95, is in the Public Record Office (FO 343). The first three volumes consist of letters from Queen Victoria, other members of the Royal Family, the Queen's private secretary, successive Foreign Secretaries, members of the German Government etc. The remaining volumes consist of Malet's letters to the Queen, Sir Henry Ponsonby, successive Foreign Secretaries etc. The collection was presented to the Foreign Office by Lord Rennell in 1936. Some further material (*c*. 100 letters to him) covering the period 1880–1908 is in Duke University Library (NUC 72-877).

MALLAM, Lieutenant-Colonel Reverend George (1895–1978)

Counsellor, British Legation, Kabul, 1932. Financial Secretary to Government, North West Frontier Province, 1939, etc.

His papers are in the Cambridge Centre for South Asian Studies. The collection includes material on the disturbances in Waziristan 1936–37, notes on 'tribal reconstruction 1941', memos etc. on the Garvi tribes of Swat and on the administration of justice in the Kurram Valley etc.

MALLET, Sir Victor Alexander Louis (1893–1969)

Minister, Stockholm, 1940–45. Ambassador, Spain, 1945–46; Italy 1947–53.

Since the entry in *Sources*, Vol. 2, p 162, a xerox copy of his memoirs is now available in Churchill College, Cambridge.

MALLORY, Air Chief Marshal Sir Trafford Leigh- (1892–1944)

AOC-in-C, Fighter Command, 1942. Air C-in-C Allied Expeditionary Air Forces, 1943–44.

His papers, 1912–69, have been placed in the Royal Air Force Museum, Hendon (ref. AC 71/24 and 74/17). The collection includes personal papers, 1917–46, letters and telegrams on his DSO, 'Copies of Reports on Wing Engagements, September 1940', a correspondence book concerning No. 8 Squadron, papers relating to German artillery signals and an envelope containing correspondence recovered from the air crash in which he was killed.

MANSERGH, General Sir (Eric Carden) Robert (1900–1970)

Military career. C-in-C, Allied Forces, Netherlands East Indies, 1946. Military Secretary, 1948–49, Deputy C-in-C, and C-in-C, Allied Forces Northern Europe, 1951–53. C-in-C, UK Land Forces, 1956–59.

In addition to the material cited in *Sources*, Vol. 2, p 163, a collection of official records covering his service in the Far East and the Dutch East Indies, 1945–46, is in the Imperial War Museum.

MARCHANT, Sir James (1867–1956)

Secretary, National Birth-Rate Commission, 1913–34. Had earlier toured Europe with Dr Barnardo's successor, investigating conditions of child life. Secretary, Cinema Psychological Inquiry, International Morals Congress. Numerous publications on religion, child welfare, venereal disease, etc.

A collection of his papers has been deposited with the Bodleian Library. It consists of correspondence from a large number of persons including William Godfrey, Archbishop of Westminster (1942–50), Cosmo Gordon Lang, Archbishop of Canterbury (1929–45), William Temple, Archbishop of Canterbury (1941), Henry Russell Wakefield, Bishop of Birmingham (1915–21), Alban Goodier, Archbishop of Bombay (1930–32), William Edwin Orchard (1927–47), and Handley Carr Glyn Moule, Bishop of Durham (1912–20).

MARKHAM, Sir (Sydney) Frank (1897–1975)

MP (Lab) Chatham, 1929–31; (Nat Lab) Nottingham South, 1935–45; (Con) Buckingham 1951–64.

Since the entry in *Sources*, Vol. 4, p 48, his World War I records have been purchased by the Imperial War Museum.

MARLING, Sir Percival Scrope (1861–1936)

Army career, Boer War, etc. Brigadier General, Potchefstroom District, South Africa, 1909–10. Served HQ, Indian Army Corps in France, World War I.

Miscellaneous of his letters and papers form part of the Marling estate, family and business papers deposited in Gloucestershire Record Office (ref D 873). The papers include accounts of events in South Africa 1899–1904, observations on the state of the German Army 1904 and manoeuvres, 1909.

MARSH, Alfred (fl 1900s)

Pioneer anarchist. Editor, *Freedom.*

His papers, which were given to Max Nettlau in 1904, have been placed in the International Institute of Social History in Amsterdam. The collection includes 12 folders of letters from Kropotkin, 1894–1904, some from Sophie Kropotkin and correspondence with C. M. Wilson, 1895–1901. There are a few letters from Carpenter, Malatesta etc.

MARSH, Sir Edward Howard (1872–1953)

Private Secretary to Winston Churchill, 1917–22 and 1924–29; to the Duke of Devonshire, 1922–24; to J. H. Thomas, 1924 and 1929–36; and to Malcolm MacDonald, 1936–37.

New York Public Library (Berg collection) has over 5,000 letters to Marsh from numerous personalities in politics and the arts. In addition, a further collection of letters received by Marsh, 1913–30, is in Birmingham University Library.

MARSHALL, Thomas Humphrey (1893–1982)

Sociologist. Professor of Sociology, London School of Economics, 1954–56. Educational adviser, British zone of Germany, 1949.

Nine boxes of his papers, 1930–80, are in BLPES.

MASSINGHAM, Henry William (1860–1924)

Journalist and author. Editor at various times of the National Press Agency, the *Star, Daily Chronicle*. Editor, the *Nation*, 1907–23.

Since the entry in *Sources*, Vol. 5, p 136, his papers and correspondence, 1874–1924, have been placed in Norfolk Record Office.

MATHER, Norman Frederick

Colonial civil servant. British Resident, Perak.

His diary and other material, is in Rhodes House Library (ref MSS Ind Ocn s 205).

MATTHEWS, Sir James (Henry John) (1887–   )

Labour local government leader.

A collection of his papers has been deposited with Southampton City Record Office and it includes files on education, 1915–67; juvenile employment and delinquency, 1920–39; planning and reconstruction, 1932–65; roads and traffic, 1951–66; industrial development, 1936–62; the Labour Party, 1932–68; and numerous other topics. Access to some files is restricted. A list is available (NRA 23206).

MATTINSON, Sir Miles (1854–1944)

Legal and political career. MP (Lib) Liverpool Walton 1886–92. Recorder of Blackburn, 1886–1922. Author of *The Law of Corrupt Practices at Elections: Selection of Precedents in Pleading*.

Some correspondence, covering the period 1884–1896, is in the House of Lords Record Office. The papers consist of letters written to him (18 items) from such people as Lord Randolph Churchill and Speaker Gully.

MAUDLING, Reginald (1917–1979)

MP (Con) Barnet, 1950–Feb 1974; Chipping Barnet, Feb 1974–1979 Economic Secretary, Treasury, 1952–5. Minister of Supply, 1955–7. Paymaster-General, 1957–9. President of the Board of Trade, 1959–61. Secretary of State for the Colonies, 1961–2. Chancellor of the Exchequer, 1962–4. Secretary of State for Home Affairs, 1970–2.

Since the entry in *Sources*, Vol. 4, p 54, some constituency papers have been acquired by Churchill College, Cambridge.

MAXWELL, General Sir John Grenfell (1859—1929)

Served Egypt, Boer War etc. Military Governor, Pretoria, 1900—01. Commander in Egypt 1908—12, 1914—15. C-in-C, Ireland, 1916. C-in-C, Northern Command, 1916—19. Member, Lord Milner's mission to Egypt, 1920.

A 52pp letter-book, with loose papers and photographs, 1898—99, is in the Sudan Archive, University of Durham. A very few letters to Maxwell concerning the 1916 rebellion in Ireland are in the British Library. George Cassar *Kitchener: Architect of Victory* states that other papers have not survived.

MAXWELL, Sir Reginald Maitland (1882—1967)

Indian Civil Service. Secretary, Government of India, Home Department, 1936. Home Member, Governor-General's Executive Council, 1938—44. Adviser to Secretary of State for India, 1944—47.

Some miscellaneous papers and other material are in the Cambridge South Asian Centre.

MAYCOCK, Sir Willoughby Robert Dottin (1849—1922)

Diplomatic career. Served with Joseph Chamberlain's Special Mission to Washington 1887. Superintendent, Treaty Department, Foreign Office 1903—13.

A collection of papers has been acquired by the Greater London Record Office. An unpublished list is available (NRA 10887). The collection consists mainly of letters to or from Maycock, mainly for the period 1889—1913. Correspondents include Lord Salisbury, Herbert Beerbohm Tree, Eyre Crowe and Sir Edward Grey.

MAYERS, Norman (1895—)

Levant Consular Service. Subsequently Minister, El Salvador. Consul-General, Sao Paulo, 1948—51. Ambassador, Ecuador.

The correspondence, cuttings and scrapbook on the Levant have been promised to the Middle East Centre, St. Antony's College, Oxford.

MAZE, Sir Frederick William (1874—1959)

Chinese consular career. Commissioner, Canton, Tientsin, Shanghai etc. Inspector-General, Chinese Maritime Customs, 1929—43. Appointed by Chinese Government, Adviser to National Board of Reconstruction, 1928.

His papers have been acquired by the School of Oriental and African Studies. A list is available (NRA 16588). There are 65 volumes of papers, relating mainly to the Chinese Maritime Customs. They include confidential letters and reports, 'semi-official' letters and the personal correspondence of the Inspector-General.

MEREDITH, Air Vice-Marshal Sir Charles Warburton (1896—1977)

Commandant-General, Southern Rhodesian Forces.

His correspondence and papers for the period 1938—45 are in the National Archives of Zimbabwe.

MELVILLE, 6th Vt
Charles Saunders Dundas (1843—1926)

Consul-General, Norway 1897—1907.

His papers, together with those of the 7th Viscount are part of the Dundas family papers. Reference should be made to the list that has been prepared (NRA 10188).

MICHELL, Roland (1847—1931)

Tutor to Prince Ibrahim Pasha in Egypt 1870—78. Chief of Statistical Department, Revenue Survey, Egypt, 1878. Commissioner at Limassol, 1879—1911.

Unpublished correspondence and papers are in the School of Oriental and African Studies. The collection includes diaries, journals etc. *c.* 1870—76 together with other papers, notes, memoranda. etc.

MIDDLETON, Richard William Evelyn (1846—1905)

Conservative Party Chief Agent, 1885—1903.

One of his letter books has survived in the extensive collection of the Akers-Douglas papers in Kent Archives Office.

MIEVILLE, Sir Walter Frederick (1855—1929)

Diplomatic and consular career. President, Egyptian Maritime and Quarantine Board of Health, 1884—97. Special mission to Vienna, Berlin and Paris, 1887.

An unpublished autobiography and other genealogical papers are in Hove Public Library.

MILLER, Major-General Charles Harvey (1894—1974)

Military service. Commander Transjordan Frontier Force, 1932—36; 5th Cavalry Brigade, 1940.

The Imperial War Museum has the papers, which include letters, a diary, other material and a photographic album relating to his service with the Transjordan Frontier Force (1932—36).

MILLER, Dr. Samuel Aaron (1912—1970)

Scientist and Zionist leader. Executive member, Zionist Federation, from 1935; later Vice President and Hon. Secretary. Member of Board of Deputies, 1946—49 and 1958—70. Chairman, British Zionist Federation, 1970.

Mrs. J. Miller (widow) of Ramat Gan, Israel, sent a collection of printed material and published works to the Central Zionist Archives. She retains many duplicated papers.

MILLS, Eric (1892—1961)

Military service, World War I. Military Governor, Gaza, 1919. Assistant Governor, Samaria, 1920. Acting Principal, Colonial Office, 1920—25. Assistant Chief Secretary to High Commissioner, Palestine, *c.* 1925. Secretary, Jerusalem and the East Mission.

Mrs. F. Newbolt (daughter) reports that her father destroyed many papers before leaving Palestine and others before his death. The Middle East Centre, St. Antony's

College, Oxford, found no papers, but has some letters from Mills to Elizabeth Monroe with comments on Palestine, and also the archives of the Jerusalem and the East Mission.

MILNE, 1st B
Field-Marshal Sir George Francis Milne (1866—1948)

Army career from 1884. Served Sudan; South Africa; World War I. Commanded British Salonika Force and Army of the Black Sea, GOC-in-C, Eastern Command, 1923—26. Chief of Imperial General Staff, 1926—33.

Since the entry in *Sources*, Vol. 2, p 170, the papers have been deposited in the Liddell Hart Centre for Military Archives, King's College, London. There are letters and correspondence relating to his career, including various orders and summaries especially concerning the Army of the Black Sea, 1916—18; dispatches relating to the peace treaty, 1920; notes and correspondence on subjects such as mechanisation, 1929, the Army and Air Force, 1931, and a collection of 25 books.

MILNER, 1st Vt
Sir Alfred Milner (1854—1925)

High Commissioner, South Africa, 1897—1905. Minister without Portfolio, 1916—18. Secretary of State for War, 1918—19; Colonies, 1919—21.

In addition to the papers cited in *Sources*, Vol. 2, p 171, a further series of papers is now available in the Public Record Office (ref. PRO 30/30). The collection includes 25 files on various topics including papers and correspondence relating to the Departmental Committee on Home Production of Food (June—Aug 1915); Secret and Confidential memos prepared by the General Staff at the War Office on various political questions in Europe; papers relating to Syria and the conflicting claims of the French and Arabs, 1919—20; correspondence and papers on Turkey and the former possessions of the Ottoman Empire (1919—20); Indian Reform Committee Papers (1919); Liquor Restrictions Committee papers (May—June 1919); memoranda and other papers relating to the Russian campaign and relations between the Baltic States and Bolshevik Russia (Aug—Oct 1919); telegrams to and from H. C. Norman, Minister Plenipotentiary to Tehran, about fighting between Persian and Bolshevik troops (Aug—Nov 1920); and papers relating to the seditious activities of the Russian Trade Delegation.

MINCHIN, Lieutenant-Colonel Charles Frederick (1862—1943)

Served India and Africa. Political Agent, Bikanir 1902. Consul-General, Khorassan and Seistan, 1904 etc.

His papers have been deposited in the Imperial War Museum.

MITRANY, David (1888—1975)

Political economist, journalist and writer. Author of *The Problem of International Sanctions* (1925), *A Working Peace System* (1943) and numerous books on Marxist problems.

The papers have been placed in the British Library of Political and Economic Science.

MOBERLEY, Brigadier Archibald Henry (1879–1960)

Assistant Director of Artillery, War Office, 1927–30.

Some World War I papers are in the Library of the Royal Artillery Institution.

MOLONEY, Con

Adjutant General, IRA.

A box of his papers has been deposited with University College, Dublin (ref P9). It is a collection of administrative letters and reports pertaining to the organisation and activities of the 2nd Southern Division of the IRA.

MOLONEY, Sir Cornelius Alfred (1848–1913)

Secretary, Gold Coast, 1879–84, Administrator of Gambia Settlement, 1884–86; Lagos 1886–90. Governor, British Honduras, 1891–97; Windward Islands, 1897–1900; Trinidad and Tobago, 1900–07.

Some material is available at Rhodes House Library, Oxford. It includes typescript and manuscript copies of despatches sent by Moloney as Governor of British Honduras to the Secretary of State for the Colonies, July-December 1894, August–December 1896 (ref MS West Indies s2–3).

MONCKTON of BRENCHLEY, 1st Vt
Sir Walter Turner Monckton (1891–1965)

MP (Con) Bristol West 1951–57. Solicitor-General, 1945. Minister of Labour and National Service 1951–55. Minister of Defence 1955–56. Paymaster-General, 1956–57.

Since the entry in *Sources*, Vol. 4, p 63, further details have become available of the Monckton papers in the Bodleian Library. The extensive collection is now catalogued (NRA 20879). The collection comprises two different deposits – one by the literary trustees (mainly of material earlier than 1950, but with some papers closed until 1999), the other by his widow, mainly dating from 1950. Much of this material is closed for 30 years. None of the papers concerning the Duke and Duchess of Windsor (1936–51 nor other members of the Royal Family are available. Enquiries concerning access should be directed to the Bodleian.

MONCKTON, Major Reginald Francis Percy (1896–1975)

Military service, World War I. Deputy Military Governor, Jericho, 1918–20. ADC and Private Secretary to High Commissioner, Palestine, 1920–5.

The Middle East Centre, St. Antony's College, Oxford, has his papers and letters home from Palestine and Transjordan (1917–25). There are a large number of letters written to his mother from Palestine. They record such events as Samuel's first visit to Es Salt and the establishment of government in northern Transjordan by Major the Hon. Fitzroy Somerset. A list is available (NRA 20811).

MONCRIEFF, Major-General Sir George Scott- (1855–1924)

Served Afghanistan 1878–80. Commander, Royal Engineers, China Expeditionary Force, 1900–01. Served Waziristan Expedition, 1901. Chief Engineer, Aldershot, 1909–11.

A typescript copy of his memoirs (2 vols) was deposited on permanent loan in the India Office Library by St. Antony's College, Oxford (Mss Eur C 259). The memoirs cover the life and attitudes of an Engineers officer, an informative account of engineering work carried out by Scott-Moncrieff and his contemporaries, and a portrayal of the events of the Afghan Campaign 1878–80, and the China Expedition.

MONEY, Major-General Sir Arthur Wigram (1866–1951)

Military service: India, South Africa and World War I. Egyptian Expeditionary Force, 1915–19. Chief Administrator, OETA Jerusalem, 1918–19.

Since the entry in *Sources*, Vol. 2, p 172, Mr. J. H. Money has moved to 25a Philbeach Gardens, London, SW5.

MONROE, Elizabeth
Mrs. Humphrey Neame (b 1905)

Scholar and historian of the Middle East. Diplomatic correspondent, *The Observer*, 1944. British representative, United Nations Sub-Committee for Prevention of Discrimination and Protection of Minorities, 1947–52. Staff, *Economist*, 1945–58. Fellow, St. Antony's College, Oxford, 1963–73.

Miss Monroe has placed her papers in the Middle East Centre, St. Antony's College, Oxford. Five files, mainly on Palestine, consist of the correspondence of Miss Monroe with persons formerly active in Middle Eastern affairs, and there are notes on interviews with R. H. S. Crossman, John Hamilton, Francis Williams, Sir A. Kirkbride, Eliahu Elath and A. Creech Jones regarding Bevin's policy over the Arabs, (1945–8).

MONSON, Sir Edmund John, 1st Bt (1834–1909)

Ambassador, Belgium, 1892; Austria, 1893–96; France, 1896–1904.

Since the entry in *Sources*, Vol. 2, p 173, an important collection of papers has been acquired by the Bodleian Library, Oxford (ref MSS Eng Hist c589–595). The collection, covering the period 1852–1905 includes correspondence while serving in Athens, Brussels and Vienna, 1889–96, and includes letters from Salisbury, Rosebery, Balfour and Stamfordham. There are papers as Ambassador in Paris, 1896–1905, including correspondence with Salisbury, Balfour, Jo Chamberlain, Queen Victoria, Edward VII, Lansdowne and Cromer. A list is available (NRA 23418). In addition, four letter books, 1899–1903, have been acquired by Ohio University Library.

MONTE, Hilde (fl 1939–1945)

Editor, German programmes, BBC, during World War II.

Her surviving papers are in the Anielewicz Museum in Memory of the Commander of the Warsaw Ghetto at the Kibbutz Haartzi Seminar, Givat Haviva in Israel.

MONTGOMERY of ALAMEIN, 1st Vt
Field-Marshal Sir Bernard Law Montgomery (1887–1976)

Military career. Served World Wars I and II. Commanded 8th Army, 1942–44 (North Africa, Sicily, Italy). C-in-C., British Group of Armies and Allied Armies, North France, 1944. C-in-C, British Army on the Rhine, and British Member of Allied Control Commission, Germany, 1945–46. Chief of the Imperial General

Staff, 1946–48. Chairman of Western European Commanders-in-Chief Committee, 1948–51. Deputy Supreme Allied Commander, Europe, 1951–58.

Since the entry in *Sources*, Vol. 2, p 174, the private papers were acquired by the Imperial War Museum in July 1982. The papers and 44 volumes of diaries, 1942–58, had previously been purchased by Times Newspapers Ltd in 1962, but under the condition that the existence of the diaries was not to be revealed during Montgomery's lifetime. The archive purchased includes extensive private correspondence with all the great war leaders: Churchill, Eisenhower, Alanbrooke, de Gaulle and Attlee. His mother had kept all his letters from the front in the 1914–18 war and afterwards, and they were returned to Montgomery on her death. The diaries begin in August 1942 and include material on the campaign from Alamein to Tunis, the Sicily and Italian campaigns; preparations and operations in North-West Europe and post-war diaries from May 1946 to September 1948. They include his period as CIGS and as Deputy Supreme Allied Commander in Europe.

MONTGOMERY, Hugh de Fellenberg (d1924)

Ulster politician. Senator. Anti-Home Ruler.

An extensive collection of papers, reflecting his prominent role in the anti-Home Rule movement, is in the Northern Ireland Public Record Office. *See* NRA 16154.

MOON, Sir (Edward) Penderel (b1905)

Indian Civil Service. Secretary, Development Board and Planning Advisory Board Government of India. Chief Commissioner, Himachal Pradesh; Manipur. Author of *The Future of India, Divide and Quit*, etc.

His correspondence and papers, 1939–52, are in the India Office Library.

MOORE, George Edward (1873–1958)

Philosopher.

Since the entry in *Sources*, Vol. 5, p 140, an important collection of his papers has been sold by his son, Timothy Moore, at Sotheby's. The collection includes correspondence, diaries and other papers. Correspondents include Bertrand Russell, Maynard Keynes and E. M. Forster. It is believed that these papers went to Cambridge University Library.

MOORE, Admiral Sir Henry Ruthven (1886–1978)

Naval career from 1902. Naval Assistant Secretary to Committee of Imperial Defence, 1921–24. Assistant Secretary, British Delegation to Washington Disarmament Conference, 1921–22, and at Geneva, 1927. Deputy Director (later Director), Plans Division, Admiralty, 1930–33. Chief of Staff to C-in-C, Portsmouth, 1938–39. Rear-Admiral Commanding 3rd Cruiser Squadron, 1939–40. Assistant Chief of Naval Staff (Trade), 1940–41. Vice Chief of Naval Staff, 1941–43. C-in-C, Home Fleet, 1944–45. Head of British Naval Mission, Washington, 1945–48. C-in-C, The Nore, 1948–50.

Contrary to the information given in *Sources*, Vol. 2, p 174, only a few papers have survived. These have now been deposited in the Imperial War Museum.

MORAN, 1st B
Charles McMoran Wilson (1882–1977)

Physician.

His papers, including manuscript notes of conversations with Churchill, 1943–46, are with the Royal College of Physicians.

MORRIS of BORTH-Y-GEST, 1st B
John William Morris (1896–1979)

Lawyer, arbitrator on industrial disputes and public servant. Liberal parliamentary candidate, 1923, 1924. A Lord of Appeal in Ordinary from 1960.

A collection of papers has been deposited with the National Library of Wales. The collection includes a large amount of his correspondence on a number of topics including the possibility of a third Welsh TV channel (1959), a proposed Parliament for Wales (1968), the use of Welsh in court and other Welsh affairs. Correspondents include Bonar Law, Baldwin, Balfour and Prince Philip. There is family correspondence 1909–62. Morris's diaries (1920–21, 1929–40, 1940–42) are held as are his legal papers (1940s–78) and papers regarding the Caernarvonshire Quarter Sessions (1939–69). There are a few political papers, including pamphlets and correspondence regarding Morris's Liberal candidacy at Ilford 1923 and 1924, and other possible candidacies (1923–38). Papers regarding committees and commissions on which he sat, including Home Office Committees on Defence Regulations (1940–45), Courts of Inquiry into the Engineering and Shipbuilding Wages Dispute (1953–54) and the Coal Mining Conciliation Scheme (1955–65), are held. There is material relating to the University of Wales (1938–74) and its expansion, and from Morris's time as Commissary of Cambridge (mainly relating to the 1968 student unrest). Miscellaneous papers (1916–75) include material on the growth of Plaid Cymru and Welsh Nationalism (1937–39) and other Welsh affairs. A small collection of his parents' papers relate to the Welsh Independent cause in Liverpool.

MORRIS, General Sir Edwin (1889–1970)

Military career.

Some papers have been transferred from the Royal Engineers Museum to the Imperial War Museum. The collection includes diaries, 1917–44, material on the war intentions of China, etc.

MORTON, Sir Desmond John Falkiner (1891–1971)

Principal Assistant Secretary, Ministry of Economic Warfare, 1939. Personal Assistant to Prime Minister, 1940–46. UK Delegate to Inter-Allied Reparation Agency.

Morton, as a matter of principle, kept no diary and burnt most of his personal papers. Some record of his personal relationship with Churchill can be found in Morton's letters to his old friend R. W. Thompson while Thompson was writing *The Yankee Marlborough*. These letters have now been published as *Churchill and Morton* (Foreword by Captain Stephen Roskill (London, 1976.)

MORTON, Sir James (1867–1943)

Industrialist. Member of Government Committees. Closely involved himself with foreign affairs.

An extensive collection of *c.* 500 files is in the Scottish Record Office (ref Morton of Darvel Muniments). An unpublished list is available (NRA 20588). There are numerous letters, notes, leaflets etc. concerning industry, foreign affairs, education and local government. There is material on Morton's advocacy of neutrality in 1914 and on his involvement *re* adult education with the Ministry of Reconstruction, 1917—18. Correspondents include A. V. Greenwood and Lord Leverhulme. Other particularly interesting items are a letter from Ramsay MacDonald asking him to serve on the Committee on New Industrial Development and a printed account of the trip to Germany made in 1936 by Lloyd George and Thomas Jones.

MOUNTBATTEN OF BURMA, 1st E
Admiral of the Fleet Louis Francis Albert Victor Nicholas Mountbatten (1900—1979)

Naval career from 1913. Commanded HMS *Kelly*, and 5th Destroyer Flotilla, 1939—41; HMS *Illustrious*, 1941. Adviser on Combined Operations, 1941—42. Supreme Allied Commander, South East Asia, 1943—46. Viceroy of India, March—August 1947. Governor-General, India, 1947—48. Flag-Officer Commanding 1st Cruiser Squadron, Mediterranean Fleet, 1948—49. Fourth Sea Lord, 1950—52. C-in-C, Mediterranean and Allied Forces, Mediterranean, 1952—54. First Sea Lord, 1955—59. Chief of UK Defence Staff and Chairman of Chiefs of Staff Committee, 1959—65.

Xeroxes of part of his papers as Viceroy and Governor-General of India, March—August 1947 are in the India Office Records (ref MSS Eur F 200). It is understood that this material is closed.

MUIRHEAD, Roland Eugene (1868—1954)

Leading Scottish Nationalist. Founder and Director, Scottish Secretariat.

In addition to the entry in *Sources*, Vol. 5, p 141, four boxes of his correspondence, together with an autobiography, have been placed in the Mitchell Library, Glasgow.

MULDOON, John (1865—1938)

Irish Nationalist MP.

Since the negative entry in *Sources*, Vol. 4, p 74, the National Library of Ireland has acquired his correspondence with Michael Davitt, T. P. O'Connor, John Redmond etc. for the period 1888—1921.

MURDOCH, Major-General Sir John Francis Burn (1859—1931)

Served Egypt, Boer War etc. Commanded Egyptian Cavalry, 1894—96; Desert Column, Battle of Firket, 1896. Inspector of Cavalry Regiments, Transvaal, etc.

His correspondence and other papers, covering the period 1894—1925, are in the National Army Museum.

MURISON, Alexander Falconer (1847—1934)

Legal career. Professor of Jurisprudence, London University, 1901—25. Editor, the *Educational Times* 1902—12. On political staff, *Daily Chronicle*. President, Society of Public Teachers of Law, 1916—17.

His papers are in the Library of University College, London.

MURRAY, General Sir Archibald James (1860–1945)

Military career from 1879. Director of Military Training, 1907–12. Inspector of Infantry, 1912–14. Chief of Imperial General Staff, 1915. GOC 1st Class, Egypt, 1916–17. GOC-in-C, Aldershot, 1917–19.

Since the entry in *Sources*, Vol. 2, p 176, the material formerly in private hands has been purchased by the Imperial War Museum from the grandson, Captain A. R. Murray, RN. The collection is particularly strong on Murray's period as GOC, Egypt, 1915–17.

MURRAY, David (fl 1934–1972)

Industrial journalist.

His correspondence and papers, 1934–72, are in the National Library of Scotland. Topics covered include the Spanish Civil War, the iron and steel industry, the Scottish Home Rule movement etc.

MURRAY, Sir Oswyn Alexander Ruthven (1873–1936)

Permanent Secretary, Admiralty, 1917–36.

In addition to the material cited in *Sources*, Vol. 2, p 177, his letters to Sir Vincent Baddely on the reorganisation of the Admiralty secretariat, 1920–21, are in the Public Record Office (ref ADM 225).

MURRAY, Sean (fl 1930s)

Communist activist. Chairman, Northern Ireland Communist Party.

His correspondence and papers are in the Public Record Office of Northern Ireland.

MYERS, Brigadier Edmund Charles Wolf (1906–   )

Commander, British Military Mission to Greek resistance, 1942–43.

The Brigadier deposited his papers in the Liddell Hart Centre for Military Archives, King's College, London in 1978. A list has been prepared (NRA 23075). The collection consists of folders of miscellaneous correspondence, signals and reports, involving Brigadier Myers' activities in Greece in 1942–45, and concerning the 1943 'political issue', miscellaneous reports, diaries and correspondence from 1942–43; three reviews written by Myers on Greece and the revised manuscript of his *Greek Entanglement*. There are miscellaneous photographs of contemporary Greece and Greeks. Reference should also be made to the Woodhouse papers also in the Liddell Hart Centre.

NAIDU, Sarojini (1879–1949)

Indian reformer and poet.

A collection of correspondence and other papers, 1897–1928, is in the India Office Library (ref MSS Eur A95). The collection includes her letters to a friend in England and an autobiographical essay on her stay in Europe, 1895–98.

NEEDHAM, Major-General Henry (1876–1965)

Military career. Served World War I. Military Attaché, Brussels, 1922–26; Paris, 1927–31. Commander, Bombay, 1931–35. Chief of Mission to Belgian Army, 1939–40.

The papers cited in *Sources*, Vol. 2, p 179, have now been presented to the Imperial War Museum. The collection includes material on North Russia, 1919, and his period as an attaché in the 1920s.

NEEDHAM, Joseph (1900–   )

Historian of science. Expert on China. Head of British Scientific Mission to China, 1942–46. Master, Gonville and Caius College, Cambridge, 1966–76.

An extensive collection of his scientific, personal and family papers was acquired by Cambridge University Library in 1976.

NELSON, Major-General Sir John (fl 1933–68)

Military career.

His memoirs, 1933–68, have been acquired by the Liddell Hart Centre for Military Archives, King's College, London.

NEWALL, 1st B
Marshal of the Royal Air Force Sir Cyril Louis Norton Newall (1886–1963)

Served European War, 1914–19. Director of Operations and Intelligence and Deputy Chief of Air Staff, 1926–31. Air Officer Commanding, Wessex Bombing Area, 1931; RAF Middle East, 1931–34. Air Member for Supply and Organisation, 1935–37. Chief of Air Staff, 1937–40. Governor General and C-in-C. New Zealand, 1941–46.

In addition to the material cited in *Sources*, Vol. 2, p 179, some papers can be found at the Public Record Office (ref AIR 8/235-299).

NEWCOMBE, Colonel Stewart Francis (1878–1956)

Expert on Arab affairs. Military career. Later Hon. Secretary, Royal Central Asian Society.

His letters to Ismet Karadoyan Bey, 1917, 1932 and 1936 are in the Middle East Centre, St. Antony's College, Oxford.

NEWTON, Sir Francis James (1857–1948)

Colonial service in Africa. Special Commissioner, Matabeleland 1894. Resident Commissioner, Bechuanaland Protectorate 1895–97 High Commissioner for Southern Rhodesia 1924–30.

An extensive collection of his papers is in the National Archives of Zimbabwe. His correspondents include Sir Charles Coghlan, 1922–27 (884 folios), J. W. Downie 1924–30 (514 folios), O. C. Du Port, Minister of Agriculture 1927–28 (64 folios), P. D. L. Flynn 1924–30 (221 folios), R. A. Fletcher 1928–30 (80 folios), Sir Sidney Sheppard, Administrator of British Bechuanaland 1888 (38 folios) etc. with other miscellaneous correspondence 1888–1939.

NICHOLAS, T. E. (1879–1971)

Poet, lay preacher and Communist.

A collection of his papers has been deposited with the National Library of Wales. The collection consists of letters from Nicholas to the donor, Mr. Williams, which refer to contemporary events. There are 99 items (1945–1969). Amongst a few miscellaneous items are several poems by Nicholas.

NICHOLL, Rear-Admiral Angus Dacres (1896–   )

Naval career. Naval Assistant Secretary, War Cabinet, 1939–41. Commanded HMS *Penelope*, 1941–42. Director of Operations Division (Foreign), Admiralty, 1942–44. Commanded HMS *Duke of York*, 1944–46, Defence Correspondent, BBC External Services, 1951–66.

The unpublished memoirs have been donated to the Imperial War Museum by the widow, Mrs. R. Nicholl. The memoirs, covering the period 1915–1951 are of most value for his service as Naval Assistant Secretary to the Committee of Imperial Defence, 1936–39, the War Cabinet Secretariat, 1939–41 and his command of the cruiser *Penelope*. Also described is the Japanese surrender, when Nicholl commanded the battleship *Duke of York* of the British Pacific Fleet.

NICHOLSON, Major-General Sir Lothian (fl 1914–1918)
Military career.

His diaries and other papers concerning his commands on the Western Front, 1914–19, have been acquired by the Imperial War Museum.

NIGHTINGALE, Major Guy Warnford (1890–   )

Army career. Served Royal Munster Fusiliers.

The papers are in the Public Record Office (ref PRO 30/71). A list is available (NRA 23396). The seven files of papers (1910–26) include a diary (Jan–Dec 1915) and letters, chiefly to his mother, from Burma (1912–14), the Western Front (1915–18), the North Russian Expeditionary Force (1918–19) and from British Forces in Silesia, Poland and Tarnow, Aden and Somaliland (1921–23) and from the 4th Battalion, Nigeria Regiment, Nigeria, 1925–26.

NOBLE, Sir Allan Herbert Percy (1908–1982)

MP (Con), Chelsea, 1945–59. Minister of State, Foreign Affairs, 1956–59. Special Ambassador, Ivory Coast.

Since the entry in *Sources*, Vol. 4, p 83, his correspondence and papers have been placed in Churchill College, Cambridge.

NOBLE, Admiral Sir Percy Lockhart Harnam (1880–1955)

Naval career from 1894. Served Grand Fleet, 1914–1919. Director of Operations Division, Admiralty Naval Staff, 1928–1930. Director of Naval Equipment, 1931–32. Commander 2nd Cruiser Squadron, 1932–34. 4th Sea Lord, 1935–37. C-in-C, China Station, 1938–40; Western Approaches, 1941–42. Head of British Naval Delegation, Washington, 1942–44.

Since the negative information cited in *Sources*, Vol. 2, pp 181–2, the surviving papers have now been placed in Churchill College, Cambridge.

NORMAN, Major-General Charles (fl 1914–1965)
Military career.

His papers, mainly concerning armour and military education, 1914–65, are in the Liddell Hart Centre for Military Archives, King's College, London.

NORMAN, George Henry Gerald (1907–)

The Times war correspondent, Middle East, 1942; Paris, 1944–52.

The Times archive has papers, mainly concerning service in Paris (1944–52).

NORTH, Major John (1894–1973)

Military career. Service General Staff, World War II, mainly writing articles for the press office. Author of such works as *Gallipoli: The Fading Vision* (1936) and *North West Europe, 1944–45* (1953).

His papers were deposited in the Liddell Hart Centre for Military Archives, King's College, London, by his widow, Mrs. Freda North, in 1977. A list is available (NRA 23076). The collection consists of 12 boxes of papers split into 5 sections: Section I contains the original typescript, correspondence and press cuttings relating to North's book *Gallipoli: The Fading Vision* (1936); Section II contains similar papers relating to his book *North West Europe 1944–45* (1953): Section III contains papers relating to his book *The Alexander Memoirs 1940–45* (1962): Section IV consists of articles by North on World War II, press cuttings, maps, and correspondence, 1936–39, 1943–45, and the 1960s: Section V contains reviews of North's *Men Fighting: Battle Stories* (1958), letters to the press by North, various articles, Sir Roger Keyes' Belgium campaign diary and personal papers.

NORTHEY, Major-General Sir Edward (1868–1953)

Military career. Served Indian Frontier, 1891–92; South Africa, 1899–1902; European War, 1914–18. Governor, Kenya, and High Commissioner, Zanzibar, 1918–22.

The papers, cited in *Sources*, Vol. 2, pp 183–184, have now been placed in the Imperial War Museum.

NOTT, Lewis Herbert William (1869–1964)

Military Governor, Tulkeram, 1915. Civil Administrator, Gaza, 1916–22. Govenor, North Palestine, 1922–28.

The Middle East Centre, St. Antony's College, Oxford, has copies of papers held by Mr. Richard Nott (son), Penkenna, Westward Ho, Devon. There are letters from Sir L. Bols, Lords Samuel and Allenby, Sir Wyndham Deedes and the Mayor of Gaza.

O'BRENNAN, Lily (Cumann na mBan)

Irish Nationalist.

A box of her papers has been deposited with University College, Dublin (ref P13). It covers the years 1921–23 and 1949, including her correspondence and diary from the period of her imprisonment, 1922–23, which refers mainly to prison conditions, hunger strikes and contemporary political events. Correspondence with Fanny Ceantt relates to house raids and general civil war conditions.

O'BRIEN, William (d1968)

Irish trade unionist.

An extensive collection of papers is in the National Library of Ireland, which acquired them after his death. The collection includes extensive material on his own political career, in the labour movement and in association with various Republican bodies. Many of the papers of James Connolly came into O'Brien's hands, and these are included in the collection; they are an important source for the earliest period of the Irish labour movement and of Irish Socialism in general. The O'Brien papers contain very extensive material relating to the activities and membership of the Irish Transport and General Workers' Union. This includes a census of the membership of the union, together with lists of its branch officers, compiled in 1918, and O'Brien's diaries as union secretary, as well as several of his personal diaries. But a very substantial proportion of the general correspondence in the collection is intimately related to the activities of this union. The William O'Brien collection also contains papers and records relating to other labour organisations. (See *Sources*, Vol. 1, pp 301–302).

O'CONNOR, General Sir Richard Nugent (1889–1981)

Military career. Served European War, 1914–18; War of 1939–45. Military Governor, Jerusalem, 1938–39. Corps Commander, Western Desert, 1940–41; France, 1944. GOC-in-C, Eastern Command, India, 1945; North Western Army, India, 1945–46. Adjutant-General to the Forces, 1946–47.

Since the entry in *Sources*, Vol. 2, p 185, the papers have now been placed in the Liddell Hart Centre for Military Archives, King's College, London.

O'DONOGHUE, Florence

Irish Nationalist.

A collection of papers is in the National Library of Ireland.

O'DONOVAN, Rossa (1831–1915)

Irish Nationalist.

Miscellaneous papers, 1873–1914, are in the National Library of Ireland (Ms 10974).

O'HEGARTY, Diarmuid (fl. 1919–1932)

Co-founder, Irish Republican Brotherhood. Secretary, Executive Council, Cumann na nGaedheal Government.

Five boxes of papers, 1919–32, are in University College, Dublin (ref P8). The collection would appear to comprise only correspondence files relating to the routine work of the Executive Council (1923–27) together with personal material and printed matter.

OLDEN, Rudolf (1885–1940)

Academic.

His papers relating to German politics, 1927–40, are in University College, London.

OLDFIELD, Major-General Sir Louis (1872–1949)

Military career.

The Imperial War Museum has his World War I letters written to a friend. They give a detailed picture of the 51st Division's operations on the Somme and impressions of the period immediately after the war.

OLIVER, Frederick Scott (1864–1934)

Businessman and publicist. Author of *Federalism and Home Rule* (1910) and *Ordeal by Battle* (1915).

Since the entry in *Sources*, Vol. 5, p 147, the papers have been acquired by the National Library of Scotland. The collection includes family correspondence and substantial correspondence with Geoffrey Dawson, Lord Milner, Lord Carson, Sir Horace Plunkett, Austen Chamberlain, Viscount Lee of Fareham, Sir Terence Humphrey Keyes, J. M. Barrie and Lionel Curtis, and letters of various other public and literary figures, such as Leo Amery, John Buchan and Stephen Gwynn. The correspondence of F. S. Oliver on public affairs concerns chiefly the progress of the war, 1914–18, and the affairs of Ireland, 1913–17.

OLIVER, Admiral Sir Geoffrey Nigel (1898–1980)

Naval career from 1915. Served during World War I. Commanded HMS *Hermione*, 1940–42. Senior Officer, Inshore Squadron, North Africa, 1942–43. British Assault Force Commander, Salerno, 1943. Commander, 21st Aircraft Carrier Squadron, 1944–45. Sea Lord and Assistant Chief of Naval Staff, 1947–48. C-in-C, East Indies Station, 1950–52; The Nore, 1953–55.

Since the entry in *Sources*, Vol. 2, p 186, his widow has deposited the papers in Churchill College Cambridge. A list is available (NRA 24831).

O'MALLEY, Ernie (fl 1920s)

Irish Republican. Commander, 2nd Southern Division. Director of Organisation, Assistant Chief of Staff, Irish Republican Army.

Some papers are in University College, Dublin (ref P17). The collection, in 22 boxes covering the period 1916–56, includes minutes, despatches, operational memoranda, staff lists, distributions of strength and reports of the southern, northern and eastern commands (1916–23), captured Free State army intelligence summaries of enemy activity (1922–4), lists of and reports on republican prisoners in captivity (1922–5), and photographs of members of the Irish Republic Army (1922–5). There are also notes of interviews with veterans of the war of independence and civil war, statements concerning their military services; typescript drafts of *The Singing Flame*, *On Another Man's Wound*, *Sean Connolly* and *Raids and Rallies*.

O'MALLEY, Sir Owen St Clair (1877–1974)

Served Foreign Office, 1911–37. Minister, Mexico, 1937–38; Hungary, 1939–41. Chargé d'Affaires, Spain (St Jean de Luz), 1938–39. Ambassador, Poland, 1942–45; Portugal, 1945–47.

Contrary to the information cited in *Sources*, Vol. 2, p 187, the papers are not in the National Library of Ireland.

OMMANEY, Rear-Admiral Erasmus Denison St. Andrew (c.1853–1936)

Naval career.

Some papers are at the National Maritime Museum. They include logs and diaries for the periods 1873–94, 1901–03.

O'NEILL, Patrick (fl 1921–1945)

Irish Nationalist. MP, Mourne, 1921–45 in Stormont Parliament.

A collection (*c.* 100 items) of correspondence, election papers and accounts are in the Northern Ireland Public Record Office. The correspondence mainly concerns the Stormont elections of 1921, 1929, and 1931.

OPPENHEIM, Lassa Francis Lawrence (1858–1919)

Whewell Professor of International Law, Cambridge University, 1908–19. Author of such works as *The Science of International Law* (1908), *The Panama Canal Conflict* (1913), etc.

Ten of his notebooks are in the Library of Trinity College, Cambridge.

OPPENHEIMER, Sir Francis (Charles) (1870–1961)

Diplomat. Consul-General, Frankfurt, 1900–11; established the Netherlands Oversea Trust and later the Société Suisse de Suiveillance Economique. Special Mission to Vienna as Financial Commissioner, May 1919.

A collection of papers has been deposited in the Bodleian Library, Oxford. The collection divides into three parts. There are 12 folders of correspondence, memoranda and press cuttings (1914–21) covering his official work, mainly relating to the Netherlands Oversea Trust, the Société Suisse de Suiveillance Economique and his special mission to Vienna as British Financial Commissioner, 1919. The literary MSS section contains autobiographical material, notes for his antiquarian publications and miscellaneous material. The personal papers section consists of miscellaneous personal financial papers, material relating to his art collections and a considerable amount of personal correspondence. Other papers are at Balliol College, Oxford. A list is available (NRA 26778).

O'REGAN, John William Hamilton (1913–)

Colonial civil servant. Served Ceylon, Jamaica, Nigeria, etc.

The papers have been deposited through the Oxford Colonial Records Project in Rhodes House Library (ref MSS Brit Emp. s 385). The papers, which are arranged chronologically, include family correspondence with his mother and brother, rough diaries, and material on immediate pre-independence matters in Ceylon, Jamaica and Nigeria. The donor's permission is needed to view the papers. A list is available (NRA 17761). The donor should be approached c/o The Communications Department, Foreign and Commonwealth Office, King Charles Street, London, WC1.

ORR, Sir Charles (William James) (1870–1945)

Colonial administrator. Resident, Northern Nigeria, 1903. Chief Secretary and Acting High Commissioner, Cyprus, 1911. Colonial Secretary, Gibraltar, 1919–26. Governor and C-in-C, Bahamas, 1926–31. Author of *The Making of Northern Nigeria* (1911), *Cyprus under British Rule* (1918).

His letters to Miss E. Leviseur, 1900–1914, are in the British Library (Add Ms 65100).

OSBORNE, Walter V. (fl 1910)

Trade unionist. At centre of the 'Osborne judgment'.

No personal archive has been located, but reference should be made to the papers relating to the 'Osborne case' (1905–11) in the National Union of Railwaymen's deposit in the Modern Records Centre, University of Warwick.

OWEN, Major-General David Lanyon Lloyd (1917–   )

Army career. Commander, Long Range Desert Group, 1943–45. Military Assistant to High Commissioner, Malaya, 1951–53. GOC, Cyprus District, 1966–68. GOC, Near East Land Forces, 1968–69.

A few papers have been placed in the Imperial War Museum. The collection includes material on the activities of the Long Range Desert Group in North Africa, the Aegean, Italy and the Balkans, 1940–45.

OWEN, Donald (fl. 1880–1952)

Colonial service. Resident, Sarawak.

His memoirs, 1880–1952, are in Rhodes House Library.

OWEN, John (1854–1926)

Anglican divine. Bishop of St. Davids, 1897–1926.

His personal papers, covering the period 1897–1926, are in the National Library of Wales.

PACKER, Admiral Sir Herbert Annesley (1894–1962)

Naval attaché, Athens, Ankara and Belgrade 1937–39. Chief of Staff to C-in-C Mediterranean 1944. A Lord Commissioner of the Admiralty and Chief of Supplies and Transport 1948–50. C-in-C, South Atlantic Station 1950–52.

The papers were presented to Churchill College, Cambridge, by his wife Lady Packer, in May 1976. Arranged in 11 sections, they consist mainly of letters written at sea, 1912–45, first to his father and later to his wife. The book written by Lady Packer *Deep as the sea* (1975) was based on these papers.

PAGET, Admiral Sir Alfred (Wyndham) (1852–1918)

Naval career. Naval attaché, Paris, St. Petersburg and Washington, 1896–99; China, 1900–01. Senior Officer, Coast of Ireland, 1908–11.

The papers, originally loaned to the Imperial War Museum for copying, have now been purchased by the Museum.

PAGET, General Sir Bernard Charles Tolver (1887–1961)

Military service, World Wars I and II, etc.; Chief of General Staff, Home Forces, 1940; C-in-C South Eastern Command, 1941; Home Forces, 1941–43; 21st Army Group, 1943; Middle East Force, 1944–46.

Lt. Colonel Sir Julian Paget, Bt. (son), 4 Trevor Street, London SW7, retains his father's personal diaries, photograph albums, etc. These are believed to be closed.

PAGET, Sir Richard (1869–1955)

Barrister and philologist.

His correspondence and papers are in the Library of University College, London.

PAISH, Sir George (1867–1957)

Economist.

One box of his papers has been acquired by BLPES (ref M 1476) to whom enquiries should be addressed. It includes his memoirs.

PALAIRET, Sir Michael (1882–1956)

Minister, Romania, 1929–35; Sweden, 1935–37; Austria, 1937–38; Greece, 1939–42. Ambassador, Greece, 1942–43. Assistant Under-Secretary, Foreign Office, 1943–45.

In addition to the information cited in *Sources*, Vol. 2, p 188, Cambridge University Library has two boxes of letters to him, 1930–56, from a Cambridge friend, C. B. Hurry.

PALMER, Right Reverend Edwin James (1869–1954)

Colonial religious leader. Bishop of Bombay, 1908–29.

Some papers are in Lambeth Palace Library. These include his letters to the Church Quarterly Review, 1903–11 and an address on the Church in South Africa, 1907.

PALMER, Sir (Herbert) Richmond (1877–1958)

Resident, Bornu Province, Nigeria 1917. Lieutenant-Governor, Northern Provinces, Nigeria 1925–30. Governor and C-in-C, Gambia 1930–33; Cyprus 1933–39.

The family papers, 1746–1946, have been placed in Lancashire Record Office.

PANET, Brigadier Henri de Lotbinière (b 1896)

Military service, World War I; Egypt and Palestine, 1935–37; Hong Kong 1938–41; Iraq and Persia, 1941–43; BLA, 1944–45. Director of Fortifications and Works, War Office, 1947–49.

The Brigadier has given his unofficial diary of service to the Royal Engineers Institution, Chatham.

PANNELL, Baron
(Thomas) Charles Pannell (1902–1980)

MP (Lab) Leeds West, 1949–Feb. 1974. Minister of Public Building and Works, 1964–6.

Since the entry in *Sources*, Vol. 4, p 97, the papers have been deposited in the House of Lords Record Office.

PARHAM, Major-General Hetman Jack (1895–1974)

Army career. Served World War II. ADC to King George VI, 1946–47. Commander, No. 3 Anti-Aircraft Group, 1946–49.

A manuscript diary of the campaign in North-West Europe, 1944, is in the Royal Artillery Institution (ref MS 110).

PARIS, Major-General Sir Archibald (1861–1937)

Chief Instructor, Royal Marine Academy 1903–05. Commander, Royal Naval Division, Defence of Antwerp 1914, Gallipoli, etc.

Twenty manuscript letters, March 1915–July 1916, dealing with the Gallipoli campaign and the role of the Royal Naval Division are in the Imperial War Museum.

PARKER, Alwyn (fl 1917)

Director of Lloyds Bank.

A collection of his papers has been deposited with the BLPES (ref Coll Misc 547). It deals mainly with his negotiations with the Turkish authorities while acting on behalf of a British Bank Consortium interested in the Anatolian Railway and the Ottoman Railway (from Smyrna to Ardin) and takes the form of reports from Parker, 1920–24, press cuttings and articles on the Baghdad Railway by Parker, 1917 etc.

PARKER, Charles A.

Medical reformer.

Letters to him, mainly concerning the State Medical Service Association, 1912–22 are in the Bodleian Library Oxford (MSS Eng lett d 266).

PARKER, John (1906–   )

MP (Lab) Dagenham, 1945–83. Parliamentary Under-Secretary, Dominions Office, 1945–6.

Since the entry in *Sources*, Vol. 4, p 97, BLPES has now acquired a collection of papers (*c.* 12 boxes).

PARRY, William John (1842–1927)

Trade unionist and author.

The papers have been acquired by the University College of North Wales at Bangor. A list is available (NRA 25543).

PATON, Frederick Noel- (1861–1914)

Secretary to Sir Edgar Vincent at Constantinople. Explored the Hadramout. Secretary, Bombay Chamber of Commerce. Director-General of Commercial Intelligence to Government of India, 1905–14.

His papers have been presented to the India Office Library by Lord Ferrier (ref MSS Eur D 842). The papers (11 vols, 1908–14) chiefly comprise his reports on various aspects of agriculture in India.

PATTERSON, Lieutenant Colonel John Henry (1867–1947)

Military service, World War I. Officer Commanding, Jewish Battalion, Palestine. Gentile Zionist Revisionist campaigner in Britain, and elsewhere. Hon. Secretary, American League for a Free Palestine.

The Jabotinsky Institute in Israel has certain files on his work (ref P 117).

PAUL, Dr. Leslie Allen (1905–)

Journalist and author. Founder of the Woodcraft Folk, 1925.

His diaries, which are held at Lloyds Bank, Hereford, will be left to Mr. Paul Wilkinson (nephew), 123 Pensicely Road, Llandaff, Cardiff, South Glamorgan. Dr. Paul's literary material and correspondence is at the University of Texas.

PAWSEY, Sir Charles Ridley (1894–1972)

Indian Civil Servant. Deputy Commissioner, Naga Hills.

Certain papers, with much material on the Naga revolt, are reported in the Cambridge Centre for South Asian Studies. Other material is reported to be in the Royal Military Museum, Sandhurst.

PAXTON, Air Vice-Marshal Sir Anthony L. (1892–1966)

Air Force career.

His papers, not at present listed but covering the years 1920–50, are in the Royal Air Force Museum (ref AC 72/27).

PEACHEY, Captain Allan Thomas George Cumberland (1896–1967)

Naval career from 1914. Active service in various stations, with commands during World War II. Commodore, Palestine and Levant, 1947–48.

An interesting collection of papers at the National Maritime Museum includes material on World Wars I and II, Palestine (eg Peachey's signals as Commodore in Palestine), Suez and NATO.

PEARCE, Sir Charles Frederick Byrde (1892–1964)

Indian Civil Servant.

His papers, 1942–60, have been placed in the India Office Records.

PEDDER, Vice-Admiral Sir Arthur Reid (1904–)

Naval career. Assistant Chief of Naval Staff (Warfare), 1953–54. Flag Officer, Aircraft Carriers, 1954–56. Commander, Allied Naval Forces, Northern Europe, 1957–59.

A tape and transcripts of his naval memoirs, 1936–60, are in Churchill College, Cambridge.

PEDLER, Sir Frederick Johnson (1908–)

Colonial service. Chief British Economic Representative, Dakar, 1942.

Since the entry in *Sources*, Vol. 2, p 191, the papers have been placed in Rhodes House Library. A list is available (NRA 26285).

PEIRSE, Air Chief Marshal Sir Richard (1892–1970)

Deputy Chief of Air Staff 1937–40. Member of the Air Council 1939. Vice-Chief of Air Staff 1940. AOC-in-C Bomber Command 1940–42. AOC-in-C India 1942–43. Allied Air C-in-C South-east Asia 1943–44.

His unlisted papers, covering the period 1913 to 1965, are in the Royal Air Force Museum (ref AC 71/13).

PELLY, Admiral Sir Henry Bertram (1867—1942)

Naval career. Commanded HMS *Tiger* off Dogger Bank and Jutland. Rear Admiral, Egypt and Red Sea Station, 1919—20.

Some papers for the period 1901—20, mainly relating to his command of the battle cruiser *Tiger*, 1914—16, are in the Imperial War Museum.

PENNEFATHER, Colonel Edward Graham (1850—1928)

Chief of Police, Mashonaland and Singapore.

Correspondence, 1890—91, relating to the occupation of Mashonaland is in the National Archives of Zimbabwe.

PENNY, Sir James Downing (1886—1978)

Indian Civil Servant, 1910—45. Deputy Secretary, Finance Department, Government of India, 1926. Officiating Commissioner, Multan, Lahore, Rawalpindi, etc. Secretary, Government of Punjab, 1941—45.

His papers and memoirs have been deposited in the India Office Library (ref Mss Eur D 823). The four volumes of memoirs describe his life and duties in the Punjab where he worked as settlement officer, commissioner and financial commissioner (1941—45) to the government. Included are printed assessment and settlement reports on the Chenab Colony (1915) and the Jhang and Gugera area of Lyallpur District (1921—23, 25).

PERCIVAL, Lieutenant-General Arthur Ernest (1887—1966)

Military career. Brigadier, General Staff, I Corps, British Expeditionary Force, 1939—40. GOC, 43rd (Wessex) Division, 1940. Assistant Chief of Imperial General Staff, 1940. GOC, 44th (Home Counties) Division, 1940—41; Malaya, 1941—42.

Since the entry in *Sources*, Vol. 2, p 192, all restrictions on access to the papers have been lifted. In addition, reference should be made to the account (also at the Imperial War Museum) of Colonel C. H. D. Wild (Percival's interpreter) on the negotiations leading to the fall of Singapore.

PERHAM, Dame Margery Freda (1895—1982)

Middle East expert.

The papers have been deposited in Rhodes House Library, Oxford. The collection comprises her entire correspondence, literary and academic.

PERRIS, George Herbert (1866—1920)

Journalist and author. Editor, *Hull Express*, 1885. On staff of *The Speaker*. Editor of *Concord*, 1898—1906. A founder, and Hon. Secretary, of Anglo-German and Anglo-Russian Friendship Committees. Secretary, Cobden Club, 1903—05. Foreign Editor, *The Tribune*, 1906—07, *Daily News*, 1908—10. Originator and Assistant Editor, Home University Library, 1912—14. War correspondent, *Daily Chronicle*, 1914—18.

Since the entry in *Sources* Vol. 5, p 157, some papers have been located in the University of London Library (see NRA 22711). They cover the period 1914—20.

PETERS, Admiral Sir Arthur Malcolm (1888–1979)

Naval career.

His papers, notebooks and logs, 1904–41, are in the National Maritime Museum.

PHILIP, Sir (James) Randall (1900–1957)

Lawyer and public servant.

Three volumes of his journal, covering the period 1947 to 1957, were presented to the National Library of Scotland (ref Acc 4157) by Lady Philip in 1966. It is now available.

PHILLIPSON, Sir Sydney (1892–1966)

Colonial civil servant. Financial Secretary, Nigeria, 1945–48. Adviser to Southern Cameroons Government on financial and constitutional matters, 1959–61.

His papers on the Southern Cameroons, 1959–1962, are in Rhodes House Library.

PICKFORD, Hon. Mary Ada (1884–1934)

MP (Con) Hammersmith North, 1931–34. Member, Indian Franchise Committee, 1931–32.

Since the entry in *Sources*, Vol. 4, p 106, letters and papers 1906–1932, including material relating to the Indian Franchise Committee, 1932, have been acquired by the India Office Records (ref MSS Eur D 1013). The papers were presented by the Imperial War Museum.

PICKLES, Frederick (fl 1880s)

Pioneer socialist.

Some relevant papers are housed in the Labour Party archives, formerly at Transport House. They consist of personal correspondence and other items relating to Socialist politics in the 1880s and 1890s. The correspondents include William Morris, Eleanor Marx, J. Bruce Glasier and Keir Hardie.

PIGGOTT, Sir Francis (Taylor) (1852–1925)

Special mission to Italy 1887. Legal adviser to Prime Minister of Japan 1887–91. Secretary to the Attorney General on the Behring Sea Arbitration 1893. Chief Justice Supreme Court, Hong Kong 1905–12. Extensive publications on law, neutrality, extradition, etc.

His papers on the special mission to Italy 1887, to discuss a proposed convention for the mutual execution of legal judgements are in the Public Record Office (FO 323/7). A further collection of papers on legal issues is in the British Library (Add MSS 42525–42554)

PINHEY, Lieutenant-Colonel Sir Alexander Fleetwood (1861–1916)

Private Secretary to the Viceroy, 1910. Resident in Hyderabad, 1912.

His papers were presented to the Cambridge Centre for South Asian Studies by Lt. Col. L. A. G. Pinhey. The papers, consisting of five boxes, include diaries and letter-books covering his work. His diary while Resident in Hyderabad, 1912–14, is particularly revealing concerning conspiracies and intrigues in the Court, with a detailed exposition of the parties involved and the relationship between the Political Agent and the State.

PIRIE, Air Chief Marshal Sir George Clark (1896—1980)

Served European War, 1914—18. Air Attaché, Washington, 1937—40. Director-General of Organisation, Air Ministry, 1943—45. Allied Air C-in-C, South East Asia, 1946—47. Inspector-General, RAF, 1948. Air Member for Supply and Organisation, 1948—50. Head of Air Force Staff, British Joint Services Mission to United States, 1950—51.

Since the negative information in *Sources*, Vol. 2, p 195, the surviving papers have been placed in the Liddell Hart Centre for Military Archives, King's College, London. The collection of papers, correspondence and diary extracts covers the period 1918—1973.

PLAYFAIR, Air Marshal Sir Patrick Henry Lyon (1889—1974)

Royal Field Artillery, Royal Flying Corps and RAF career, from 1910. Air Officer Commanding in Chief, India, 1940—42.

Since the entry in *Sources*, Vol. 2, p 195, his previously unpublished memoirs have now been published as *'Pip' Playfair* (Arthur Stockwell Ltd, Ilfracombe, Devon, 1980).

POLAK, Henry (1882—1959)

Lawyer and humanitarian.

His papers have been deposited in Rhodes House Library, Oxford.

PORTEOUS, James A. A. (d 1979)

Economist and Scottish Nationalist.

Some papers have been deposited in the National Library of Scotland (ref Acc 7585). Porteous was Assistant Secretary, Scottish National Development Council, Economic Committee and the collection comprises two boxes containing files of reports, minutes and other papers of the Committee, 1936—39.

POWELL, Richard (1889—1961)

Indian police career, 1908—47. Inspector-General of Police, Jammu and Kashmir, 1946—47

His correspondence and other papers, 1947—60, have been acquired by the India Office Library (ref MSS Eur D 862), having originally been part of the Lothian papers. The papers relate chiefly to events in Kashmir, 1946—47.

POWELL, Wilfred (1853—1942)

Consul for Samoa, 1885 and Deputy Commissioner for the Western Pacific. Successively Consul at Stettin, Philadephia, Pennsylvania etc. Promoted Consul-General 1913. Fellow of the Royal Colonial Institute.

Personal papers, letters and notebooks, with miscellaneous maps, photographs, lantern slides, etc, are in the library of the Royal Commonwealth Society. The material falls into three main groups: letters and reports relating to the affairs of Samoa 1885—89; routine consular business, and documents on Powell's consular appointments, pay, transport, etc.

POWER, Admiral Sir Manley (Lawrence) (1904–1981)

Naval career. Fifth Sea Lord and Deputy Chief of Naval Staff, 1957–59. C-in-C, Portsmouth, Allied C-in-C, Channel, and C-in-C, Home Station (Designate) 1959–61.

In addition to the papers described in *Sources*, Vol. 2, p 197, his autobiography is in Churchill College, Cambridge.

POWLETT, Admiral Armund Temple (1841–1925)

Naval career. Commodore of the Training Squadron 1889–91. Superintendent of Sheerness Dockyard 1892–94. Second-in-Command in the Channel 1896–97.

Six volumes of his letter-books are in the National Maritime Museum (*see* NRA 20663). They cover his commands of HMS *Avon* in Chinese waters 1874–75, *Spiteful* and *Sirus* off West Africa 1876–77. *Champion* in China 1883–86 and *Benbow* in the Mediterranean 1888–89.

POWNALL, Lieutenant-General Sir Henry Royds (1887–1961)

Military career. Served India, European War of 1914–18, etc. Military Assistant Secretary, Committee of Imperial Defence, 1933–38. Director of Military Operations and Intelligence, War Office, 1938–39. Chief of General Staff, British Expeditionary Force, 1939–40. Inspector-General of Home Guard, 1940. Commanded British Troops in Northern Ireland, 1940–41. Vice Chief of Imperial General Staff, 1941. C-in-C, Far East, Dec. 1941–Jan. 1942, Persia-Iraq, 1943. GOC Ceylon, 1942–43. Chief of Staff to Supreme Allied Commander, South East Asia 1943–44.

Since the entry in *Sources*, Vol. 2, p 198, some of the papers have now been deposited in the Liddell Hart Centre for Military Archives, King's College, London. This material includes very full diaries, 1933–36, and 1938–45, together with letters and extracts from reports. Mr. J. W. Pownall-Gray retains certain papers which are to go to the Centre after his death.

PRESTIGE, George Leonard (1889–1955)

Acting General Secretary, Church of England Council on Foreign Relations.

His diary for November-December 1949 has been presented to Lambeth Palace Library by the Reverend R. H. Collier (son-in-law). The diary records the visit Prestige made to the Vatican, with the approval of Archbishop Fisher, to explore the possibility of conversations on reunion between the Anglican and Roman Catholic Churches.

PRETTY, Air Marshal Sir Walter (Philip George) (1909–1975)

Air Force career. Director-General of Organisation, Air Ministry, 1958. AOC-in-C, Signals Command, 1961–64. Deputy Chief of the Defence Staff (Personnel and Logistics), 1964–66.

His papers are in the Royal Air Force Museum (ref AC 75/24-25, 76/12. They cover the period 1928–56 and include letters, notebooks, press-cuttings etc.

PRIDHAM, Vice-Admiral Sir (Arthur) Francis (1886–1974)

Naval career. Flag Officer, Humber Area, 1939–40. President of the Ordnance Board, 1941–45.

In addition to the autobiography cited in *Sources*, Vol. 2, p 199, his war diary (1914—18) is also deposited at Churchill College, Cambridge.

PRITT, Denis Nowell (1887—1972)

MP (Lab, later Ind Lab) Hammersmith North, 1935—50.

The papers, cited in *Sources*, Vol. 4, p 115, have now been deposited in BLPES. They include political and legal papers, 1938—61, in the form of correspondence, printed papers, occasional diary notes and press cuttings which deal with a wide variety of topics including the Peoples Convention, 1941—42; the 1945 Election; trips to Socialist countries, 1946—61; Pritt's work as an MP; the Korean War; Jomo Kenyatta; China; Hungary; Ghana; the Reichstag fire; chemical warfare; the Munich agreement; the Helsinki Conference, etc. There are also books, addresses and speeches by Pritt from the 1930s to 1972.

PROUDFOOT, David (fl 1920s—1940s)

Communist. A leader of the Fife Miners.

His papers, together with his correspondence with George Allen Hutt, the Communist journalist and author, have been deposited in Methil Public Library, Fife. A list is available (NRA 22259). The papers relate mainly to the United Mineworkers of Scotland (1920s—1940s). They contain minutes, papers and accounts relating to the National Union of Mineworkers (Scotland) and to the Methil Cooperative Society, 1931—34. There are files relating to several Scottish Mineworkers Associations, to the Methil Trades and Labour Council, the General Strike in Fife, the Communist Party, the Young Communist League and the National Minority Movement.

There are two boxes of letters, 1924—42, from Proudfoot to Hutt, notes by Proudfoot and a file of miscellaneous important documents. There are also a number of pamphlets, press cuttings etc.

PUGH, Major-General Lewis Owain (b1907)

Military career.

The papers have been donated to the Imperial War Museum by his widow. The collection includes records of the raid on Axis shipping in Goa in 1943, correspondence relating to his command of the 49th Infantry Brigade in Java in 1945 and much correspondence concerning the employment of the Gurkhas in Brunei from 1966 to 1980.

PURDIE, Robert (Bob) (1940—   )

Extra-parliamentary Left activist. Active in Young Socialists, Socialist Labour League. Member, Central Committee, IMG, 1967—74. Organiser, Anti-Internment League, 1972—73.

A collection of pamphlets, duplicated papers and other records acquired by Purdie is in the Modern Records Centre University of Warwick (see NRA 20864). Many of the papers reflect his involvement with the situation in Ireland. There are duplicated papers and correspondence relating to the Irish Solidarity Campaign, the Troops Out Movement and the Anti-Internment League, various journals and publications from the Republican movement (Provisionals and Officials and its supporters) *c.* 1969—75; also papers of the Vietnam Solidarity Campaign with publications (VSC *Bulletin*, Indochina, etc.), 1966—72, and notes for speeches and articles by Bob Purdie. Correspondence, duplicated bulletins and other material originating with, or relating to, the IMG, especially their view on Ireland, are included in the papers, together with (copies) correspondence on the relationship to the Bertrand Russell Peace Foundation, 1967. Researchers should note that all unpublished material relating to the IMG is closed.

PURSEY, Commander Harry (1891—1980)

Naval career from 1907. Served ten years on lower deck in World War I and thereafter until 1936. Journalist and lecturer. MP (Lab) Hull East, 1945—70.

Since the entry in *Sources*, Vol. 2, pp 199—200, his naval papers have been acquired by the National Maritime Museum. The collection includes correspondence with Lionel Yexley. His parliamentary and constituency papers, 1936—1970, have been placed in the Brynmor Jones Library, University of Hull.

QUILLIAM, Brigadier Cyril David (1899—1972)

Military career. *The Times* correspondent, Middle East, 1945—51.

Letters and cuttings from Nokrashy Pasha, Lester Pearson and others concerning the trial and death sentence of the former Egyptian Prime Minister, Ibrahim Abdel Hadi in 1953 are in St. Antony's College, Oxford. There are some further papers in the archives of *The Times*.

RABINOWICZ, (Kuasnik) Oskar Kurt (1902—1969)

Financier, author and Zionist in Britain, Austria and the United States. Served Jews College and Jewish Historical Society, London, after 1939.

His papers are in the Jabotinsky Institute in Israel, and his library is at the Hebrew University.

RAGLAN, 4th Lord
Major Hon. Fitzroy Richard Somerset (1885—1964)

Military career, World War I. Political Officer, Palestine, 1919—21.

Copies of his Transjordan papers, including material relating to the installation of Amir Abdullah, and minutes of Churchill's Jerusalem Conference, 1921, are in the Middle East Centre, St. Antony's College, Oxford.

RAINIER, Admiral John Harvey (1847—1915)

Naval career. Served East Indies Station 1884—87. Served anti-slavery patrols off East Africa. Relieved Kandanos in Crete, 1897. Created Rear-Admiral 1901, Vice-Admiral 1905.

The papers (9 volumes, 2 files) were presented to the National Maritime Museum in 1948 by Captain J. W. Rainier. They consist of logs 1862—97 (with gaps) and miscellaneous loose papers concerning the disturbances in Crete and the relief of Kandanos.

RAMSAY, Dr. Mary (fl 1930—1957)

Scottish Nationalist.

Her papers, covering the period *c.* 1930—1957, have been presented to the National

Library of Scotland by Dr. W. N. M. Ramsay. They reflect her involvement with the Scottish Nationalist movement and include several letters of Hugh MacDiarmid.

RANCE, Major-General Sir Hubert Elvin (1898–1974)

Military career. General Staff, Western Command, 1943–45. Director of Civil Affairs, Burma, 1945–46. Governor, Burma, 1946–48, Trinidad and Tobago, 1950–55.

Since the entry in *Sources*, Vol. 2, p 201, his letters and papers covering the period 1945 to 1972 (four boxes) have now been presented to the India Office Library. At present there are restrictions on access to the papers. The collection, mainly comprising correspondence with the Burma Office, is particularly concerned with political and constitutional developments in Burma between 1945 and 1948. Correspondents include Lord Mountbatten and Malcolm MacDonald. There are also correspondence, press cuttings and related papers concerning his return visit to Burma in 1956 as an official guest of the Burmese government.

RANKIN, Air Commodore A. J. (1896–1974)

Air Force career.

His papers, not at present listed but covering the period 1918–68, are in the Royal Air Force Museum (ref AC 74/4, 10).

RANKIN, John (1890–1973)

MP (Lab) Glasgow Tradeston, 1945–55; Glasgow Govan, 1955–73.

Since the negative information in *Sources*, Vol. 4, p 121, some correspondence, 1946–49 and material on John Maclean is now in the Mitchell Library, Glasgow.

READY, General Sir Felix Fordati (1872–1940)

Army career. Served Sudan etc. GOC, Northern Ireland District, 1926–28. Quarter-Master General to the Forces, 1931–35.

His diaries of the Sudan campaign (1897) are in the National Army Museum.

REAY, 11th B
Donald James Mackay (1830–1921)

Governor of Bombay 1885–90. Under-Secretary for India 1894–95. Chairman, London School Board 1897–1904. First President of the British Academy 1901–07.

Some of his papers are housed at the School of Oriental and African Studies. The collection (one trunk covering the years 1884–90) contains material on his Governorship of Bombay. There are military and naval papers, reports on railways, irrigations, etc., and minutes and memoranda on such subjects as the Abkari administration.

RECKITT, Maurice Bennington (1888–1980)

Writer and philosopher. Founder member, National Guilds League.

Since the entry in *Sources*, Vol. 5, p 163, the papers have now been deposited in Sussex University Library.

REDCLIFFE-MAUD, Lord
John Primatt Redcliffe-Maud (1906—1982)

Diplomat and public servant.

The papers have been placed in the BLPES.

REDESDALE, 1st B
Algernon Bertram Freeman-Mitford (1837—1916)

Attaché in Japan 1866—70. Secretary to the Board of Works 1874—86. MP (Con) Stratford-on-Avon 1892—95. Accompanied HRH Prince Arthur's Mission to Japan, 1906.

The family papers, 18th-20th century, were deposited by Lord Redesdale in Gloucestershire Record Office in 1964 (NRA 17639). The papers of the 1st Baron Redesdale comprise *c.* 250 letters received 1872—1916, *c.* 80 semi-official letters 1875—86 relating to the Board of Works and miscellaneous further letters of appointment, honours, personal accounts, etc.

REES, Alwyn D. (1911—1974)

Noted political writer in Welsh circles. Editor of the periodical, *Barn.*

A collection of his papers has been deposited at the National Library of Wales. The collection includes papers relating to the University of Wales (1930s—1974) including general correspondence, 1955—74; the Welsh language in the University, 1965—74; disciplinary measures against students attending the Tryweryn trial (1963); proposed defederalisation of the University (1960—66); and miscellaneous printed material, lectures, notes and reviews. There are articles and notes, 1966—74, relating to the Welsh periodical *Barn*, together with a substantial collection of correspondence including letters from Alun Talfan Davies, Gwynfor Evans, Sir Albert Evans Jones, J. Enoch Powell, D. J. Williams and others. The papers include correspondence and printed material relating to the Welsh language campaign, 1965—74, and correspondents include Lord Denning, Tom Ellis, Gwynfor Evans, Lord Gardiner, Lord Hailsham and C. O. Williams, Archbishop of Wales. There are 2 folders on broadcasting in Wales, *c.* 1960—74; a folder on the National Eisteddfod, 1972—74; and 2 folders on Welsh politics, *c.* 1960—74. General correspondence covers the years 1935—74.

REES, Brigadier-General Hubert Conway (1882—1948)

Military career, World War I.

His papers have been deposited in the Imperial War Museum by his daughters, Mrs. L. S. Dodd and Miss A. V. Rees. The collection centres round his unpublished 'Personal Record of the First World War' which describes his various commands during the war. There are detailed accounts of the fighting at Gheluvelt on 31 October 1914, the opening of the Battle of the Somme and of the 150th Brigade's resistance to the 1918 German spring offensive. There is also an almost verbatim record of his interview with the Kaiser after he had been taken prisoner on 28 May 1918.

REID, Baron
James Scott Cumberland Reid (1890—1975)

MP (Con) Stirling and Falkirk Burghs, 1931—35; Glasgow Hillhead, 1937—48. Solicitor-General for Scotland, 1935—41. Lord Advocate, 1941—5.

Since the entry in *Sources*, Vol. 4, p 127, some papers have been deposited in the House of Lords Record Office by Lady Reid (ref Hist Coll 232). The material comprises notebooks used by Lord Reid when hearing Appeals in the House of Lords and the Privy Council. The material is not open for public inspection.

REID, Major-General Denys Whitehorn (1897–1970)

Army career. Served World War I and World War II. Commanded 10th Indian Division in Italy.

His papers are at the Imperial War Museum. The collection consists of autobiographical and miscellaneous Indian Army papers, including service in Mesopotamia in World War I, campaign papers as Commander of the 29th Indian Infantry Brigade 1940–42, papers concerning the Italian campaign and the 10th Indian Division and post-war papers and miscellanea.

RENDEL, 1st B
Stuart Rendel (1834–1913)

Businessman and Politician. MP (Lib) Montgomeryshire, 1880–94. Managing Director, Armstrong Whitworths.

His correspondence and business papers are in Tyne and Wear Archives Office. Other letters, including material on Western relations with China, are in the National Library of Wales.

RENDEL, Sir George William (1889–1979)

Diplomat.

Since the entry in *Sources*, Vol. 2, p 205, his correspondence and papers have been placed in the National Library of Wales.

RENTON, 1st B
Sir David Lockhart-Mure Renton (1908–   )

MP (Nat Lib) Huntingdon, 1945–50; (Nat Lib and Con) 1950–68; (Con) 1968–79. Parliamentary Secretary, Ministry of Fuel and Power, 1955–7. Parliamentary Secretary, Ministry of Power, 1957–8. Joint Parliamentary Under-Secretary, Home Office, 1958–61. Minister of State, Home Office, 1961–2.

Since the entry in *Sources*, Vol. 4, p 129, the papers have now been deposited in the House of Lords Record Office, to whom enquiries should be addressed.

REY, Lieutenant-Colonel Sir Charles Fernand (1877–1968)

Served Board of Trade; Ministry of Munitions; Ministry of National Service, and Ministry of Labour (World War I). Chief British Representative, Inter-Allied Commission for Food Supply to Germany, 1919. Served Unemployment Grants Committee, 1927–29. Resident Commissioner, Bechuanaland, 1930–37.

In addition to the material cited in *Sources*, Vol. 2, p 206, his original diaries as Resident Commissioner in Bechuanaland, 1929–37, are in the Botswana National Archives. The Hoover Institution on War, Revolution and Peace has typewritten copies of them.

RICHARDS, Charles (fl 1950—1976)

Director, East African Literature Bureau, 1948—63. Director, Christian Literature Fund, 1965—75.

His papers, c. 1950—76, are in the Library of the School of Oriental and African Studies.

RICHARDSON, Sir George Lloyd Reily (1847—1931)

Army career. Commanded Cavalry Brigade, China Expeditionary Force, 1900—01; Agra Brigade, 1903; 6th Poona Division, 1904—08.

A few documents on the Ulster crisis, 1914, are in the National Army Museum (ref Acc 5705/30).

RICHARDSON, Hugh (fl 1920s—30s)

Pacifist and Quaker.

Some papers for the period 1911—31 are in the Peace Collection, Friends Historical Library, Swarthmore College. The collection includes correspondence, notes and articles on peace, several peace plays and journals of his European travels, 1921—31. The papers include letters from German prisoners of war on the Isle of Man.

RICHMOND, Ernest Tatham (b 1874)

Political Secretary in Palestine to Chief Secretaries Deedes and Clayton, 1920—24. Chief Adviser to High Commissioner on Moslem Affairs.

Sir John Richmond (son) reported that all his father's political files concerning Palestine were destroyed by fire in 1926. He retains a number of letters written by his father from Palestine, but access is only granted after careful consideration.

ROACH, Edward Keith (1885—1954)

Colonial administrative service, Sudan and Palestine. Administrator, Jerusalem District, 1926—31. District Commissioner, Northern Palestine, 1931—37; Jerusalem, 1937—43. Author. Joint editor, *Handbook of Palestine and Trans-Jordan*.

The Middle East Centre, St. Antony's College, Oxford, has his two-volume unpublished diaries and memoirs, *Pasha of Jerusalem*.

ROBBINS, Lord
Lionel Charles Robbins (1898—1984)

Economist, public servant and academic.

His papers are to be placed in BLPES, to which enquiries should be addressed.

ROBERTS, Brian (1912—   )

Antarctic administrator.

A collection of his papers has been deposited with the Scott Polar Research Institute, University of Cambridge (ref MS 1308). The collection includes around a dozen typescript journals of Roberts' expeditions, 1930—71, to various countries including Canada, Iceland, USSR and Greenland. It also includes typescript personal journals on the 1st—6th Antarctic Treaty Consultative Meetings, 1961—70 (access to which is restricted); on the 1959 Antarctic Conference, Washington; on the Antarctic

Treaty Meeting of Experts on Logistics, Tokyo 1980; and a volume entitled *Antarctic 1960–61: United States Operation 'Deep Freeze 61'*. The latter part of the collection consists mainly of official documents, all closed until various periods after 1989. These papers include the official documents pertaining to the Antarctic Treaty Consultative Meetings 1–8 (1961–1975, 8 vols); the official records of the Antarctic Conference 1959 (2 vols typescript); the Antarctic Treaty Meetings on Telecommunications, final Report 1969; and documents pertaining to the 1972 conference on the conservation of Antarctic seals. There is a volume of correspondence (not restricted) relating to the Scott Polar Research Institute, 1930–64.

ROBERTS, Cecil Edric Mornington (1892–1976)

Author.

The papers have been placed in Churchill College, Cambridge. The collection comprises 15 boxes of diaries, correspondence and other papers. A list is available (NRA 23858).

ROBERTS, Reginald Arthur (1874–1940)

Colonial civil servant. Chief Political Officer, Agbor Expedition, 1906. Consul, Dahomey, 1911. Senior Resident, Southern Provinces, Nigeria, 1914. Acting Lieutenant-Governor, 1922–24.

Papers concerning Nigeria, including letters as Senior Resident, 1895–1928 are in Rhodes House Library.

ROBERTSON, Sir Robert (1869–1949)

Scientist. Director of Explosives Research, Royal Arsenal, Woolwich. Government Chemist, 1921–36. Treasurer, Royal Institution, 1929–46.

His papers have been deposited in the Library of the University of Dundee. The collection includes articles and talks by Sir Robert, minutes and correspondence regarding the reorganisation of the National Physical Laboratory, 1919–27, and correspondence on scientific matters, particularly concerning the use of Sir Robert's ideas in World War II. Correspondents include Lord Rayleigh, Sir James Irvine and C. P. Snow.

ROBERTSON, Field-Marshal Sir William Robert, 1st Bt (1860–1933)

Military career. Director of Military Training, 1913–14. Chief of General Staff, BEF, 1915. Chief of Imperial General Staff, 1915–18. GOC in C, Eastern Command, 1918. C-in-C, British Army on the Rhine, 1919–20.

The three volumes of papers, 1916–17, cited in *Sources*, Vol. 2, p 210 are not in the Public Record Office. There are, however, three volumes of his correspondence with Archibald Murray in the British Library.

ROBINSON, Commander Charles Napier (1849–1936)

Journalist and naval expert. Assistant Editor, *Army and Navy Gazette*, 1884. Staff of *The Times*, 1895. Editor, *Brassey's Naval Annual* from 1929.

The papers are in the Naval Library, Ministry of Defence.

ROBINSON, Wright (1876–1960)

Labour activist. Editor, *Liverpool Forward*. Manchester Councillor. Lord Mayor of Manchester, 1941–42.

A collection of papers was deposited in Manchester Central Library in December 1977 by Councillor Norman Morris, son-in-law (ref M284). The collection of diaries, autobiography and letters to his family and friends reflects all aspects of his political and trade union involvement. Amongst his correspondence with politicians, 1911–60, are letters from C. R. Attlee, Aneurin Bevan, Ernest Bevin, Wilfrid Burke, Barbara Castle, Sir Stafford Cripps, Hugh Dalton, Lord Darwen, Sir Wyndham Deedes, Hugh Gaitskell, Lord Geddes, J. Ramsay MacDonald, Angus Maude, Herbert Morrison, Morgan Philips, Alf Robens, Sir Ben Bowen Thomas, George Tomlinson, Ellen Wilkinson and Lord Woolton.

ROBSON, William (1895–1980)

Professor of Public Administration, London School of Economics, 1947–62.

The papers have been deposited in BLPES, to which enquiries concerning access should be addressed.

ROCH, Walter Francis (1880–1965)

MP (Lib) Pembrokeshire, 1908–18.

Since the entry in *Sources*, Vol. 4, p 138, his diaries and albums, 1932–56, have been placed in the National Library of Wales.

RODGERS, Sir John 1st Bt (1906–   )

MP (Con) Sevenoaks, 1950–79. Parliamentary Secretary, Board of Trade, 1958–60.

Since the entry in *Sources*, Vol. 4, p 139, his papers have been promised to Kent Record Office, to whom enquiries should be addressed.

RODWELL, Sir Cecil Hunter- (1874–1953)

On staff of Lord Milner 1901–03. Imperial Secretary in South Africa 1904–18. Governor of Fiji and High Commissioner for the Western Pacific 1919–24. Governor of British Guiana 1925–28. Governor of Southern Rhodesia 1928–34.

His correspondence and other papers, 439 folios, covering the period 1926–34, are in the National Archives of Zimbabwe.

ROE, Brigadier William Carden (1894–1977)

Military career. Commander, Southern Area, East Africa, 1946. Commander, British Advisory Staff, Polish Resettlement Corps, 1947–49. ADC to King George VI, 1946–49.

The papers have been acquired by the Imperial War Museum.

ROLFE, Eustace Neville (1845–1908)

Diplomatic career. Consul-General, Naples.

A collection of papers is available in Norfolk and Norwich Record Office. The collection, which covers the period 1867–1908, includes correspondence, diaries and other papers. The seven volumes of correspondence include letters from Rosebery and Kitchener. A list is available (NRA 17981).

ROLLIN, Aaron

Jewish labour historian. Trade unionist.

The Modern Records Centre, University of Warwick, has his working papers and also papers relating to union organisation in the tailoring industry, especially in London in the 1930s and 1940s. The collection also includes rare pamphlets and some papers of W. Wess, the anarchist.

ROSS, Colonel Sir John (fl 1890s)

Chief Commissioner, Dublin Metropolitan Police. Secretary to missions to the Vatican, 1880, 1890.

His letters, journals etc, for the period 1880–1920 are in the Public Record Office of Northern Ireland.

ROWNTREE, (Benjamin) Seebohm (1871–1954)

Social reformer. Writer on social questions. Manufacturer.

Since the entry in *Sources*, Vol. 5, p 170, the papers which were formerly in the Institute of Social and Economic Research have now been deposited in the Borthwick Institute.

ROYDEN, Dr. Agnes Maude (1867–1956)

Feminist.

Some papers are in the Fawcett Library, City of London Polytechnic.

RUSSELL, Sir Thomas Wentworth (1879–1954)

Egyptian civil service. Known as 'Russell Pasha'. Commandant, Cairo City Police, etc.

Photocopies of the papers which remained with his widow are in the Middle East Centre, St. Antony's College, Oxford. The material includes letters to his family 1904–22, despatches concerning political assassinations, 1922, and papers on the murder of the Sirdar, Sir Lee Stack, November 1924 and the subsequent trial.

RUTHVEN, Colonel (Christian) Malise Hore- (1880–1969)

Army career. Commanded 151st (Durham Light Infantry) Brigade. ADC to the King 1932–33. Secretary to Governor-General of the Union of South Africa 1933–36.

His reminiscences of the Boer War, together with his letters and diaries as Secretary to the Governor-General of South Africa 1933–36, are in the Imperial War Museum.

RYAN, Desmond (fl 1924–1964)

Irish republican. Author. Editor of *The Torch*. His published works include *James Connolly, His Life, Work and Writings*, 1924; *The Invisible Army*, 1932; *Remembering Sion*, 1934; *Unique Dictator, a study of Eamon de Valera*, 1936; *The Phoenix Flame, a Study of Fenianism and John Devoy*, 1937; and *Sean Treacy and the Third Tipperary Brigade*, 1945.

A collection of his papers (23 boxes, 1902–64) is in the Archives Department, University College, Dublin (ref LA 10). The collection includes drafts of published and unpublished works, scripts for radio, book reviews, working notebooks and reference material on nationalist and socialist topics (1934–64). There is correspondence relating to his editorship of *The Torch* and articles for publication (1941–

4); personal correspondence and material relating to family affairs (1924—64); correspondence on literary, historical and political matters with publishers, individuals such as Ernest Blythe, Austin Clarke, Bulmer Hobson, William O'Brien, Patrick Pearse and George Russell and with political and trade union groups such as the Labour Party, the Irish Congress of Trade Unions and the Irish Anti-Partition Society (1924—64).

SALMOND, Marshal of the Royal Air Force Sir John Maitland (1881—1968)

Director-General, Military Aeronautics; Member, Army Council 1917. Director, Armament Production, Ministry of Aircraft Production, and Director General, Flying Control and Air Sea Rescue, Air Ministry, World War II.

His papers have now been placed in the Royal Air Force Museum (1914—1943, not yet listed, ref AC 71/20, 73/14).

SAMSON, Air Commodore Charles Rumney (1883—1931)

Air Force career. Served World War I. Antwerp, Ypres etc. Commanded Brigade of French Territorials.

The papers are in the Imperial War Museum. The collection includes his personal file, log books, personalia, early aviation papers and information relating to the official history *War in the Air*.

SANDFORD, Sir Folliott Herbert (1906—   )

Assistant Under-Secretary of State, Air Ministry, 1944—47; Deputy Under-Secretary, 1947—58.

His diary of experiences in West Africa, 1942—44, is in Churchill College, Cambridge.

SANDFORD, Sir George Ritchie (1892—1950)

Colonial civil service from 1915. Financial Secretary, Palestine, 1940—44. Chief Secretary, Tanganyika, 1944—46. Administrator to East Africa High Commission, 1948—50.

It is understood that any surviving papers are with Mrs. D. Sandford (sister-in-law), 1 Carlton House, 36 Denmark Road, Exeter.

SAPTE, Herbert Langton (1853—1923)

ADC to High Commissioner in Cyprus, 1879. Military Secretary to High Commissioner, South Africa, 1889. Mission to Portuguese East Africa 1891. Business associate of Cecil Rhodes.

His correspondence (35 folios, 1891—93) relating to his mission to Manica is in the National Archives of Zimbabwe.

SAVILE, Lieutenant-Colonel Robert Vesey (1873—1947)

Army career. Provincial Governor in the Sudan; Bahr-el-Ghazal Province 1908, Kordofan 1909. Served in reconquest of Darfur expedition 1916. Governor of Darfur 1917—23.

His diaries for the period 1902—05 and 1910—21 can be found in the Sudan Archive, Oriental Section, University of Durham. They mainly concern tours in Kordofan, Darfur and Northern Kasala.

SCAMP, Sir Athelstan Jack (1913–1977)

Industrial arbitrator and conciliator. Personnel Director, GEC, 1962. Chairman, Motor Industry Joint Labour Council. Member, numerous government inquiries. Seconded to Department of Economic Affairs as Industrial Adviser, 1965–66.

Certain papers have been deposited by Lady Scamp in the Modern Records Centre, University of Warwick (ref MSS 178). The papers consist of four boxes relating to Scamp's work in industrial relations arbitration, 1965–77 and his work as chairman of the Motor Industry Joint Labour Council. They include proceedings and reports of inquiries with related documentation and correspondence. Access to these papers is strictly limited.

SCHLATER, General Sir Henry (fl 1898–1927)

Military career.

Copies of his correspondence and papers, 1898–1927 are in the Liddell Hart Centre for Military Archives, King's College, London.

SCOBIE, Lieutenant-General Sir Ronald MacKenzie (1893–1969)

Assistant Adjutant-General, War Office, 1938–39. Deputy Director of Mobilisation, 1939–40, GOC, 70th Division, Tobruk, 1941; Malta, 1942; Greece, 1944–46.

Since the entry in *Sources*, Vol. 2, p 218, a diary in six volumes has been deposited in the Imperial War Museum. The diaries give an invaluable account of the measures taken to suppress the Communist revolution in Greece from December 1944 to January 1945 and the efforts to re-establish a stable government and economy. Extensive quotations from the diaries appeared in Henry Maule's *Scobie, Hero of Greece* (1975).

SCOTT, Alexander MacCallum (1874–1928)

MP (Lib) Glasgow Bridgeton, Dec 1910–22.

Contrary to the information cited in *Sources*, Vol. 4, p 156, the papers have now been deposited, not at the University College, Buckingham, but in Glasgow University Library.

SCOTT, Sir (James) George (1851–1935)

Colonial service, Burma, Siam and Indo-China. Chargé d'affaires, Siam, 1893–94 British Commissioner, Burma-China Boundary Commission, 1898–1900. Superintendent and Political Officer, Southern Shan States, 1902–10. Author.

In addition to the material cited in *Sources*, Vol. 2, p 219 his letter book as Minister in Bangkok, 1889–1898 is in the Library of the School of Oriental and African Studies.

SCOTT, Sir Robert (1903–1968)

Colonial administrative service, Uganda, Palestine, Gold Coast. Administrator, East African Commission, 1950–54. Governor, Mauritius, 1954–59.

Many papers, used in drafting his books *A Survey of Palestine* (3 volumes), *Memorandum on the Administration of Palestine under the Mandate* (Jerusalem, 1947) were destroyed in 1946 at the King David Hotel. Rhodes House, Oxford, has his personal correspondence (1928–58), and his uncompleted reminiscences.

SCOTT, Sir Robert Heatlie (1905–   )

Civil servant and diplomat.

Some papers, 1923–82, are in the National Library of Scotland.

SCOTTER, General Sir William

Military career.

Copies of correspondence and memoranda, etc., are in the Liddell Hart Centre for Military Archives, King's College, London.

SCRIVENOR, Sir Thomas Vaisey (1908–   )

Colonial service, Tanganyika, Palestine, Malta and Nigeria. Deputy High Commissioner, Basutoland, Bechuanaland and Swaziland, 1953–60.

In addition to the papers cited in *Sources*, Vol. 2, p 220, one box of his papers and speeches as Deputy High Commissioner for Basutoland, the Bechuanaland Protectorate and Swaziland, 1953–60, is in the Centre for South African Studies, University of York.

SEABROOKE, Sir James Herbert (1852–1933)

Indian civil service. Assistant Secretary, Revenue and Statistics Department. Deputy Clerk of the Council, 1912–19. Joint Secretary, Military Department, 1915–19.

Twelve letters from India to his wife, and one to his daughter, 1911–12, describing his activities in India, particularly his participation in George V's Coronation Durbar, are in the National Library of Wales (ref 14588E).

SELWYN-LLOYD, Baron
(John) Selwyn Brooke Lloyd (1904–1976)

MP (Con) The Wirral, 1945–76. Minister of State, Foreign Office, 1951–4. Ministry of Supply, 1954–5. Minister of Defence, 1955. Secretary of State for Foreign Affairs, 1955–60. Chancellor of the Exchequer, 1960–2. Lord Privy Seal and Leader of the House of Commons, 1963–4. Speaker of the House of Commons, 1971–6

Since the entry in *Sources*, Vol. 4, p 160, some 450 boxes of his political papers have been deposited in Churchill College, Cambridge by the trustee of his estate. There are restrictions on access.

SEYMOUR, Admiral Sir Edward (1840–1929)

Naval career from 1852. Service in China, Egypt, etc. C-in-C, China Station, 1898–1901; Devonport 1903–05.

In addition to the material in the National Library of Scotland and in McGill University Library, his journal, 1898–1901, while C-in-C of the China Squadron is in the Naval Historical Branch Library of the Ministry of Defence.

SEYMOUR, Sir Horace James (1885–1978)

Minister, Persia, 1936–39. Assistant Under-Secretary, Foreign Office, 1939–42. Ambassador, China, 1942–46.

Since the entry in *Sources*, Vol. 2, p 221, six boxes of papers, correspondence and photographs relating to his diplomatic career have been deposited by his widow in Churchill College, Cambridge (NRA 23859).

SHAW, Flora (d 1929)

Author and writer. Colonial Editor, *The Times*. Wife of Lord Lugard. Joint Founder of the War Refugees Committee.

Papers covering the period 1890 to 1901 can be found in the archives of *The Times*. In addition, Lord Lugard's own papers deposited in Rhodes House Library, Oxford, contain not only correspondence with his wife, but a rough sketch of his career written by Lady Lugard and other family correspondence. Some of the material in Rhodes House was provided by Major Lugard (brother) for the use of Dame Margery Perham and is reserved until 1995.

SHAW, Lieutenant-General Sir Frederick Charles (1861—1942)

Army career. Commanded 9th Infantry Brigade, 1913—15, 13th Division etc. Director, Home Defence, War Office, 1915. Chief of General Staff, Home Force, 1916—18. C-in-C, Ireland 1918—20.

The Imperial War Museum has his diary for the period June—September 1915 when in command of the 13th Division at Gallipoli. This gives a detailed account of the operations at Cape Hellas and Anzac.

SHAW, Sir Walter Sidney (1863—1937)

Colonial legal service. Chief Justice, Straits Settlements 1921—25. Chairman, Commission of Enquiry into Disturbances in Palestine, 1929.

The Middle East Centre, St. Antony's College, Oxford, has only a few papers (ref Luke collection) on the 1929 disturbances. No other collection of papers has been located.

SHINWELL, Baron
Emanuel Shinwell (1884—   )

MP (Lab) Linlithgowshire, 1922—24 and 1928—31; Seaham, 1935—50; Easington, 1950—70. Financial Secretary, War Office, 1929—30. Parliamentary Secretary, Department of Mines at the Board of Trade, 1924 and 1930—1, Minister of Fuel and Power, 1945-7. Secretary of State for War, 1947—50. Minister of Defence, 1950—1.

Since the entry in *Sources*, Vol. 4, p 165, the papers have been placed in BLPES.

SHOENBERG, Sir Issac (1880—1963)

Television pioneer. Director, Electrical and Musical Industries (EMI).

His correspondence and papers, 1910—63, are in the Institute of Electrical Engineers.

SHOWERS, Lieutenant-Colonel Herbert Lionel (1861—1916)

Indian Political Department. Political Agent, Zhob. British Commissioner, Mewar Enquiry Committee. Served Sudan.

The papers have been deposited at the Centre for South Asian Studies, Cambridge.

SIEFF, Rebecca Doro
Lady Sieff (fl 1930s–50s)

Chairman, Women's International Zionist Organisation. President, Federation of Women Zionists of Great Britain and Ireland. Chairman, Women's Appeal Committee for Jewish Women and Children Refugees.

The Federation of Women Zionists, in London, holds her assorted correspondence and reports (1931–50s), as President of the Women's International Zionist Organisation and in connection with her work in rescuing children from Germany before World War II. Further material survives in the main Women's International Zionist Organisation archives in Tel Aviv, Israel. For the papers of Lord Sieff, see *Sources*, Vol. 5, p 180.

SIMMONS, Charles James (1893–1975)

MP (Lab) Birmingham Erdington, 1929–31; Birmingham West, 1945–50; Brierley Hill, 1950–59. Junior Lord of the Treasury, 1946–49; Parliamentary Secretary, Ministry of Pensions, 1949–51.

Since the entry in *Sources*, Vol. 4, p 167, the papers have been deposited in the Social Sciences Department, Birmingham Reference Library. The collection consists of personal papers, notes for sermons and addresses, political memoranda, etc.

SIMON, 1st Vt
Sir John Allsebrook Simon (1873–1954)

MP (Lib) Walthamstow (Essex SW), 1906–18; Spen Valley, 1922–31; (Lib Nat) Spen Valley, 1931–40. Solicitor-General, 1910–13. Attorney-General, 1913–15. Secretary of State for Home Affairs, 1915–16 and 1935–7; Foreign Affairs, 1931–5. Chancellor of the Exchequer, 1937–40. Lord Chancellor, 1940–5.

Since the entry in *Sources*, Vol. 4, p 167, his correspondence, diaries and papers, 1890–1953, have been placed in the Bodleian Library, Oxford. The collection has been listed (NRA 24981).

SIMON, Sir Francis Eugene (1893–1956)

Physicist. Closely involved with German refugee question in inter-war period. Professor of Thermodynamics, Oxford University, 1945–56. Member, Atomic Energy Project 1940–1946.

The papers have been placed with the Royal Society. The material, mainly scientific, but with some personal papers, includes laboratory notebooks and working papers, lectures and addresses, drafts of publications, press cuttings, etc. No material is earlier than 1924. A list is available (NRA 13900).

SINCLAIR, Admiral Sir Hugh (1888–1939)

Naval career.

His journals and scrapbooks have been placed in the National Maritime Museum.

SKEFFINGTON, Francis Sheehy (1878–1916)

Writer. Socialist, pacifist and feminist. Editor. *Irish Citizen*, 1912. Vice-Chairman, Irish Citizen Army.

An important collection of his papers, and those of his wife Hanna, are in the National Library of Ireland. The collection contains many letters from leaders of women's organisations and left-wing groups in Britain during the first forty years of this century.

SKEFFINGTON, Hanna Sheehy

Feminist. Founder, Women Graduates Association, 1903.

See above entry.

SKOULDING, Air Commodore Francis Arthur (1896–1974)

Royal Flying Corps and RAF service, from 1915. Middle East, China, India and US.

The Imperial War Museum has his reports of service, including air operations over Somaliland (1919–20), and visits to Palestine (1920) Egypt, Shanghai and Hong Kong.

SKRINE, W. F. de V. (fl 1922)

Sarawak civil servant.

His papers are in Rhodes House Library. The collection includes correspondence, 1909, 1911–28, while in the service of the Sarawak government, including letters from Sir C. V. Brooke. There are also diaries, 1910–12, 1914–17, official memoranda and correspondence relating to administration of provinces 1913–29.

SLESSOR, Marshal of the Royal Air Force Sir John (1897–1979)

Air Representative, Anglo-French conversations, 1939, and Anglo-American Staff conversations 1941. Assistant Chief of Air Staff, Casablanca Conference 1942–43. AOC-in-C, Coastal Command 1943. C-in-C, RAF Middle East and Mediterranean 1944–45.

His papers are at the Royal Air Force Museum (ref AC 75/28).

SLIM, 1st Vt
Field-Marshal William Joseph Slim (1891–1970)

Army career. Commanded 1st Burma Corps, 15th Indian Corps, 14th Army. C-in-C, Allied Land Forces, SE Asia, 1945–46. Chief of Imperial General Staff, 1948–52. Governor-General and C-in-C, Australia, 1953–60.

Since the entry in *Sources*, Vol. 2, p 224, an important collection of papers has been acquired by Churchill College, Cambridge. The collection comprises 12 boxes of private correspondence, military papers, articles etc. Churchill College also has Slim's letters to his ADC, Nigel Bruce, covering the period 1949–69. There are also xeroxes of letters from Slim to H.R.K. Gibbs and Field-Marshal Lord Birdwood, 1942–63, as well as xeroxes of letters to his daughter, 1940–59.

SMALL, William (d 1903)

General Secretary, Lanarkshire Miners Union. Founder member, Scottish Labour Party and ILP.

A small amount of material is in the National Library of Scotland (ref Acc 3350). Although a largely posthumous collection (1 box, 1899–1953) assembled by his daughter Miss Belle Small, it includes letters of Small to her, 1902, a semi-autobiographical story *A Dour De'il's Miracle and Sequel* written by William Small, 1899, and scripts of a BBC programme on him, 1948.

SMILES, Sir Walter Dorling (1883—1953)

MP (Con) Blackburn, 1931—45; (Ulster Unionist) Down, 1945—50; Down North, 1950—53.

Since the entry in *Sources*, Vol. 4, p 170, the papers have now been deposited in the Public Record Office of Northern Ireland. The collection includes biographical and genealogical notes, newspaper cuttings relating to his career, *c.* 1930—53, election literature, *c.* 1945—50, brief notes for speeches, together with some Russian papers, 1916—17, and Indian papers, *c.* 1925—29. (Sir Walter served during World War I in the British armoured division operating in Russia and during the 1920s he was employed administering a tea estate in Assam.)

SMITH, Sir Allen Chalmers (1893—1980)

Colonial legal career. Puisne Judge, Trinidad, Gold Coast. Chief Justice, Sierra Leone.

The papers are in Rhodes House Library (ref Mss Brit Emp S 442). A list is available (NRA 22912). The collection includes files on judgements in the West Indies, 1938—43, and in West Africa, 1944—50. There is also some correspondence between Smith and the Colonial Office.

SMITH, Brian Abel- (b 1906)

Academic. Professor of Social Administration, University of London.

The papers have been promised to BLPES, to which enquiries should be addressed.

SMITH, Sir Charles Bean Euan- (1842—1910)

Military and diplomatic career. Consul-General, Zanzibar, 1887—91. Minister, Tangier 1891—93. Minister-Resident, Bogota, 1898—99.

Correspondence for the period 1877—1883 was acquired by the India Office Library in 1977.

SMITH, Captain Gordon Gordon- (fl 1939—1945)

Diplomat.

His correspondence and papers, 1930—45, concerning the Yugoslav legation in Washington are in the British Library (Add MSS 60743-744).

SMITH, Sir Henry Babington (1863—1923)

Private Secretary to the Earl of Elgin, Viceroy of India 1894—99. British representative on Council of Administration of Ottoman Public Debt, 1900. President 1901. Secretary to Post Office 1903—09. President, National Bank of Turkey, 1909. Chairman, Royal Commission on the Civil Service 1915.

Some of his papers are at the Middle East Centre, St. Antony's College. The collection includes papers relating to the Baghdad Railway negotiations, the Mahssousshe Steamship negotiations, the Ottoman Bank, irrigation schemes in Mesopotamia and the Council of Foreign Bondholders. Correspondents include Sir E. Cassel, Lord Revelstoke and Sir Arthur Nicolson. Further papers are believed to be with Trinty College, Cambridge.

SMITH, Sir James Robert Dunlop (1858–1921)

Indian Civil Service. Political Agent, Phulkian States. Private Secretary to the Viceroy, 1905–10. Political ADC, Secretary of State for India, 1910–21.

In addition to the papers at the India Office Library (see *Sources*, Vol. 2, p 225), his diary of the Paris Peace Conference (1919) is in the Bodleian Library.

SMITH, Major-General Lionel Charles (1899–1976)

Army career.

An unlisted collection of papers is in the Imperial War Museum. It would appear to consist only of Operational Orders for 1st Corps, Royal Artillery, July–September 1944.

SMITH, Air Commodore Sydney W. (1889–1971)

Air Force career.

Some papers and correspondence covering the period 1913–70, are in the Royal Air Force Museum (ref AG 72/7, 32, 74/14).

SMITH, Sir William Alexander (1854–1914)

Founder, the Boys' Brigade.

A collection of his papers, including diaries, correspondence, and an unpublished biography have been preserved. *See* NRA 20767.

SNOW, Lieutenant-General Sir Thomas D'Oyly (1858–1940)

Army career from 1879. Commands during World War I; Western Command, 1918–19.

Since the entry in *Sources*, Vol. 2, p 226, the papers previously in family hands have been deposited in the Imperial War Museum.

SORLEY, Air Marshal Sir Ralph (1898–1974)

Assistant Chief of Air Staff (Technical Requirements), 1941. Controller of Research and Development, Ministry of Aircraft Production 1943–45. Member of the Air Council.

His papers, covering the period 1915–71, are in the Royal Air Force Museum (ref AC 75/27). The collection includes publications, diaries, log books, photographs, correspondence, papers and typescripts.

SOUCHAIR, Sir Sa'id Pasha (d 1934)

Government service in Palestine, Sudan etc.

The Sudan Archive, School of Oriental Studies, University of Durham, includes Souchair's papers. There are papers concerning Palestine (1918–19); Syria (1918–20); correspondence with Sir George Schuster, (1924–29); personal material, e.g. draft letters to Faisal, etc. especially concerning Syria and its finance, (1919–20); his projected appointment to Palestine, 1920; and relations with Transjordan (1922–23).

SOWREY, Air Commodore John (1892—1967)

Air Force career.

Papers, together with papers of Air Commodore William Sowrey are in the Royal Air Force Museum (ref AC 70/3, 5, 74/1). Most of the material concerns World War I, but some papers refer to East Africa, where William Sowrey was ADC during the Abyssinian campaign 1940—42.

SOWREY, Air Commodore William (1894—1968)

See above entry.

SPENCE, (James) Lewis (Thomas Chalmers) (1874—1955)

Scottish Nationalist. Sub-Editor *The Scotsman*, 1899—1904; Editor, *The Edinburgh Magazine* 1904—05; Sub-editor *The British Weekly*, 1906—09. Nationalist candidate, North Midlothian by-election, January 1929.

The papers have been placed by Miss Rhoda Spence in the National Library of Scotland (ref Acc 5916). The collection includes correspondence, with related documents, 1925—31, concerning the Scottish National Movement and the National Party of Scotland and a corrected typescript of Lewis Spence's *Freedom for Scotland*.

SPICER, Gerald Sydney (1874—1942)

Foreign Office career. Private Secretary to Sir T. Sanderson, Permanent Secretary for Foreign Affairs, 1903—06.

The Board of Deputies' Archive holds Spicer's correspondence and papers, 1921—24, concerning the League of Nations Union. Lawrence Graham & Co. (solicitors), London are in touch with Spicer's daughters.

SPRY, Sir John (Farley) (1910—   )

Chief Inspector, Land Registration, Palestine, 1944—48. Administrative and legal career, Kenya, Tanganyika, etc.

Correspondence, reports and memoranda relating to land law and land tenure in Palestine, 1919—48, are in the Middle East Centre, St. Antony's College, Oxford.

STACK, Augustine (1880—1929)

MP (Sinn Fein) Kerry West, 1918—22.

Since the entry in *Sources*, Vol. 4, p 181, some papers have been placed in the National Library of Ireland.

STAMFIELD, Claude (fl 1930s)

Welsh Hunger Marcher. Organiser, National Unemployed Workers Movement.

A diary covering his experiences as a hunger marcher is in University College, Swansea.

STANFORD, J. K.

Indian civil Service. Deputy Commissioner, Myitkyina, 1933—36.

Seven letter-books of his correspondence etc. are in the India Office Library (MSS Eur E 244).

STARKIE, William Joseph Myles (1861–1921)

Resident Commissioner for Irish National Education.

Correspondence concerning the Irish National Education Commission can be found in Dublin University Library.

STEVENSON, 1st B
James Stevenson (1873–1926)

Politician.

A collection of papers has been deposited in Sussex University Library. A list is available (NRA 23420). The collection includes a diary, 1921–26, correspondence, 1918–26, and other papers.

STEWART, Commander Archibald Thomas (1876–1968)

Naval career. Served HMS *Cornwallis* in Dardanelles, firing the opening shot of the bombardment. Senior British Naval Officer, Bizerta, 1917–19.

His logs and other papers were acquired by the National Maritime Museum in 1963.

STEWART, Sir Michael Hugh Shaw- (1854–1942)

MP (Con) Renfrewshire East, 1886–1906.

Certain papers, almost all relating to the Ardgowan Estates, have been listed by the NRA Scotland and are now deposited in Strathclyde Regional Archives (see NRA 14672).

STOCKWELL, General Sir Hugh Charles (1903–   )

Military career.

The Liddell Hart Centre for Military Archives, King's College, London has certain papers. They include reports and correspondence relating to service as Commander, Sixth Airborne Division, Palestine, 1947–8, including the illegal transhipment of Jews, the protection of oil installations and the withdrawal of British forces. His Suez papers are also there.

STOKES, Brigadier-General William Henry (1894–1969)

Army career, Royal Army Ordnance Corps.

His papers concerning the Royal Army Ordnance Corps during World War I and World War II have been placed in the Imperial War Museum.

STOKES, William Henry (1894–1978)

Trade unionist. Served various public bodies, e.g. Chairman, Midland Regional Board for Industry, 1945–50; Iron and Steel Corporation, etc.

A collection of papers has been placed in the Modern Records Centre, University of Warwick (ref MSS 180). A list is available (NRA 21924). The collection consists of the minute book of the National Minority Movement, Coventry District (1925), minutes of meetings of the 'Ministry of Production. Midland Regional Board' 1942–44, files of minutes, reports, correspondence and notes by Stokes relating to the Midland Regional Board 1940–45 (3 files). There are 2 files apparently belonging to G. B. King, Regional Controller, Ministry of Production on the 'Future of

250

Regional and District Organisation 1943–45' and the 'Re-conversion of Industry'. These contain memos, correspondence and notes. There is a volume of minutes of the AEU shop stewards, Humber Works, Coventry, 1950–63, and in 1979 a deposit was made of notes, press cuttings and circulars relating to the Coventry Toolroom Dispute 1971.

STOPES, Marie Carmichael (d 1958)

Birth control pioneer.

In addition to the papers cited in *Sources*, Vol. 5, p 187, further papers are in the Contemporary Medical Archives Centre, Wellcome Institute. These have now been listed (NRA 24915).

STOPFORD, Robert Jemmett (1895–1978)

Served European War, 1914–18. Banking career, 1921–28. Member of Runciman Mission, 1938. Liaison Officer for Refugees with Czech Government, 1938–39. Served World War II, Washington Embassy and War Office.

Since the entry in *Sources*, Vol. 2, p 232, substantial additional papers have been added to the collection in the Imperial War Museum. This additional deposit includes World War I diaries and letters together with material concerning his period at Washington. There is also an important collection of papers (5 vols, 2 boxes, covering the years 1928–77) in the India Office Library (ref MSS Eur E 346). The collection comprises private and demi-official correspondence, notes, and photographs as Private Secretary to Sir John Simon 1928–30 and as Secretary to the Conservative Delegation to the Round Table Conference 1930–31, together with explanatory notes dated 1976–77.

STORRS, Sir Ronald (1881–1955)

Served Egyptian Government. Military Governor, Jerusalem, 1917–20. Civil Governor, Jerusalem and Judea, 1920–26. Governor and C-in-C, Cyprus, 1926–32; Northern Rhodesia, 1932–34.

Since the entry in *Sources*, Vol. 2, p 232, an important set of papers has been purchased by Camellia Investments Ltd.

STRANG, 1st B
Sir William Strang (1893–1978)

Diplomatic Service, 1919–53. Assistant Under-Secretary, Foreign Office, 1939–43. UK Representative, European Advisory Commission, 1943–45. Political Adviser to C-in-C, Germany, 1945–47. Permanent Under-Secretary, Foreign Office (German Section), 1947–49; Foreign Office, 1949–53. Chairman, Royal Institute of International Affairs, 1958–65.

Since the entry in *Sources*, Vol. 2, p 233, certain of Strang's papers were given in May 1981 to Churchill College, Cambridge. A list is available (NRA 24829). Enquiries concerning access should be made to Churchill College.

STREETEN, Brigadier Gilbert (1890–1974)

Military service, World War I, Royal Engineers in Egypt; World War II in Palestine and Egypt.

The Imperial War Museum has his autobiography (1890–1970) including an account of anti-terrorist measures for which he was responsible as Commandant, Royal Engineers in Palestine (1938–40), and details of routine duties there (Chapter III).

STRICKLAND, General Sir (Edward) Peter (1869–1951)

Army career. Commanded 6th Division, Ireland, 1919–22, 2nd Division, 1923–26. GOC, British troops in Egypt, 1927–31.

The papers have been presented to the Imperial War Museum by his step-daughters, Lady Harrod and Mrs E. Le Strange. The collection consists of diaries, official papers, reports and photographs, 1899–1922. Topics covered include the Sudan, West Africa, his period as GOC 1st Division, 1916–18 on the Western Front, and his command of the 6th Division in Ireland. The collection includes intelligence reports, captured IRA documents and military orders relating to his Irish command.

STRINGER, Alderman Sidney (1889–1969)

Midland Labour politician. Leader of the Labour majority, Coventry City Council, 1938–67. Mover of the controversial motion in 1954 for Coventry to abandon civil defence.

A collection of his papers has been deposited in the Modern Records Centre, University of Warwick (ref MSS 24). The collection includes over 200 letters concerning the civil defence controversy, 1954 and a small group of papers re. Coventry City policy, mainly on housing and housing finance, 1958, 1966–67. Some similar material has been deposited in Coventry Record Office.

STUART, Sir Campbell (1885–1972)

Civil servant. Served in Washington, 1917. Deputy Director of Propaganda in Enemy Countries, 1919. Managing editor, *Daily Mail*, 1921. Director of *The Times*, 1919–60. Managing Director, 1920–4. Chairman, Imperial Communications Advisory Committee, and its successor, the Commonwealth Communications Council, 1933–45. Director of Propaganda in Enemy Countries, 1939–40.

Since the entry in *Sources*, Vol. 5, p 190, the Imperial War Museum has acquired an important collection of papers. The collection includes propaganda leaflets, minutes of consultative committee meetings, etc. The deposit comprises an important record of the top-level planning of British propaganda.

Further details are now available of the papers deposited in the Library of the Royal Commonwealth Society. The collection includes memoranda, reports and correspondence on a number of topics including Sir Campbell's investigation of the relationship of the Pacific Cable Board and the cable service in the West Indies (2 folders); 13 files of reports on the Imperial Communications Advisory Committee (*c.* 1929–44) including correspondence with the Treasury and Committee of Imperial Defence; 6 files relating to the Commonwealth Communications Council (operative from 1944) including verbatim notes of its first 19 sessions in 1944, interim reports on the future organisation of Imperial and Commonwealth telecommunications and Commonwealth Communications Council minutes, August 1945. The collection also includes some personal miscellanea.

SUETER, Rear-Admiral Sir Murray (1872–1960)

Director, Air Department, Admiralty, 1912–15. Member, Advisory Committee on Aeronautics, 1908–17. Superintendent of Aircraft Production 1915–17. Commander, RNAS units, South Italy, 1917–18.

An unlisted collection of his papers, covering the period 1913–19, is in the Royal Air Force Museum, Hendon (ref AC 74/12).

SULLIVAN, Timothy D. (1865–1911)

Lord Mayor of Dublin.

Some of his letters, together with those of his brother, Alexander Martin Sullivan, MP (1869–73) are in the Healy-Sullivan family papers deposited in University College, Dublin (ref P6).

SWEETMAN, Roger

Irish nationalist.

Papers in the possession of Brigid Sweetman were used by Leon O Broin in his book *Revolutionary Underground: The Story of the Irish Republican Brotherhood, 1854–1924*.

SWINLEY, Captain Casper Silas Balfour (1898–   )

Naval career. Chief Staff Officer, C-in-C, Malta 1942. Chief of Naval Information, Admiralty 1947. Commodore and Chief of Staff, Royal Pakistan Navy, 1953–54.

His papers were placed in Churchill College Cambridge in 1970 and 1971. The collection covering the period 1916–51, includes memoirs, diaries, newspaper cuttings, etc. The papers have been arranged in three groups: a memoir (1898–1941) written by Swinley, with copies of some of his diaries (1919–26); his 'scrapbooks', which consist of collections of letters and copies of letters; and a third group of items which do not fit the above categories. The correspondence includes letters from Admiral Sir Gerald Dickens and there is material on war-time Naval Conferences, plans for invasion, etc. For a variety of reasons, not all the papers are open to general inspection. Application to see these papers should be made to Dr. Swinley, Broughtons, near Newnham, Gloucestershire. A list is available (NRA 15456).

SYMES, Major-General George William (1896–1980)

Military career.

A diary in twelve volumes, covering the period 1940–48, has been given to the Imperial War Museum by his widow. The diaries are of particular value for the preparations and initial stages of the second Chindit expedition, the circumstances in which Lentaigne succeeded Wingate in March 1944 and the growing agitation for Burmese independence.

SYMON, Sir Alexander (Colin Burlington) (1902–1974)

Deputy High Commissioner, India, 1946–49. Assistant Under-Secretary of State, Commonwealth Relations Office, 1949–52. High Commissioner, Pakistan, 1954–61.

His papers, covering the period 1930–74, are in the India Office Library. The collection also includes his wife's papers.

TAIT, W.

Secretary, National Executive Council, British Section, International Socialist Labour Party.

A collection of papers has survived in private hands (*see* NRA 24342). The collection includes letters to him on early socialist activities as well as MBs (1896–1914) of the Edinburgh and Leith branch of the Social Democratic Federation.

TALBOT, Sir Adelbert (Cecil) (1845–1920)

Resident, Persian Gulf, 1891–94. Deputy Secretary, Indian Department, Government of India, 1894–96. Resident, Kashmir, 1896–1900.

The papers in the India Office Library (ref MSS Eur E 354) consist of his letters to Muriel Brown, 1884 onwards.

TALBOT, Vice-Admiral Arthur George (1892–1960)

Director, Anti-Submarine Warfare Division, Admiralty 1940. Naval Commander Eastern Assault Force, Normandy Invasion. Head, British Naval Mission to Greece, 1946–48.

His papers have been placed in the Imperial War Museum. The collection relates to his service as Director of Anti-Submarine Warfare at the Admiralty 1939–40.

TALBOT, Vice-Admiral Sir Cecil Ponsonby (1884–1970)

Naval career.

The Imperial War Museum has diaries covering his career, 1899–1932, with special reference to the submarine service.

TALBOT, Sir George John (1861–1938)

Lawyer.

Certain papers (c. 624 items, 1888–1935) are in the House of Lords Record Office (ref Hist Coll 108). The collection consists of Fee and other Account Books and miscellaneous personal, business and legal correspondence.

TALBOT, Colonel Hon. Milo George (1854–1931)

Military career, India, the Sudan etc. DAAG, HQ, Nile Expedition, 1897–99. Accompanied Sir Reginald Wingate's mission to the Senussi, 1916–17.

Some papers have been deposited in Rhodes House Library, Oxford (ref MSS Brit Emp s 424). There are letters to his brother and sister, 1876–1904, papers on survey and intelligence duties in Egypt and the Sudan, and letters to his wife written whilst with Wingate's mission to the Senussi.

TALLENTS, Sir Stephen George (1884–1958)

Civil servant and administrator. Chief British Delegate for Relief in Poland, 1919. British Commissioner, Baltic Provinces, 1919–20. Secretary, Empire Marketing Board, 1926–33; Principal Assistant Secretary, Ministry of Town and Country Planning, 1943–46.

The papers have been placed in the Institute of Commonwealth Studies. A list is available (NRA 21999). The collection includes 45 files on the origins of the Empire Marketing Board, the 1930 Imperial Conference, the EMB Reconstruction Committee etc. There is further material on the break-up of the Empire Marketing Board, July–August 1933 and correspondence with John Grierson. There are numerous minutes, reports, drafts, etc.

TANCRED, Edith Mary (1872–1956)

Historian of the women's police movement.

A collection of surviving papers has been deposited in Leeds Archives Department (ref Acc 1187). The collection includes 4 volumes of newspaper cuttings about women police in Britain, Ireland and South Africa (1917–41), a box of pamphlets and letters etc. re women police and the National Council of Women (1919–51), a box file of reports on women police throughout the world (1923–41), a box file of correspondence re women police and local authorities and a box file of miscellaneous papers. There are minutes of evidence of the 1928 Royal Commission on Police Powers and Procedure (Oct 1928–Jan 1929), the report of an Unofficial Commission (1935) by the South African Temperance Alliance, and an album of press cuttings on various subjects (1928–54) such as Welfare Centres, young offenders, cruelty to children, etc. There is a memo of the National Council of Women –Scottish Standing Committee (1934–35) with particular reference to censorship and juveniles and the Cinematograph Exhibitors Association.

TANGYE, Wing Commander N.

Air Force career, World War II. Liaison Officer with US Strategic Air Force (Europe).

His transcript diary, kept while serving as RAF Liaison Officer on the personal staff of the Commanding General, US Strategic Air Force (Europe), July–October 1944, is in the Imperial War Museum. The diary is very revealing of Anglo-American relations from both the British and the American viewpoint.

TASKER, Sir Theodore James (b 1884)

Indian Civil Service. Commissioner, Coorg, 1923–26. Loaned to the Government of the Nizam of Hyderabad as Revenue Secretary, 1927–35 and Member of Council 1935–42.

His papers, covering the period 1927–72, have been placed in the India Office Library. At the time of writing, the collection was closed.

TATLOW, Canon Tissington (1876–1957)

General Secretary, Student Christian Movement 1903–29. Honorary Secretary, World Conference on Faith and Order 1913–27. Founder and first Secretary of the Anglican Fellowship, 1912.

A collection of papers is held by Lambeth Palace Library. It includes papers for the period 1912–39, including his work as Secretary of the Faith and Order Conferences, 1918 and copy letters to Archbishop Lang.

TAYLOR, (Francis) John (1912–1971)

Anglican divine. Principal, Wycliffe Hall, Oxford. Bishop of Sheffield, 1962–71. Author of *The Church of God* (1946).

A collection of his papers has been deposited at Sheffield Central Library by Archdeacon Johnson. They are closed until 2021, but dispensation may be sought from Archdeacon Johnson. The collection consists of 14 files of correspondence between Bishop Taylor and Archdeacon Johnson, 1933–71 (BTP 1–14) comprising letters dealing with theology and the episcopate and general topics. There are 10 files of manuscript and typescript notes for Taylor's sermons and lectures, *c.* 1940–70 (BTP2, 1–10), 14 printed pamphlets, mostly by Taylor, 1943–61; a folder of press cuttings and a box of miscellaneous material.

TAYLOR, Sir Geoffrey Ingram (1886—1975)

Aerodynamicist. Nuclear scientist, who worked on first nuclear explosion in New Mexico.

His papers are in Trinity College, Cambridge.

TAYLOR, Robert Arthur (1886—1934)

MP (Lab) Lincoln 1924—31.

Since the entry in *Sources*, Vol. 4, p 198, his diary of a visit to Canada and the USA in 1928 has been placed in the Brynmor Jones Library, University of Hull.

TAYLOR, Sir Thomas Murray (1897—1962)

Academic and lawyer. Principal and Vice-Chancellor, University of Aberdeen, 1948—62; formerly Professor of Law, 1935—48. Executive Committee, World Council of Churches.

The papers have been placed in Aberdeen University Library. The collection includes copies of published works, 1946—65, manuscripts and typescripts of sermons, speeches etc. 1936—62, legal opinions 1936—48 and papers relating to his public work. This latter group includes material on the Enquiry into Crofting Conditions, 1951—54, the Crofters' Commission, 1951—61, the World Council of Churches, 1948—59 and General Assemblies, 1931—58. There is extensive correspondence concerning religious and university business.

TEICHMAN, Sir Eric (1884—1944)

Diplomat and expert on China. Chinese Secretary, Peking Legation 1922—27. Counsellor 1927—36, 1942—44.

His letters are in Bristol University Library.

TEMPEST, Brigadier-General Roger Stephen (1876—1948)

Military career. Served Boer War, World War I. Commanded 43rd Infantry Brigade 1917—18. Present at Festubert, Loos, the Somme.

The collection forms part of the estate papers and other correspondence of the Tempest family of Broughton, in the possession of H. R. Tempest, Broughton Hall, Skipton. A list is available (NRA 19695). The papers include World War I correspondence and papers, some diaries, personal letters to his parents and miscellaneous estate and legal papers.

TENNANT, Sir William Robert (1892—1969)

Indian Civil Service, 1919—47.

His letters and reminiscences, 1916—49, have been deposited in the India Office Library. Particularly interesting are the letters from Simla residents, dated 1948—49, commenting on the changes brought about by Independence.

THESIGER, Wilfred Patrick (1910—)

Diplomat and explorer. Explored Danakil country of Abyssinia and the Aussa Sultanate, 1933—34. Served Sudan Political Service. Author of *Arabian Sand*.

A collection of his diaries and papers, 1934—56, is in the archives of the Royal

Geographical Society. The collection relates mainly to travels in Africa and the Middle East.

THOMAS, Sir Ben Bowen (1899—1977)

Educationalist, author and UNESCO official.

A collection of his papers has been deposited with the National Library of Wales. The collection includes correspondence from Sir Percy Watkins, 1926—39, and Thomas Jones, 1927—55, relating to Coleg Harlech and education in Wales; papers and official documents relating to the ITA and the grant of new television contracts, 1967; papers relating to the Rural Development Board in Wales, 1968—69; papers relating to the establishment of a Welsh Language Council, March—Sept 1973: correspondence and diaries relating to journeys to the Far East, Europe and North and South America as member and chairman of the Executive Board of UNESCO, 1945—65; and miscellaneous material.

THOMAS, Sir (Thomas) Shenton Whitelegge (1879—1962)

Colonial service. Governor, Nyasaland, 1929—32; Gold Coast, 1932—34, Straits Settlements (and High Commissioner, Malay States), 1934—42.

Since the entry in *Sources*, Vol. 2, p 240, his papers and other correspondence have been acquired by Rhodes House Library.

THOMSON, Sir George Paget (1892—1975)

Nuclear physicist.

One box of his papers concerning the Maud Committee is in Churchill College, Cambridge.

THORNLEY, Sir Colin Hardwick (1907—   )

Colonial administrative service. Principal Private Secretary to Secretary of State for the Colonies, 1941—45. Governor, British Honduras, 1955—61. Director-General, Save the Children Fund, 1965—74.

Sir Colin Thornley stated that he lost his papers in the British Honduras hurricane disaster of 1961.

THOROLD, Air Vice-Marshal Henry Karslake (1896—1966)

Air Force career. Deputy Director of Equipment, Air Ministry, 1938—39. HQ British air forces in France 1940; Takoradi (West African Reinforcement Route) 1940—42. AOC No. 92 Group Bomber Command 1943—45. Head of Air Section, British Military Mission in Moscow, 1945.

Some miscellaneous papers, 1940—42, mainly concerning the West African Reinforcement Route are in the Imperial War Museum.

THWAITES, General Sir William (1868—1947)

Military career. Director of Military Intelligence, War Office, 1918—22. GOC-in-C, British Army on the Rhine, 1927—29. Director General, Territorial Army, 1931—33.

L. & W. Wilkinson (solicitors and executors), Blackburn, Lancashire, have information on the General's surviving papers.

TITMUSS, Richard M. (1907—1973)

Professor of Social Administration, London School of Economics, 1950—73.

A collection of 142 boxes of his papers, *c.* 1939—73, has been deposited in BLPES. A summary handlist is available.

TODD, Baron
Sir Alexander Todd (1907—   )

Professor of Organic Chemistry, Cambridge, 1944—71. President, British Association for the Advancement of Science, 1969—70. Chairman, Royal Commission on Medical Education, 1965—68.

A collection of his papers has been deposited with Cambridge University Archives, The University Library, Cambridge. Readers should contact the Keeper of Archives. The collection consists of a group of letters, circulars, minutes, reviews and press cuttings (1963—71) relating to the Royal Commission on Medical Education, 1965—68. Principal correspondents include the members of the Commission, Lord Platt, Sir George Godber, Sir Frank Lee, Sir John Wolfenden and T. S. Black-Kelly.

TOFAHRN, Paul

Assistant General Secretary, International Transport Workers Federation (ITWF)

Certain papers have been deposited by his widow in the Modern Records Centre, University of Warwick. They are of most value for the ITWF in the inter-war years but also include some material on the International Federation of Workers in the Food Industry for the 1930s. The main ITWF deposit is also at Warwick (ref MSS 159).

TOTTENHAM, Sir (George) Richard (Frederick) (1890—1977)

Indian career. Secretary, Government of India, Defence Department, 1932—37. Additional Secretary and Secretary, Home Department, 1940—46.

A microfilm of his memoirs is in the care of the Cambridge Centre for South Asian Studies. There is considerable material on the Imperial Conference, political movements and internal security, the Indian National Congress, etc.

TOVEY, Admiral of the Fleet Lord
John Cronyn Tovey (1887—1971)

Naval career. C-in-C, Home Fleet, 1940—43; C-in-C, The Nore, 1943—46.

His papers have been deposited in the National Maritime Museum.

TOWNSHEND, Major-General Sir Charles Vere Ferrers (1861—1924)

Entered Royal Marines, 1881. Served Sudan; South Africa; European War, 1914—18. MP (Ind) The Wrekin, 1920—22.

Since the entry in *Sources*, Vol. 2, p 242, a scrapbook relating to Kut, and two files of correspondence, one containing letters from Field-Marshal Earl Kitchener of Khartoum to General Townshend, the other relating to Colonel A. J. Barker's research for *The Neglected War* and *Townshend of Kut*, have been given by Colonel Barker to the Liddell Hart Centre for Military Archives, King's College, London.

TOYNBEE, Arnold Joseph (1889–1975)

Historian and writer. Member, Foreign Office Political Intelligence Department, 1918; British Delegation to the Paris Peace Conference, 1919. Director, Foreign Research and Press Service, Royal Institute of International Affairs, 1939–43. Director, Foreign Office Research Department, 1943–46.

Since the entry in *Sources*, Vol. 2, p 242, the papers have been deposited in the Bodleian Library Oxford. A list has been prepared, but the permission of the donor is required to consult both the list and the papers.

TREVASKIS, Sir (Gerald) Kennedy (Nicholas) (1915–   )

Colonial civil servant. British Military Administration, Eritrea, 1941–50. Political Officer, Western Aden Protectorate, 1951. High Commissioner for Aden and the Protectorate of South Arabia, 1963–65. Publications on Eritrea and South Arabia.

Six boxes of his papers, covering the period 1944–66, are in Rhodes House Library, Oxford (ref MSS Brit Emp s 367). Two boxes are concerned with Eritrea, the remaining four with Aden. Boxes 5 and 6, containing recent correspondence, are not at present available for research. A handlist is available (NRA 13845).

TRIPE, William Borrowdale (1906–   )

Colonial Administrative Service, Tanganyika, 1929–50. Military service, World War II, in Middle East. Arab affairs adviser, Tripolitania, 1944.

The Middle East Centre, St. Antony's College, Oxford, has his secret study on Transjordan (1941). Rhodes House, Oxford, has 4 boxes, including correspondence, reports, memoranda, etc. (1928–45), covering his war service in the Middle East.

TUDOR, Major-General Sir (Henry) Hugh (1871–1965)

Military career. Served South Africa, World War I etc. Chief of Police, Ireland, 1920.

In addition to the information in *Sources*, Vol. 2, p 244, the Royal Artillery Institution holds his diary.

TULLOCK, Major-General Sir Alexander Bruce (1838–1920)

Army career. Special service officer, C-in-C, Mediterranean Fleet, 1882. Head of Intelligence Department, Egypt. Military adviser to Australian colonies, etc.

Some papers, including Intelligence Reports on Egypt, *c.* 1885 have been placed in Monmouthshire Record Office.

TWEEDSMUIR OF BELHELVIE, Baroness,
Priscilla Jean Fortescue Buchan, Lady Tweedsmuir (1915–1978)

MP (Con) Aberdeen South, 1946–66. Minister of State, Scottish Office, 1970–2; Foreign and Commonwealth Office, 1972–4.

Since the entry in *Sources*, Vol. 4, p 214, her correspondence and papers, 1945–74, have been placed in the National Library of Scotland.

TWEEDY, Owen (1888–1960)

Journalist and civil servant. Assistant Oriental Secretary to Allenby, 1919–24.

Middle East correspondent, *Daily Telegraph* and *Financial Times*, from 1926. Government Press Officer, Palestine, 1936–43. Director of Ministry of Information and Propaganda, Minister of State's Office, Cairo, 1941–43.

The Middle East Centre, St. Antony's College, Oxford, has his diary, scrapbooks of press cuttings and letters home etc. (1926–52).

TYLER, Sir Henry Hewey Francis Macdonald- (1877—1962)

Political Officer, Civil Administration, Mesopotamia, 1917–20. Secretary of Indian Central Committee, Indian Statutory Commission, 1928–29.

The papers which form part of the family archive dating back to 1750, have been placed in the Northern Ireland Public Record Office. A list is available (NRA 21036). The correspondence (1901–24) and diaries (27 vols., 1901–29) cover almost all his career in India and Mesopotamia. His typescript memoir, notes on the Arab rising and various press cuttings are also in the collection.

TYSON, Sir John Dawson (1893—1976)

Indian Civil Service. Secretary to the Agent of the Government of India in South Africa, 1927–29. Private Secretary to the Governor of Bengal 1930–35, 1938 1945–47.

His papers have been placed in the India Office Library. The collection includes copies of detailed weekly letters written home, 1920–48, but there are also notes on V. S. Srinivasa Sastri's tour of duty in South Africa, 1927–29 and on Sir John Anderson, 1st Viscount Waverley, as Governor of Bengal, 1932–37.

VAUGHAN, Dame Helen Charlotte Isabella Gwynne- (1879—1967)

Commandant, Women's Royal Air Force, 1918–20. Director, Auxiliary Territorial Service, 1939–41. Member, Royal Commission on Food Prices, 1924.

Her papers, together with two volumes of diaries, are in the Museum of the Womens Royal Army Corps, Queen Elizabeth Park, Guildford, Surrey. Some of the papers are closed to AD 2100.

VERNEY, Major-General Gerald Lloyd (1900—1957)

Military career. Served World War II. Commanded 1st Guards Brigade, 6th Guards Tank Brigade, 7th Armoured Division, etc. Author of *The Desert Rats* (1954).

The papers were deposited at the Liddell Hart Centre for Military Archives, King's College, in November 1977 by his son, Major P. V. Verney. A list is available (NRA 23079).
 The collection is in five parts. Part 1 relates to the 6th Guards Tank Brigade and contains papers covering Operation Bluecoat, the operations of 8 Corps south of Caumont (Normandy) in July 1944; Part 2 relates to the operations of the 7th Armoured Division August–November 1944; Part 3 relates to the 1st Guards Brigade (February 1944 to May 1945) and its actions in Italy. Part 4 consists of various pamphlets on military matters and Part 5 consists of 40 campaign maps.

VERNEY, Lieutenant-Colonel Sir Ralph (1879—1959)

Military Secretary, Viceroy of India, 1916–21.

His letters (three files of typed copies), as Military Secretary to the Viceroy, 1916–21, are in the India Office Library (ref Mss Eur D 921).

VERNON, Wilfred Foulston (1882–1975)

MP (Lab) Dulwich, 1945–51.

Since the entry in *Sources*, Vol. 4, p 216, two folders of his correspondence were placed in BLPES in February 1977 (ref Coll Misc 521). The correspondence is with Morgan Phillips and left-wing members of the Labour Party concerning the telegram of congratulation sent to the left section of the Italian Socialist Party led by Pietro Nenni.

VINCENT, Sir (Harold) Graham (b 1891)

Private Secretary, successive Prime Ministers, 1928–34. Principal Private Secretary, 1934–36. Principal Assistant Secretary, Committee of Imperial Defence, 1936–39; Ministry of Food, 1939–40; Works and Buildings and Town and Country Planning, 1940–44; Production 1944–46; Civil Aviation, 1946–49.

A memoir on British political affairs, 1932–38 (written *c.* 1970) was given by the author in 1975 to the Brotherton Library, University of Leeds. The memoir is mainly an account of Baldwin's efforts to promote rearmament in the 1930s. There are also a few original letters, e.g. one from Swinton (*c.* 1936), one from Inskip (*c.* 1938) and a copy of a lengthy memo from Vincent to Bridges criticising the hopeless state of administrative organisation for defence.

VINCENT, Air Marshal Stanley Flamank (1897–1976)

Air Force career. AOC, 13 Group, Scotland, 1943; 221 Group, SE Asia Air Forces, Burma, 1944–45. SASO Fighter Command 1945–48.

Drafts and correspondence relating to his autobiography are in Churchill College, Cambridge.

VINCENT, Sir William Henry Hoare (1866–1941)

Indian Civil Servant.

Some 226 folios of his papers as Judicial Commissioner, Chota Nagpur, 1908, are in the India Office Library (ref Mss Eur D 698). Part of the collection concerns the 1908 dispute in Champaran between the Bettiah Raj and the Motihari Indigo Concern which Vincent arbitrated.

VON DONOP, Major-General Sir Stanley Brenton (1860–1941)

Commissioned in Royal Artillery, 1880. Director of Artillery, War Office, 1911–13. Master-General of the Ordnance and 4th Military Member of Army Council, 1913–16. Commander, Humber Garrison, 1917–20.

Since the entry in *Sources*, Vol. 2, p 248, all restrictions on access to the papers in the Imperial War Museum have been lifted. In addition, the Public Record Office has an important collection of papers, 1910–34, mainly relating to the munitions crisis (W.O. 79).

WAKEHURST, 2nd B
Hon. John de Vere Loder (1895–1970)

Politician and colonial governor. MP (Con) Leicester East, 1924–29; Lewes, 1931–36. Governor, New South Wales, 1937–46; Northern Ireland, 1952–64.

The papers described in *Sources*, Vol. 2, p 248 were deposited in the House of Lords Record Office in 1976 by the Dowager Lady Wakehurst. The collection includes a typescript of his unpublished memoirs and of a work entitled *Mediterranean Background*, accounts of visits to South America, Australia and French North Africa, copies of Intelligence Summaries from Turkey, 1918, personal scrap books, press-cuttings, election material and a few papers relating to Northern Ireland. These Northern Ireland papers are not open to public inspection.

WALLACE, Walter Ian (b 1905)

Indian Civil Service 1928–47. Defence Secretary to the Government of Burma at Simla, 1942–44. Chief Secretary to the Government of Burma, 1946.

Two boxes of his papers covering the period 1930–1957 are in the India Office Library (ref MSS Eur E 338).

WALLIS, Sir Barnes (Neville) (1887–1979)

Inventor of Geodetic construction, and of the weapon which destroyed Moehne and Eder Dams, and penetration bombs.

Two boxes of his papers are in Churchill, College, Cambridge. The papers consist of his aeronautical research files, 1940–58.

WALLIS, Leonard George Coke (1900–1974)

Indian Political Service. Deputy High Commissioner, Pakistan, 1947–52.

His papers, 1947–61, 46 folios, have been presented to the India Office Records (ref MSS Eur D 1002).

WALSH, Major-General Ridley P. Pakenham (1888–1966)

Military career. British Representative, International Commission, Teschen, 1919–20. AAG War Office, 1934–35. Engineer in Chief, BEF, 1939–40. GOC, Northern Ireland District, 1940–41. Controller General, Army Provision (EG) 1943–46.

A collection of his diaries (23 volumes, 1927–47) is in the Royal Engineers Corps Library. Further papers are in the Liddell Hart Centre for Military Archives, King's College, London.

WARD, Mary Augusta
Mrs. Humphrey Ward (1851–1920)

Novelist and social worker. Founded the Passmore Edwards Settlement and the Play Centres of London, 1897. A founder of the Women's National Anti-Suffrage League.

In addition to the entry in *Sources*, Vol. 5, pp 199–200, further papers are available in Honnold Library, Claremont, California. In addition, four boxes of papers, mainly literary, are in Washington University Library.

WARDROP, General Sir Alexander (1872–1961)

Military service, World War I. Commander, Palestine, *c*. 1922. GOC, Northern Command, 1933–37.

Mr. L. Plowman (executor) of Godden Holme & Co. (solicitors), London S.W.1, knows of no papers, and there is no surviving family.

WARING, Walter (1876—1930)

MP (Lib) Banffshire, 1907—18; (Co Lib) Blaydon, 1918—22; Berwickshire and East Lothian, 1922—3.

The papers in family possession, cited in *Sources*, Vol. 4, p 223, have now been acquired by the Scottish Record Office.

WARNER, Sir George Redston (1879—1978)

Diplomat.

Since the negative entry in *Sources*, Vol. 2, p 250, his diaries and other correspondence, 1906—78, have been deposited in Hampshire Record Office.

WATT, Air Chief Commandant Dame Katherine Watson (1899—1971)

Director, Womens Auxiliary Air Force, 1939—43. Missions to the Middle East and North America 1943—44.

Her papers, not at present listed, covering the period 1939—70 are in the Royal Air Force Museum (ref AC 72/17).

WAUCHOPE, Major-General Sir Author Grenfell (1874—1947)

Chief of British Section, Military Inter-Allied Commission of Control, Berlin, 1924—27. High Commissioner and C-in-C, Palestine and Transjordan, 1931—38.

His observations on the future potential development of German industry, 1924—25, are in the Public Record Office (WO 32/57-98). Five volumes of his personal albums are in the Black Watch Regimental Museum, Balhousie Castle, Perth.

WAVERLEY, 1st Vt
Sir John Anderson (1882—1958)

Secretary, Ministry of Shipping, 1917—19. Chairman, Board of Inland Revenue, 1919—22. Joint Under-Secretary to Lord Lieutenant of Ireland, 1920. Permanent Under-Secretary, Home Office, 1922—32. Governor of Bengal, 1932—37. MP (Ind National) Scottish Universities, 1938—50. Lord Privy Seal, 1938—39; Home Secretary, 1939—40. Lord President of the Council, 1940—43. Chancellor of the Exchequer, 1943—45.

In addition to the material cited in *Sources*, Vol. 2, p 252, the India Office Records have acquired his official and private correspondence as Governor of Bengal, 1932—37.

WEBB, Sir Charles Morgan (1872—1963)

Indian Civil Service. Deputy Commissioner, Burma, 1901. Chief Secretary, Government of Burma, 1918.

Copies of correspondence (1920) with J. A. Stewart, Deputy Commissioner at Kyaukse, are in the India Office Library.

WEDGWOOD, 1st B
Josiah Clement Wedgwood (1872—1943)

MP (Lib) Newcastle-under-Lyme, 1906; (Lab) 1919—42. Chancellor of the Duchy of Lancaster, 1924.

Since the entry in *Sources*, Vol. 4, p 228, his correspondence and papers have been placed in the Library of the University of Keele by his grand-daughter, Dr. N. J. Pease.

WEINER, Abraham (1876–1952)

Historian and pioneer Zionist. Lecturer in Modern History, King's College, London.

Miss Joyce Weiner (daughter), 36 Lower Lake, Battle, Sussex, has a collection of her father's unpublished MSS, essays, lectures and reviews, and some printed material concerning his work for the Zionist movement. Miss Weiner gave her father's collection of pamphlets to the Weizmann Institute and to the Weiner Library.

WELBY, 1st B
Reginald Earle Welby (1832–1915)

Assistant Financial Secretary, Treasury 1880. Auditor of the Civil List 1881. Permanent Secretary, Treasury, 1885–94.

A collection of his letters, together with government publications etc., covering the period 1852–1911, is available in BLPES. Further papers relating to Imperial Defence 1888–91 are in the British Library (Egerton MSS 3291). Further papers form part of the Welby (Allington) MSS in Lincolnshire Archives Office (NRA 5901).

WELLESLEY, Hon. Frederick Arthur (1844–1931)

Military attaché in Russia, 1871–78. First Secretary in Austria 1878–79. Colonel of the Coldstream Guards.

His papers were presented to the Public Record Office by Sir Victor Wellesley (FO 519). They include seven volumes of his entry books of dispatches to the British Ambassador at St. Petersburg, 1871–77, official and semi-official correspondence with the Foreign Office 1877–79 and miscellaneous papers collected by Wellesley for his published works.

WELLS, Frederick Arthur (1901–1971)

Academic and Public Servant. Professor of Industrial Economics.

The papers have been placed in the University of Nottingham Library. A list is available (NRA 21600). The collection includes papers of the building industry National Joint Council, legal actions in the Industrial Court (1917–53), arbitration papers, notes on economics, correspondence and notes for his book on the hosiery industry, minutes of evidence etc. for the various committees on which he served, material on the National Coal Board, reports on the state of industry after the war, numerous publications and press cuttings.

WENLOCK, 3rd B
Beilby Lawley (1849–1912)

Governor of Madras 1891–96. Lord of the Bedchamber to the Prince of Wales, 1901–10.

His papers can be found in Hull University Library and in the India Office Library. The papers at Hull University Library (which had originally been deposited by T. Forbes-Adam in the East Riding Record Office and were transferred in 1974)

264

include records of his official duties as Governor of Madras, 1891–96, and are on permanent loan at the India Office Library. There is also extensive correspondence with Lord George Hamilton in the Hamilton papers, also at the India Office Library.

WESTER WEMYSS, 1st B
Admiral of the Fleet Sir Rosslyn Erskine Wemyss (1864–1933)

Naval career from 1877. Commodore, Royal Naval Barracks, 1911–12. Rear-Admiral, 2nd Battle Squadron, 1912–13. Commanded squadron of troops landing in Gallipoli, 1915. C-in-C, East Indies and Egypt, 1916–17. 1st Sea Lord, 1917–19.

Since the entry in *Sources*, Vol. 2, p 253, his papers have been deposited by his daughter in Churchill College, Cambridge. A list is available (NRA 24833).

WESTON, Bertram John (1907–   )

Colonial Civil Service. Assistant Commissioner, Nicosia, 1937. Government Secretary, Acting Governor and C-in-C, St. Helena 1960–63.

His papers are in Rhodes House Library. They include introductory notes etc. on the Cyprus problem 1957, a political appreciation of the Cyprus position 1959, correspondence with the Colonial Secretary and the Governor of Cyprus 1954–60, and minutes and papers during his period at St. Helena 1960–63, including a report on the administration of Ascension 1962.

WHITE Arthur John Stanley (b 1896)

Indian Civil Service. Deputy Commissioner, Burma, 1928–34. (during the Burma Rebellion, 1931–32). Secretary to Government of Burma, 1934. Deputy Secretary-General, later Secretary-General, British Council.

Some papers have been presented to the India Office Library (ref MSS Eur E 356). The collection, covering the period 1922–36, comprises four boxes of letters, reports and memoirs.

WHITEHOUSE, Sir George (1857–1938)

Builder of the Uganda Railway, subsequently its Manager and Chief Engineer, 1895–1903.

The papers are in Rhodes House Library, Oxford (ref Mss Afr s 1046). The collection includes nine volumes of diaries and correspondence relating to his period in Uganda.

WICKS, Harry (1905–   )

Communist. Member, Central Committee, Young Communist League. Editor, railway rank-and-file publication, *Victoria Signal*. Expelled from Communist Party 1932, along with Groves and Flower. Subsequently involved with Trotskyist movement.

Some material has been deposited in the Modern Records Centre, University of Warwick (ref MSS 102). The collection comprises duplicated study notes on Marxist economics, the history of the Russian Communist Party and the history of the Labour movement in Europe.

WIGG, Baron
George Edward Cecil Wigg (1900—1983)

MP (Lab) Dudley, 1945—67. Paymaster-General, 1964—7. Member, Racecourse Betting Control Board, 1957—61; Horserace Totalisator Board, 1961—4; Chairman, Horserace Betting Levy Board, 1967—72. President, Betting Office Licencees Association, 1973—83.

Since the entry in *Sources*, Vol. 4, p 236, the papers have been acquired by BLPES.

WILKIE, Alexander Mair (1917—1966)

Colonial civil servant. British Resident Commissioner, New Hebrides.

His notes, memoranda etc. are in Rhodes House Library (MSS Brit Emp s 383). The papers, 5 boxes, covering the period 1935—69, concern Kenya, the Western Pacific etc. His correspondence as British Resident Commissioner in the New Hebrides is not at present available for research.

WILKINSON, Gerald Hugh (1909—1965)

British Liaison Officer with MacArthur in the Philippines, 1942. Served British Security Co-ordination, New York, 1943—45.

Six boxes of his war journals and other papers have been placed in Churchill College, Cambridge.

WILKINSON, Sir Hiram Shaw (1840—1926)

Consular service. British Commissioner for the Settlement of Claims after the Canton riots 1883. Chief Justice, Supreme Court of China and Korea, 1900—05.

His papers are in the Northern Ireland Public Record Office (ref D 1292). The collection consists of *c*. 1,000 documents, and includes both personal and official correspondence. Some correspondence refers to Ireland, including letters concerning the 1918 Irish Convention and a threatening letter from the Irish Republican Army in March 1922. A list is available (NRA 25886).

WILLIAMS, Alfred Martyn (1897—)

MP (Con) Cornwall North, 1924—9.

Since the entry in *Sources*, Vol. 4, p 228, copies of his brief memoirs of his naval career have been placed in the Imperial War Museum.

WILLIAMS, Harold Whitmore (d 1928)

Journalist, closely involved in Russian emigré work after 1917.

In addition to the papers cited in *Sources*, Vol. 5, p 206, additional material can be found in the papers of his wife, A. V. Tyrkova-Williams in Columbia University Library. The collection includes papers, letters, manuscripts and reports on the political situation in South Russia in 1919.

WILLIAMS, William Hugh (1857—1938)

Colonel; Vice-Consul, Asia Minor, 1895—97.

His journal (1877—1884) is in the National Army Museum.

WILLIAMSON, Group Captain Hugh Alexander (1885–1979)

Career in naval aviation.

Four boxes of his memoirs, naval aviation and personal papers have been placed in Churchill College, Cambridge. A list is available (NRA 25831).

WILLIS, Admiral Sir Algernon Osborne (1889–1976)

Naval career from 1904. Chief of Staff, Mediterranean Fleet, 1939–41. C-in-C, South Atlantic Station, 1941–42; Levant Station, 1943; Mediterranean Fleet, 1946–48; 2nd Sea Lord and Chief of Naval Personnel, 1944–46.

The papers cited in *Sources*, Vol. 2, were placed in Churchill College, Cambridge, in 1976. They have been listed (NRA 20290). The collection includes correspondence relating to his entry in the Navy (before the Fisher reforms) and early log books (1905–08). There is little else prior to 1919. There are diaries of operations in the Baltic, 1918–19, and of the Australasian cruise, 1920. There is correspondence 1933–34, (when he commanded HMS *Kent* and HMS *Nelson*), some papers for 1935–38, an events diary, August 1947–January 1948, correspondence with the Cabinet Office Historical Section, a paper on 'Churchill and the War at Sea, 1939–45', his war memoirs, letters to the press, press cuttings, etc.

WILLIS, Bob (fl 1945–1969)

Trade Unionist. General Secretary, London Society of Compositors etc.

Certain papers have been deposited in the Modern Records Centre, University of Warwick by the head office of the National Graphical Association. The papers consist of his files as General Secretary of the London Society of Compositors/London Typographical Society and as Joint General Secretary of the National Graphical Association, 1945–69. The papers include material deriving from his TUC activities and his membership of the National Board for Prices and Incomes (1965–67), in addition to London Society of Compositors records.

WILLOCK, Air Vice-Marshal Robert Peel (1893–1973)

Air attaché, British Embassy, China, 1933–36. Director of Staff Duties, Air Ministry, 1938. AOC, Iraq and Persia, 1943–44. Deputy Head, RAF Delegation, Washington 1944–46. Civil Air Attaché, Washington, 1946–47.

Certain papers relating to his service career, 1914–60, have been placed in the Imperial War Museum.

WILSON, Sir Garnet Douglas (1885–1975)

Local political leader. Lord Provost of Dundee, 1940–46.

His papers, correspondence and speeches, covering the period 1921–75, have been deposited in Dundee District Archives.

WILSON, Sir Horace (1882–1972)

Civil service career. Permanent Secretary, Ministry of Labour, 1921–30; Treasury, 1939–42. Chief Industrial Adviser, HM Government, 1930–39.

Since the entry in *Sources*, Vol. 2, p 258, some Private Office papers have become available at the Public Record Office.

WIMBERLEY, Major-General Douglas Neil (b 1896)

Military career. Served European War, 1914–18; North Russia, 1919; India, North West Frontier, 1930; War of 1939–45. GOC, 46th Division, 1941. Divisional Commander, 51st Highland Division, 1941–43. Commandant, Army Staff College, 1943–44. Director of Infantry, War Office, 1944–46.

Since the entry in *Sources*, Vol. 2, p 258, a copy of the unpublished biography has been placed in the Imperial War Museum.

WINCOTT, Leonard (fl 1930s–40s)

Naval mutineer, Invergordon.

One box of his memoirs is in Churchill College, Cambridge.

WINGATE, Sir Francis Reginald (1861–1953)

Governor-General, Sudan, 1899–1916. High Commissioner, Egypt, 1917–19.

In addition to the papers in the Sudan archive (see *Sources*, Vol. 2, p 259), a collection of papers can be found in Duke University Library. The papers, 345 items covering the period 1884–1955 include correspondence, reports, maps and clippings, chiefly 1890–91, when Wingate was Director of Military Intelligence in Egypt. The papers are chiefly concerned with military operations and with political and economic affairs in the Sudan. The correspondents include Wingate's superiors and subordinates in London, Cairo, southern Egypt and the eastern Sudan.

WINGATE, Sir Ronald Evelyn Leslie (1889–1978)

Indian Political Service, World Wars I and II. Member of Joint Planning Staff, War Cabinet. Author.

In addition to the entry in *Sources*, Vol. 2, p 259, his papers on service in Iraq, 1920 und in Muscat 1919–22 are in St. Antony's College, Oxford.

WINTERBOTHAM, Group Captain Frederick William (1897–   )

Service with the Air Staff and Foreign Office 1929–45. Chief of Air Intelligence, World War II.

His papers, not at present listed, covering the period 1934–43 are in the Royal Air Force Museum (ref AC 72/23).

WITHERS, Sir John James (1863–1939)

MP (Con) Cambridge University, 1926–39.

Although no papers have been located, over 300 letters to Oscar Browing, *c*. 1883–1912, can be found in the Browning papers.

WOODBURN, Arthur (1890—1978)

MP (Lab) Clackmannan and East Stirlingshire, 1939—70. Parliamentary Secretary, Ministry of Supply, 1945—7. Secretary of State for Scotland, 1947—50.

Contrary to *Sources*, Vol. 4, p 253, correspondence and papers have survived and have been acquired by the National Library of Scotland (Acc 7656). The collection covers the period 1907—1978 and includes political, personal and family correspondence, speeches, lectures etc. as well as the draft of an autobiography.

WOODHOUSE, Colonel Hon. Christopher Montague (1917—)

Head of the British Military Mission to German-occupied Greece. Secretary-General, Allied Mission to supervise Greek elections, 1946. Director-General, Royal Institute of International Affairs, 1955—59. MP (Con) Oxford, 1959—66, 1970—74. Parliamentary Secretary, Ministry of Aviation, 1961—62. Joint Under-Secretary of State, Home Office, 1962—64.

Three boxes of his papers were placed in the Liddell Hart Centre for Military Archives, King's College, London, in February 1976. A list has been prepared (NRA 23080). The first box contains SOE documents, 1942—44. The second box consists of an official report on SOE operations in Greece, 1945; a report by him on the Allied Military Mission in Greece, 1942—44; and reports of the BBC Monitoring Service, 1948—50. The third box contains personal accounts of operations in Greece, written by Woodhouse and G. K. Wines. A letter of recommendation is needed to consult the papers. Reference should also be made to the Myers papers also held by the Liddell Hart Centre.

WOODS, Henry Charles (1881—1939)

Author and journalist. Vice-Consul, Adana, Asia Minor, 1910. Special Correspondent, *The Times*, in the Balkans, 1911. Military and diplomatic correspondent, *Evening News*, 1914—15.

Some papers are with the archives of the Royal Geographical Society. The material includes diaries and notebooks, 1905—28, relating to political and economic affairs.

WORTLEY, Major-General Edward James Montagu-Stuart- (1857—1934)

Army career. Served Tel-el-Kebir, Nile Expedition etc. Military attaché, Drummond Wolff special mission to Turkey, 1885. Military attaché, Paris, 1901—04. Commanded 10th Infantry Brigade, 1908—12; North Midland Division, 1914 and 65th Division in Ireland.

Some papers are in the Bodleian Library, Oxford (ref. Eng Hist D 256). They relate mainly to the *Daily Telegraph* incident and include letters from his wife, 1907—08.

WRIGHT, Stanley Fowler (1873—1953)

Commissioner of Customs and Personal Secretary, Inspector-General of the Chinese Maritime Customs.

The papers and books have been bequeathed to the Library of Queen's University, Belfast. The collection, which fills 14 shelves, includes not only numerous official printed papers and reports but also Wright's notes and papers for his various published works (e.g. *Hart and the Chinese Customs*, Belfast, 1950), some of Wright's own official papers, personal notebooks, notes based on Foreign Office archives, etc. There also also books in Chinese, books and pamphlets on China, etc. Some of the papers of Sir Robert Hart (*q.v.*) are also in this collection.

WYNNE, General Sir Arthur Singleton (1846—1936)

Military career. Commanded 11th Infantry Brigade, 1900—01. Commanded 6th Division, 1904—05. Military Secretary, Headquarters, 1906—11.

His letters and papers have been deposited in the National Army Museum (ref 7508-32). The collection covers his service in Afghanistan, 1878—79, Egypt 1882—85, the Boer War 1899—1902, and the King's Own Yorkshire Light Infantry, 1913—27.

YORKE, Peter (fl 1940s—1950s)

Industrialist. Director, British Omnibus Companies Public Relations Committee.

His papers concerning the anti-nationalisation campaign of which he was director are in the Public Record Office (PRO 30/84). They cover the period 1944—57.

YOUNG, Douglas (1882—1967)

British Consul, Archangel, 1915—18; critic of allied intervention.

His correspondence and papers, (12 vols, 1900—41) were presented in October 1980 to the British Library (Add MSS 61844—61855).

YOUNG, Douglas (1913—1973)

Poet, playwright and Scottish Nationalist. Chairman of the Scottish National Party, 1942—45. Resigned from SNP, 1948.

The papers were bought by the National Library of Scotland with the help of the Arts Council of Great Britain (ref Acc 6419, 7085). The collection (140 boxes), covering the period 1931—73, includes manuscripts and typescripts of poems, articles, reviews and lectures, correspondence with such people as C. M. Grieve, Naomi Mitchison and Edwin Muir, documents and correspondence relating to PEN, the Scottish National Party, etc. The collection fully reflects all Young's political activities in the national and labour movements, particularly events surrounding the schism in the SNP, 1942, nationalist politics during the 2nd World War, and the Covenant campaign thereafter.

YOUNG, Sir Frederick (1817—1913)

Advocate of Imperial Federation.

In addition to the Royal Commonwealth Society papers (see *Sources*, Vol. 5, p 209), the journal of his South African mission, 1889, is in the Library of the School of Oriental and African Studies.

YOUNGHUSBAND, Sir Francis Edward (1863—1942)

Soldier and explorer. Transferred to Indian Foreign Department 1889. Resident, Indore 1902—03. Led expedition to Lhasa 1903—04. Resident, Kashmir, 1906—09.

An important collection of papers has been deposited in the India Office Library. A journal (2 vols.) of his journey from Kashmir to Sinkiang, August-October 1889, is in the Royal Geographical Society Library.

YPRES, 1st E of
Field Marshal Sir John Denton Pinkstone French, 1st Vt French, (1852—1925)

Served Sudan, South Africa etc. Chief of Imperial General Staff, 1911—14. C-in-C, Expeditionary Forces in France, 1914—15; Home Forces, 1915—18. Lord Lieutenant, Ireland, 1918—21.

In addition to the information given in *Sources*, Vol. 2, p 262, there have been important acquisitions of relevant papers by the Imperial War Museum. The Museum has purchased 99 letters from French to Mrs. Winifred Bennett, his mistress. With a very few exceptions the letters were written between January 1915 and January 1916 and provide an almost daily record of Sir John French's thoughts and activities during the most important appointment of his career. While a significant proportion of the correspondence is of a purely personal nature, Sir John French also wrote in great detail about the conduct and progress of the operations under his command on the Western Front, his relations with the British government and allied commanders and the course of events in other theatres of operations. There are, in particular, lengthy accounts of the planning for, and development of, the battles of Neuve Chapelle, Festubert and Loos as well as of the German offensive in the Ypres area in April 1915. In addition to this purchase, Sir John French's granddaughter, Lady Patricia Kingsbury has lodged with the Museum for safe keeping the diaries kept by Sir John during the South African and the First World Wars.

YSTYWTH, 1st B
Matthew Lewis Vaughan-Davies (1840—1935)

MP (Lib) Cardiganshire, 1895—1920.

Since the entry in *Sources*, Vol. 4, p 258, the papers have been placed in the National Library of Wales.

APPENDIX I

A note on archives since 1951

The last decade has seen a far greater awareness of the need to preserve very recent papers. Accordingly, material more recent than 1951 is rapidly flowing into archive repositories. Although this volume includes many papers, both of organisations and individuals, of later date than 1951, it has not attempted any form of systematic enquiry. The results of that enquiry, when it has been carried out, will form the basis of the next volume in this series. The following brief appendix lists those members of parliament elected after 1951 whose constituency correspondence has already been deposited. Normally, such papers remain closed. Among these papers so far located are: Lord Avebury (Eric Lubbock), Hull University Library; Lord Boyle, Brotherton Library, University of Leeds; Derek Coombs, Modern Records Centre, University of Warwick (ref MSS 132); John Ellis, Hull University Library; Michael English, Nottinghamshire Record Office, Fred Evans, South Wales Miners' Library, University of Swansea; Gwynfor Evans, National Library of Wales; Martin Flannery, Sheffield City Library (NRA 22744); Bernard Floud, Hull University Library; Patricia Ford (now Lady Fisher), Northern Ireland Public Record Office; William Hamling, Modern Records Centre, University of Warwick; Frank Hooley, Sheffield City Library (NRA 22261); Lord Hooson, National Library of Wales; Will Howie, Hull University Library; Peter Jackson, Hull University Library; Aubrey Jones, Churchill College, Cambridge; Anne Kerr, Hull University Library; John Mackintosh, National Library of Scotland (ref Dep 323, NRA list 24817); Kevin McNamara, Hull University Library; Joan Maynard, Sheffield City Library (NRA 22260); John Mendelson, South Yorkshire Record Office (NRA 24911); Airey Neave, House of Lords Record Office, Stan Newens, Essex Record Office; John Osborn, Sheffield City Library (NRA 22694); John Prescott, Hull University Library; Christopher Price, Hull University Library; Vivian Simpson (Stormont politician), Northern Ireland Public Record Office; William Wilson, Modern Records Centre, University of Warwick (ref MSS 76); and David Winnick, Hull University Library.